The Comprehensive Guide to
LEGAL RESEARCH, WRITING & ANALYSIS

VOLUME 1

Moira McCarney, Ruth Kuras, Annette Demers
with Shelley Kierstead

D1224634

2013
Emond Montgomery Publications
Toronto, Canada

Emond Montgomery Publications Limited
60 Shaftesbury Avenue
Toronto ON M4T 1A3
http://www.emp.ca/lawschool

Printed in Canada.

We acknowledge the financial support of the Government of Canada through the Canada Book Fund for our publishing activities.

Publisher, Professional division: Bernard Sandler
Director, editorial and production: Jim Lyons
Production editor: Andrew Gordon
Copy editors: Jim Lyons, Nancy Ennis, Kate Hawkins, Jamie Bush
Permissions editor: Nancy Ennis
Proofreader: David Handelsman
Indexer: Paula Pike
Designer: Tara Wells
Cover image: ARENA Creative / Shutterstock

ISBN 978-1-55239-600-1

The Library and Archives Canada CIP record for this book is available from the publisher on request.

Contents

PART I   BECOMING A COMPETENT LAWYER

PART II   LEGAL RESEARCH

PART III   LEGAL ANALYSIS

Preface

At the Faculty of Law, University of Windsor, legal skills training has been an important component of the curriculum for many years. A legal writing program was identified as a first-year requirement in 1969, even before the law school had a physical home. Currently, successful completion of a mandatory legal writing and research course, which introduces legal research methodologies, analysis, writing, and oral advocacy, is required of all first-year law students. Upper-year students can supplement their skills education with additional coursework, including advanced legal research.

The first-year course has been taught by many faculty since its inception. In recent years, the program has been further developed by Ruth Kuras and Moira McCarney, both of whom joined the faculty in the mid-1990s.

Building on the work of their predecessors, along with Ruth's knowledge in fostering academic success, and Moira's additional expertise in education and course design, together they developed what is colloquially known as "the LRW manual". In the developmental process for more than a decade, it includes explanatory notes, tools, problems, and assignments, and forms the basis for this guide, which has been created to assist students in acquiring the essential competencies associated with legal research, problem solving, and communication.

Now, for the first time, this resource is being made available in an expanded form to others interested in legal writing and research across Canada. The materials have been rounded out with updated research chapters prepared by Annette Demers, Acting Law Librarian at the Paul Martin Law Library, whose vision provided the impetus for the launch of this project, and a team of legal research experts from across the country. We are indebted to the contributions of authors Nadine Hoffman, Christine Press, and Kim Clarke from Alberta; Donna Sikorsky from Manitoba; Michèle LeBlanc from New Brunswick; Jennifer Adams from Nova Scotia; Lucie Rebelo from Quebec; Greg Wurzer from Saskatchewan; and Laurie Brett for her contribution to the British Columbia chapter.

This work has benefited significantly from the contribution of Professor Shelley Kierstead of Osgoode Hall Law School, York University. Professor Kierstead, a renowned expert in the field of legal research and writing, conducts cutting-edge research in the field. Through her research expertise, and her experience teaching legal research and writing to law students in Canada, Professor Kierstead has enriched these materials extensively.

The final contributor to the team is Rose Faddoul, a practising lawyer for many years, who is currently Review Counsel at Community Legal Aid, a legal aid clinic at the Faculty of Law, University of Windsor. In her position as Review Counsel, she helps students transfer the learning they have received in law school to legal practice.

The authors are also grateful to the following individuals for their valuable technical advice: Richard Sage, Research Librarian, Legislative Library of the Legislative Assembly of Ontario; and Ingrid Ludchen, Chief Legislative Editor, Legislative Editing and Publishing Services Section of the Department of Justice.

This guide could not have been completed without the efforts of our outstanding student researchers. Not only did they undertake numerous assigned tasks in a professional manner, as the project developed they provided insightful ideas from the perspective of the student learner, many of which we incorporated into the final text. We owe a debt of gratitude to law students Chuck Andary, Noah D. Schein, Andrew McLean, Erika Ramage, and Timothy Morris, together with all the students who contributed to earlier versions of the manual.

The authors thank and acknowledge the funding support of the Faculty of Law at the University of Windsor and the Law Foundation of Ontario to this project.

However, the author team's vision to create a distinctive work of benefit to law students and lawyers could not have been realized without Paul Emond and his team at Emond Montgomery Publications. At its inception, Paul encouraged us, thoughtfully listened to our ideas, and ultimately gave the go-ahead.

Our sincerest thanks go to Bernard Sandler, Ruth Epstein, and Debbie Hogan. Bernard's extraordinary attention to every aspect of the book's development is truly appreciated. His dedication to the work and his willingness to problem-solve with us on issues as they arose smoothed the development process. Moreover, his unflagging support for the work as it progressed inspired our efforts. Ruth's contributions to the project at critical junctures were very much appreciated, while Debbie's creative ideas and enthusiasm facilitated the journey to print.

The author team believed that to engage the reader, the form of the book must promote the understanding of its content. The editorial and production team translated and integrated our ideas into a product that exceeded our expectations. We thank Tara Wells for her inspired creative design, Nancy Ennis for her tireless efforts in securing permission to use the numerous sources that appear in the text, and David Handelsman for his indefatigable proofreading.

Finally, we are profoundly indebted to Jim Lyons for his rigorous oversight that ensured the highest standard for this work.

Foreword

By The Honourable Thomas A. Cromwell, Supreme Court of Canada

When I took legal research and writing as a law student in the early 1970s, the course seemed mostly concerned with learning the difference between round and square brackets and finding one's way around the library. Of course, there was also a memo to do on some impenetrable problem designed, it seemed at the time, to show that we could neither think nor write.

How times have changed. Legal research and writing courses now expose students to a vast world of legal materials, help develop their skills of analysis and clear expression and introduce them to professional interactions with clients, opposing parties and tribunals.

This, of course, is as it should be. Every good lawyer needs to be able to research effectively, write clearly and analyze insightfully. While to some extent there is more art than science in this domain, nonetheless some core competencies can be taught and learned. And they should be taught and learned in the context of what lawyers do and what their professional responsibilities are.

The authors of this new work set out to facilitate and systematize both the teaching and the learning of legal research, writing and analysis. Their efforts, it is my pleasure to report, constitute a significant and welcome addition to the available materials.

The authors' approach is thorough, well organized and detailed. They go beyond the merely technical to address matters such as how to elicit facts, build a research plan, construct effective legal arguments and write clear and compelling opinions and submissions. They invite the reader to reflect on the lawyer's role and on matters of professional responsibility. They offer help with making the transition from the classroom to law school legal clinics and to practice. This book has a wide sweep and deep coverage.

In short, I envy the chance that current law students will have to benefit from the breadth and depth of this book.

Thomas A. Cromwell
Ottawa
7 July 2013

PART I

Becoming a Competent Lawyer

Foundations

1

CONTENTS

LEARNING OUTCOMES

By the end of this chapter, you should be able to:

- Appreciate the expectations for legal competence within the practice of law
- Identify how the acquisition of skills, abilities, and knowledge contributes to legal competence
- Appreciate why cultural competence can be considered an essential legal competency
- Understand the significance of legal research in law school and professional practice
- Understand the legal research process
- Understand the structure of the Canadian legal system

This chapter introduces two topics that are foundational for the activities in this text, and the practice of law generally. The first section considers the meaning of legal competence and how it infuses the study and practice of law. The second section describes the Canadian legal system and explains the development of the system of laws that will be discussed in later chapters.

I. Expectations: Developing Competence

Law is a self-governing profession that serves the public interest. To be accepted into the legal profession, aspiring lawyers are assessed on their competence to practise law. Moreover, throughout the duration of their practice, lawyers must demonstrate that they are maintaining their competence.

Practising law is not a right; it is a privilege accompanied by obligations. For example, lawyers must understand that:

- Colleagues drawn from their professional ranks are authorized to establish competence standards of practice that all members of the profession are required to meet.
- Lawyers have a duty to inform their governing body of the activities they have undertaken to maintain competence.
- Lawyers have a professional obligation to educate themselves about current developments and best practices in the profession.

- In the event of complaints, lawyers' work is subject to review by their governing body.
- Lawyers who fail to maintain minimum competence standards may be provided with advice and directed to take remedial action. The most severe sanction is disbarment, which occurs when, for the protection of the public, the lawyer's governing body revokes the lawyer's licence to practise law.

Similarly, law students' work will be subject to correspondingly intense scrutiny at times. It is not just graded results, such as those obtained from written examinations, that assess competence. The practice of law requires the completion of numerous multi-faceted tasks, frequently in the context of dispute avoidance or dispute resolution. Law students will have opportunities to undertake activities that demonstrate their ability to apply their developing knowledge, and in these instances it is their preparation, methods chosen, processes followed, choices made, and judgments and decisions reached that will be reviewed and evaluated.

Within this framework, the question remains: What is competence and how do you achieve it? At the beginning of your legal studies, it may be difficult to give meaning to the concept of competence and identify the steps required to reach this goal. Previous educational experiences will have shown that disciplined study,

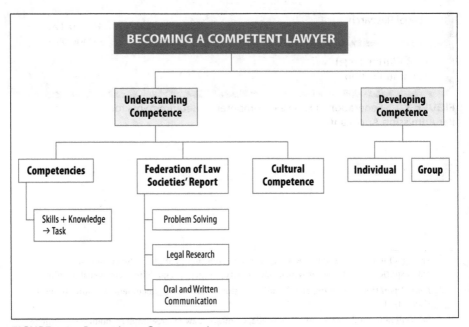

FIGURE 1.1   Becoming a Competent Lawyer

facilitated by those with expert knowledge, is essential to achieving an understanding of any given subject. But how does one establish professional competence that meets the standard necessary to maintain public service and protection?

Law societies, created through legislation, identify in general terms the areas of competence expected of lawyers who practise under their jurisdiction. Professional competence guidelines can be found on law society websites.[1] Recently, the Federation of Law Societies of Canada examined this issue from a national perspective. Its recommendations are found in the final report of the Task Force on the Canadian Common Law Degree.[2] Included in the report is a recommendation to establish a uniform national requirement for entry to bar admission programs. This would require applicants to demonstrate the range of competencies illustrated in Figure 1.2, in skills, ethics and professionalism, and substantive legal knowledge. Implementation of the task force recommendations continues to be discussed.[3]

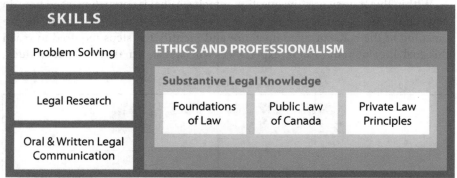

FIGURE 1.2 Federation's Proposed Competency Requirements for Bar Admission Applicants

---

1   See e.g. Ontario's *Rules of Professional Conduct* can be found at <http://www.lsuc.on.ca/with.aspx?id=671>. Other provincial law society competence guidelines are available online.

2   *Final Report* (October 2009) at 7-9, online: <http://www.flsc.ca/_documents/Common-Law-Degree-Report-C(1).pdf>.

3   See Federation of Law Societies of Canada, Common Law Degree Implementation Committee, *Final Report* (August 2011), online: <http://www.flsc.ca/_documents/Implementation-Report-ECC-Aug-2011-R.pdf>.

II. Competence and Competencies

The meaning of a "competency" may be better understood by considering the following working definition.

> A competency can be defined as "a combination of skills, abilities, and knowledge needed to perform a specific task".[4]

To achieve competence, law students must develop a set of competencies, or requisite tools, that frame the practice of law. Competencies develop from interactive experiences where skills, abilities, and knowledge integrate to form new learning, which can then be applied to specific legal problems. The skills-based competencies identified by the Task Force on the Canadian Common Law Degree are shown in Figure 1.3.

How do law students ensure that the choices they make during law school will lead to the development of necessary competencies? For example, one of the Federation's problem-solving competencies is the ability to "identify relevant facts". At first glance, achieving this competency appears straightforward. Fact assessment is required in many law school courses; evaluation of this competency typically occurs through the use of hypothetical examination questions where students apply the law to a novel set of facts.

However, does success on a law school hypothetical examination question transfer directly to competency in fact assessment in a client interview, such as a law student would experience as a volunteer in a live-client clinic setting? Not necessarily. In the clinic setting, where the law student must discover the facts through the interview process (rather than merely sifting through a set of facts provided on an examination hypothetical question), fact assessment is bundled with other competencies, such as interviewing competencies, which in turn are multi-faceted.[5]

---

4   This definition has been adopted by Richard A Voorhees, "Competency-Based Learning Models: A Necessary Future" in Richard A Voorhees, ed, *Measuring What Matters: Competency-Based Learning Models in Higher Education*, New Directions of Institutional Research No 110 (San Francisco: Jossey-Bass, 2001) at 8. This book summarizes the data and policy implications arising from a project that assessed, in part, competency-based issues across post-secondary education. The definition adopted by Voorhees comes from the report of the National Postsecondary Education Cooperative (NPEC) Working Group on Competency-Based Initiatives in Postsecondary Education, *Defining and Assessing Learning: Exploring Competency-Based Initiatives* (Washington, DC: US Department of Education, September 2002).

5   Fact gathering during a client interview is discussed in Chapter 14.

Problem-Solving Competencies	Legal Research Competencies	Oral and Written Legal Communication Competencies
• Identify relevant facts • Identify legal, practical, and policy issues; conduct the necessary research arising from these issues • Analyze research results • Apply the law to the facts • Identify and evaluate the appropriateness of alternatives for resolution of the issue or dispute	• Identify legal issues • Select sources and methods; conduct legal research relevant to Canadian law • Apply techniques of legal reasoning and argument (e.g. case analysis and statutory interpretation) to analyze legal issues • Identify, interpret, and apply research results • Effectively communicate research results	• Communicate clearly in English or French • Identify the purpose of the proposed communication • Use correct grammar, spelling, and language suitable to the purpose/audience of the communication • Effectively formulate and present well-reasoned and accurate legal argument, analysis, advice, or submissions

FIGURE 1.3   Task Force on the Canadian Common Law Degree: Skills-Based Competencies Summary

You can take different paths to become a competent lawyer. Your own interest in a specific area of law can be the starting point. For example, competence is required of both a family law lawyer and one whose work includes corporate or criminal law; only the subject matter differs. Within that framework, establishing skills-based competencies goes beyond merely achieving an abstract or theoretical understanding of the subject that could be demonstrated on an examination; an ability to apply this knowledge and the associated skills is required as well. Therefore, seeking out opportunities that allow the demonstration of acquired knowledge and skills should enhance the development of competence.

Considering basic learning principles such as those derived from Bloom's taxonomy[6] can provide a valuable perspective to help you evaluate the skills you are learning, not only from your course work, but from extracurricular and co-curricular activities as well.

---

6   David R Krathwohl, "Revising Bloom's Taxonomy" (2002) 41:4 Theory into Practice 212.

III. Applying Bloom's Taxonomy

Bloom's taxonomy, developed more than 50 years ago, provides an organizational structure to assess the expectations for students' learning. It has general application to many fields of study, including law.[7] Six primary categories with associated subcategories identify the levels at which learning can take place. They include knowledge, comprehension, application, analysis, synthesis, and evaluation. The revised version (see Figure 1.4) uses descriptive verbs to identify the categories of learning. These are:

- Remember
- Understand
- Apply

- Analyze
- Evaluate
- Create

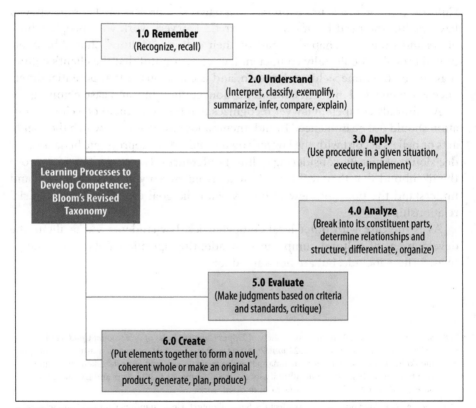

FIGURE 1.4   Bloom's Revised Taxonomy: Categories of Learning

---

7   Paul D Callister, "Time to Blossom: An Inquiry into Bloom's Taxonomy as Hierarchy and Means for Teaching Legal Research Skills" (2010) 102:2 Law Libr J 191.

Law students can monitor the development of their competencies by ensuring that they examine what and how they are learning, and by selecting courses and co-curricular and extracurricular activities that include opportunities for learning in a variety of situations. For example, law school hypotheticals typically evaluate levels 1, 2, and 3 learning. However, in order to develop competence, law students must also be exposed to learning opportunities at the other three levels during the course of their studies. Activities that include problem-based learning and clinical and experiential learning are well suited to provide exposure to these higher-level learning opportunities.

IV. Cultural Competence

Cultural competence is not expressly mandated as a professional competency of lawyers, but the need for it can be inferred.[8] Lawyers work with people whose views and values are shaped in part by their culture. "Culture" should be interpreted broadly. A culturally competent lawyer is mindful that the client's culture may not be the same as his or her own, and is conscious of that potential difference when engaged in client communication, counselling, and case planning.

A culturally competent lawyer recognizes that the assessment of a client's situation should not be influenced by judgments about the degree to which the client's acts or beliefs accord with the lawyer's own standards of appropriate behaviour or decision making. By considering cultural differences, law students can improve the likelihood that they will learn how to avoid stereotypical assumptions, and understand the point of view of others, with the goal of enhancing beneficial relationships.[9]

As is the case with other legal competencies, law students can facilitate the development of cultural competence by adopting specific habits and perspectives.[10] These include, but are not limited to:

---

8   *Supra* note 1. Rule 2.01 of the Law Society of Upper Canada's *Rules of Professional Conduct* (Toronto: LSUC, adopted by Convocation 22 June 2000) states that a "competent lawyer" must have and apply the skills, attributes, and values in a manner appropriate to each matter undertaken on behalf of a client. Because clients differ in cultural aspects, the rule implies that lawyers and law students must be aware that cultural issues may factor into client work.

9   See e.g. Rose Voyvodic, "Lawyers Meet the Social Context: Understanding Cultural Competence" (2006) 84:3 Can Bar Rev 563 for a discussion of developing cultural competence in a clinical law setting.

10 See Susan Bryant & Jean Koh Peters, "Five Habits for Cross-Cultural Lawyering" (2001) 8 Clinical L Rev 33 for a discussion of the value of adopting specific habits to enhance cross-cultural awareness when working with clients.

- recognizing that one's own cultural awareness is essential to developing this competency
- identifying one's own cultural values is also essential to developing this competency; one can compare and contrast one's values with others' values, and begin to anticipate where cultural differences may give rise to similar or different beliefs
- recognizing that interactions with others, including student colleagues, professors, clients, lawyers, and the judiciary, will be shaped, often subtly, by personal cultural values
- recognizing that shared cultural values often enhance group cohesiveness while unexplored differences can interfere with its development
- recognizing that unrecognized or unacknowledged differences can interfere with problem or dispute resolution
- recognizing that cultural biases can result in judgmental positions that may impede problem resolution
- recognizing that finding both the similarities and the differences between oneself and others can help resolve these differences
- recognizing that law is neither created nor interpreted in a cultural vacuum; historical events play a role, and the meaning of law must be considered in the light of cultural variables at play when law was created and interpreted

Learning to become a culturally competent lawyer begins in law school. As a law student, you should be mindful of cultural competence when assisting clients during volunteer or employment activities, when engaged in pro bono work, when discussing contentious legal and policy issues in class, when interpreting the facts in a law school hypothetical problem, and when studying how legislation is created and cases are decided.

V. Introduction to Legal Research as a Skill of a Competent Lawyer

As noted earlier, the Federation of Law Societies of Canada has identified the legal research competencies that new lawyers must demonstrate. Part II of this text describes the knowledge, skills, and habits a law student needs to learn to become a competent legal researcher; this section explains how legal research fits into law school studies and legal practice. The following section provides an overview of the Canadian legal system; later chapters build on this information, and describe how laws are made and disseminated.

A. The Role of Legal Research in Law School and in Professional Practice

Legal research is considered both by law schools and by the law societies that regulate lawyers to be a set of essential skills that a competent lawyer must demonstrate. As such, legal research is an important component of the law school experience. In addition to legal research faculty, law librarians in law schools, in law firms, and in county law libraries provide expertise in legal research, and they are an important resource both to law students and to lawyers in practice.

Law students, articling students, lawyers, and paralegals must be skilled at legal research and familiar with the current best practices and methods in order to keep current with changes to both legislation and case law.

Most law schools offer many opportunities to develop legal research skills. For beginning legal researchers, advice and assistance are available from law librarians, legal research faculty, or legal research methods texts, in print or online. Law librarians may hold training sessions to teach legal research methods. Legal research and writing courses focus on incorporating legal research tasks with writing activities. Some courses require students to prepare legal memoranda, facta, or other documents used in legal practice; other courses provide students with an opportunity to develop legal knowledge through essay preparation. Law school clinics and mooting teams also provide valuable opportunities to build legal research skills in a practical context. Editorial positions on law journals and research assistantships for professors also provide opportunities for law students to hone legal research skills.

B. The Legal Research Process

Most lawyers advocate for others. Advocacy is the process by which a lawyer persuasively advances the client's position. To be a persuasive advocate, one must be well informed and well organized when meeting with clients, and when conducting legal research.

Ascertaining the facts of a client's legal problem is the first step in the process of legal problem solving. The next step is assessing the client's legal rights and obligations. To do this, one must understand the basis of the client's legal problem, which often requires legal research. Once the research is complete, and once the results are applied to the client's legal issues, the lawyer communicates this information to the client and others.

As discussed earlier, lawyers are governed by the law society that regulates lawyers in the jurisdiction in which they operate. Law societies, which operate as self-regulating organizations, are empowered to establish rules, bylaws, and standards of appropriate professional conduct for the lawyers they govern. For example, rule 2.01 of Ontario's *Rules of Professional Conduct* establishes that lawyers in Ontario have a professional obligation to conduct competent legal research.[11]

A lawyer must be fully informed of the client's particular factual situation, and of the relevant law that applies. In order to develop legal research skills, a lawyer must:

- know how laws are made and disseminated
- keep up to date with changes to the law
- know how to complete historical legal research
- understand how legal information is distributed
- perform legal research efficiently and cost-effectively, using both print and online sources
- supervise others who conduct legal research on the lawyer's behalf

The legal research process involves several steps. Legal researchers must know how to:

- locate legislation (statutes and regulations)
- backdate statutes to determine their historical development
- update statutes to determine their development since enactment
- locate bills
- locate case law, also called judicial decisions
- interpret the results of research using primary and secondary sources of law
- apply the law to the facts of the client's legal issue

The research process is schematically represented in Figure 1.5. In practice, research problems are generated by clients' legal issues. To answer the issues, the lawyer must locate and review the controlling law. It is often useful to consider legislation first. Depending on the type of legal issue, backdating the legislation to find its historical roots may be necessary. Determining whether bills have been proposed that will amend existing legislation may be required, followed by finding and studying relevant judicial decisions. Once the primary law (legislation and case law) has been located, it must be interpreted. If the researcher is unfamiliar with the area of law, or unsure what legislation applies, it can be helpful to start with secondary sources, such as an authored treatise or article. (Secondary sources are discussed in Chapter 7.) Finally, the lawyer uses the information gathered to provide the client with legal advice.

---

11 *Supra* note 1.

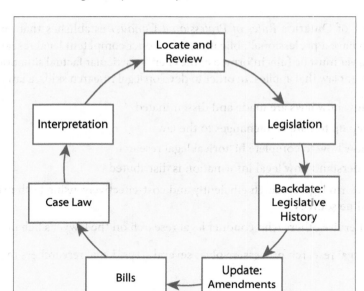

FIGURE 1.5 The Legal Research Process

VI. Overview of the Canadian Legal System

A. Canada's Bijural Legal System

Canada has two legal systems: the common-law system in all provinces and territories except Quebec, and the civil-law system in Quebec. The systems reflect Canada's historical evolution of domestic law.[12] The ability to find, analyze, and write about the law requires an understanding of the structure of domestic law.

B. The Common-Law System

Canada's common-law system is based on a legal system inherited from England, beginning in 1766 with the implementation of English common law and constitutional practices.[13] The common law developed from court decisions made by judges. Judges relied on prior decisions of other judges to decide cases before them, resulting in the application of a "common" law. This led to the compilation and publication of law reporters, which are books that record court decisions.

---

12 Domestic legal issues may have an international or foreign component. See Chapter 8, Introduction to International and Foreign Legal Research in a Canadian Context.

13 See Richard A Yates, Ruth Whidden Yates & Penny Bain, *Introduction to Law in Canada*, 2d ed (Toronto: Prentice Hall Allyn, 2000) at 15-18.

Some reporters are arranged by topic; others cover decisions of particular courts; still others focus on decisions of courts within certain geographical boundaries. Many modern reporters can be accessed in both print and electronic form.

A key aspect of legal research is finding cases that deal with questions that are relevant to the problem being analyzed. Court structures are discussed later in this chapter. For now, it is enough to know that there is a hierarchy of court authority. Judges and members of administrative tribunals render decisions about the merits of parties' disputes. Where a court of higher authority than the one deciding a case has established principles based on a similar set of facts, the lower court is required to follow that decision. That is why, within legal discourse, decisions of the Supreme Court of Canada are important. The Supreme Court of Canada is now the final court of appeal for Canada.[14] Where the Supreme Court of Canada has established principles on a particular subject matter, other courts in Canada must uphold those principles unless the court determines that the facts or issues before it are sufficiently different to warrant different treatment.

Legislation is created by each level of government—federal, provincial/territorial,[15] and municipal. Legislation creates new law, and can also change existing law. For example, the common-law definition of marriage as being the union of a man and a woman has been changed by the *Civil Marriage Act*[16] to allow for the marriage of same-sex partners.

Once legislation comes into force, part of the judicial role involves interpreting the meaning and application of legislation in specific factual contexts. In essence, within a common-law system, a researcher will find that research problems may involve legislation, judge-made rules, or a combination of both.

In Canada, the *Constitution Act, 1867*[17] and the *Constitution Act, 1982*,[18] which includes the *Canadian Charter of Rights and Freedoms*,[19] provide the legal framework both to create laws and to consider their operation.[20] Within this framework, federal and provincial/territorial levels of government exist, all of which have individual and overlapping spheres of responsibility.

---

14 Prior to 1949, the Judicial Committee of the Privy Council in England was the final court of appeal for Canada. Certain cases could be appealed from provincial courts of appeal directly to the Judicial Committee without first being heard by the Supreme Court.

15 Unless otherwise noted, references to provincial legislatures and courts should be understood to include territorial legislatures and courts.

16 SC 2005, c 33.

17 (UK), 30 & 31 Vict, c 3, reprinted in RSC 1985, App II, No 5 [*Constitution Act, 1867*].

18 Being Schedule B to the *Canada Act 1982* (UK), 1982, c 11.

19 Part I of the *Constitution Act, 1982*, being Schedule B to the *Canada Act 1982* (UK), 1982, c 11.

20 Because Canada is a constitutional monarchy, Queen Elizabeth II is the official head of state. The Queen's designated representative in Canada is the Governor General.

The federal level of government comprises distinct but interconnected branches[21]: executive (the prime minister and Cabinet, which includes ministers responsible for specific portfolios and which can pass orders in council[22] approved and signed by the Governor General); legislative (Parliament, consisting of the House of Commons and Senate, whose members debate bills before passage into legislation; and judicial (courts and tribunals, which consider the application of the law, including its constitutional validity). Legislation encompasses both statutes and regulations. Regulations are subordinate or delegated legislation as they derive their authority from an enabling act.[23]

C. The Civil-Law System

The civil-law system is the basis for Quebec's legal regime. Civil law is based on a civil code that consists of a number of broadly stated principles intended to provide guidance for the resolution of disputes. Judges interpret civil code provisions to determine parties' rights and obligations. When interpreting civil code provisions, judges consider the writings of legal scholars in the areas at issue. In addition, the Quebec legislature enacts legislation. Further, legislation enacted by the federal Parliament governs citizens of all provinces and territories. See the Quebec chapter for detailed information regarding the origins and history of Quebec law, and how to research Quebec legislation.

D. Overview of Court Structure in Canada: Federal and Provincial

The Canadian court system is outlined in Figure 1.6 and is discussed below.

1. Federal Courts

In 1875, Parliament established the Supreme Court of Canada as the general court of appeal for Canada. The court hears appeals from provincial superior courts, the Federal Court of Appeal, and the Court Martial Appeal Court. The Supreme Court

---

21 <http://www.canada.gc.ca/aboutgov-ausujetgouv/structure/menu-eng.html>. Provincial and territorial governments have a similar structure.

22 <http://www.collectionscanada.gc.ca/databases/orders/index-e.html?PHPSESSID=33>; see also <http://www.pco-bcp.gc.ca/index.asp?lang=eng&page=secretariats&sub=oic-ddc&doc =gloss-eng.htm>.

23 For a history of delegated legislation in Canada, see Audrey O'Brien & Marc Bosc, eds, *House of Common Procedure and Practice*, 2d ed (Ottawa: House of Commons, 2009), online: Parliament of Canada <http://www.parl.gc.ca/procedure-book-livre/>, ch 17, Delegated Legislation, "Historical Perspective".

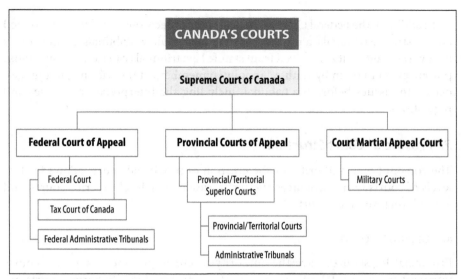

FIGURE 1.6   Canadian Court System

of Canada is the highest court in Canada and, since 1949, the final general court of appeal for Canada. The federal government may also request the Supreme Court of Canada's opinion on reference cases that consider specific legal questions.

Pursuant to section 101 of the *Constitution Act, 1867*, the Federal Court of Appeal, the Federal Court, the Tax Court, and the Court Martial Appeal Court were authorized for the better administration of the laws of Canada. The Federal Court, created in 1971, specializes in certain areas of federal law pursuant to the *Federal Courts Act*,[24] such as intellectual property and immigration.[25] The Tax Court specializes in taxation matters.[26] The Court Martial Appeal Court hears appeals from the courts martial, or military trial-level courts, dealing with matters related to Canadian Forces personnel.[27] Decisions of the Tax Court and Federal Court may be appealed to the Federal Court of Appeal, and further appealed to the Supreme Court of Canada for a final decision.

---

24 RSC 1985, c F-7.

25 For further information regarding the Supreme Court of Canada, see <http://www.scc-csc.gc.ca>; for the Federal Court, see <http://www.fct-cf.gc.ca>; for the Federal Court of Appeal, see <http://www.fca-caf.gc.ca>. The Federal Court succeeded the Exchequer Court, established in 1875. As of 2003, the Federal Court and the Federal Court of Appeal are separate courts.

26 For further information about the Tax Court of Canada, see <http://www.tcc-cci.gc.ca>.

27 For further information regarding the military court system in Canada, see <http://www.cmac -cacm.ca>.

In addition, the Federal Court of Appeal reviews decisions of federally appointed administrative tribunals, a process called judicial review. Tribunals are not courts of law. Their authority is derived from statute law; tribunals can exercise only those powers given to them by statute. Appointed members of the tribunal, not judges, decide the issues before the tribunal, including the interpretation of rules and regulations.[28]

2. Provincial Court Structure

The constitutional authority for the creation of provincial courts allows for two levels of courts in the provinces and territories: higher-level superior courts, and lower-level provincial courts.[29]

a. SUPERIOR COURTS

Provincial legislatures have the authority to create provincial superior courts pursuant to section 92(14) of the *Constitution Act, 1867*. Superior courts are subdivided into the superior trial court and the superior appeal court. These courts can decide matters in any area of law except where a statute has expressly given jurisdiction over the area to another entity.

Across Canada the name of the provincial superior trial court varies by jurisdiction.[30] Decisions from the provincial superior trial court may be appealed to the provincial superior appeal court. The name of this court also varies by jurisdiction. In Ontario, it is called the Court of Appeal for the Province of Ontario. Decisions from provincial superior appeal courts may be appealed, if leave is granted or by right, directly to the Supreme Court of Canada.

b. PROVINCIAL COURTS

The lower-level provincial court system generally has a civil and a criminal division. It may include specialized courts such as family court, youth court, and small claims court, but this varies from province to province. Appeals from the provincial courts are heard by the provincial superior appeal court.

---

28   Some examples of federally appointed tribunals are the Canada Employment Insurance Commission and the Immigration and Refugee Board.

29   Nunavut has a territorial superior court only, the Nunavut Court of Justice, a circuit court that hears all cases originating in Nunavut: see <http://www.nucj.ca>. Sentencing circles and alternative dispute resolution systems (ADR) are also implemented at the provincial/territorial level in Canada: see the Department of Justice Canada website at <http://www.justice.gc.ca/eng/dept-min/pub/ccs-ajc/page3.html>.

30   For example, the provincial Superior Trial Court is called the Court of Queen's Bench in Manitoba, the Superior Court of Justice in Ontario, and the Supreme Court in British Columbia.

The Ontario court system is outlined in Figure 1.7 and is discussed below.[31]

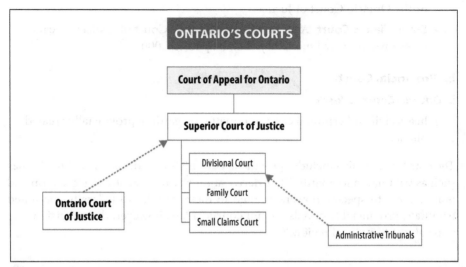

FIGURE 1.7   Ontario Court System

Ontario

The Ontario court system has two divisions: Superior Court and Provincial Court.

a. Superior Court

i. *Appeal level: Court of Appeal for Ontario*

- hears appeals from the Superior Court of Justice and the Ontario Court of Justice

ii. *Trial level: Superior Court of Justice*

The Superior Court of Justice has three branches:

- **Divisional Court:** A specialized appeal court that is a branch of the Superior Court of Justice; it hears some civil appeals and statutory appeals from provincial administrative tribunals, and it conducts judicial review.
- **Family Court:** Both federal and provincial laws govern aspects of family law. In some locations in Ontario, a Unified Family Court has been created

---

31   For further information about the Ontario court system, see <http://www.ontariocourts.on.ca/coa/en> and <http://www.ontariocourts.on.ca/scj/en/>. For information about the court structure found in other provinces and territories, consult the relevant jurisdiction.

to consider matters arising from both jurisdictions. In other locations, these matters are decided separately in either the Superior Court of Justice or the Ontario Court of Justice.

- **Small Claims Court:** A branch of the Superior Court of Justice; it hears cases involving civil monetary claims up to $25,000.

b. Provincial Court

i. *Ontario Court of Justice*

- hears civil and criminal cases and matters regarding provincially created offences

The court system also includes provincial administrative decision-making bodies such as tribunals and boards. They derive authority from enabling legislation and must adhere to specific powers granted to them. Similar to federally appointed tribunals, provincial tribunals are not courts of law; however, their decisions are also subject to judicial review.[32]

VII. Overview of This Guide

Legal research, writing, and advocacy are not course-specific; the skills and knowledge obtained by working through the material in this guide apply to many aspects of the law school curriculum, and infuse the practice of law. The information contained in this guide, supported by both the appendixes and the online components, is designed to assist you in developing competence in these foundational legal skills.

Part I Becoming a Competent Lawyer	
Chapter 1	Introductory concepts: competence, legal system
Chapter 2	Basics of factual and issue analysis: considered in each chapter, applied in Chapters 11-14

---

32 Some examples of provincially appointed tribunals are the Human Rights Tribunal of Ontario and the Landlord and Tenant Board. Courses focusing on a detailed analysis of administrative tribunals and the judicial review process are offered at many law schools.

Problem Analysis: Facts and Issues

2

CONTENTS

This chapter explains how fact assessment and issue analysis provide the foundation for advanced legal problem solving. Subsequent chapters build on this discussion to explore the essentials of legal research, analysis, and communication.

I. Dispute Analysis: Begin with the Facts

Whether one intends to practise law in a courtroom or to pursue an alternative legal career, every lawyer must understand the dispute resolution process. The basis of a dispute is revealed by its facts, presented to the lawyer by the client during one or more interviews. As the factual basis for the dispute is uncovered, the lawyer begins to explore the underlying legal issues. On the basis of this preliminary assessment, the lawyer will decide whether or not legal research is required to answer the issues.

As the legal basis for the dispute becomes apparent, the lawyer may identify gaps in the factual record. To strengthen the factual record, the lawyer may reinterview the client, seek additional witnesses, and procure relevant documents or other tangible evidence of the dispute. Ultimately, the basis of the dispute is revealed in sufficient detail to enable the lawyer to offer the client legal advice about potential dispute outcomes and resolution options.

Fact analysis has two aspects. The first involves discovering the facts. The second involves sorting and organizing the facts, and classifying them as either relevant or irrelevant to the dispute. Relevant facts are those that relate directly to some aspect of the legal issue; they are often described as material facts. Irrelevant facts are those that are incidental to the dispute and do not aid the dispute resolution process. A third category of facts is connector facts. These may be difficult to classify as either relevant or irrelevant; however, they serve the important function of connecting relevant facts and thus aid in understanding the narrative of the dispute.

Undertaking a thorough fact assessment is a professional obligation;[1] therefore, developing a systematic approach to discover the facts ensures that the lawyer compiles an accurate factual record before the fact assessment and classification process begin.[2] See Figure 2.1.

II. Preliminary Fact Assessment: Gather and Organize the Facts

At its most basic level, fact discovery involves determining:

- the parties to the dispute, and
- the incidents of the dispute.

Once this basic information is obtained, the details surrounding these broad categories can be explored.

Whether interviewing a client[3] or solving a law school hypothetical, one can ascertain most facts through six questions of discovery,[4] followed by a critical analysis of the responses. Once the facts are revealed, the lawyer must determine how the facts can be substantiated should the legal dispute reach a court or tribunal for resolution.[5]

---

1 See e.g. Law Society of Upper Canada, *Rules of Professional Conduct* (Toronto: LSUC, adopted by Convocation 22 June 2000), r 2.01(1)(b).

2 Law school evaluation techniques may only partially assess a student's ability to factually analyze a client's legal issue, if hypothetical problems on an examination are the sole measure of this skill. While hypothetical problems can assess issue spotting and fact organization, they cannot assess fact discovery. Part V of this text builds on the information in this chapter, and discusses how students can develop their legal skills by preparing themselves for practice-based clinical and experiential learning opportunities.

3 Interviewing comprises a complex skill set on its own. See Chapter 14 for an introduction to this topic.

4 The pervasive nature of these six questions as a tool of analysis is evident by how frequently Kipling's "Six Honest Serving Men" is referenced in various online sources. Rudyard Kipling, *Just So Stories* (Cornwall, UK: Stratus Books, 2009) at 38.

5 Students intending to become litigators should include a course on evidence in their upper-year studies. Such a course will explore *inter alia* the rules of evidence that are applied to witness testimony, documentary, and real evidence.

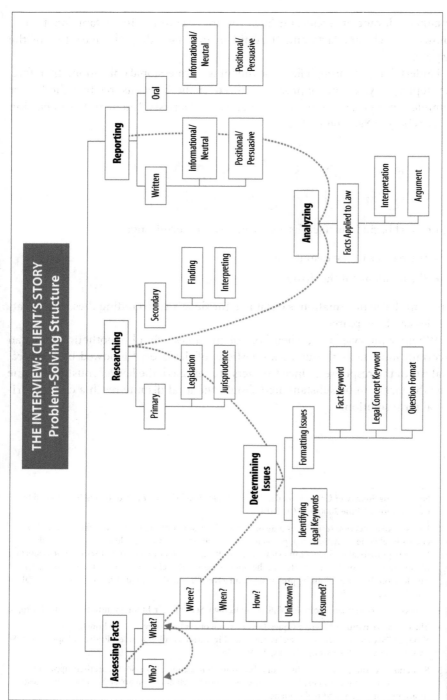

FIGURE 2.1 Problem Analysis Structure

A. Who?

"Who" is often the first question asked.

- Who is the client?
- Who are the parties to the dispute, and what is their relationship to each other?
- Who are the potential witnesses, and what do they know?
- Do any of the parties have a specific title or role?
- Do any of the parties have a specific interest in the outcome of the dispute?
- Is the client the person who has been harmed (the "plaintiff"), or the person who may be liable for harm caused to someone else (the "defendant" or "accused")?

Note and record the details. The relevance of details will be determined after the issues have been framed and the research has been completed.

B. What?

"What" prefaces the second set of questions, and may be inextricably linked to "who."

- What happened?
- What was said or done and by whom?
- What privilege or harm is claimed or alleged?
- What consequence may be forthcoming?
- What remedy is being sought?
- What legal action is contemplated, or what other form of dispute resolution is being considered (for example, mediation)?
- What other facts must be located or confirmed?

Ensure that the relationships between and among the parties, and the activities leading to the dispute, have been considered and recorded.

C. When, Where, How?

These three questions help to clarify and expand the foundation of the narrative.

- When did the relevant acts occur? Dates, times, and seasons may be important. Individuals may not always recall or relate factual detail in a linear or sequential manner, so develop questions to obtain an accurate record.

Create timelines, charts, or diagrams to clarify the sequence of events and the relationships between and among persons and events, and to identify any gaps in that understanding.

- Where did the events occur? Identify the country, province, city, street, building, or place. Jurisdiction in a dispute—i.e. the authority of those entitled to act—may be a significant fact, and is often revealed by the question "where."

- How did the events unfold? Focus on details of the client's story. How does the client perceive or feel about the situation? The emotional tone may be relevant to the decisions made before and after the dispute occurred, and may provide a basis for exploring settlement or dispute resolution options.

Ensure that the relationships among the parties, the events, and the time and location are known. Identify unknown details for later investigation.

D. Why?

"Why" examines the reasons that events and actions occurred and the decisions that were made before, during, and after the dispute. The question can be asked at any time during the fact assessment.

- Why did the parties act as they did?
- Why were specific acts taken or omitted? Reasons, beliefs, explanations, and motivations may help to identify a motive, a defence, or a justification.

Answering "why" may help sort out relevant from irrelevant facts; it may also provide a starting point to explore dispute resolution options.

E. Unknown/Assumed?

This category includes facts that may be relevant but are, as yet, not fully ascertained. Categorizing facts as "unknown" or "assumed" ensures that relevant facts are not overlooked or ignored.

- What facts are yet to be determined? Note the relationships between and among the known facts. Identify any inconsistencies or gaps.

- Because disputes arise from differing versions of similar facts, one of the categories of unknown facts is anchored in some aspect of the other party's version of the events. How can this information be obtained?

- Assumed facts are those that have been assumed to be accurate during the fact-gathering process, but that lack additional proof to confirm their accuracy. How might these assumptions be verified?

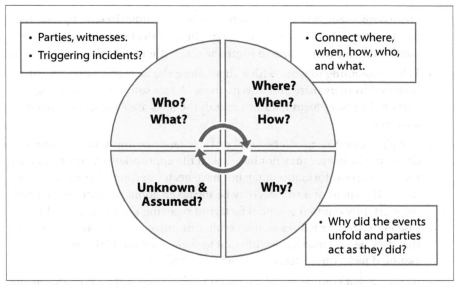

FIGURE 2.2   Preliminary Fact Assessment: Gather and Organize the Facts

- At the completion of the fact analysis, determine the additional facts to be discovered, and consider how that information might be acquired.
- Undetermined facts are common. Because they may hold the key to the eventual resolution of the legal issue, they must be identified.
- By the conclusion of the analysis, the more material facts there are that are unknown, assumed, or unverifiable, the more difficult it will be for the lawyer to provide a sound legal opinion. Undetermined facts, therefore, may result in a qualified legal opinion.

III. Fact Assessment: Additional Factors

- Analysis of the facts is an ongoing process. In the fact assessment stage, work with available information. Be flexible. Certain facts will acquire either greater or lesser significance as the research progresses.
- Facts and law are interrelated, so sorting relevant from irrelevant facts is critical to a legal analysis. However, relevance cannot be determined until the legal research is complete. Therefore, avoid premature conclusions and be prepared to review and reconsider the facts once the relevant law has been assessed.
- When organizing the facts, use visual aids such as charts, diagrams, time-lines, and mind maps to establish connections between and among the facts. Ultimately, the law will be applied to the facts in a legal argument.

Once organized, the facts can be more readily synthesized and presented for this purpose. To test your understanding of the facts, ask whether you could explain them clearly to someone else without referring to your notes.

- When beginning to work with a client, draft the facts as a narrative but be prepared to reorganize and rewrite them. A fact summary at this stage is a first draft only. Reformulate and redraft the facts after the law has been analyzed.

- Not all relevant facts will be known. The client may not know an important detail, or the lawyer may not have asked the appropriate questions during the interview. Information may not have been interpreted or recorded correctly. The client or a witness may be mistaken about the facts or may have inadvertently omitted essential facts, not realizing their relevance. Occasionally, clients or witnesses may omit, minimize, or disguise some facts that they believe may be detrimental to their position. Unknown or assumed facts, once identified, can be verified later.

- Be aware that your personal values and beliefs may not be the same as the client's. Avoid injecting a personal or subjective standard of analysis or decision making during the fact-gathering process. Remain objective at all times.

- The relevance of facts is usually determined by primary law (legislation and case law). Therefore, to determine a fact's relevance, it is necessary to thoroughly research primary sources. Secondary sources such as commentaries on the law can help suggest the scope or applicability of the law to all the relevant facts. Secondary sources are discussed in Chapter 7.

- Once the facts have been reviewed, consider your research approach. As a general guideline, among primary sources, legislation (if it exists) should be reviewed first and case law (if it exists) should be reviewed next.

- Flexibility is the key in legal research. For example, researching legislation may take precedence over case law, but you may find relevant legislation by reading a case on point, or a journal article may provide the necessary context for understanding the relevant primary law.

- Whatever research approach you take, ensure that you record your steps in a systematic manner by using both a research plan and a research log or some other form of checklist. A research plan sets out the research that must be done, and identifies research tools to accomplish the plan. A research log records the specific steps that were actually taken. Research plans and logs are related, but they are likely to differ as research steps are adapted during the process.[6]

---

6   See Chapters 3 to 8 for legal research methodology and Chapter 9 for guidelines to complete research plans and logs.

IV. Frame the Legal Issues Using Keywords

After the facts have been reviewed, the legal issues must be framed. Legal issues are legal questions that arise from the specific facts of a client's legal problem. These questions are formulated and then analyzed on the basis of the facts and the law. For certain legal problems, a policy analysis may be required. Frequently, legal research must be undertaken before the answers to the issues posed can be determined.

Legal issues must focus on the application of the law to the facts of a specific client. To ensure this focus, every legal issue should be drafted as a question in order to provide direction to the research or analysis to be undertaken. The legal issue must also contain specific fact keywords derived from the client's facts and legal concept keywords that apply to the facts. A legal issue that does not contain both a fact keyword and a legal concept keyword is imprecise, as can be seen in the hypothetical that follows. See Task 2.1.

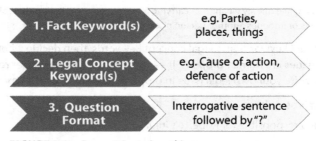

FIGURE 2.3   Formatting a Legal Issue

TASK 2.1

Issue Drafting: Hypothetical

Read the following fact hypothetical and identify both fact keywords and legal concept keywords. Then, frame the legal issue.

On 15 June 2011, Theo and Roberto, two friends who were avid hockey fans, stopped by Derry's Bar and Grille to watch the final game of the Stanley Cup. The bar, located in Blissville, Ontario, was a popular gathering place for sports fans because of its big-screen televisions. Theo and Roberto had watched many of the earlier games in the series, and were excited because their favourite teams were in the final. Roberto was a Bruins fan, while Theo supported the Canucks.

After Boston won 4–0 in Game 7, Roberto jumped onto a table with several other fans and began to celebrate the victory by dancing and singing. During the celebration, a full bottle of beer tipped over and spilled on Theo. Overcome by anger, Theo picked up the empty bottle and intentionally swung it at Roberto's head. The bottle shattered when it hit Roberto's right temple. Roberto fell, hit his head on the table, and lost consciousness. Frightened, Theo ran out of the bar, but was arrested by police before he crossed the border to the United States.

Theo is your first client following your graduation from law school. He wants to know if he committed assault pursuant to the *Criminal Code*. Assume that Roberto did not consent to Theo's actions.

Now, review the law concerning this problem found in section 265 of the *Criminal Code*.

265(1) A person commits an assault when
(a) without the consent of another person, he applies force intentionally to that other person, directly or indirectly;
(b) he attempts or threatens, by an act or a gesture, to apply force to another person, if he has, or causes that other person to believe on reasonable grounds that he has, present ability to effect his purpose; or
(c) while openly wearing or carrying a weapon or an imitation thereof, he accosts or impedes another person or begs.

List the fact keywords and legal concept keywords, then decide whether the following issues are framed properly. If yes, why? If no, why not? After reviewing the issues, write your own legal issue in proper format for this fact hypothetical.

- What is assault?
- Is Theo responsible for Roberto's injury?
- Theo's defence to the assault of Roberto.

V. Preliminary Problem Analysis: Formulating a Legal Issue

Once the legal issue has been drafted, legal research and preliminary analysis to understand the client's legal position can begin. The governing legal rules are found in primary sources, which include both legislation and judicial decisions, or case law. Secondary sources provide the means to help locate and interpret primary law. Finding and understanding relevant primary and secondary sources is the subject matter of subsequent chapters.

Once the law that applies to the relevant facts has been analyzed and synthesized, the information needed to generate a "theory of the case" should be available. A theory of the case provides a framework for explaining the facts as they relate to the law. In many situations, developing a sound theory is an essential step in providing competent legal advice to the client should the legal issue proceed to a dispute resolution forum.[7]

VI.   Issue Drafting: Additional Factors

- A properly framed legal issue for this hypothetical is: "Did Theo assault Roberto pursuant to section 265 of the *Criminal Code*"? The fact keywords are Theo and Roberto. The legal concept keywords are assault and section 265 of the *Criminal Code*.

- Always review the issues after framing them to ensure that they include the three components of a properly framed legal issue. A legal issue that does not contain both a fact keyword and a legal concept keyword is imprecise, and a legal issue that is not phrased as a question does not provide research or analytical direction.

- Examine the legal issues as provided above. "What is assault?" does not contain a fact keyword. "Is Theo responsible for Roberto's injury?" does not contain a legal concept keyword. "Theo's defence to the assault of Roberto" is not phrased as a question. Imprecise issue formation at this point may lead to a vague discussion about the law that is unrelated to the client's concern.

- Sometimes you may be asked to research a topic without being given detailed facts. In those cases, instead of naming a particular person, use a generic fact keyword such as "person" or "individual".

- The correct framing of a legal issue requires a full review of primary law (legislation, case law, or both). Secondary legal sources such as authored treatises are also critical resources that assist in framing a legal issue, because the author will have analyzed the area of law and referenced the relevant case law and legislation. (Secondary sources are discussed in Chapter 7.) Once the relevant legal principles are known, the law must be applied to the facts of the case. If the issue as framed does not support a discussion of law that explores legal arguments applied to the facts of the case, the issue is not framed appropriately, and may result in an incomplete analysis.

- It often happens that a legal issue must be redrafted after the research has been completed because additional legal points are discovered that require review. Issue drafting is like fact drafting: both require revision. Do not rely on the first attempt at issue drafting.

---

7   This topic is considered in Chapter 14.

- A legal analysis may consider policies underlying the relevant law at issue, particularly if the case involves a challenge to the law's constitutionality. Policy issues follow the same format as legal issues, including the three components of proper formation.
- For complex issues, use subissues to organize the analysis. Subissues must be answered separately first; the results must then be integrated in order to answer the primary issue fully. Subissues follow the same format as the primary issue of which they are a part.
- Use subissues sparingly, if at all. In the body of a legal document, subheadings can be used more effectively to organize the analysis.

Consider the example of Roberto and Theo. Assume that Theo did not intend to hit Roberto but merely to capture his attention. Because Roberto was distracted by the noise in the bar, he hit his head on the bottle that Theo was holding. To convict Theo of this criminal offence, the Crown attorney must establish that he both had a "guilty mind" (*mens rea*) and voluntarily committed a "guilty act" (*actus reus*). If the research leads to cases that consider both terms, and if enough facts exist to support legal arguments related to both concepts, subissues examining the concepts of *mens rea* and *actus reus* may be appropriate. In that case, the broader primary issue could be divided into subissues as follows:

1. Did Theo assault Roberto pursuant to section 265 of the *Criminal Code*?
   a. Will the Crown be able to establish *mens rea* for the assault charge?
   b. Will the Crown be able to establish *actus reus* for the assault charge?

VII. Summary

Fact assessment and issue analysis provide the foundation for legal problem solving of disputes. Understanding the facts and formulating the issues are essential steps in the process of exploring potential dispute resolution outcomes. Most of the facts of a dispute can be ascertained through six questions of discovery: who, what, when, where, how, and why. Analysis of the facts is an ongoing process, and must be reviewed as further information becomes available. Once the facts have been reviewed and research into primary legal sources has been undertaken, the legal issues can be framed. Legal issues focus on the application of the law to the facts of the dispute. Together, fact assessment and issue analysis form the basis on which legal advice for resolving the dispute can be offered.

PART II

Legal Research

The Federal Law-Making Process

3

I. How a Bill Becomes a Federal Statute

The authority to create federal legislation resides with the Parliament of Canada, which comprises two chambers: the House of Commons and the Senate. Federal legislation includes both statutes and regulations. This section describes the statute creation process; section III describes the regulation process.

All prospective statutes begin as bills. Before becoming law, every bill is scrutinized by both the House and the Senate. After both the House and Senate pass a bill, it becomes an "act".[1] Once it receives royal assent and comes into force, the new act has the status of legislation, and is enforceable as federal law.

The process by which a bill becomes a federal statute is shown in Figure 3.1.

---

1 An act may also be referred to as "annual statute", "source law", "unrevised statute", "enacted version", or "session law". The use of these terms reflects the form of a statute as first enacted, and does not refer to a statute that has been amended, revised, or consolidated.

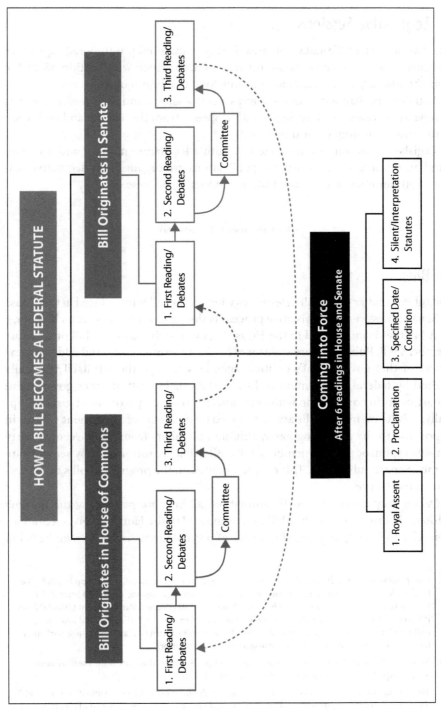

FIGURE 3.1   Federal Legislation Creation Process: Mind Map

A. Legislative Sessions

The Parliament of Canada operates during sequentially numbered legislative sessions. Legislative sessions are opened in accordance with section 38 of the *Constitution Act, 1867*[2] and may continue for a maximum of five years.

Usually, a parliament is divided into several sessions, and each session consists of separate sittings. Sessions begin with a Speech from the Throne and end when Parliament is prorogued or dissolved.[3]

Legislative sessions are identified by both a legislature number and a session number. Because many legislative publications are organized by legislative session, both numbers are required when conducting bill research.

41st Parliament, 1st Session

B. Bills

The subject matter of the bill determines whether the bill is introduced in the House or Senate; however, the legislative process is the same for bills in each chamber.

A bill that is introduced in the House begins as either a public bill or a private member's bill. Public bills are sponsored by the governing party, and address some aspect of that government's political agenda, although the bill itself is usually drafted by federal Department of Justice staff, or by staff of other government departments in conjunction with personnel from the Department of Justice. Typically, private members' bills are introduced by members of Parliament who sit in opposition to the governing party, although members from the governing party may also sponsor private members' bills. Bills that are introduced by senators are termed Senate public bills. This chapter focuses on the progress of bills that originate in the House.

When they are ready for dissemination, all bills are printed by the Queen's Printer.[4] At this stage, a public bill that originated in the House receives a number from C-1 to C-200, sequenced in order of presentation. A private member's bill

---

2   *Constitution Act, 1867* (UK), 30 & 31 Vict, c 3, ss 38, 50 reprinted in RSC 1985, App II, No 5. For further details about the commencement of parliamentary sessions, see Audrey O'Brien & Marc Bosc, eds, *House of Commons Procedure and Practice*, 2d ed (Ottawa: Parliament of Canada, 2009) [O'Brien & Bosc] ch 8, "The Parliamentary Cycle" at "Opening of a Parliament and a Session", online: <http://www.parl.gc.ca/procedure-book-livre/>. For further details about how parliamentary sessions are ended, see *ibid* at "Prorogation and Dissolution".

3   Based on Parliament of Canada, "FAQ", online: <http://www2.parl.gc.ca/CommitteeBusiness/SiteFaq.aspx?CmteInst=joint&Language=E&Mode=1&Parl=40&Ses=3> [FAQ].

4   The Queen's Printer is designated by the Minister of Public Works and Government Services under the authority of the *Department of Public Works and Government Services Act*, SC 1996, c 16, s 19.

that originated in the House is given a sequential number beginning with C-201.[5] A bill that originated in the Senate is given a reference number beginning with an S rather than a C. The bill is then added to the LEGISinfo[6] website and is distributed to members of Parliament and to libraries.

Both the bill number and the legislature and session numbers are required to locate a bill in print or online.

C. First Reading Stage

For bills beginning in the House, the first reading of the bill is added to the House agenda and the bill is read for the first time. The House agenda is documented in the *Journals of the House of Commons of Canada* ("*Journals*"), while the Senate agenda is found in the *Journals of the Senate*. The Index to House and Senate *Journals*, organized by legislature and session number, document the dates of each bill's progress through Parliament.

The daily comments made by ministers and other members of Parliament are recorded in the *Debates of the House of Commons of Canada* ("*Debates*"), while senators' comments are recorded in the *Debates of the Senate of Canada*. Parliamentary *Debates*, known as *Hansard*,[7] are organized first by legislature and session number and then by date. The date that a bill passes a particular legislative phase is used to find debates about a bill's progress.

The following excerpt illustrates first reading debate commentary.[8]

OATHS OF OFFICE

Right Hon. Stephen Harper (Prime Minister, CPC) moved for leave to introduce Bill C-1, respecting the administration of oaths of office.

Mr. Speaker, I seek the unanimous consent of the House to have the bill printed.

(Motions deemed adopted and bill read the first time)

The Speaker: Does the right hon. Prime Minister have the consent of the House to have the bill printed?

Some hon. members: Agreed.

***

---

5   See Parliament of Canada, "Bills: Private Members' Bills", online: <http://www.parl.gc.ca/LEGISINFO/Home.aspx?ParliamentSession=41-1&BillType=Private+Member%E2%80%99s+Bill&Page=1>.

6   See Parliament of Canada, LEGISinfo, online: <http://www.parl.gc.ca/LegisInfo>.

7   This is the name of the person who originally kept debate records. For a full history of the earliest publishing of the Debates, see Elizabeth Nish, ed, *Debates of the Legislative Assembly of United Canada 1841* (Montreal: Presses de l'École des Hautes Études Commerciales, 1970) vol 1 at xviii.

8   Canada, *House of Commons Debates*, 41st Parl, 1st Sess, No 2 (3 June 2011) at 15 (Hon Stephen Harper, PM).

D. Second Reading Stage

After passing first reading, the bill is scheduled for second reading.[9] The introducing minister or member of Parliament may explain the basis for the bill, followed by debate, which provides members of Parliament with the opportunity to comment on the bill. Following debate, a motion is made to dispose of second reading, followed by a recorded vote. If a majority of those voting support the bill, it proceeds; if a majority vote against the bill, it is defeated. A bill that passes second reading may be referred to one or more committees for further study before being scheduled for third reading.

The following excerpt illustrates second reading debate commentary.[10]

FAIR AND EFFICIENT CRIMINAL TRIALS ACT

The House resumed consideration of the motion that Bill C-2, An Act to amend the Criminal Code (mega-trials) be read the second time and referred to a committee.

***

The Acting Speaker (Mr. Bruce Stanton): Order, please. It being 2:09 p.m., pursuant to an order made earlier today, it is my duty to interrupt the proceedings at this time and put forthwith the question on the motion for second reading now before the House. The question is on the motion. Is it the pleasure of the House to adopt the motion?

Some hon. members: Agreed.

(Motion agreed to, bill read the second time and referred to a committee)

***

E. Committee Stage

Committees of the House or Senate, made up of members of Parliament or senators, have a particular mandate or area of expertise. Standing committees meet routinely,[11] while special committees meet as required.[12] After finishing its work, the committee reports to Parliament. The final report may include proposed amendments to the bill, which may or may not be adopted.

---

9   As noted in the *Journals*.

10 Canada, *House of Commons Debates*, 41st Parl, 1st Sess, No 10 (16 June 2011) at 467.

11 Current standing committees of the House include Finance, Transport, and Justice and Legal Affairs.

12 FAQ, *supra* note 3.

Recent committee reports are now available online through the Parliament of Canada website.[13] Committee reports that are not available online are available in print in most large libraries.

F. Third Reading Stage

After the committee reports to Parliament, the bill proceeds to third reading (in amended form if committee recommendations have been accepted). Discussions at this stage are recorded in the *Debates*. After third reading, a bill is passed if a majority of those voting support the bill.

Once the bill passes through the House, it is sent to the Senate, where it undergoes a similar review. A bill that originates in the Senate follows the same process, finalizing its journey in the House.

G. Royal Assent

Once a bill passes all six readings in both the House and the Senate, it receives royal assent. The Governor General, the Queen's representative in Canada, signs the bill, symbolizing the Queen's consent to its enactment. Notification of royal assent is recorded in the *Debates*.[14]

ROYAL ASSENT

The Right Honourable David Johnston, Governor General of Canada, signified royal assent by written declaration to the bills listed in the Schedule to this letter on the 29th day of November, 2011, at 4:15 p.m. Bills assented to Tuesday, November 29, 2011:

An Act to give effect to the Agreement between the Crees of Eeyou Istchee and Her Majesty the Queen in right of Canada concerning the Eeyou Marine Region (*Bill C-22, Chapter 20, 2011*)

A third Act to harmonize federal law with the civil law of Quebec and to amend certain Acts in order to ensure that each language version takes into account the common law and the civil law (*Bill S-3, Chapter 21, 2011*)

An Act to amend the National Defence Act (military judges) (*Bill C-16, Chapter 22, 2011*)

---

13   Parliament of Canada, House of Commons Committees, online: <http://www.parl.gc.ca/CommitteeBusiness>.

14   Canada, *Senate Debates*, 41st Parl, 1st Sess, No 34 (29 November 2011) at 1640.

H. Publication of Statutes: Enacted and Consolidated Versions—Print and Online

Once a bill receives royal assent, it is published. The act as it first appears in the *Canada Gazette*, Part III and the *Statutes of Canada* is the enacted version, also referred to as an annual statute, source law, or session law. The current version of the statute, which includes all amendments, is the consolidated version. This version may be referred to as a consolidated statute or a revised statute.

After receiving royal assent, an act is sent to the Clerk of the Parliaments. The Clerk retains the original copy[15] on file, and creates a certified copy under seal that is sent to the Queen's Printer, first for dissemination in the *Gazette*, Part III, the Justice Laws Annual Statutes online, and later for dissemination in the *Statutes of Canada*, which are the permanent annual statutes publication.

The *Statutes of Canada*, which are abbreviated as SC in legal citations, are published each year in one or more volumes, and contain all statutes enacted during that year. The SC also identifies the parliamentary session during which the legislation was passed.

Acts are given a chapter number and are ordered within the annual volume(s) by date of enactment. The chapter number identifier is used to locate an act. For example, *An Act to amend the Citizenship Act*, in the SC 2005 volumes, has been assigned chapter number 17.[16]

Locating the Enacted Version of a Statute

When completing legislative research, record the information source and methods used. This is used to complete a legislative history, described later in this chapter, and a research log, described in Chapter 9.

---

15   For certainty, the Clerk's copy supersedes all others in case of discrepancies.

16   A detailed table of contents in the SC helps users to locate the relevant act. Each set of the SC also provides several tables, which will be described in Chapter 4.

TASK 3.1

Locating an Enacted Version of a Statute in Print: Official

1. Locate the annual *Statutes of Canada* (not the *Revised Statutes of Canada*) in the library.

2. Use the act's citation reference to locate the relevant volume containing the year and chapter number of the enacted statute. Finally, locate the act using its chapter number.

3. Historical annual Statutes can be found in print and on HeinOnline in Session Laws, from 1792 to the present.

TASK 3.2

Locating an Enacted Version of a Statute Online: Authoritative

Enacted versions of statutes are found online after 2000.

1. On the Justice Laws website, <http://laws-lois.justice.gc.ca>, go to Annual Statutes.

2. Using the citation reference, select the relevant year and locate the statute.

Department of Justice Laws	
Home » Laws Website Home » 2005 Annual Statutes	
Laws	**2005 Annual Statutes**
Constitutional Documents	The Annual Statutes accessible on this page are the Public General Acts as they were enacted by Parliament in each calendar year. They include new Acts as well as Acts that amend existing Acts. More information on Annual Statutes
Consolidated Acts	
Consolidated Regulations	
Annual Statutes	2012 2011 2010 2009 2008 2007 2006 2005 2004 2003 2002 2001
Statutes Repeal Act: Reports and Repeals	
Search	2005, c. 1 *(Bill C-14)* *Assented to*
Basic Search	Tlicho Land Claims and Self-Government 2005-02-15
Advanced Search	2005, c. 2 *(Bill C-7)* *Assented to*
Resources	An Act to amend the Department of 2005-02-24
Table of Public Statutes and Responsible Ministers	Canadian Heritage Act and the Parks Canada Agency Act and to make related amendments to other Acts

Enacted versions of federal statutes can be found in the *Canada Gazette*, which is the government's official newspaper.

Locating an Enacted Version of a Statute Online: Official

On the *Canada Gazette* website, <http://www.gazette.gc.ca>, Gazettes from the current session of Parliament are listed under Latest Publications, while Gazettes from previous parliamentary sessions are located in the Archives, <http://www.gazette.gc.ca/archives/archives-eng.html>.

- Locate the relevant statute's year of enactment. The individual issues of the *Canada Gazette* published that year are shown.

- The *Canada Gazette*, Part III is organized by year, volume, issue number, and page. The chapter numbers for each statute published in the *Statutes of Canada* are listed. PDFs include bookmarks for each statute chapter number.

- If a recent act has not yet been published in the *Canada Gazette*, Part III, locate the version of the statute at royal assent, which is provided on the LEGISinfo website, <http://www.parl.gc.ca/LEGISINFO>.

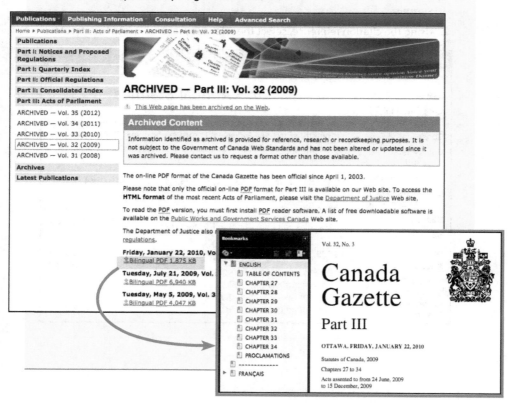

All bills must receive royal assent before becoming law. However, not all acts take effect on royal assent; others come into force at a later date. Determining the "coming into force" date of legislation is the final step in the process of a bill becoming law.

I. Locating Coming into Force Information for Acts

The coming into force (CIF) date of legislation must be confirmed to ensure that the law was in force at the relevant time under consideration.

Following a bill's successful passage through the House and the Senate, it receives royal assent. An act may come into force immediately upon receiving royal assent, but the date of royal assent is not always the date that the act takes legal effect. Some acts come into force only after they are "proclaimed". Others come into force on specific dates, or when certain conditions are met, while others are silent as to their coming into force. Moreover, an act can come into force as a whole, or sections of the act can come into force on various dates. Staggered implementation may be necessary when the statute amends other acts, or when it alters the operation of a regulatory structure.

In some instances, the CIF date can be established without difficulty. Statutes in force on royal assent or on a specified date provide the CIF date in the statute itself. Statutes that are silent about their CIF rely on interpretive legislation that fixes their CIF date.

The most challenging aspect of CIF research involves acts whose CIF date comes into force on proclamation. Statutes that are in force on proclamation do not specify the CIF date in the act itself; therefore, additional steps must be taken to locate the CIF, adding complexity to the research process.

Once the CIF date is located, according to the *Interpretation Act*,[17] "[j]udicial notice shall be taken of a day for the coming into force of an enactment that is fixed by a regulation that has been published in the *Canada Gazette*". *Black's Law Dictionary*[18] defines "judicial notice" as "[a] court's acceptance, for purposes of convenience and without requiring a party's proof, of a well-known and indisputable fact".

Accordingly, for statutes that are proclaimed, once the proclamation is located and referenced, the CIF date will be acceptable in court without the need for additional proof.

---

17   RSC 1985, c I-21, s 6(3).

18   *Black's Law Dictionary*, 9th ed, *sub verbo* "judicial notice".

The steps by which a federal act comes into force can be conceptualized as shown in Figure 3.2.

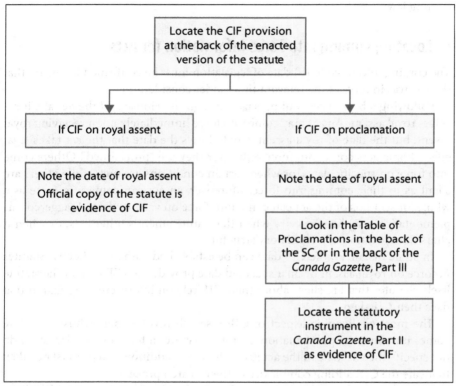

FIGURE 3.2 Steps to Locate CIF of Acts

The examples that follow illustrate the steps to take to locate CIF dates in most situations.

1. Steps for Finding CIF Information for Acts: Online and Print

TASK 3.4

Locating Coming into Force Online: Royal Assent

When did the *Fairness for Military Families (Employment Insurance) Act*, SC 2010, c 9 come into force?

1. On the Justice Laws website, locate the enacted version of the *Fairness for Military Families (Employment Insurance) Act*, SC 2010, c 9.

2. Locate the CIF provision. Section 5 states: "This Act comes into force on the first Sunday after the day on which it receives royal assent".

3. If the section provides that the Act comes into force on royal assent, or if it otherwise refers to the date of royal assent, turn to the title page or the first page of the Act and locate the royal assent statement. The *Fairness for Military Families (Employment Insurance) Act* was assented to on 29 June 2010. Therefore, it came into force on 4 July 2010, which was the first Sunday after the date of royal assent.

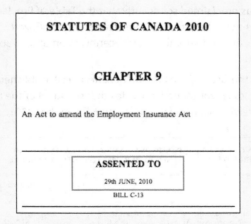

STATUTES OF CANADA 2010

CHAPTER 9

An Act to amend the Employment Insurance Act

ASSENTED TO

29th JUNE, 2010

BILL C-13

TASK 3.5

Locating Coming into Force Online: Proclamation

When did the *Immigration and Refugee Protection Act*, SC 2001, c 27, s 4 come into force?

1. On the Justice Laws website, locate the enacted version of the statute and find the CIF provision. Section 275 states that the provisions of this Act come into force on a day or days to be fixed by order of the Governor in Council. Accordingly, this statute did not come into force on royal assent. However, record the date of royal assent (1 November 2001) because it will be required to complete a legislative history.

2. Locate the Table of Proclamations, which is published as an appendix in the last volume of the annual *Statutes of Canada* (print publication) each year, and is available online in the final pages of each issue of the *Canada Gazette*, Part III. A link is provided on the Justice Laws website to the *Canada Gazette*. The steps below outline the process when using the online version.

   a. From the *Canada Gazette*, Part III Archives page, choose the relevant year (2001).

   b. In the 2001 volume, review the dates and select one of the issues published after the date of royal assent (1 November 2001).

   c. In the PDF version, review the Table of Proclamations. If the relevant statute is not included in this table, close the PDF and select the next issue. Continue until you locate the CIF information.

   d. If the Act was proclaimed so recently that the Table of Proclamations does not contain the relevant information, link to the *Canada Gazette*, Part II, and review only those published after the most recent version of the Table of Proclamations found in Part III.

   e. In this case, the issue of the *Canada Gazette*, Part III published on Wednesday, 13 February 2002, vol 24, no 5 provides that section 4 of the *Immigration and Refugee Protection Act* came into force on 6 December 2001.

PROCLAMATIONS OF CANADA AND ORDERS IN COUNCIL RELATING TO THE COMING INTO FORCE OF ACTS — 22 NOVEMBER, 2001 TO 19 DECEMBER, 2001		
————	Date in force	Canada Gazette Part II
Canada Business Corporations Act and the Canada Cooperatives Act and to amend other Acts in consequence, An Act to amend the, S.C. 2001, c. 14, in force..	24 Nov., 2001	SI/2001-114 Vol. 135, p. 2806
Constitution Act, 1982, Constitution Amendment, 2001 (Newfoundland and Labrador), effective	6 Dec., 2001	SI/2001-117 Vol. 135, p. 2899 Extra No. 6, p. 1
Customs Act and to make related amendments to other Acts, An Act to amend the, S.C. 2001, c. 25, sections 1, 3 to 23, 31 to 35, 37 to 44, subsection 45(1), sections 46, 48 to 52, 54 to 62, 64 to 71, subsections 72(2) and 74(2), sections 75 to 87, subsections 88(1) and 91(1) and sections 99 to 111, in force..............................	29 Nov., 2001	SI/2001-115 Vol. 135, p. 2896
Immigration and Refugee Protection Act, S.C. 2001, c. 27, sections 1 and 4, in force..	6 Dec., 2001	SI/2001-119 Vol. 135, p. 2901

TASK 3.6

Locating Coming into Force in Print: Royal Assent or Proclamation

When did the *Canada Student Financial Assistance Act*, SC 1994, c 28 come into force?

Online searching is not always possible. If the statute's CIF predates Justice Canada's online coverage, use print sources.

1. Locate the Act in the 1994 print volume of the annual *Statutes of Canada*. If the CIF section provides that the Act comes into force on royal assent, or if it otherwise refers to the date of royal assent, turn to the title page or the first page of the Act and record the date of royal assent.

2. If the Act did not come into force on royal assent, but came into force on a date to be proclaimed, continue with the following steps.

   a. Locate the Table of Proclamations, which is published near the end of the last volume of each annual set of volumes of the *Statutes of Canada*.

   b. Proclamations might be made immediately, but if the proclamation is not in the Table of Proclamations in the year the Act received royal assent, examine the Table of Proclamations in subsequent years until you locate the proclamation.

   c. Statutes are listed in the Table of Proclamations in alphabetical order by statute title and chapter number.

   d. Review the information in the column to the right of the statute. The date of coming into force is provided, along with the volume number and page number in the *Canada Gazette*, Part II where the statutory instrument can be found.

   e. In this case, the *Canada Student Financial Assistance Act*, SC 1994, c 28 came into force on 1 August 1995. Although the statutory instrument that brought the Act into force is not identified by its citation, the document location is provided; therefore, select the relevant volume number and page reference in the *Canada Gazette*, Part II to locate the CIF document.

PROCLAMATIONS OF CANADA AND ORDERS IN COUNCIL RELATING TO THE COMING INTO FORCE OF ACTS—1 JANUARY, 1995 TO 31 DECEMBER, 1995		
—	Date in force	Canada Gazette Part II
Canada Business Corporations Act and to make consequential amendments to other Acts, An Act to amend the, S.C. 1994, c. 24, sections 21 and 22 and subsection 24(2), in force	30 May, 1995	Vol. 129, p. 1647
Canada Grain Act and respecting certain regulations made pursuant to that Act, An Act to amend the, S.C. 1994, c. 45, in force	1 Aug., 1995	Vol. 129, p. 2457
Canada Shipping Act and to amend another Act in consequence thereof, An Act to amend the, S.C. 1993, c. 36,		
—paragraph 660.2(2)(c) of the Canada Shipping Act, as enacted by section 6, in force	31 July, 1995	Vol. 129, p. 2200
—paragraphs 660.2(2)(a) and (b) and subsections 660.2(3) to (6) of the Canada Shipping Act, as enacted by section 6, —paragraphs 662(1)(i) and (k) of the Canada Shipping Act, as enacted by subsection 7(2), —section 8, and —sections 10 and 11, in force	15 Aug., 1995	Vol. 129, p. 2200
Canada Student Financial Assistance Act, S.C. 1994, c. 28, in force	1 Aug., 1995	Vol. 129, p. 2190
Canadian Environmental Assessment Act, S.C. 1992, c. 37, sections 1 to 60, 71, 72, 74, 76 and 77, in force	19 Jan., 1995	Vol. 129, p. 274

2. Other CIF Circumstances: Online and Print

- Regardless of whether the statute itself states that it comes into force on royal assent, proclamation, or a specified date, or is silent as to its coming into force, the CIF provisions come into force on royal assent.[19]
- Statutes that do not specify a CIF date are deemed to be in force on royal assent through the operation of the *Interpretation Act*.[20]
- When CIF information is provided for some sections of an act but not others, the sections of the act not included in the specified CIF provisions come into force on royal assent.[21]
- From time to time, a statute or statute section may never be brought into force. The *Statutes Repeal Act*[22] disposes of certain unproclaimed acts.

Regardless of how a statute comes into force, the date of royal assent must always be recorded, along with any reference to the *Canada Gazette* in the case of acts proclaimed or otherwise brought into force. This information is used in creating CIF statements (discussed later in this chapter) and legislative histories (discussed in Chapter 4), and is an essential component of a research log (discussed in Chapter 9).

As well as determining how an act comes into force, legal researchers must be able to locate and track a bill at each stage of its passage through Parliament.

II. How to Track a Bill That Is Currently in Parliament

A. Why Track a Bill?

Practising lawyers, legal scholars, and students must be able to track a bill through each stage of its development, because this information may be relevant to the interpretation of the legislation. Merely understanding the law-making process is not sufficient. Determining the reasons for the bill's enactment, including discussions held during debates, is an essential legal research competency.

---

19   *Interpretation Act, supra* note 17, s 5(3).

20   *Ibid*, s 5(2).

21   *Ibid*, s 5(4).

22   SC 2008, c 20.

B. Introduction to LEGISinfo

While historical research requires the use of print sources, bills currently before Parliament can be tracked online using the Library of Parliament's online tool LEGISinfo, which is a collaborative effort of the Senate, the House of Commons, and the Library of Parliament. According to its website:[23]

> LEGISinfo is an essential research tool for finding information on legislation before Parliament. This tool provides electronic access to a wide range of information about each bill, such as:
>
> - details on the passage of the bill through the Senate and House of Commons;
> - text of the bill as introduced at First Reading and its most recent version if it is amended during the legislative process;
> - votes;
> - major speeches at second reading;
> - coming into force data;
> - legislative summaries from the Parliamentary Information and Research Service of the Library of Parliament; and
> - government press releases and backgrounders (for government bills).

C. Finding a Bill: How LEGISinfo Is Organized

The home page for LEGISinfo lists all bills that have been introduced during the current legislative session. (See Figure 3.3.) Although recently enacted bills are listed first, they are further categorized to promote ease of access:

- To view bills in order by bill number, choose Sort By: Bill Number directly above the list of bills. (This is the default view.)
- To view bills that were before Parliament during a previous legislative session, choose the legislature and session number under Refine Your Search: Parliament - Session.

Bills can be searched quickly by bill number or title (see Figure 3.4), and the results can be sorted by bill number or by Parliament and session.

---

23   <http://www.parl.gc.ca/LegisInfo/AboutLegisInfo.aspx>.

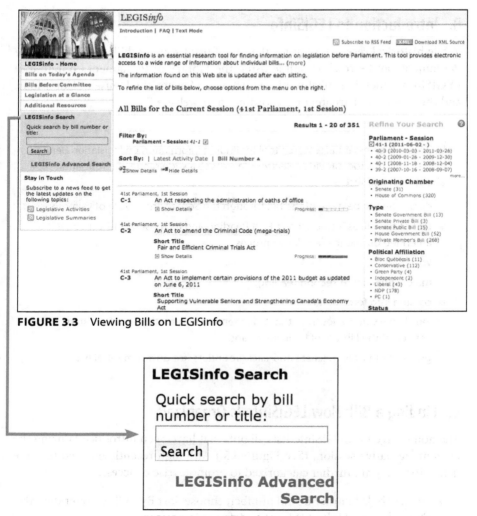

FIGURE 3.3   Viewing Bills on LEGISinfo

FIGURE 3.4   LEGISinfo Search Function

Bill searches can be refined using preset options under Refine Your Search. These options allow searches to be organized by:

- originating chamber (House or Senate)
- type of bill (public or private member's)
- sponsoring member of Parliament/political affiliation
- status of the bill

Use the Advanced Search feature to construct more complex searches.

D. Viewing Bills Online

Once you have located the relevant bill, open it to view the bill's content page. Since a bill can be amended at each stage in the legislative process, different versions of the bill are available. To see the full text of the bill, under "Latest Publication" select "All Published Versions". This displays links to the full text of the bill as it appeared during each stage in the legislative process.

E. Determining the Status of Bills

To examine the bill at any stage in the legislative process, return to the bill's information page.

As shown in Figure 3.5, the bill's information page provides essential information that can be organized to complete a legislative history. (The steps for constructing a legislative history are explained in Chapter 4.)

Legislature and Session Number	41st Parliament, 1st Session
Bill Number	C-2
Bill Title	An Act to amend the Criminal Code (mega-trials)
Sponsor	Minister of Justice (includes a link to more information about the Minister)
Bill Stage	Royal assent (includes the date of royal assent: 2011-06-26)
Status of the Bill (Table)	The status table shows the dates of the bill's passage in the House and Senate.

FIGURE 3.5   Bill Information Available on LEGISinfo

F. Viewing Debates

Information obtained from debates can be used to determine the intent of the legislation. Debates of the House and Senate contain verbatim transcripts of discussions during a bill's passage.

TASK 3.7

Locating Recent Debates

Use LEGISinfo to locate recent debates online.

1. Open the bill's information page and select the relevant legislative stage.

2. Choose "Show Sittings" to display the enumerated Chamber Sitting, then click the date of the sitting to link to the Debate.

3. At the top right of the page, choose "Print format" to view the PDF version.

   ■ The PDF is a copy of the actual contents of the print version of the Debates, so the page numbers in the PDF can be used for citation purposes.

   ■ The Debate can also be viewed and searched online, but particular passages cannot be cited by page number.

   ■ The Debates of the date of the sitting include statements by members, oral questions, routine proceedings, government orders, and adjournment proceedings. The Contents of the Debate are found at the end of the PDF and at the beginning of the online version.

4. Scroll through the Contents, or use the PDF reader's search function, to search for keywords and phrases such as unique words from the title of the bill.

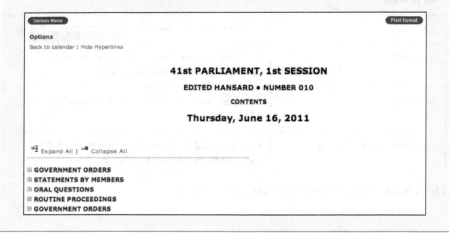

G. Historical Versions of Bills and Debates

On occasion, you will need to conduct legal research using historical materials that are not available online. Print sources of bills and debates are available in most university and law libraries and can be consulted where online sources are insufficient. Locating historical legal information is a multistep process because bills and debates are located in separate volumes, organized by Parliament and session. Locating historical versions of bills and debates is discussed in Chapter 4.

H. Legal Citation of Federal Bills, Federal Statutes; and Creating a CIF Statement: Format

There are a number of methods of citing Canadian legal sources, but the source most frequently used in Canadian law schools is the *Canadian Guide to Uniform Legal Citation*,[24] which has been adopted by several courts and law journals. While this text has adopted many of the McGill Guide conventions, it suggests alternatives where necessary to provide relevant information about primary sources of law.

1. Bills

Locating a bill at each stage of its development requires an understanding of its legal citation elements. The citation of a federal bill includes the following information, in the following order:

1. bill number

2. long title of the bill

3. session number

4. legislature number

5. year

6. pinpoint reference, if desired, to a clause, abbreviated as "cl" for a single clause and "cls" for multiple clauses

7. additional information about the status of the bill, if desired

Citations to bills include the legislative session in which the bill originated. The legislative session includes a reference to both the session number (such as "1st Sess") and legislature number (such as "38th Parl"). Bills originating in the House begin with "C-", while bills originating in the Senate begin with "S-".

---

24   7th ed (Toronto: Carswell, 2010) [McGill Guide].

For example:

> Bill C-61, *An Act to amend the Copyright Act*, 2nd Sess, 39th Parl, 2008, cl 4

2. Statutes

Once a bill passes third reading in both chambers and becomes an act, its citation format alters. The citation of a federal statute includes the following information, in the following order:

1. official short title as stated in the statute, or the long title of the statute if a short title is not specified
2. designation of the statute as first published as an annual Statute of Canada ("SC"), or as subsequently consolidated and published in its revised form as a Revised Statute of Canada ("RSC")
3. year of publication of either the annual or the revised statute
4. chapter reference
5. pinpoint reference, if desired, to a section, abbreviated as "s" for a single section and "ss" for multiple sections

For example:

Statutes of Canada	*Wage Earner Protection Program Act*, SC 2005, c 47, s 2
Revised Statutes of Canada	*Wages Liability Act*, RSC 1985, c W-1, s 3

3. CIF Information Statement

A CIF statement communicates the essential details of a statute's coming into force. Although the McGill Guide does not recommend a format for a CIF statement, it does suggest a citation format for the *Canada Gazette*, which is included in a CIF statement. However, the recommended format for citing the *Canada Gazette* omits essential information required in a complete CIF statement.

The following CIF information summary includes all essential information:

> The *Canada Student Financial Assistance Act*, SC 1994, c 28 came into force in accordance with section 29 of the Act on 1 August 1995 by Order of the Governor in Council, as evidenced by *Order Fixing August 1, 1995 as the Date of the Coming Into Force of the Act*, SI/95-77 published in the *Canada Gazette*, Part II, 9 August 1995, vol 129, no 16, page 2190.

The CIF statement in the format recommended by the McGill Guide is as follows:

> The *Canada Student Financial Assistance Act*, SC 1994, c 28 came into force in accordance with section 29 of the Act on 1 August 1995 by Order of the Governor in Council, as evidenced by *Order Fixing August 1, 1995 as the Date of the Coming Into Force of the Act*, SI/95-77, (1995) C Gaz II, 2190.

Although the McGill Guide states that it is not necessary to include a full citation to a *Canada Gazette* when citing orders in council or regulations,[25] for research purposes *Canada Gazette* location information is preferred. Noting the date, volume, issue, and page number ensures that the CIF information can be located if proof of CIF information is required. Therefore, when completing a CIF statement, include the location information as noted in the first example.

III. How a Regulation Becomes Law at the Federal Level

A discussion of the process by which legislation is created begins with statutes and concludes with regulations. Regulations are termed subordinate legislation because they derive their existence and authority from statute, yet they perform important functions on their own, and have the same force in law as statutes.

A. Regulatory Authority: The Enabling Act

Regulations may be created to explain the details of an act's application. Other regulations are created to bring statutes into force, as discussed earlier. Understanding the process by which regulations are created is central to understanding how to locate and work with them.

The authority to make regulations is derived from an enabling statute, as the following example indicates (emphasis added):

> 11. **The Governor in Council may make regulations** providing for the establishment and operation of a program to provide special interest-free or interest-reduced periods to borrowers or classes of borrowers, including the terms and conditions of the granting or termination of the periods, the making,

---

25   *Ibid* at ch 2.6.1.

continuation or alteration of agreements between borrowers and lenders when the periods are granted or terminated and the authorization of lenders to grant or terminate the periods and otherwise administer the program.

Source: *Canada Student Loans Act*, RSC 1985, c S-23, s 11.

B. How a Regulation Is Created

When determining whether regulations have been created pursuant to a statute, consider the following points:

- Does the statute contain enabling language that allows the creation of regulations? If the statute does not contain enabling language, then regulations cannot be created.
- If the statute contains enabling language, is the language mandatory or permissive? In the example above, the use of the word "may" indicates that the creation of regulations is permitted but not mandatory. If the word "shall" had been used instead, the creation of regulations would be mandatory.

Once a regulation has been prepared by the authorized body,[26] it is submitted in both official languages to the Clerk of the Privy Council, who reviews it in consultation with the Deputy Minister of Justice.[27] After examination (and any necessary revision), the regulation is submitted again in both official languages to the Clerk of the Privy Council, and the regulation is registered.[28] Regulations are also scrutinized by a standing committee of the House and of the Senate,[29] but are not otherwise scrutinized by Parliament.

All regulations must be published in the *Canada Gazette*, Part II within 23 days of being registered.[30]

C. Steps for Finding CIF Information for Regulations

As with statutes, regulations must come into force in order to take effect. Unless otherwise stated, regulations come into force on the day they are registered.[31]

---

26 *Statutory Instruments Act*, RSC 1985, c S-22, s 2. Regulations include rules of the court and many other types of instruments.

27 *Ibid*, s 3(2).

28 *Ibid*, s 6.

29 *Ibid*, s 19.

30 *Ibid*, s 11(1).

31 *Ibid*, s 9.

The steps for finding CIF information for regulations are shown in Figure 3.6.

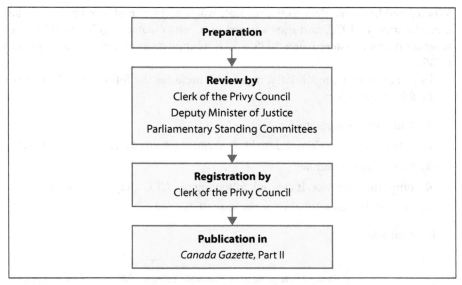

FIGURE 3.6   Steps for Finding CIF Information for Regulations

The process for locating unrevised and consolidated regulations is described in Chapter 4.

TASK 3.8

Finding CIF Information for Regulations

1. Locate the regulation as it appeared when it was originally registered.

2. Determine whether the regulation contains a CIF provision. Most regulations do not contain such a provision. For those that do, the provision specifies the date on which the regulation, or sections of it, comes into force.

3. For all regulations that do not contain additional CIF information, the date of registration displayed at the beginning of the regulation is the date the regulation came into force, pursuant to section 9 of the *Statutory Instruments Act*.

OTTAWA, THURSDAY, DECEMBER 23, 2010	OTTAWA, LE JEUDI 23 DÉCEMBRE 2010
Registration SOR/2010-312 December 23, 2010	Enregistrement DORS/2010-312 Le 23 décembre 2010
CRIMINAL CODE	CODE CRIMINEL
Regulations Amending the Regulations Establishing a List of Entities	**Règlement modifiant le Règlement établissant une liste d'entités**

D. Legal Citation of Federal Regulations

When providing a regulation citation, note whether it was registered before the last consolidation in 1978, and thus appears as a consolidated regulation (CRC), or whether it was registered after 1978, and thus appears as an unrevised regulation (SOR).

The citation of a consolidated regulation includes the following information, in the following order:

1. name of the regulation
2. reference to the *Consolidated Regulations of Canada*, abbreviated "CRC"
3. CRC chapter number
4. pinpoint reference, if desired, following the CRC chapter number
5. year of the consolidation or revision, if desired

For example:

> *Pacific Pilotage Regulations*, CRC 1978, c 1270

The citation of an unrevised regulation includes the following information, in the following order:

1. name of the regulation, if desired
2. reference to the *Statutory Orders and Regulations*, abbreviated "SOR"
3. year of the regulation, shown as two digits for years prior to 2000 (e.g. "98" for a 1998 regulation) and four digits for years including and after 2000 (e.g. 2013)
4. SOR regulation number
5. pinpoint reference following the SOR regulation number, if desired

For example:

> *Pacific Hake Exemption Notice*, SOR/86-750

IV. Meaning of Official Sources, Authoritative Sources, and Unofficial Sources of Legislation: Guide to Publications

Legislation is published in various formats. While the government is responsible for the initial official publication of legislation, others may subsequently reproduce it. Commercial publishers and some non-commercial publishers of legal information typically reproduce legislation on their online platforms or in their print publications. These unofficial sources of law may be preferred by legal researchers for a variety of reasons. Some unofficial sources can be navigated more quickly than official sources, and they often have added value, such as links to judicial decisions that have considered the legislation, or summaries of leading cases that have interpreted the legal principles derived from the legislation.

In most legal research situations, any source of legislation may be consulted. However, if a matter goes to court, lawyers are required to substantiate the applicable legislation in support of their argument, so the official version of legislation must be provided.

A. Legislative Foundations of Official Publications

For legal research and court purposes, an "official" source refers exclusively to Government of Canada publications, including legislation and judicial decisions. Official sources are also known as "primary" sources of law because they are the original source of the legal rules and interpretations of the law published by the government or issuing court.

Providing an official version ensures that all parties are referring to the same version of the legislation or case, and that their references to paragraphs or page numbers are identical. This ensures accuracy and consistency, which helps to protect the interests of clients and the integrity of the justice system.

Official sources of federal legislation are discussed below. Official sources of provincial legislation are discussed in Chapter 5 and in specific provincial research chapters, and official sources of judicial decisions are discussed in Chapter 6.

The statutory authority to provide a court with an official copy of legislation begins with the *Publication of Statutes Act*:[32]

---

32   RSC 1985, c S-21, ss 4, 5, 9.

> 4. The Clerk of the Parliaments shall have a seal of office and shall affix the seal to certified copies of all Acts required to be produced before courts of justice, either within or outside Canada, and in any other case in which the Clerk of the Parliaments considers it expedient.
>
> 5. All copies of the Acts certified by the Clerk of the Parliaments pursuant to section 4 shall be held to be duplicate originals and to be evidence of those Acts and of their contents as if printed under the authority of Parliament by the Queen's Printer.
>
> ...
>
> 9. The Clerk of the Parliaments shall furnish the Queen's Printer with a certified copy of every Act of Parliament as soon as it has received royal assent.

Furthermore, the *Canada Evidence Act*[33] confirms that documents published by the Queen's Printer are acceptable for evidentiary purposes in court.

> 19. Every copy of any Act of Parliament, public or private, published by the Queen's Printer, is evidence of that Act and of its contents, and every copy purporting to be published by the Queen's Printer shall be deemed to be so published, unless the contrary is shown.
>
> 20. Imperial proclamations, orders in council, treaties, orders, warrants, licences, certificates, rules, regulations or other Imperial official records, Acts or documents may be proved
>
> > (a) in the same manner as they may from time to time be provable in any court in England;
> >
> > (b) by the production of a copy of the *Canada Gazette*, or a volume of the Acts of Parliament purporting to contain a copy of the same or a notice thereof; or
> >
> > (c) by the production of a copy of them purporting to be published by the Queen's Printer.

In summary, if the source is not designated by statute as "official", it is not official evidence of the law for courtroom use, and is considered to be an unofficial source of law. This includes most web-based and commercial publications. Therefore, whenever possible, provide a copy of the law obtained from the *Canada Gazette* and other publications by the Queen's Printer for use in court.

---

33 RSC 1985, c C-5, ss 19-20. Because of the legal distinction between official and unofficial sources of legislation, only methods of locating official sources are described in this chapter and in Chapter 4; methods of locating unofficial sources of legislation are discussed in Chapter 7. The same guideline applies to matters adjudicated in provincial court, which are subject to provincial evidence laws, as explained in specific provincial research chapters.

Some versions of Government of Canada publications, while not official, are considered authoritative and are preferable to unofficial versions. Authoritative publications are most commonly found on government websites.

B. Official and Authoritative Publications: Online and Print

1. Canada Gazette

The *Canada Gazette* is published in print and online. The print and online versions are governed by different regulations and therefore must be considered separately.

Pursuant to applicable legislation, a copy of a statute taken from the print version of the *Canada Gazette*, Part III provides appropriate evidence for use in a federal court.[34] Similarly, a copy of a regulation taken from the print version of the *Canada Gazette*, Part II is acceptable evidence for use in a federal court.[35]

Pursuant to statutory authority,[36] the online version of the *Canada Gazette*, in PDF form, is now considered to be an official version of the law, under the *Canada Gazette Publication Order*.[37]

2. Statutes of Canada

The *Statutes of Canada* are published in print and online. The print and online versions are governed by different regulations and therefore must be considered separately. At the time of publication of this text, the print version is official, while the online Justice Laws Annual Statutes collection is merely authoritative.

Sections 10, 11, and 12 of the *Publication of Statutes Act*[38] provide the authority by which statutes are published in the *Statutes of Canada*. Furthermore, the *Publication of Statutes Regulations*[39] set out the details of this publication.

However, while the Act confers authority to the Governor in Council to prescribe regulations about the manner in which statutes are to be printed, to date no further regulations have been filed to confirm that the content of the Annual Statutes collection on the Justice Laws website is official.

---

34   *Statutory Instruments Regulations*, CRC, c 1509, s 12. See also *Publication of Statutes Act, supra* note 32, s 12.

35   *Statutory Instruments Regulations, supra* note 34, s 11(2).

36   *Supra* note 26, s 10.

37   SI/2003-58, s 1. Effective 1 April 2014, there will no longer be a requirement to distribute and sell the print version of the *Canada Gazette* pursuant to *Statutory Instruments Regulations*, CRC, c 1509, ss 19-20, as amended by *Regulations Amending the Statutory Instruments Regulations*, SOR/2013-85.

38   *Supra* note 34, ss 10-12.

39   CRC, c 1367.

According to the Chief Legislative Editor, Department of Justice, Canada:

> The data of the Acts that are included in the Annual Statutes collection on the Justice Laws Website is taken from the *assented to* versions of Acts that are published, within days after royal assent, by the Speaker of the House of Commons or the Speaker of the Senate. It is this same data that is later published in the *Canada Gazette*, Part III and in the bound volumes of the Annual Statutes of Canada, printed by the Queen's Printer.[40]

Accordingly, the Annual Statutes collection on the Justice Laws website should be considered authoritative and not official.

3. Revised Statutes of Canada

The *Revised Statutes of Canada* are published in print and online. Pursuant to the *Legislation Revision and Consolidation Act*,[41] which governs official consolidations of law at the federal level, both the print version of the *Revised Statutes of Canada* and the online version of consolidated statutes published on the Justice Laws website are considered official sources. (The difference between consolidated and revised statutes is discussed in Chapter 4.)

4. Other Primary Sources of Law

Additional primary sources of law include the *Debates* of the Senate and House of Commons. The print version and the PDF version of *Debates* on the LEGISinfo website are considered official, because both contain the seal of the Crown. The HTML version on the LEGISinfo website does not contain the seal of the Crown, so it is not considered official and should not be used in court.

Most government legislative publications are considered authoritative for the purposes of legal research. As a result, one can rely on the contents of such publications.

---

40 Email from Ingrid Ludchen, Chief Legislative Editor, Legislative Services Branch, Department of Justice, Canada, to Annette Demers (10 April 2013).

41 RSC 1985, c S-20, ss 28 and 31.

C. Summary

A statute or regulation has "official" status when it bears the seal of the Crown. The seal is located:

- at the beginning of the print version of each print volume of the *Statutes of Canada* and the *Revised Statutes of Canada*
- on the consolidated version of statutes on the Justice Laws website, but not on the online version of the Annual Statutes
- at the beginning of the *Canada Gazette* in PDF, but not in HTML

If an official version is not available, an authoritative version from a government source is preferred to an unofficial source.

A PDF of the original may be used but an HTML version may not be substituted, because this format makes it difficult to direct the court and opposing counsel reliably to page numbers.

D. Guide to Publications and Status of Commonly Used Publications Tables

Figures 3.7 and 3.8 summarize the publications described in Chapters 3 and 4, the information they provide, their date coverage, their status as official or authoritative sources, and their location, both online and print. If a publication is available in print, the full set of the publication, including historical material, is likely available at most law libraries.

FIGURE 3.7 Guide to Publications

Publication	What It Is	Print	Online
Orders in Council	Law made by the executive	**AVAILABLE:** Yes/ intermittent **COVERAGE:** Historical to present **AUTHORITY:** Official	**URL:** <http://www.collectionscanada.gc.ca/databases/orders/index-e.html> **COVERAGE:** 1867-1910 **AUTHORITY:** Authoritative **and** **URL:** <http://www.pco-bcp.gc.ca/oic-ddc.asp?lang=eng&Page=secretariats> **COVERAGE:** 1990 to present **AUTHORITY:** Authoritative
Canada Gazette	The official newspaper of the government Part I contains notices. Part II contains regulations. Part III contains statutes as enacted.	**AVAILABLE:** Yes **COVERAGE:** Historical to present **AUTHORITY:** Official	**URL:** <http://www.gazette.gc.ca/gazette/home-accueil-eng.php> **COVERAGE:** Most recent 5-year period (currently, 2013-2008) **AUTHORITY:** Official/authoritative. The PDF version has been official since 1 April 2003. Neither the HTML version nor the PDF version prior to 1 April 2003 is official; however, both are authoritative.* **and** **URL:** <http://www.gazette.gc.ca/archives/archives-eng.html#older> **COVERAGE:** 1841-2007 (currently) **AUTHORITY:** This is a scanned, PDF version of the historical copies of the *Gazette*, as reproduced by Library and Archives Canada. It is a reproduction of an official version and thus reliable in most instances. However, note the disclaimer provided on the site.
Bills	Libraries collect copies of bills for each legislative session. Bills are available from each legislative stage.	**AVAILABLE:** Yes **COVERAGE:** Historical to 17 September 2012** **AUTHORITY:** Authoritative	**URL:** <http://www.parl.gc.ca/LEGISINFO> **COVERAGE:** 37th Parl, 1st Sess to present (29 January 2001 to present) **AUTHORITY:** Authoritative
Journals of the House of Commons of Canada and *Journals of the Senate of Canada*	The daily agenda for the House and Senate	**AVAILABLE:** Yes† **COVERAGE:** Historical to 17 September 2012** **AUTHORITY:** Authoritative	**URL:** <http://www.parl.gc.ca> **NAVIGATION:** Use the Site Map **COVERAGE:** 35th Parl, 1st Sess to present (17 January 1994 to present) **AUTHORITY:** Authoritative

Publication	What It Is	Print	Online
Debates of the House of Commons of Canada (*Hansard*)	Organized by legislative session and then by day. Contains verbatim transcript of proceedings.	**AVAILABLE:** Yes **COVERAGE:** Historical to 17 September 2012** **AUTHORITY:** Authoritative	**URL:** <http://www2.parl.gc.ca/Sites/LOP/ReconstitutedDebates/index-e.asp> **COVERAGE:** 1st Parl, 1st Sess to 1st Parl, 5th Sess (1867-1872) **and** **URL:** <http://www.parl.gc.ca> **NAVIGATION:** Use the Site Map **COVERAGE:** 35th Parl, 1st Sess to present (1994 to present) **AUTHORITY:** Authoritative
Debates of the Senate of Canada	Organized by legislative session and then by day. Contains verbatim transcript of proceedings.	**AVAILABLE:** Yes **COVERAGE:** Historical to 17 September 2012** **AUTHORITY:** Authoritative	**URL:** <http://www2.parl.gc.ca/sites/lop/reconstituteddebates/index-e.asp> **COVERAGE:** 1st Parl, 1st Sess to 1st Parl, 5th Sess (1867-1872) **and** **URL:** <http://www.parl.gc.ca> **NAVIGATION:** Use the Site Map **COVERAGE:** 35th Parl, 1st Sess to present (1994 to present) **AUTHORITY:** Authoritative
Committee reports	Reports prepared by parliamentary committees	**AVAILABLE:** Yes **COVERAGE:** Historical to 17 September 2012** **AUTHORITY:** Authoritative	**URL:** <http://www.parl.gc.ca> **NAVIGATION:** Use the Site Map **AUTHORITY:** Authoritative **COVERAGE:** 35th Parl, 1st Sess to present (1994 to present)
Statutes of Canada	The permanent collection of federal laws as enacted	**AVAILABLE:** Yes **COVERAGE:** Historical to present **AUTHORITY:** Official	**URL:** <http://laws-lois.justice.gc.ca/eng> **NAVIGATION:** Go to Annual Statutes **AUTHORITY:** Authoritative **COVERAGE:** 2001 to present

*   *Canada Gazette*, Important Notices, online: <http://canadagazette.gc.ca/in-ai-eng.html>.

**   After 17 September 2012, publications are available only in electronic format. See <http://publications.gc.ca/site/eng/news/2012/2012-11-eng.html>.

†   The print version of this publication ceased from 1993 (34th Parl, 3rd Sess) to 2004 (38th Parl, 1st Sess). This gap is only partially covered in the online version.

Because there are no "official" methods to complete legal research, choose the most efficient, cost-effective approach using the most authoritative sources available. Official sources may not be required for basic research needs. However, when possible, official sources should be used for courtroom purposes. Figure 3.8 summarizes the sources that are considered "official", "authoritative", and "unofficial" for court purposes.

FIGURE 3.8 Status of Commonly Used Publications

Publication	Printer	Status
Canada Gazette, print	Queen's Printer	Official
Canada Gazette, online	Queen's Printer	Official
Statutes of Canada, print	Queen's Printer	Official
Annual Statutes database on Justice Laws website	Justice Canada	Authoritative
Revised Statutes of Canada, print	Queen's Printer	Official
Consolidated Acts database on Justice Laws website	Justice Canada	Official
Debates, print	Canada Government Publishing	Authoritative
Debates, online	Parliament of Canada	Authoritative
Journals of the House, print	Public Works and Government Services	Authoritative
Journals of the House, online	Parliament of Canada	Authoritative
Secondary sources	Various	Unofficial; use copy from original or PDF, not HTML

Locating and Working with Federal Statutes and Regulations

4

LEARNING OUTCOMES

By the end of this chapter, you should be able to:

- Understand how federal statutes and regulations are amended, revised, and consolidated
- Locate official current and prior revised and consolidated versions of statutes and regulations, in print and online
- Update revised and consolidated federal statutes and regulations
- Understand how to complete period-in-time research
- Complete historical federal legislative research (backdating)
- Compile a legislative history
- Locate private statutes

Research Tasks

Chapter 3 described the process by which Parliament creates statutes and regulations. Chapter 4 builds on that information and explains how to solve research problems, working with statutes and regulations that have come into force.

It is important to be aware that legislation is published in two versions. First, statutes are published as enacted, while regulations are published as registered. Second, both statutes and regulations are published in a consolidated form. Further, both versions are published in two formats: in print and online. The complexity of federal legal research becomes apparent when it is recognized that competent legal research requires the use of both versions (enacted or registered, and consolidated) and both formats (print and online). However, the versions have different functions, and the choice of whether to use a print or online format is dictated by the nature of the research issue.

I. How Federal Statutes Are Amended, Consolidated, and Revised

A. The Purpose of an Amending Statute

Amending statutes are created to alter some aspect of an existing statute. An amending statute may change some wording of the existing statute, replace or repeal sections or entire parts, or repeal the statute in its entirety. Once an amending statute has fulfilled its purpose, it has no future effect.

The following example illustrates the amendment process (see Figure 4.1):

> The *Motor Vehicle Safety Act* was first enacted in 1993. Subsequently, the government decided to change the definition of the term "vehicle", and an amending statute was created.[1] Once the bill amending the *Motor Vehicle Safety Act* was passed in the House and Senate, received royal assent, and came into force, section 2 of the amending statute, titled the *Ensuring Safe Vehicles Imported from Mexico for Canadians Act*, SC 2011, c 1, amended the definition of "vehicle" in the pre-existing *Motor Vehicle Safety Act*.

When conducting research, it is essential that you determine the amendment history of a statute. There is no limit to the number of times a statute can be amended; the longer it has been in existence, the greater the chance is that it has changed. Therefore, a fundamental issue to be determined is whether the required version of the statute is:

---

1   Creation of the statute followed the process described in Chapter 3.

- the version as first enacted, as described in Chapter 3
- the current version containing all amendments, as described in the next section
- the version as it existed at a specific historical point in time, as described later in the chapter

FIGURE 4.1   Example of an Amending Statute

	Original Statute	Amending Statute
Title	*Motor Vehicle Safety Act*, SC 1993, c 16, s 2	*Ensuring Safe Vehicles Imported from Mexico for Canadians Act*, SC 2011, c 1, s 2
Definition of "vehicle"	"Vehicle" means any vehicle that is capable of being driven or drawn on roads by any means other than muscular power exclusively, but does not include any vehicle designed to run exclusively on rails.	"Vehicle" means any vehicle that belongs to a prescribed class of vehicles.

B. Updating Statutes to Include Amendments: The Initial Solution—Revised Statutes of Canada: Print Consolidations

The *Statutes of Canada* (SC) provide the version of the statute as first enacted. However, as legislation is amended, the original version of the statute ceases to be current. The initial solution was to publish a revised version of the statute that contained amendments to the statute as enacted. Several revisions have been undertaken; the most recent version of the *Revised Statutes of Canada* (RSC) was published in 1985, and the version before that in 1970.

The *Revised Statutes of Canada*, 1985 (RSC 1985) were compiled by the Statute Revision Commission. The commission was given legislative authority to both consolidate and revise the law.[2]

---

2   *Revised Statutes of Canada, 1985 Act*, RSC 1985, c 40 (3d Supp) and *Statute Revision Act*, SC 1974-75-76, c 20. Similar authority was provided in prior statutes enacted to authorize previous versions of the RSC.

To consolidate the law, the commission examined all statutes that were published in the RSC 1970, removed those acts that were repealed between 7 October 1970 and 31 December 1984, added all new substantive acts, and incorporated all amendments to statutes that were enacted during the period. In summary, the RSC 1985 included all substantive laws in force as of 31 December 1984, and it consolidated all amendments to those laws. Figure 4.2 summarizes the inclusions in and omissions from the RSC 1985.

FIGURE 4.2   Summary of Inclusions in and Omissions from the 1985 Consolidation

Revised Statutes of Canada, 1985	
Included	**Omitted**
Statutes in the RSC 1970, in force, that were amended	Some statutes in force, but not amended between 1970 and 1985
Substantive acts enacted after 1970 and their amendments	Amending and repealing statutes (non-substantive)
Substantive acts enacted between 1986 and 1988 (supplements)	Repealed statutes

Statutes from the prior 1970 consolidation that were not repealed form the basis of the RSC 1985. However, their chapter numbers were changed to reflect an alphanumeric identification that corresponded to their place in the new set.

The origin of each statute published in the RSC 1985 is noted in section 1 of the statute as it appears in the consolidation. This historical information line is used to backdate a statute, which will be described later in this chapter.

Substantive statutes[3] that were enacted between 1970 and 1985 were included in the RSC 1985. They were integrated into the remaining contents of the RSC 1970 (as outlined above) and the entire set was organized alphanumerically. All statutes were organized alphabetically and given a new chapter number that corresponded to their place in the set.

The *Canadian Human Rights Act*, SC 1976-77, c 33 became the *Canadian Human Rights Act*, RSC 1985, c H-6.

---

3 Substantive statutes are created to regulate some aspect of the law. Amending statutes, in contrast, are created to change some aspect of a substantive statute; they have no continued purpose once they have amended the substantive statute. Some statutes have a dual function: they have a specific substantive purpose, and they also amend other substantive law.

The statute's origins (SC 1976-77, c 33) are provided in section 1 of the RSC 1985 version of the statute. See Figure 4.3.

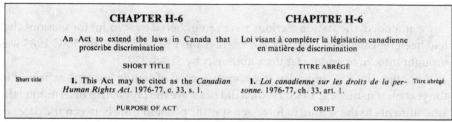

FIGURE 4.3   Example of the Origins of a Statute Referred to in the Revised Statutes

Some statutes were not included in the 1985 statute revision. Amending statutes that were enacted between the RSC 1970 and the RSC 1985 and that did not create a substantive act, but merely amended other acts, were not included in the RSC. Although the amending statutes themselves were not reproduced as independent statutes within the RSC, the amendments they enacted were integrated into the substantive statutes in the RSC. Also omitted from the RSC 1985 were statutes that were not repealed and remain in force but that had no new amendments between 1970 and 1984.

> The *Criminal Law Amendment Act, 1977*, SC 1976-77, c 53 does not appear in the RSC 1985 because its only purpose was to amend criminal legislation.
>
> The *Canada Corporations Act*, RSC 1970, c C-32 does not appear in the 1985 consolidation because it was not revised between 1970 and 1984; however, it has not been repealed and remains in force.

A useful research tool is the Table of Concordance, published as a separate volume in the RSC 1985. It details the status of every statute contained in the RSC 1970, along with every statute enacted between 7 October 1970 and 31 December 1984.

Seemingly anomalous inclusions in the RSC 1985 are substantive statutes enacted between 1 January 1986 and 12 December 1988, along with amendments to those statutes made during these years. These are contained in four supplemental volumes to the RSC 1985. (A fifth supplement contains the *Income Tax Act*.) The inclusion of these later statutes is understandable if one recognizes that rapid information organization and dissemination of legal information was far more difficult before the digitization of legislation. Though the revision is named "1985", it was not completed and published until 1989.

Enacted version: *Divorce Act*, SC 1986, c 4, assented to 13 February 1986.
Revised version: *Divorce Act*, RSC 1985, c 3 (2d Supp).

Once amended, the statute sections were renumbered to account for sections that had been repealed or added.[4] When the revision was complete, the RSC 1985 was brought into force under statutory authority by SI/88-227.

Although the RSC provides an accurate record of statute law as it appeared in the year of its name (e.g. 1985, 1970), it did not solve the problem of determining the amendments to the statute in force at a specific point in time between the dates of consolidation.

C. Updating Statutes to Include Amendments: The Current Solution—Revised Statutes of Canada: Online Consolidations

The print version of the *Revised Statutes of Canada, 1985* is no longer current; in fact, it increasingly lost currency with each new substantive and amending statute enacted after its publication. Currently, all amendments are incorporated into each statute, and the Department of Justice consolidates the law and makes these consolidations available online on the Department of Justice website (Justice Laws).[5]

The online consolidations are permitted by legislative authority. In 2009, the *Legislation Revision and Consolidation Act* came into force.[6] Pursuant to the Act, the Statute Revision Commission retains the authority to revise statutes. This includes removing repealed sections, incorporating amendments, and renumbering sections.[7] However, there is no immediate intent to produce a new printed set of the *Revised Statutes of Canada*.[8]

---

4   The Statute Revision Commission's authority to revise statutes, including the authority to renumber statutes and to renumber statute sections, was also set out in the *Statute Revision Act*, RSC 1985, c S-20, s 6(d). (This Act has been succeeded by the *Legislation Revision and Consolidation Act*, *infra* note 7.)

5   Department of Justice, "Consolidated Acts", online: <http://laws-lois.justice.gc.ca/eng/acts/>.

6   RSC 1985, c S-20, as amended by the *Personal Information Protection and Electronic Documents Act*, SC 2000, c 5.

7   *Legislation Revision and Consolidation Act*, RSC 1985, c S-20, ss 3-4, 5-7.

8   Email from Ingrid Ludchen, Chief Legislative Editor, Legislative Editing and Publishing Services Section, Department of Justice, to Annette Demers (7 February 2011): [Ludchen (7 February 2011)]: "There are no plans to print a consolidation of the entire statute book in paper form, which is a costly and time-consuming undertaking. The consolidated Acts and regulations provided free of charge on the Justice Laws website have had official status (that is, they have evidentiary value in

Although the Statute Revision Commission maintains the ability to revise statutes, the Department of Justice, through the office of the Chief Legislative Editor of Canada, now has the authority to consolidate the law and to make these consolidations available online in an electronic format.[9] The authority to consolidate, however, does not include the authority to renumber chapters or to renumber sections of an act.[10] The Act delineates consolidation dissemination,[11] and establishes the official nature of such consolidations for use in a courtroom.[12]

In summary:

- Official current consolidations of the law are now available on the Department of Justice's Justice Laws Consolidated Acts online.
- A new print revision is not being considered; the RSC 1985 is the most recent print revision available.
- Most of the current consolidations that appear on the Justice Laws website were compiled using the RSC 1985 as their starting point; therefore, citations to RSC 1985 can be used to locate statutes as they appeared in the print volumes of the RSC 1985 as well as some statutes in the current consolidations on the Justice Laws website.

---

accordance with section 31 of the *Legislation Revision and Consolidation Act*) since June 1, 2009. Anyone can, at any time, print out a consolidation of any Act or regulation that has been included on the Justice Laws Website. The consolidations are usually current to within three or four weeks of an amendment's coming into force. (This timeframe has to do with the timing of the publication in the *Canada Gazette*, Part II of amendments and coming into force information.)"

9   *Legislation Revision and Consolidation Act, supra* note 7, s 26.

10   Ludchen (7 February 2011), *supra* note 8, "The Statute Revision Commission referred to in the *Legislation Revision and Consolidation Act* has authority to *revise* Acts, and, since 2009, to *revise* regulations. It is the Minister of Justice that has been authorized to maintain a *consolidation* of public statutes and regulations. These consolidations are made available in unilingual HTML and bilingual PDF printable formats and are updated weekly on the Justice Laws Website."

11   *Legislation Revision and Consolidation Act, supra* note 7, ss 28-30.

12   *Ibid*, s 31(1).

D. Legal Citation of Revised and Consolidated Statutes

Chapter 3 set out the basic format for citation of bills, regulations, and statutes as enacted. There are additional variants when citing to a revised and consolidated statute.

> ■ A statute as it appeared in the RSC 1985 is cited to RSC 1985.
>
> ■ A statute that was included in the RSC 1985 and that remains in force, thus appearing in the current consolidations online, is cited to RSC 1985.
>
> ■ A statute that was last consolidated before 1970, and was not included in the RSC 1985 print revision but that remains in force, thus appearing in the current consolidations online, is cited to its RSC consolidation, e.g. 1970.
>
> ■ A statute as it appeared in the *Statutes of Canada* is cited to SC. This includes a statute that was in existence before the RSC 1985 but that was not included in the revision yet remains in force, thus appearing in the current consolidations online.
>
> ■ A statute that was enacted after 1985 that remains in force, thus appearing in the current consolidations online, is cited to SC.

Although the *Canadian Guide to Uniform Legal Citation*[13] provides a generally accepted format for legal citation of revised and consolidated statutes, there is a legislative basis for some acceptable variations to the McGill Guide recommendations, as the following examples illustrate.

Several variations of the same statute may exist:

> *Statute Revision Act*, RSC 1985, c S-20.[14]
> *Legislation Revision and Consolidation Act*, RSC 1985, c S-20.[15]
> *Legislation Revision and Consolidation Act*, RSC, c S-20.[16]

---

13 7th ed (Toronto: Carswell, 2010) [McGill Guide].

14 This Act originally appeared in the *Revised Statutes of Canada*, 1985 under this title.

15 This Act has been substantially amended and its title has been changed; however, because it was not repealed, it continues to be cited to RSC 1985.

16 This citation is permitted by authority of the *Revised Statutes of Canada, 1985 Act*, RSC 1985, c 40, s 9 (3d Supp). See also the *Interpretation Act*, RSC 1985, c I-21, s 40(1).

E. Guide to Publications in This Section

A summary of statute publications discussed in this section, along with their availability online and in print, is provided in Figure 4.4. One may assume that publications available in print form, including historical material, will be available at most law libraries.

FIGURE 4.4   Summary of Statute Publications and Print/Online Availability

	Description	Print	Online
Revised Statutes of Canada, 1985	A collection of revised federal statutes compiled by the Statute Revision Commission	**AVAILABLE:** Yes **COVERAGE:** Historical statutes and their amendments in force as of 31 December 1984 **AUTHORITY:** Official	**AVAILABLE:** HeinOnline Session Laws Library
Revised Statutes of Canada, historical versions	Revised federal statutes	**AVAILABLE:** Yes **COVERAGE:** Historical content **AUTHORITY:** Official	**AVAILABLE:** HeinOnline Session Laws Library
Consolidated acts	Federal statutes consolidated by the Department of Justice	**AVAILABLE:** No **COVERAGE:** Current **AUTHORITY:** Official	**AVAILABLE:** Yes **URL:** <http://laws.justice.gc.ca/eng/acts>

II. Locating and Updating Revised and Consolidated Federal Statutes Including Amendments

Chapter 3 explained the process to locate statutes as first enacted, while section I of this chapter explained the amendment process. Section II explains how to locate the amended versions of statutes that have been revised and consolidated.

A. Locating Revised Statutes Using Official Sources: Print and Online

If you are required to locate historical versions of statutes not available online, use the following method. The *Interpretation Act*, RSC 1985, c I-21 will be used for the following examples.

TASK 4.1

Locating Historical Versions of Revised Statutes: Print—Official

1. In a law library, use the library catalogue to locate the RSC 1985. Select chapter I-21, using the Table of Contents to navigate the multiset series.

2. The RSC is organized in alphabetical order by statute title, and each act is given an alphanumeric chapter number that reflects the first letter in its title as well as its numerical position within the set. Turn to chapter I-21 to view the statute.

3. The coming into force sections may be removed when the statute is revised. If the original version of the statute as first enacted is required, follow the steps to backdate a statute, described later in this chapter.

Locating Current Consolidations of Revised Statutes: Online—Official

1. On the Justice Laws website, go to Consolidated Acts.

2. From the alphabetical list of statutes, select "I" and locate the *Interpretation Act*.

3. If the statute is required for courtroom use, choose the PDF version, which is marked by the seal of the Crown. Review the currency statement provided on the title page of the document to determine the date the statute was last updated.

4. The coming into force sections are removed when the statute is revised. If the original version of the statute as first enacted is required, follow the steps to backdate a statute, described later in this chapter.

5. If a current consolidation is required for courtroom use, update the statute to the present date using the steps provided later in this chapter.

B. Locating Statute Amendments

At certain times—for example, when completing period-in-time research—amendments to statutes that were made subsequent to the last print consolidation must be located. The amendment information line found in the revised consolidated statutes can be used to locate this information.

The *Access to Information Act*, RSC 1985, c A-1, section 77 will be used for the following example.

Locating Statute Amendments Using Consolidated Acts: Online and Print—Official

■ On the Justice Laws website, go to Consolidated Acts. Locate and review section 77 of the *Access to Information Act*.

■ The amendment information line is located at the end of the section. It contains citation references to two amendments to the designated section: "R.S., 1985, c. A-1, s. 77; 1992, c. 21, s. 5; 2006, c. 9, s. 163". This can be interpreted as:

> Section 77 of the *Access to Information Act* appearing in the *Revised Statutes of Canada*, 1985 at chapter A-1 was first amended by the statute that appears at SC 1992, chapter 21, section 5. It was later amended by the statute that appears at SC 2006, chapter 9, section 163.

- If required, using the citation reference, locate the amending statutes as they were first enacted in the print or online versions of the *Statutes of Canada*.
- The print version of the RSC contains similar amendment information for the statute and can be used to locate amending information. However, the print version of the RSC cannot be used to determine any amendments made to legislation subsequent to the last revision in 1985; therefore, its use is limited to situations when historical research is required. This point will be discussed in greater depth in the discussion on historical research later in this chapter.

C. Locating Statute Amendments Using the Table of Public Statutes: Online and Print—Authoritative

The Table of Public Statutes is a comprehensive reference tool that can be used to find:

- a list of substantive statutes currently in force for the online version (or in force on the date the table was compiled for the print version)
- amendments made to substantive statutes and their corresponding citation references after the date of the last print consolidation
- coming into force information for each amendment with corresponding citation references

The Table of Public Statutes is found in the annual volume of the *Statutes of Canada*, and contains all amendments to the statutes made since the last print revision in 1985. A current version of the Table of Public Statutes (entitled "Table of Public Statutes and Responsible Ministers") is maintained on the Justice Laws website.

TASK 4.4

Locating Statute Amendments Using the Table of Public Statutes: Online and Print—Official

On the Justice Laws website, locate the Table of Public Statutes. Within the table, locate the *Access to Information Act* and examine the accompanying references:

Access to Information Act — R.S., 1985, c. A-1

(Accès à l'information, Loi sur l')

Minister of Justice (for purposes of paragraph (b) of the definition "head" in section 3, subsection 4(2), paragraphs 77(1)(f) and (g) and subsection 77(2)); President of the Treasury Board (for all other purposes of the Act) (SI/83-108)

s. 3, 1992, c. 21, s. 1; 2002, c. 8, par. 183(1)(a); 2006, c. 9, s. 141
s. 3.01, added, 2006, c. 9, s. 142
s. 3.1, added, 2006, c. 9, s. 142
s. 3.2, added, 2006, c. 9, s. 142
s. 4, 1992, c. 1, s. 144 (Sch. VII, item 1)(F); 2001, c. 27, s. 202; 2006, c. 9, s. 143
s. 11, 1992, c. 21, s. 2
s. 12, R.S., c. 31 (4th Supp.), s. 100(E); 1992, c. 21, s. 3
s. 13, 2000, c. 7, s. 21; 2004, c. 17, s. 16; 2005, c. 1, ss. 97 and 107, c. 27, ss. 16 and 22(1); 2006, c. 10, s. 32; 2008, c. 32, s. 26; 2009, c. 18, s. 20
s. 16.1, added, 2006, c. 9, s. 144
s. 16.2, added, 2006, c. 9, s. 89
s. 16.3, added, 2006, c. 9, s. 145
s. 16.4, added, 2005, c. 46, s. 55 (**see** 2006, c. 9, s. 221)
s. 16.5, added, 2005, c. 46, s. 55 (**see** 2006, c. 9, s. 221)
s. 18, 2006, c. 9, s. 146
s. 18.1, added, 2006, c. 9, s. 147
s. 20, 2007, c. 15, s. 8
s. 20.1, added, 2006, c. 9, s. 148
s. 20.2, added, 2006, c. 9, s. 148
s. 20.4, added, 2006, c. 9, s. 148
s. 21, 2006, c. 9, s. 149

All amendments made to the statute since 1985 are listed in order, followed by a citation reference to the amending statute. As noted previously, section 77 was amended twice:

s. 77, 1992, c. 21, s. 5; 2006, c. 9, s. 163

Section 77 of the *Access to Information Act* was first amended by section 5 of the statute enacted in 1992 at chapter 21. Section 77 was later amended by section 163 of the statute enacted in 2006 at chapter 9.

- Also included in the table is coming into force (CIF) information for all amendments. To locate CIF information, scan the table. CIF information is listed after all amendments to the statute are identified.

■ The first amendment to section 77, by SC 1992, c 21, s 5, was brought into force on 1 October 1992 by Statutory Instrument SI/92-126. The CIF for the second amendment would be found using the citation reference for that amendment.

```
CIF, 1991, c. 3, s. 10 in force 21.04.91 see SI/91-58
CIF, 1991, c. 6, s. 22 in force 09.09.91 see SI/91-117
CIF, 1991, c. 16, s. 21 in force 01.12.91 see SI/91-158
CIF, 1991, c. 38, s. 25 in force 26.11.91 see SI/91-161
CIF, 1992, c. 1, s. 2, s. 143 (Sch. VI, Item 1)(E), s. 144 (Sch. VII, Items 1 to
    3)(F), s. 145 (Sch. VIII, Item 1)(F) and s. 147 in force on assent 28.02.92
CIF, 1992, c. 21, ss. 1 to 5 in force 01.10.92 see SI/92-126
CIF, 1992, c. 33, s. 68 in force 09.05.95 see SI/95-61
CIF, 1992, c. 34 in force on assent 23.06.92
CIF, 1992, c. 36, s. 37 in force 01.01.93 see SI/92-153
```

D. Updating a Statute: Determining Coming into Force

A statute may have been amended since the last date of consolidation.[17] To update a statute, determine whether amendments have come into force between the currency date of the most recent official consolidation available and the current date.

TASK 4.5

Updating a Statute Using the Canada Gazette to Locate Recent Amendments: Online—Official

Update the *Interpretation Act*, RSC 1985, c I-21, s 6 to the most current version.

1. On the Justice Laws website, locate the official copy of the statute consolidation. Review the currency statement provided on the title page of the statute.

2. Locate the *Canada Gazette*, Part III. Determine whether any issues of the *Gazette* have been published subsequent to the currency date.

3. If new issues have been published, review the Table of Proclamations in the issue of the *Canada Gazette*, Part III published after the currency date. Examine the acts that have come into force since the currency date to determine whether a new statute has amended the statute.

4. If there are no new issues of the *Canada Gazette*, Part III published after the currency date, turn to the *Canada Gazette*, Part II.

---

17 Department of Justice Canada, "Frequently Asked Questions", online: Department of Justice <http://laws-lois.justice.gc.ca/eng/FAQ/#g5_5>.

5. For each issue published after the currency date, locate the Table of Contents and review the list of statutory instruments (SIs) and statutory orders (SORs). (Although the majority of amendments to statutes will be found in an SI document, on occasion an amendment to a statute will be found in an SOR— e.g. SOR/2011-233, which amends a schedule to an act.)

6. If an amending statute is located that may amend the Act, locate the amending statute using the citation reference. If the amending statute has not yet been made available on the Justice Laws website under Annual Statutes, and if it has not yet been published in the *Canada Gazette*, Part III, use the "royal assent" version of the text as found on the LEGISinfo website. See Chapter 3.

In summary, statutes exist in two versions, the original version as enacted, and the amended version as revised and consolidated. Moreover, they are published in both print and online formats. The issue being researched will determine the version and format to be used. Complete research requires locating statutes in both versions and formats.

Whether the statute under review was recently enacted or has been revised and consolidated several times, one of the most challenging tasks for the novice researcher is determining the date that the statute came into force.

To determine the CIF date for the original version of the statute as enacted, review the steps in Chapter 3. To determine the CIF date for revised and consolidated statutes, refer to the sections below.

1. *Revised Federal Statutes: Print*

The RSC 1985 was proclaimed in force on 21 December 1988.[18] All acts contained in the set came into force on that date. Therefore, when referring to a statute as it appeared in the print version of the *Revised Statutes of Canada*, assume that it is in force.

2. *Consolidated Federal Statutes: Online*

When referring to a statute as it appears on the Justice Laws website online consolidation, note that the entire statute or only specific sections of it may be in force. The content found in this version is evidence of the law.[19]

---

18 *Revised Statutes of Canada, 1985 Act, supra* note 2, ss 72(1), (2), (3), by order of the Governor in Council, SI/88-239.

19 *Legislation Revision and Consolidation Act, supra* note 7, s 31(1).

This version must be updated as described earlier in this chapter to ensure that any statute amendments that have recently come into force have been located. Prior consolidations on the federal Justice Laws website can be considered official.[20]

3. Table of Public Statutes: Online

As described earlier in this chapter, the current version of the Table of Public Statutes provides CIF information for every amendment made to every statute since the last consolidation of statutes in 1985.

III. Steps for Locating Regulations as Registered

Regulations serve several functions. Some bring statutes into force, others provide rules to implement aspects of the statute. Regulations can also be amended. Both the version of the regulation as first registered and the version of the regulation as amended, revised, and consolidated are used in legal research.

A. How Regulations Are Published, Organized, and Cited

The official versions of federal regulations are published in the *Canada Gazette*, Part II, available at most libraries and online.[21] The *Canada Gazette* is the only publication, in print or online, that provides a copy of federal regulations as they appear when they were originally registered. The Justice Laws website, the Canadian Legal Information Institute (CanLII), and commercial research services such as Westlaw and LexisNexis Quicklaw do not reproduce this content. Instead, these products provide a consolidated version of regulations as amended.

To locate a regulation, a citation is required. Regulations as first registered appear as either a statutory order (SOR) or a statutory instrument (SI). The citation contains the following elements:

---

20   *Ibid.* Confirmed in email from Ingrid Ludchen, Chief Legislative Editor, Legislative Editing and Publishing Services Section, Department of Justice, Canada, to Annette Demers (9 February 2011) [Ludchen (9 February 2011)]. According to Ludchen (7 February 2011), *supra* note 8: "Our new website should make point-in-time searching easier still, by setting out the timeframes of the various versions of an enactment, so the points in time are visible at a glance. Because of the availability of these online consolidations, there is no longer a need for a revision of statutes simply to provide a consolidation of the laws, a consolidation that would be out of date as soon as the next amendment is enacted. The newly appointed Statute Revision Commission is currently reviewing the possibility of revising certain specific Acts and regulations identified as laws that would benefit from a revision."

21   Government of Canada, *Canada Gazette*, Part II <http://www.gazette.gc.ca/rp-pr/p2/index-eng.html>.

- "SOR" or "SI"—abbreviations for "Statutory Orders and Regulations" and "Statutory Instrument"
- year—the year the regulation was registered
- number—the document number

SOR/92-279 and SI/95-77

In the first example, "SOR" indicates that this is a statutory order, "92" indicates that the statutory order was registered in 1992, and "279" is the document number. In the second example, "SI" indicates that this is a statutory instrument, "95" indicates the year it was registered, and "77" is the document number.

B. Locating a Citation to a Regulation as Registered: Online

Citations to federal regulations appear in the Consolidated Index of Statutory Instruments to the *Canada Gazette*, Part II. This is available in print, while the most current version is also available online on the *Canada Gazette*, Part II website.

Within the Consolidated Index, locate Table II, Table of Regulations, Statutory Instruments (Other Than Regulations) and Other Documents Arranged by Statute. This table is organized in alphabetical order by title of enabling act; therefore, to use this table, the title of the enabling act is required.

FIGURE 4.5   Table II Within the Consolidated Index

C. Locating Regulations as Registered

TASK 4.6

Locating Regulations as Registered Using Official Sources When the Name of the Regulation Is Known: Print

Locate the regulation *Ontario Rules of Practice Respecting Reduction in the Number of Years of Imprisonment Without Eligibility for Parole*, SOR/92-270 (subsequently repealed).

1. In the library, locate the *Canada Gazette*, Part II print volumes. Examine the set of volumes published in the year in which the regulation was filed (1992).

2. In the 1992 volume, note the SOR citation reference at the top corner of each page. This helps to navigate the volume, as SORs are printed in the *Canada Gazette* in numerical order by document number.

3/6/92   *Canada Gazette Part II, Vol. 126, No. 12*   *Gazette du Canada Partie II, Vol. 126 N° 12* | SOR/DORS/92-270 |

| Registration | Enregistrement |
| SOR/92-270 11 May, 1992 | DORS/92-270 11 mai 1992 |

| CRIMINAL CODE | CODE CRIMINEL |

| **Ontario Rules of Practice Respecting Reduction in the Number of Years of Imprisonment Without Eligibility for Parole** | **Règle de procédure de l'Ontario concernant la réduction du délai préalable à la libération conditionnelle** |

The Chief Justice of the Ontario Court, pursuant to subsection 745(5) of the Criminal Code, hereby revokes the Ontario Rules of Practice Respecting Reduction in the Number of Years of Imprisonment Without Eligibility for Parole* and makes the annexed Ontario Rules of Practice respecting reduction in the number of years of imprisonment without eligibility for parole, in substitution therefor.

Dated at Toronto, Ontario, May 11, 1992

En vertu du paragraphe 745(5) du Code criminel, le juge en chef de la Cour de l'Ontario abroge les Règles de procédure de l'Ontario concernant la réduction du délai préalable à la libération conditionnelle* et établit en remplacement la Règle de procédure de l'Ontario concernant la réduction du délai préalable à la libération conditionnelle, ci-après.

Fait à Toronto (Ontario), le 11 mai 1992

THE HONOURABLE F. W. CALLAGHAN
Chief Justice of the Ontario Court

Juge en chef de la Cour de l'Ontario
L'HONORABLE F. W. CALLAGHAN

TASK 4.7

Locating Regulations as Registered by Citation Using Official Sources: Online

■ To find a regulation within the *Canada Gazette*, Part II online, you must use the citation for the regulation. To locate SOR/92-279, review the most current issue of the Consolidated Index to the *Canada Gazette*, Part II online.

■ While recent issues of the *Gazette* are provided on the main page, older versions appear in the Archives. Go to Part II: Official Regulations to view the issues of the *Gazette* from 1998 to 2013. To navigate, select the year and then review the list of issues to locate the SOR or regulation being searched.

Publications ▾	Publishing Information	Consultation	Help	Advanced Search

Part I: Notices and Proposed Regulations	Part II: Official Regulations	Part III: Acts of Parliament
Volume 147 (2013)	Volume 147 (2013)	ARCHIVED — Volume 35 (2012)
ARCHIVED — Volume 146 (2012)	ARCHIVED — Volume 146 (2012)	ARCHIVED — Volume 34 (2011)
ARCHIVED — Volume 145 (2011)	ARCHIVED — Volume 145 (2011)	ARCHIVED — Volume 33 (2010)
ARCHIVED — Volume 144 (2010)	ARCHIVED — Volume 144 (2010)	ARCHIVED — Volume 32 (2009)
ARCHIVED — Volume 143 (2009)	ARCHIVED — Volume 143 (2009)	ARCHIVED — Volume 31 (2008)
ARCHIVED — Volume 142 (2008)	ARCHIVED — Volume 142 (2008)	
		Archives
Part I: Quarterly Index	**Part II: Consolidated Index**	ARCHIVED — 1841-2007
Volume 147 (2013)	Volume 147 (2013)	
ARCHIVED — Volume 146 (2012)	ARCHIVED — Volume 146 (2012)	
ARCHIVED — Volume 145 (2011)	ARCHIVED — Volume 145 (2011)	
ARCHIVED — Volume 144 (2010)	ARCHIVED — Volume 144 (2010)	
ARCHIVED — Volume 143 (2009)	ARCHIVED — Volume 143 (2009)	
ARCHIVED — Volume 142 (2008)	ARCHIVED — Volume 142 (2008)	

To access older versions of the *Gazette* published between 1841 and 1997, go to 1841-1997 under Archives and then select the link to "Library and Archives Canada (LAC)".

■ At the Library and Archives Canada website, go to Search the *Canada Gazette*. Select "Find an Issue" and choose "Part II (1947-1997)" from the drop-down Title menu.

■ Enter the year of the regulation to be located in the "Year" field (1992), then select "Submit".

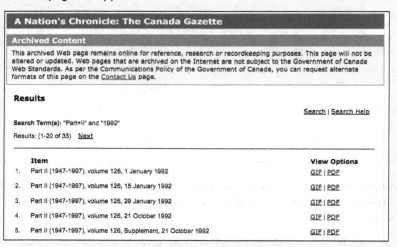

- A results page will appear.

- Use the document number of the SOR to start the search. For example, to locate SOR/92-10, select the first issue in 1992. To locate SOR/92-279, try one of the later issues in 1992.

- The SOR range covered in each issue of the *Gazette* is stated on the title page. The issue that includes SOR/92-279 is vol 126, no 12 (3 June 1992).

- Scroll to the end of the *Gazette* issue to view the Table of Contents. SORs are listed in order by document number. The page number is provided in the far right column (2085).

Vol. 126, No. 12

Canada Gazette

Part II

OTTAWA, WEDNESDAY, JUNE 3, 1992

Statutory Instruments 1992

SOR/92-270 to 334 and SI/92-99 to 104

Pages 2048 to 2460

- Scroll to that page to view the regulation: *Securities Dealing Restrictions (Banks) Regulations*, SOR/92-279.

3/6/92 *Canada Gazette Part II, Vol. 126, No. 12*			SOR/92-270–334 SI/92-99–104	
TABLE OF CONTENTS	**SOR**	**Statutory Instruments (Regulations)**		
	SI:	**Statutory Instruments and Other Documents (Other than Regulations)**		
Registration No.	P.C. 1992	Departments	Name of Statutory Instruments or Other Documents	Page
SOR/92-270		Justice	Ontario Rules of Practice Respecting Reduction in the Number of Years of Imprisonment without Eligibility for Parole	2048
SOR/92-271	1026	Agriculture	Saskatchewan Canola Order	2060
SOR/92-272	1027	Finance	Securities Dealing Restrictions (Trust and Loan Companies) Regulations	2064
SOR/92-273	1028	Finance	Investments (Canadian Companies) Regulations	2074
SOR/92-274	1029	Finance	Investments (Foreign Companies) Regulations	2076
SOR/92-275	1030	Finance	Investments (Canadian Societies) Regulations	2077
SOR/92-276	1031	Finance	Vested Assets (Foreign Companies) Regulations	2079
SOR/92-277	1032	Finance	Life Companies Borrowing Regulations	2081
SOR/92-278	1033	Finance	Securities Dealing Restrictions (Cooperative Credit Association Regulations	2083
SOR/92-279	1034	Finance	Securities Dealing Restrictions (Banks) Regulations	2085
SOR/92-280	1035	Finance	Securities Dealing Restrictions (Insurance Companies) Regulations	2087
SOR/92-281	1036	Finance	Property and Casualty Companies Borrowing Regulations	2089
SOR/92-282	1037	Finance	Resident Canadian (Banks) Regulations	2091

IV. How Federal Regulations Are Amended, Consolidated, and Revised

Chapter 3 discussed the purpose of regulations and described the manner in which they were created, first registered, and brought into force. However, just as statutes can be amended, revised, and consolidated, so too can regulations.

A. Consolidated Regulations of Canada

The *Consolidated Regulations of Canada* (CRC) are published and disseminated pursuant to the *Legislation Revision and Consolidation Act*.[22] The most recent print consolidation of regulations was published in 1978 and includes regulations in force on the date of the consolidation.

All amendments to regulations were incorporated within the content. The substantive regulations that remained in the set were then organized in alphabetical order by the enabling act title and given a chapter number.[23]

---

22   *Supra* note 7, ss 6, 10, 11, 21.

23   Not every regulation was included in the final set. The CRC provides a table that specifies the results of the regulation review process.

> The *Machinery Sales Tax Remission Order*, CRC 1978, c 797 was made pursuant to the *Financial Administration Act*.

The new set of the CRC was brought into force as a whole by statutory authority, and the year was added to the title: CRC 1978.

Although researching regulations in print form may be required from time to time when conducting historical research, most regulation research can now be done online. Both current and prior consolidated versions of regulations published on the Justice Laws website are considered official.[24] The Department of Justice's authority to consolidate regulations is provided by the *Legislation Revision and Consolidation Act*.[25]

B. Legal Citation of Consolidated Regulations

As it does for bills and statutes, the McGill Guide provides recommendations for citing regulations.[26] Chapter 3 discussed the basic format for regulations as first registered. Additional variants are possible in citations of consolidated regulations, as summarized below. Further, note should be made of the legislation that provides the basis for these rules, as well as acceptable alternatives to those provided in the McGill Guide.

> ■ A regulation as it appeared in the CRC 1978 is cited to CRC 1978.
>
> ■ Regulations in the current online consolidation on the Justice Laws website that were included in the CRC 1978 and that have not been repealed are cited to CRC 1978 pursuant to section 24 of the *Legislation Revision and Consolidation Act*.
>
> ■ A regulation that was enacted after the CRC 1978 is cited as it appeared when registered, using its SOR number. Example: *Federal Book Rebate (GST/HST) Regulations*, SOR/98-351.
>
> ■ A regulation as registered and that has not been repealed is cited using its SOR number.

---

24   *Legislation Revision and Consolidation Act, supra* note 7, s 31(c). Confirmed by Ludchen (9 February 2011).

25   *Supra* note 7, ss 27, 28, 29, 31(1).

26   *Supra* note 13 at ch 2.6.

As the following examples illustrate, in citations of consolidated regulations, statutory authority[27] provides alternatives to the forms recommended by the McGill Guide:

- *Machinery Sales Tax Remission Order*, CRC 1978, c 797.[28]
- *Machinery Sales Tax Remission Order*, CRC, c 797.[29]
- *Machinery Sales Tax Remission Order*, RRC, c 797.[30]
- *Machinery Sales Tax Remission Order*, RR, c 797.[31]

V. Locating and Updating Consolidated Regulations Including Rules of Court

The following steps to locate regulations can be used to locate the current consolidated version of federal court rules.

A. Locating Current Consolidations of Regulations Using Official Sources: Online

TASK 4.8

Locating Current Consolidated Regulations by Title

Locate the *Machinery Sales Tax Remission Order*, CRC 1978, c 797.

1. On the Justice Laws website, go to Consolidated Regulations and locate the *Machinery Sales Tax Remission Order*.

2. The PDF version is marked by the seal of the Crown, and should be used at court.

---

27   *Legislation Revision and Consolidation Act, supra* note 7, s 20(1).

28   This is the citation style preferred by the McGill Guide, and it is used to refer to content as it originally appeared in the CRC 1978.

29   This is the format used by the Justice Laws website to cite consolidated regulations that originally appeared in the CRC 1978 and that are currently in force and included in the online consolidation.

30   This format is permitted by section 20(1) of the *Legislation Revision and Consolidation Act, supra* note 7.

31   This format is permitted by section 20(1) of the *Legislation Revision and Consolidation Act, ibid.*

3. Locate the currency statement provided on the title page of the document.

4. Update the regulation. On the *Canada Gazette*, Part II website, examine each issue published after the currency date. Locate the Table of Contents. Review the list of statutory orders. Look for new regulations that have come into force that would amend the regulation. If no regulation is found that amends the subject regulation, updating is complete.

5. If an amending regulation is found, select the linked SOR citation to view.

2011-01-19	*Canada Gazette Part II, Vol. 145, No. 2*		SOR/2010-316—317	SI/2011-1—4

TABLE OF CONTENTS	SOR:	Statutory Instruments (Regulations)		
	SI:	Statutory Instruments and Other Documents (Other than Regulations)		

Registration number	P.C. number	Minister	Name of Statutory Instrument or Other Document	Page
SOR/2010-316		Environment	Order 2010-87-12-02 Amending the Domestic Substances List..................	44
SOR/2010-317		Environment	Order 2010-66-12-01 Amending the Domestic Substances List..................	49
SI/2011-1	2011-2	Prime Minister	Order Terminating the Assignment of the Honourable Peter Kent	50
SI/2011-2	2011-3	Prime Minister	Order Terminating the Assignment of the Honourable Diane Ablonczy and Assigning the Honourable Diane Ablonczy to Assist the Minister of Foreign Affairs (Americas and Consular Affairs)............................	51
SI/2011-3	2011-4	Prime Minister	Order Assigning the Honourable Ted Menzies to Assist the Minister of Finance	52
SI/2011-4	2011-5	Prime Minister	Order Assigning the Honourable Julian Fantino to Assist the Minister of Human Resources and Skills Development	53

TASK 4.9

Locating Current Consolidated Regulations by Citation

Locate SOR/81-677.

1. On the Justice Laws website, go to Advanced Search. In the "Chapter registration #" field, enter SOR/81-677. Under "Search in", choose "Regulations".

2. Search. A list of search results will appear at the bottom of the page, below the search boxes.

3. Update the regulation. On the *Canada Gazette*, Part II website, examine each issue published after the currency date. Locate the Table of Contents. Review the list of statutory orders. Look for new regulations that have come into force that would amend the regulation. If no regulation is found that amends the subject regulation, updating is complete.

4. If an amending regulation is found, select the linked SOR citation to view.

5. Update the regulation as described in the previous example.

TASK 4.10

Locating Current Consolidated Regulations by Title of Enabling Act

Locate current regulations under the *Access to Information Act*.

1. On the Justice Laws website, go to Consolidated Acts and locate the *Access to Information Act*.

2. Select the yellow "R" box next to the Act to view regulations made pursuant to the Act.

Access to Information Act

R.S.C., 1985, c. A-1   ⤓ **PDF** [338 KB]   [R]

---

3. Alternatively, link to the statute to view the Table of Contents. Regulations are listed at the bottom of the page.

B. Locating Consolidations of Regulations Using Official Sources: Historical Research—Print

If online searching is unavailable, use print sources to locate previous versions of revised regulations, such as the CRC 1978.

TASK 4.11

Locating Historical Regulations: Print

Locate the *Machinery Sales Tax Remission Order*, CRC 1978, c 797.

- At a law library, use the library catalogue to locate the *Consolidated Regulations of Canada*. Locate the regulation at chapter 797.

C. Locating Consolidated Regulations Using the Canada Gazette: Historical Research—Print and Online

When historical research of regulations is required, use the Consolidated Index of Statutory Instruments to the *Canada Gazette*, Part II. Consolidated indexes are available online on the *Canada Gazette* website and the Library and Archives Canada website.[32] They are also available in print in most large university libraries. The index itself is a consolidation of regulations from 1955 to today.

TASK 4.12

Locating Consolidated Regulations by Title of Enabling Act

Using the *Bank Act*, SC 1991, c 46 for this example, determine whether a regulation exists affecting the cost of borrowing.

1. On the Justice Laws website, go to the Consolidated Index of Statutory Instruments and select the most recent index. The index is maintained on the *Canada Gazette* website. Go to Quarterly Index and Consolidated Index and select the most recent Consolidated Index.

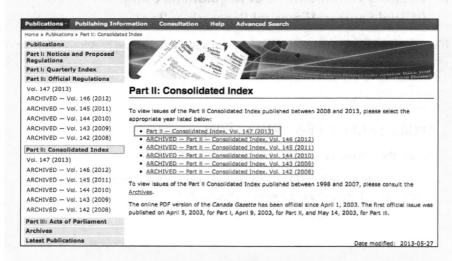

■ Section I of the document is organized in alphabetical order by regulation title. Each regulation is followed by the title of its enabling act.

---

32   Library and Archives Canada, online: <http://www.collectionscanada.gc.ca>.

■ Section II of the document is organized in alphabetical order by title of enabling act. Below the title of each enabling act, each regulation made pursuant to the act is listed. Each section of the regulation that has been amended is also listed. Each of these listings is followed by a citation to the regulation(s) that amended that particular section.

2. Turn to section II of the index. Locate the *Bank Act*. Review the regulations made pursuant to the *Bank Act*. Locate this regulation: *Cost of Borrowing (Banks) Regulations*, SOR/2001-101.

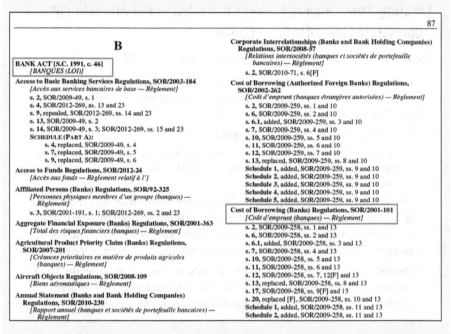

87

B

BANK ACT [S.C. 1991, c. 46]
[BANQUES (LOI)]

Access to Basic Banking Services Regulations, SOR/2003-184
[Accès aux services bancaires de base — Règlement]
s. 2, SOR/2009-49, s. 1
s. 4, SOR/2012-269, ss. 13 and 23
s. 9, repealed, SOR/2012-269, ss. 14 and 23
s. 13, SOR/2009-49, s. 2
s. 14, SOR/2009-49, s. 3; SOR/2012-269, ss. 15 and 23
SCHEDULE (PART A):
   s. 4, replaced, SOR/2009-49, s. 4
   s. 7, replaced, SOR/2009-49, s. 5
   s. 9, replaced, SOR/2009-49, s. 6
Access to Funds Regulations, SOR/2012-24
[Accès aux fonds — Règlement relatif à l']
Affiliated Persons (Banks) Regulations, SOR/92-325
[Personnes physiques membres d'un groupe (banques) — Règlement]
s. 3, SOR/2001-191, s. 1; SOR/2012-269, ss. 2 and 23
Aggregate Financial Exposure (Banks) Regulations, SOR/2001-363
[Total des risques financiers (banques) — Règlement]
Agricultural Product Priority Claim (Banks) Regulations, SOR/2007-201
[Créances prioritaires en matière de produits agricoles (banques) — Règlement]
Aircraft Objects Regulations, SOR/2008-109
[Biens aéronautiques — Règlement]
Annual Statement (Banks and Bank Holding Companies) Regulations, SOR/2010-230
[Rapport annuel (banques et sociétés de portefeuille bancaires) — Règlement]

Corporate Interrelationships (Banks and Bank Holding Companies) Regulations, SOR/2008-57
[Relations intersociétés (banques et sociétés de portefeuille bancaires) — Règlement]
s. 2, SOR/2010-71, s. 6[F]
Cost of Borrowing (Authorized Foreign Banks) Regulations, SOR/2002-262
[Coût d'emprunt (banques étrangères autorisées) — Règlement]
s. 2, SOR/2009-259, ss. 1 and 10
s. 6, SOR/2009-259, ss. 2 and 10
s. 6.1, added, SOR/2009-259, ss. 3 and 10
s. 7, SOR/2009-259, ss. 4 and 10
s. 10, SOR/2009-259, ss. 5 and 10
s. 11, SOR/2009-259, ss. 6 and 10
s. 12, SOR/2009-259, ss. 7 and 10
s. 13, replaced, SOR/2009-259, ss. 8 and 10
Schedule 1, added, SOR/2009-259, ss. 9 and 10
Schedule 2, added, SOR/2009-259, ss. 9 and 10
Schedule 3, added, SOR/2009-259, ss. 9 and 10
Schedule 4, added, SOR/2009-259, ss. 9 and 10
Schedule 5, added, SOR/2009-259, ss. 9 and 10
Cost of Borrowing (Banks) Regulations, SOR/2001-101
[Coût d'emprunt (banques) — Règlement]
s. 2, SOR/2009-258, ss. 1 and 13
s. 6, SOR/2009-258, ss. 2 and 13
s. 6.1, added, SOR/2009-258, ss. 3 and 13
s. 7, SOR/2009-258, ss. 4 and 13
s. 10, SOR/2009-258, ss. 5 and 13
s. 11, SOR/2009-258, ss. 6 and 13
s. 12, SOR/2009-258, ss. 7, 12[F] and 13
s. 13, replaced, SOR/2009-258, ss. 8 and 13
s. 17, SOR/2009-258, ss. 9[F] and 13
s. 20, replaced [F], SOR/2009-258, ss. 10 and 13
Schedule 1, added, SOR/2009-258, ss. 11 and 13
Schedule 2, added, SOR/2009-258, ss. 11 and 13

3. To view an official, current consolidation of the regulation, on the Justice Laws website, go to Consolidated Regulations and locate the regulation.

D. How Federal Regulations Are Amended, Consolidated, and Revised

Regulations, like statutes, can be amended. Understanding the amendment process is essential when conducting period-in-time research.

TASK 4.13

Locating Amendments to Regulations Using the Amendment Information Line: Official—Online

Locate the *Advance Payments for Crops Regulations*, CRC 1978, c 446, s 5.

■ On the Justice Laws website, go to Consolidated Regulations and locate the regulation. Find section 5, and examine the amendment information line: "SOR/82-817, s. 1; SOR/83-835, s. 2".

■ This information line can be interpreted as:

> Section 5 of the *Advance Payments for Crops Regulations* was amended in 1982 by regulation SOR/82-817, s 1. It was later amended in 1983 by the regulation that appears at SOR/83-835, s 2.

■ If the research problem requires that you locate these amending regulations, follow the steps to locate a regulation as registered by citation as described earlier in this chapter. Note the CIF information for any relevant regulation amendments to determine the exact date that the amendments took effect.

■ Alternatively, the Consolidated Index of Statutory Instruments, on the *Canada Gazette* website, contains a cumulative list of all regulation amendments between 1 January 1955 and the date shown on the title page.

In summary, as with statutes, regulations exist in two versions: the original version as registered, and the consolidated version as amended and revised. Moreover, they are published in both print and online formats. Although most regulation research can be completed online using official sources, occasionally you will need to conduct historical research using print sources. Competence in researching regulations requires that you be able to locate regulations in both versions and both formats.

To determine the CIF date for the original version of a regulation as registered, review the steps in Chapter 3. To determine CIF information for consolidated regulations, refer to the following sources:

- *Consolidated Regulations of Canada* (print version, 1978). The last printed version of the *Consolidated Regulations of Canada* was published in 1978. This set came into force by Order SI/79-131 on 15 August 1979.

- Consolidated Regulations on the Justice Laws website. As with statutes, when relying on a regulation as it appears in the online collection, assume that it was brought into force.[33]

VI. When to Use Prior Versions of Statutes and Regulations: Period-in-Time Research

The Department of Justice regularly consolidates federal statutes and regulations, and researchers will usually work from a current consolidation that has been updated. However, not all legal research requires locating the most current version of a statute or regulation. One may need to locate legislation as it appeared at a particular period or point in time (PIT research).

A. Determining the Relevant Date or Time Frame

To determine whether period-in-time research is required:

- Examine the relevant facts and determine the issues to be researched. Identify the date the issue arose and the relevant time frame.
- Review the governing statute and any other relevant documents, such as a contract or agreement, and consider any relevant time limitations or conditions.
- Review the *Interpretation Act*[34] and any relevant limitations legislation or any other interpretive materials (such as cases, rules, or regulations) for any further direction with respect to the operation of time.

Examples of laws and rules to consult in determining relevant dates and time limitations are shown in Figure 4.6.

Once the relevant time frame has been determined, unless otherwise stated in the relevant act itself, or in the *Interpretation Act* or other interpretive materials, the law that governs the matter is the law that was in force on the date(s) of the event that caused the legal issue. The *Interpretation Act* explains the operation of time for federal matters, and the effect of amending and repealing statutes on matters at various stages in judicial proceedings.[35]

---

33 *Legislation Revision and Consolidation Act, supra* note 7, s 31(1).

34 *Interpretation Act, supra* note 16, ss 26-30 provide information about calculating time.

35 *Ibid*, ss 43, 44.

FIGURE 4.6 Examples of Relevant Dates for Research Purposes

Governing Law or Rule	Version of the Law
Rules of court, rules of a tribunal, or process-related rules	Usually the current version
Evidence Act*	Usually the current version
Court fees and forms	Usually the current version
Statute-based situations	Review the statute and applicable sections in conjunction with the facts to determine the applicable time frame.
Criminal law	The date the offence was alleged to have occurred.**
Tort law	The date(s) the tort was alleged to have occurred. If the matter is based in common law regarding property or civil rights, the common-law principles in force at the time apply.** Provincial limitations acts may also apply.
Contract law	The date(s) outlined in the contract. Matters governed by statute may contain additional conditions.**

   * RSC 1985, c C-5.

  ** *Interpretation Act*, RSC 1985, c I-21, ss 8.1, 43, 44.

This general rule applies to the substantive law governing the matter. Some laws and regulations (in particular the Rules of Procedure, Rules of Evidence, court forms, and fees regulations) may govern the actual conduct of the action, so a current version of these will be required in most circumstances.

If the matter is statute-based and if the statute that governs the matter is a prior version of the statute, the prior version must be located.

Before proceeding, review, if necessary, the processes that enact statutes, bring statutes into force, and amend statutes, because a thorough understanding of these concepts, discussed earlier, is necessary to understand period-in-time research.

TASK 4.14

Determining Statute Amendments in Force at a Specific Period in Time Using the Table of Public Statutes: Official

Section 239 of the *Criminal Code*, RSC 1985, c C-46 criminalizes attempted murder. Determine whether the section had been amended since the *Criminal Code* was last revised in 1985.

- On the Justice Laws website, locate the Table of Public Statutes. Find the *Criminal Code* information. Locate section 239, review the amendments, and locate the CIF information for each amendment to that section. Although it is not expressly stated, each amending statute reference refers to a statute as enacted (SC).
   – Amendments to s 239: "1995, c. 39, s. 143; 2008, c. 6, s. 16; 2009, c. 22, s. 6".
   – Section 239 of the *Criminal Code* was amended three times:
      1. By SC 1995, c 39, s 143: CIF, ss 141 to 150, in force 1 January 1996. See SI/96 2.
      2. By SC 2008, c 6, s 16: CIF, ss 2 to 17, in force 5 January 2008. See SI/2008-34.
      3. By SC 2009, c 22, s 6: CIF, ss 1 to 19, in force 10 February 2009. See SI/2009-92.

B. Locating Prior Amendment Information

On the basis of the dates provided in the Table of Public Statutes that the *Criminal Code* was amended, a timeline can be created that reflects the changes to section 239 since 1985. As discussed earlier in this chapter, the consolidations of law on the Justice Laws website build on the statutes in the RSC 1985. Amendments are added to this content over time. The starting point is often, but not always,[36] the RSC 1985.

Prior Version— 21 December 1988	Prior Version— 1 January 1996	Prior Version— 5 January 2008	Current Version— 10 February 2009
Criminal Code, RSC 1985, c C-46, s 239	1 January 1996 (CIF date for SC 1995, c 39, s 143)	5 January 2008 (CIF date for SC 2008, c 6, s 16)	10 February 2009 (CIF date for 2008, c 22, s 6)

---

36 The consolidation also contains substantive acts that were enacted after 1985. Accordingly, many statutes in the consolidation are cited directly to the *Statutes of Canada* instead of the RSC 1985. In that case, the statute as it appears in the SC will be the foundation on which all future amendments will be built for creation of the current consolidation. Also note that if the Table of Public Statutes provides information that a new section has been "added" by a particular statute, then the statute that added the amendment will be the basis on which future amendments will be built.

Once the version of the statute has been determined before and after each amendment, assess the facts of the issue and determine the applicability of amendments as follows:

- If the matter occurred between 1985 and the day before 1 January 1996, use section 239 as it appeared in the RSC 1985.
- If the matter occurred between 1 January 1996 and the day before 5 January 2008, use section 239 as it appeared in the RSC 1985, including the amendments that came into force on 1 January 1996.
- If the matter occurred between 5 January 2008 and the day before 10 February 2009, use section 239 as it appeared in the RSC 1985, including the amendments that came into force on 1 January 1996 and 5 January 2008.
- If the matter occurred after 10 February 2009, use section 239 as it appears on the current consolidation online.

VII. Locating Prior Versions of Statutes

Once the relevant time frame has been established as explained in section VI above, the relevant legislation can be located.

A. Locating Prior Versions of Statutes Using Official Sources: 2003 and On—Online

Prior versions of consolidated statutes on the Justice Laws website can be considered official.[37] Currently, the Justice Laws website can be used to view previous versions of statutes from the present date back to 1 January 2003.[38] This archive continues to grow with the addition of new materials.

TASK 4.15

Locating Prior Versions of Statutes Using Official Sources

Examine the *Criminal Code* as it appeared on 10 January 2008.

1. On the Justice Laws website, go to Advanced Search.
   - In the Title field, enter a term from the title of the statute (e.g. "criminal"). In the Date field, use the drop-down calendar to choose the date ("2008-01-10"). Ensure that "Show Titles only" is checked. Search.

---

37   *Legislation Revision and Consolidation Act, supra* note 7, s 31(1).
38   The *Income Tax Act* and its regulations go back to 31 August 2004.

- On the results page, select the Code from the list of results, then select the version of the Code that was in force during the relevant period ("In force from 2008-01-01 to 2008-04-16").

2. Alternatively, on the Justice Laws website, go to Consolidated Acts.

- Locate the Code.

- At the top of the document, note the Code's currency statement. For versions of the Code earlier than the current version, select "Previous Versions".

- Select the version of the Code that was in force during the relevant period ("In force from 2008-01-01 to 2008-04-16").

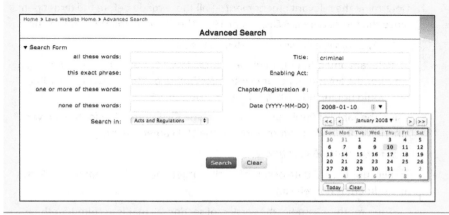

B. Creating a Prior Version of a Statute Using Official Sources: 1985-2003

Although the last print RSC was 1985, the online consolidations on the Justice Laws website only go back to 1 January 2003. Accordingly, to obtain a prior version of a statute using official sources with a relevant date between 1985 and 2003, it is necessary to manually create the statute using official sources by:

- locating the amendments to the relevant section of the statute
- determining which of the amending statutes were in force prior to the relevant date
- compiling the prior version

TASK 4.16

Creating a Prior Version of a Statute Using Official Sources

Examine the *Criminal Code*, RSC 1985, c C-46, s 95 (Possession of Weapon Obtained by Commission of Offence) as it appeared on 3 December 1995.

1. On the Justice Laws website, locate the amendment information for section 95 as described earlier in this chapter. Amendments to section 95:

   ■ 1991, c 28, s 8, c 40, ss 9, 37; 1993, c 25, s 93; 1995, c 39, s 139; 2008, c 6, s 8; 2012, c 6, s 5

2. Determine the relevant amendments—all those made before the target date. Since the target date is 3 December 1995, the relevant amendments include:

   ■ 1991, c 28, s 8, c 40, ss 9, 37; 1993, c 25, s 93

   Relevant amendments might also include 1995, c 39, s 139, depending on whether the amendment came into force before or after 3 December 1995, but would not include 2008, c 6, s 8 or 2012, c 6, s 5.

3. Using the Table of Public Statutes, locate the CIF information for the relevant amendments. The CIF information for the 1995 amendment:

   ■ in force 01.01.96 *see* SI/96-2

   Because the CIF date occurs after the target date of 3 December 1995, this amendment is not relevant.

   Thus, for this example, the version of section 95 that is required for the relevant date of 3 December 1995 will be a consolidation of only these statute sections:

   ■ RS, 1985, c C-46, s 95; 1991, c 28, s 8, c 40, ss 9, 37; 1993, c 25, s 93

4. To compile the prior version, record the statute section as it appeared in the RSC prior to the target date. In many cases, this will be the statute as published in the RSC 1985; or, in the case of a statute that was enacted after the previous consolidation, a copy of the statute section as enacted.

5. Copy each relevant amending statute and provide a complete citation for each amending statute.

6. Locate the statutory instrument or CIF information for each amending statute section.

VIII.   Locating Prior Versions of Regulations

Period-in-time research for regulations also requires the researcher to begin by determining the relevant date.

A.   Locating Prior Versions of Regulations on the Justice Laws Website

Prior versions of consolidated regulations on the Justice Laws website can be considered official. The Department of Justice continues to publish new consolidated versions of regulations online, adding to its collection of archived material.

Currently, the Justice Laws website can be used to view previous versions of regulations back to 22 March 2006.[39]

TASK 4.17

Locating Prior Versions of Regulations Using the Title of the Regulation: Online—Official

Locate the *Access to Basic Banking Services Regulations*, SOR/2003-184, made pursuant to the *Bank Act*, SC 1991, c 46 as it appeared on 25 January 2009.

1. On the Justice Laws website, go to Consolidated Regulations and locate the regulation by its title.

2. Where a previous version of the regulation is available, the currency statement includes a link entitled "Previous Versions".

3. Select the version of the regulation that was in force during the relevant period ("In force from 2006-03-22 to 2009-02-11").

---

39   With the exception of versions of the *Income Tax Act* and its regulations, which go back to 31 August 2004.

TASK 4.18

Locating Prior Versions of Regulations Using the Title of the Enabling Act: Online—Official

Locate SOR/2003-184, made pursuant to the *Bank Act*, SC 1991, c 46, as it appeared on 25 January 2009.

1. On the Justice Laws website, go to Consolidated Acts and locate the Act.

2. Select the yellow "R" next to the title of the Act. Alternatively, select the Act title and scroll down the page, past the Table of Contents, to "Regulations made under this Act". Select the relevant regulation.

Consolidated Acts
A B C D E F G H I J K L M N O P Q R S T U V W X Y Z
Bank Act
S.C. 1991, c. 46   R   ⬇ PDF [3756 KB]

3. Where a previous version of the regulation is available, the currency statement includes a link entitled "Previous Versions".

   ■ Select the version of the regulation that was in force during the relevant period ("In force from 2006-03-22 to 2009-02-11").

B. Creating a Prior Version of a Regulation Using Official Sources: 1978-2006

Although the most recent CRC was 1978, the earliest prior version on the Justice Laws website is 2006. Accordingly, there may be some instances in which neither an official consolidation nor a revision of a regulation exists. To create a prior version of a regulation section:

- Locate relevant amending regulations.
- Determine which of the amending regulations were in force prior to the relevant date.

TASK 4.19

Creating a Prior Version of a Regulation Using Official Sources: 1978-2006

Locate the *Immigration and Refugee Protection Regulations*, SOR/2002-227, s 52 as it appeared on 25 June 2003.

- On the Justice Laws website, locate the regulation section and its amendment information line. Note the amending information:
  - SOR/2003-197, s 1; SOR/2003-260, s 1; SOR/2004-167, s 14(F); SOR/2010-54, s 3; SOR/2010-195, s 2(F); SOR/2011-125, s 2

- Choose the relevant amending regulations. Since the target date is 25 June 2003, the following amendments are relevant if they were in force before the target date: SOR/2003-197, s 1 and SOR/2003-260, s 1. The amendments SOR/2004-167, s 14(F) and SOR/2011-125, s 2 are not relevant.

- Locate the CIF information for both the 2003 regulations to determine whether these particular amendments were in force on the relevant date. To do so, locate the SOR in the *Canada Gazette*, Part II by using the Consolidated Index in the *Gazette*, and note their registration dates.
  - SOR/2003-197, s 1, registered 5 June 2003
  - SOR/2003-260, s 1, registered 8 July 2003

- The first regulation was registered before the target date and is relevant; the second regulation was registered after and is not.

- Thus, the version of section 52 required for the relevant date of 25 June 2003 will be a consolidation of these sections:
  - SOR/2002-227, s 52; SOR/2003-197, s 1

- To compile the prior version, record the regulation section as it appeared in the CRC prior to the relevant date or, in the case of a regulation that was registered after the previous consolidation, copy the regulation section as enacted. In this example, use SOR/2002-227, s 52, which was the original regulation number.
  - Copy each regulation section that amended this section, provide a complete citation for each amending regulation, and copy the registration dates.

IX. Backdating Legislation

A. Purpose

Backdating legislation involves locating prior versions of statutes and regulations, starting from the most current consolidation. It is frequently required when completing historical research. To ensure that legislation is accurately backdated, a legislative history should be completed.

While online research is possible if a statute or statute section was enacted within the last decade, print sources must be consulted if the search time frame pre-dates the year 2000.

Compiling a legislative history is required in the following situations:

1. *A court is required to interpret a statute.* The legislative intent behind a statute can be explored by examining parliamentary debates. The minister or member of Parliament who introduces the bill will state the purpose or rationale of the proposed legislation. As the bill passes through the House and Senate, debates and discussion at committees provide a contextual framework for the bill's passage into law.

2. *The constitutionality of the law is in question.* When a law is subject to constitutional challenge, debates and committee reports can reveal the reasons for the creation of the legislation, including its purpose. Backdating a statute will reveal the citation of a statute as first enacted and published in the *Statutes of Canada*. Once the date has been determined, the debates can be located.

3. *The historical development of legislation is being studied.* Law professors and practising lawyers often write and teach about the law's development. Understanding the key stages of the enactment of legislation is required to comment accurately on the origin and development of the law.

A legislative history begins with a citation to a statute (session law/enacted version). Thus, in order to complete a legislative history in this circumstance, you must first backdate the statute.

X. Backdating Federal Statutes

Most research with statutes begins by locating the current consolidation of the statute on the Justice Laws website as described earlier in this chapter.

Statutes found in the current online consolidation that were included in the print version of the RSC 1985 include a historical information line located just below section 1 of the Act. This line provides a citation to the statute on which the revision was based.

For example:

- *Access to Information Act*, RSC 1985, c A-1: This revision is based on SC 1980-81-82-83, c 111, Schedule I "1".
- *Agricultural Products Marketing Act*, RSC 1985, c A-6: This revision is based on RSC 1970, c A-7, s 1. Note that the information line specifies only "RS"; that is, this revision is based on the prior revised version, or the RSC 1970.

These earlier citation references could be located to learn more about the statute's origins.

The online consolidation also contains statutes enacted after the print version of the RSC 1985 was published. The backdating process for these statutes is less complex, because the statute's current citation refers to the enacted version of the statute, which can be located in the annual *Statutes of Canada*, either in print or online. Such statutes do not include a historical information line below section 1.

For example:

- *Agreement on Internal Trade Implementation Act*, SC 1996, c 17. This statute was enacted after 1985, and is the originating act.

A. Locating an Originating Act Using Official Sources

The complexity of backdating a statute increases if an enacted version of a statute has repealed an earlier version. The following example illustrates the steps to take to trace a statute back to its earliest origins.

Locating an Originating Act Using Official Sources

Backdate the *Youth Criminal Justice Act* to its origin.

- On the Justice Laws website, go to Consolidated Acts and locate the Act. Note its citation to the 2002 annual statutes: SC 2002, s 1. Go to Annual Statutes and locate the Act. Review the end of the Act, and locate section 199, which repeals the *Young Offenders Act*, RSC 1985, c Y-1.

- The *Young Offenders Act* originated today's *Youth Criminal Justice Act*. Locate the *Young Offenders Act* in the print version of the RSC 1985. Review the title page. Section 1 provides a citation to the Act on which this consolidation is based. The citation will refer to the RSC 1970, unless the statute was enacted or replaced after 1970, as in this case.

CHAPTER Y-1	CHAPITRE Y-1
An Act respecting young offenders	Loi concernant les jeunes contrevenants
SHORT TITLE	TITRE ABRÉGÉ
Short title **1.** This Act may be cited as the *Young Offenders Act*. 1980-81-82-83, c. 110, s. 1.	**1.** *Loi sur les jeunes contrevenants*. 1980-81- 82-83, ch. 110, art. 1. Titre abrégé

- Thus, the *Young Offenders Act* as consolidated in the RSC 1985 was based on a statute passed in the 1980-81-82-83 volume of the *Statutes of Canada*. Locate and review the statute that appears at SC 1980-81-82-83, c 110. Note that a statute as enacted in the SC either creates a new law or amends or repeals a previous act. Amending and repealing information is located near the end of the statute. This statute, at section 80, repeals the *Juvenile Delinquents Act*, RS (i.e. RSC 1970), c J-3.

REPEAL
Repeal R.S., c.J-3   **80.** The *Juvenile Delinquents Act* is repealed.

- Locate the statute as it appeared in RSC 1970, c J-3. Review section 1 of the Act to determine the statute that originated this version. This consolidation is based on the prior consolidation, RSC 1952, c 160.

CHAPTER J-3
An Act respecting juvenile delinquents
Short title   **1.** This Act may be cited as the *Juvenile Delinquents Act*. R.S., c. 160, s. 1.

- Locate the statute as it appeared in RSC 1952, c 160. Review section 1 of the Act to determine the statute that originated this version. This consolidation is based on the version that appeared in SC 1929, c 46.

CHAPTER 160.

An Act respecting Juvenile Delinquents.

SHORT TITLE.

1. This Act may be cited as the *Juvenile Delinquents* Short title. *Act.* 1929, c. 46, s. 1.

INTERPRETATION.

- Locate the statute as it appeared in SC 1929, c 46. This is the statute as enacted, so it could be the earliest version of the Act, or it could have repealed and replaced the previous enactment. Go to the end of the Act to locate the repealing section, if any. Section 46 repeals the *Juvenile Delinquents Act*, RSC 1927, c 108.

Repeal.   **46.** Chapter one hundred and eight of the Revised Statutes of Canada, 1927, entitled the *Juvenile Delinquents Act*, is hereby repealed.

- Locate the statute as it appeared in RSC 1927, c 108. Review section 1 of the Act. The Act on which this consolidation was based appeared in SC 1908, c 40.

CHAPTER 108.

An Act respecting Juvenile Delinquents.

SHORT TITLE.

1. This Act may be cited as the Juvenile Delinquents Short title. Act. 1908, c. 40, s. 1.

INTERPRETATION.

- Locate the statute as it appeared in SC 1908, c 40.
- Review the closing sections of this Act. This Act does not repeal any other act, so this is the earliest version of the *Juvenile Delinquents Act*, which was the precursor to the *Youth Criminal Justice Act*.

To summarize:

Backdating the statute reveals that the *Youth Criminal Justice Act*, SC 2002, c 1 was originated by the *Young Offenders Act*, RSC 1985, c Y-1, which in turn was originated by the *Juvenile Delinquents Act*, SC 1908, c 40.

B. Locating an Originating Statute Section Using Official Sources: Print

Locating an Originating Statute Section Using Print Sources

Locate the statute section that originated section 9(2) of the *Canada Evidence Act*, RSC 1985, c C-5.

■ Locate section 9(2) of the statute as it appears in the print version of the RSC 1985. As with the online versions of consolidated statutes, amending information is provided at the end of each statute section. This note identifies all of the statutes that, when read together, were combined to create this consolidation.

Section 9 of the Act provides this citation: RS, c E-10. Since the RSC 1985 is a consolidation that is based on the previous consolidation plus amendments, section 9 of the Act appears in the RSC 1970 as chapter E-10. It was not amended between 1970 and 1985. Locate the statute as it appeared in the RSC 1970.

■ Locate section 9. Examine the citation: RS, c 307. Since the RSC 1970 is a consolidation that is based on the previous consolidation plus amendments, section 9 of the Act appeared in the RSC 1952 as chapter 307. It was amended by the statute that appears at SC 1968-69, c 14, section 2.

■ Locate the statute as it appeared in the prior consolidation, RSC 1952, c 307. Locate section 9. Section 9(2) was not included in this consolidation.

■ On the basis of the foregoing analysis, the amending statute that was enacted at SC 1968-69, c 14, section 2 may provide the origins of section 9(2) of the *Canada Evidence Act*, RSC 1985, c C-5. The final step is to locate and review section 2 of the statute as it appeared in SC 1968-69, c 14, which confirms that section 9(2) was added by this amending statute.

In summary:

Section 2 of *An Act to Amend the Canada Evidence Act*, SC 1968-69, c 14 originated section 9(2) of the *Canada Evidence Act*, RSC 1985, c C-5.

XI. Backdating Federal Regulations

A. Locating an Originating Regulation Using Official Sources: Print

To locate originating regulations, you must first understand the organization of the *Consolidated Regulations of Canada*. The Table of Contents to the CRC 1978 can be found at the end of the CRC set. It includes two primary finding aids. The Table of Contents indicates that the set of regulations is organized alphabetically by title of enabling act. Each regulation is given a chapter number based on its location in the set. The table provides chapter numbers and page numbers. A schedule to the CRC 1978 explains the disposition of existing regulations during the consolidation process. Examine the first page of the schedule to locate a list of acronyms and code references used throughout the CRC. Documents included comprise:

- Privy Council documents
- SOR regulations from 1948 to 1955
- SOR consolidation in 1955
- SOR registered from 1954 to 1977

Locating an Originating Regulation Using Print Sources

Locate the regulation that originated the *Designated Areas Firearms Order*, CRC 1978, c 430.

■ Find the regulation as it appears in the print CRC 1978. Notice that neither the date nor the SOR is provided in this consolidated version.

■ Locate the Consolidated Index of Statutory Instruments (*Canada Gazette*, Part II) for the year prior to the 1978 consolidation to find out the SOR and registration date for this regulation.

– The *Designated Areas Firearms Order* was registered on 28 January 1972 as evidenced by SOR/72-22, which is located in the *Canada Gazette*, Part II from 9 February 1972, page 185.

85

STATUTES Regulations and other documents	Date made	No.	Date Registered	1955 Consolidation or Canada Gazette Part II Date	Page Com
COOPERATIVE CREDIT ASSOCIATIONS ACT, *RSC 1970, c. C-29*					
Cooperative Credit Associations Investment (Special Shares) Regulations	22/10/74	SOR/74–594	23/10/74	13/11/74	2785 n
Protection of Securities (Cooperative Credit Associations) Regulations	3/ 2/76	SOR/76–100	4/ 2/76	25/ 2/76	451 n
COPYRIGHT ACT, *RSC 1970, c. C-30*					
Act Extended to Certain Countries		SOR/62–313		22/ 8/62	868 n
		SOR/62–423		14/11/62	1171 n
		SOR/64–319		12/ 8/64	809 n
		SOR/65–93		10/ 3/65	295 n
		SOR/67–140		12/ 4/67	501 n
		SOR/69–52		12/ 2/69	263 n
Copyright Fees Order	10/ 9/73	SOR/73–548	18/ 9/73	10/10/73	2379 n
Copyright Rules	16/ 8/78	SOR/78–665	22/ 8/78	13/ 9/78	3447 xr
				C 55	664
CORPORATIONS AND LABOUR UNIONS RETURNS ACT, *RSC 1970, c. C-31*					
Corporations and Labour Unions Returns Regulations		SOR/63–9		9/ 1/63	21 n
CRIMINAL CODE, *RSC 1970, c. C-34*					
Approved Instruments Order	23/ 8/74	SI/74–110	11/ 9/74	11/ 9/74	2452 r
	22/ 1/78	SI/78–23	8/ 2/78	8/ 2/78	522
Approved Roadside Screening Device Order	15/ 9/76	SI/76–111	13/10/76	13/10/76	2780 n
	15/ 3/78	SI/78–49	12/ 4/78	12/ 4/78	1391 xr
British Columbia County Court Summary Conviction Appeal Rules, 1976	19/ 8/76	SI/76–123	27/10/76	27/10/76	2862 n
Certain Provisions of Section 3 of the Criminal Law Amendment Act, 1977 Proclaimed in Force January 1, 1979	18/ 7/78	SI/78–131	9/ 8/78	9/ 8/78	3296
Criminal Appeal Rules, 1972, amendment	21/ 6/76	SI/76–87	28/ 7/76	28/ 7/76	2157
Criminal Appeal Rules, Yukon Territory, 1973	6/ 9/73	SI/74–21	13/ 2/74	13/ 2/74	482 n
Designated Areas Firearms Order	27/ 1/72	SOR/72–22	28/ 1/72	9/ 2/72	185 n

■ Locate the SOR in the *Gazette* as evidence of the originating regulation. This confirms that the *Designated Areas Firearms Order*, SOR/72-22 is the originating regulation.

While proclamations are currently found in the *Canada Gazette*, Part II, this was not always the case. The Table of Proclamations as published in SC 1974-75-76 until SC 1978-79 refers to the *Canada Gazette*, Part I for proclamations. After that, the Table of Proclamations refers to the *Canada Gazette*, Part II for proclamations.[40]

XII. Compiling a Legislative History

A legislative history is a comprehensive summary of the development of legislation that may include information from the time of bill creation to, in some circumstances, the repeal of the statute itself. Completing a legislative history requires knowledge of the information contained in both Chapters 3 and 4. It also requires maintaining a complete record of source documents reviewed. While screen captures and downloads can be used for information located online, typically photocopies are required for print sources. When photocopying research materials, photocopy the first (title) page and the second (copyright) page of the source to ensure that the information is available to properly cite it.

When compiling a legislative history for a lawyer, you should first ascertain the purpose of the history—how it will be used. Sometimes, a brief history will suffice; in other cases, if the legislation will be analyzed in court, a more comprehensive legislative history is required. For example:

Question: What was the status of Bill C-4, *An Act to amend the Youth Criminal Justice Act and to make consequential and related amendments to other Acts*, at dissolution of the House during the 40th Parliament, 3rd Session?

Brief answer: On 3 May 2010, the bill received second reading and was referred to the Standing Committee on Justice and Human Rights in the House of Commons.[41]

---

40   Prior to SC 1974-75-76, the *Canada Gazette* was published as a single newspaper.

41   Parliament of Canada, LEGISinfo <http://www.parl.gc.ca/LegisInfo/BillDetails.aspx?Language =E&Mode=1&billId=4343885>.

A. Key Components of a Legislative History

Bill number and bill title
Parliament and session number
Introducing minister or member

For both the House and the Senate:

- First, second, and third reading recorded vote dates and the corresponding page number for each in the *Debates*

- Whether referred to committee and, if so, the name of the committee, the committee's disposition of the bill, along with the corresponding page number in the *Debates*, with a citation to the committee report itself

- Date of royal assent or proclamation and a citation to the proclamation

- Date of coming into force and by what authority, including the citation to the statutory order or statutory instrument as published in the *Canada Gazette*, Part II

- Citation to the year and chapter in the annual *Statutes of Canada* where the Act was finally published

Attach copies of the actual *Debates* and committee reports where required.

B. Sample Legislative History

Bill number: C-128

Title of bill: *An Act to amend the Criminal Code and the Customs Tariff* (child pornography and corrupting morals)

Introducing member: Campbell, Kim, Minister of Justice

Parliamentary session: 34th Parliament, 3rd Session

Progress (House):

Stage	Date	Location in the Debates
First reading	13 May 1993	page 19365
Second reading	3 June 1993	page 20328
Standing Committee on Justice and the Solicitor General	Reported with amendments 15 June 1993	page 20843
Third reading	15 June 1993	page 20883

Progress (Senate):

Stage	Date	Location in the Debates
First reading	16 June 1993	page 3530
Second reading	17 June 1993	page 3580
Committee on Legal and Constitutional Affairs	Reported with no amendment 22 June 1993	page 3637
Third reading	23 June 1993	page 3697
Royal assent	23 June 1993	page 3707

In force: 1 August 1993

By authority of: *Order of Governor in Council, SI/93-155*

Enacted as: SC 1993, c 46

C. Finding the Status or the Legislative History of a Bill Recently Before Parliament

Chapter 3 describes the bill-making process and explains how the LEGISinfo website can be used to track bills currently before Parliament. LEGISinfo can also be used to find the status of bills from previous sessions, back to 29 January 2001.

TASK 4.23

Reading Debates: Tips

When reading the *Debates*, consider:

■ At first reading, a motion is passed without debate. Note the page number in the *Debates* where the results of the motion are recorded. This page number corresponds to the date of first reading.

■ At second reading, a motion is made, the debate occurs, and the motion results are recorded. On the Legislative History Table, note the first page where the debates begin. On the Legislative History Table, this page number corresponds with "Debates on Second Reading". If you are compiling a research log, note the page number and speaker's name if required to refer directly to specific submissions.

■ Usually, the motion for second reading is passed at the end of debate. On the Legislative History Table, note the page number in the *Debates* where the results of the motion are recorded. This page number corresponds to the date of second reading. Motion results are provided at the end of debate on the topic. For example:

June 9, 1993	COMMONS DEBATES	20595
	Routine Proceedings	
Madam Deputy Speaker: Pursuant to Standing Order 68(2), the motion is deemed adopted.	the representation they have received from the unions they are forced to be members of.	

■ The motion at second reading may refer the bill to committee. Note the committee name in the legislative history. If relevant, refer to committee meetings directly using LEGISinfo. At a minimum, provide information about the date on which the committee reported, and, if necessary, the page number in the *Debates* of this report.

D. Finding Debates, Committee Reports, and Journals

Recent committee reports can be found on the LEGISinfo website. *Debates of the House of Commons* and *Debates of the Senate of Canada* are available online from the 35th Parliament, 1st Session (17 January 1994) to the present. Historical committee reports can be found in print form at most libraries. Use the library online catalogue to search for the committee as author. Standing committees are shelved as a series.

If you are searching for a special committee, search for the committee by author, or use the title or subject of the report, if known. The indexes to the *Journals* of the House and Senate at one time indexed sessional reports by subject.

The print versions, which include historical volumes of the *Debates* of both the House of Commons and the Senate, are available in most large libraries. The *Debates*, whether in print or online, are organized by day. Use all of the relevant dates in the legislative history to find information.

The *Journals of the House of Commons of Canada* and the *Journals of the Senate of Canada* are available in most large libraries. Indexes provide long-term historical information on the status of bills. They are now available online through the Parliament website from the 35th Parliament, 1st Session (17 January 1994) to the present. Note that some libraries temporarily stopped receiving the print volumes of the *Journals* between 1993 and 2004.

E. Creating a Legislative History

Example:

What was the status of House Bill C-11, *An Act to amend the Immigration and Refugee Protection Act and the Federal Courts Act* at the end of the 40th Parliament, 3rd Session?

Summary statement: This bill was enacted as the *Balanced Refugee Reform Act*, SC 2010, c 8 and received royal assent on 29 June 2010. It came into force[42] in accordance with section 42 of the Act:

> CIF, 2010, c 8: ss 3 to 6, 9, 13, 14, 28, 31, 32, 39, and 40 in force on royal assent, 29 June 2010; s 8 repealed before coming into force—see 2011, c 8, s 6; ss 1, 2, 7, 10 to 12, 14.1, 15(3) and (4), 17 to 27, 29, 30, 33 to 37, and 38 come in force on 29 June 2012 or on any earlier day or days that may be fixed by order of the Governor in Council—see s 42(1); ss 15(1), (2), and (5) and 16, 16.1, 27.1, and 37.1 come into force 12 months after the day s 15(3) comes into force, or on any earlier day that may be fixed by order of the Governor in Council—see s 42(2)—not in force.

---

42   As noted in the Table of Public Statutes (updated to 2011, c 19 and *Canada Gazette*, Part II, vol 145, no 24 (23 November 2011), online: <http://laws-lois.justice.gc.ca/eng/TablePublicStatutes/I.html>.

SAMPLE LEGISLATIVE HISTORY

Bill number: C-11

Title of bill: *An Act to amend the Immigration and Refugee Protection Act and the Federal Courts Act*

Introducing member: Kenney, Jason, Minister of Citizenship, Immigration and Multiculturalism

Parliamentary session: 40th Parliament, 3rd Session

Progress (House):

Stage	Date	Location in the Debates
First reading	30 March 2010	page 1089
Debates on second reading	26 April 2010 27 April 2010 29 April 2010	page 1943 page 2045 page 2118
Second reading	29 April 2010	page 2140
Standing Committee on Citizenship and Immigration	Reported with amendments 11 June 2010	page 3720
Debates on third reading	15 June 2010	page 3880
Third reading	15 June 2010	page 3893

Progress (Senate):

Stage	Date	Location in the Debates
First reading	15 June 2010	page 794
Debates on second reading	16 June 2010 17 June 2010	page 818 page 840
Second reading	17 June 2010	page 842
Standing Committee on Social Affairs, Science and Technology	Reported without amendments 28 June 2010	page 924
Debates on third reading	28 June 2010	page 932
Third reading	28 June 2010	page 935
Royal assent	29 June 2010	page 961

Enacted as: SC 2010, c 8

F. Finding the Status of a Bill for Statutes Passed After 2001: Online

Compiling a Full Legislative History for Statutes Passed After 2001: Online

Provide a full legislative history for *An Act Respecting Immigration to Canada and the Granting of Refugee Protection to Persons Who Are Displaced, Persecuted or in Danger*, SC 2001, c 27.

- Locate the enacted version of the statute on the Justice Laws website. Open the PDF for the Act that appears as chapter 27 and review the title page of the statute. Note the Parliament and session number, bill number, and date of royal assent on the Legislative History Table.

- On the LEGISinfo website, select the Parliament and session number (37th Parliament, 1st Session). Locate the bill in the list of bills provided.

- Compile the legislative history as described earlier in this chapter.

G. Finding the Status of a Bill for Statutes Passed After 2003: Print

Compiling a Full Legislative History for Statutes Passed After 2003: Print

Provide a full legislative history for *An Act to Amend the Citizenship Act,* SC 2005, c 17.

1. Locate the print *Statutes of Canada.* Select the 2005 volume, which includes chapter 17. Note the spine of this volume, which provides the Parliament and session number.

2. Locate the statute. The date of royal assent is provided. Turn to the preceding page. A full legislative history table is provided.

LEGISLATIVE HISTORY / HISTORIQUE				
An Act to amend the Citizenship Act – Bill S-2 (Introduced by: Senator Noël A. Kinsella) Loi modifiant la Loi sur la citoyenneté – Projet de loi S-2 (Déposé par : Le sénateur Noël A. Kinsella)				
House of Commons / Chambre des communes		Senate / Sénat		
Bill Stage / Étape du projet de loi	Date	Bill Stage / Étape du projet de loi	Date	
First Reading / Première lecture	2004-11-15	First Reading / Première lecture	2004-10-06	
Debate(s) at Second Reading / Débat(s) à la deuxième lecture	2004-11-30 2005-02-10	Debate(s) at Second Reading / Débat(s) à la deuxième lecture	2004-10-20	
Second Reading / Deuxième lecture	2005-02-16	Second Reading / Deuxième lecture	2004-10-20	
Committee / Comité	Citizenship and Immigration / Citoyenneté et immigration	Committee / Comité	Social Affairs, Science and Technology / Affaires sociales, sciences et technologie	
Committee Meeting(s) / Réunion(s) du comité	2005-02-24	Committee Meeting(s) / Réunion(s) du comité	2004-10-27	
Committee Report / Rapport du comité	2005-02-25	Committee Report / Rapport du comité	2004-10-28	
Debate(s) at Report Stage / Débat(s) à l'étape du rapport		Debate(s) at Report Stage / Débat(s) à l'étape du rapport		
Report Stage / Étape du rapport	2005-05-04	Report Stage / Étape du rapport		
Debate(s) at Third Reading / Débat(s) à la troisième lecture		Debate(s) at Third Reading / Débat(s) à la troisième lecture		
Third Reading / Troisième lecture	2005-05-04	Third Reading / Troisième lecture	2004-11-02	
Royal Assent : May 5, 2005, Statutes of Canada, 2005, chapter 17 Sanction royale : 5 mai 2005, Lois du Canada (2005), chapitre 17				

3. Compile the legislative history as described earlier in this chapter.

As of May 2009, the *Canada Gazette,* Part III, which publishes statutes as enacted, also began to include legislative history tables for published statutes.[43]

43 Parliament of Canada, *Canada Gazette,* Part III <http://www.gazette.gc.ca/rp-pr/p3/index-eng.html>.

H. Finding the Status of a Bill for Statutes Passed After the RSC 1985: Print

Compiling a Full Legislative History for Statutes Passed After the RSC 1985: Print

Provide a full legislative history for *An Act to Establish the Department of Industry, Science and Technology, to Repeal the Department of Regional Industrial Expansion Act and to Make Consequential Amendments to Other Acts*, SC 1990, c 1.

■ Find the statute in the print volumes of the 1990 *Statutes of Canada*. Record the Parliament and session number using the information provided on the spine or title page of the volume (34th Parliament, 2nd Session).

■ The *Statutes of Canada* volumes, beginning with SC 1968-69, include a Table of Contents that provides the bill number.

■ The date of royal assent is provided on the first page of the statute: 30 January 1990. Use the date of royal assent to navigate the *Debates*.

■ Find 30 January 1990 in the *Debates*. Locate the royal assent information for this statute and record it in the table.

■ If an index to the *Debates* for the session is available, use it to locate the bill by title or by subject. However, an index is not always available.

■ Locate the *Journals of the House of Commons* in the library. Use the year and Parliament and session number to locate the relevant volumes of the *Journals*. Select the last volume for the session, because this one contains the index.

■ In the index, all elements of the legislative history are listed, followed by the page number in the *Journals* for the day on which this agenda item was heard in the House. Note the information from this page, and select each corresponding page in the *Journals* to find the relevant dates. For example, the index notes that first reading of the bill appears on page 80-1.

■ Turn to page 80-1 of the volume of the *Journals* and find the date of first reading, which is located at the top of the page: 12 April 1989. Use the page numbers in the index to navigate the *Journals* and find the dates for each remaining element in the legislative history. Then, use the dates to find the page numbers in the *Debates*.

I. Finding the Progress of Bills: Other Tools

Canadian Legislative Pulse	An online subscription service that tracks federal and provincial bills (CCH, Wolters Kluwer).
Canada Statute Citator	The Weekly Bulletin Service updates the status of bills introduced in the current parliamentary session in both the House of Commons and the Senate. Available in print in some libraries and online at <http://www.carswell.com/products/canada-statute-citator> (Canada Law Book, Thomson Reuters Canada).
Status of House Business	Provides the status of bills before the House for particular sessions of Parliament. Lists bills and includes key components of a legislative history except *Debates* page numbers. Available online at <http://www.parl.gc.ca/HousePublications/Publication.aspx?Pub=status>.
Canada Legislative Index	Service developed by the BC Courthouse Library that included bill status information. Discontinued several years ago, now revamped in an online subscription format (Quickscribe). Some libraries may have the *Canada Legislative Index* binders for historical research of bills.

FIGURE 4.7   Other Tools for Finding the Progress of a Bill

XIII. Researching Private Statutes: Print and Online

Also found on the Justice Laws website is the Table of Private Statutes, which indexes most federal private acts published in the *Statutes of Canada* since 1867. The table also includes amendments and repeals and is updated annually.

Researching private statutes occurs infrequently, because a private statute affects only specific individuals, not the public at large. However, if you are required to locate a private act, review the Table of Private Statutes and select an appropriate heading. Acts are grouped under general headings and then listed alphabetically. Only the table is available online. The statutes themselves can be located in the print statutes using the citation reference.

Researching Provincial and Territorial Legislation: An Introduction

5

CONTENTS

Publisher's Note

See Volume 2 for specific provincial research chapters.

I. Overview

The Canadian Constitution vests authority to create legislation in both the federal government and each provincial and territorial government. The division of powers between the federal, provincial, and territorial governments ensures that each jurisdiction can enact legislation under its exclusive constitutional authority. Accordingly, developing research competence requires an understanding of not only the processes to research federal legislation as discussed in Chapters 3 and 4, but also the methods and techniques to conduct research in each provincial and territorial jurisdiction.

Once you are proficient with the federal legislative research process, that knowledge can be applied to learn comprehensive research techniques for each province or territory. The following discussion introduces some of the research terms and concepts that are explained in more depth in each provincial research chapter.

II. Comparison of Federal, Provincial, and Territorial Research Processes

To begin, compare the mind map below illustrating the provincial and territorial bill passage process with the one found at Figure 3.1 in Chapter 3 describing the federal process, and note both the similarities and differences.

A. Why Is Legislation Created?

As with federal legislation, each provincial and territorial government identifies issues that require resolution through the enactment of legislation. The legislation may be created to address some aspect of the government's mandate, to solve an identified problem, or to create a new program. As with federal legislation, new law can be created through the passage of statutes and regulations, and existing statutes and regulations can be amended or repealed. Over time, jurisdictions revise and consolidate their statutes; however, not every jurisdiction officially revises and consolidates its regulations; e.g. Alberta does not.

B. Who Is Responsible for the Creation of Legislation and How Is It Created?

The same process used to create federal legislation is used to create provincial and territorial legislation. However, the terminology used and the steps taken vary

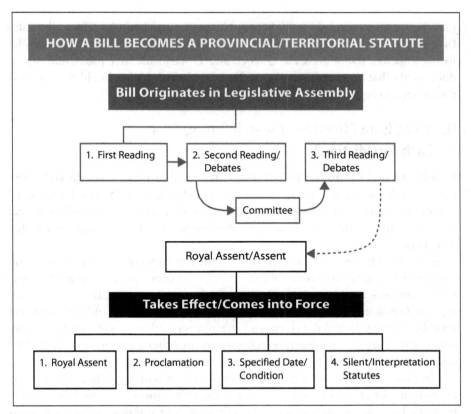

FIGURE 5.1   Provincial/Territorial Legislation Creation Process: Mind Map

somewhat across jurisdictions. In the initial legislative step to create a statute, a member of the Legislative Assembly (called the National Assembly in Quebec) introduces a bill. The bill may be sponsored either by a member of the governing party or by a member of the opposition. Both government bills, which affect the general population, and private bills, which affect only a specific group, organization, or individual, may form the basis of newly created statutes.

The provinces and territories have only one body that considers a bill's passage into law. As a result, bills are read only three times in the legislature before they receive royal assent. As with federal statutes, each provincial and territorial enacted statute must take effect before it becomes enforceable law.

C. When Does Legislation Take Effect?

Although the coming into force process for provincial statutes is similar to that for federal statutes, the terminology and the steps taken vary somewhat across jurisdictions. For example, Nova Scotia, Nunavut, and Manitoba refer to the dates that statutes come into force, while Prince Edward Island and Saskatchewan refer to the effective dates. As well, Quebec and Ontario identify proclamations as documents that bring statutes into force, while British Columbia identifies these documents as regulations.

D. What Is an Effective Research Protocol for Each Jurisdiction?

Despite the overall similarities between federal and provincial/territorial legislative research, there are differences across jurisdictions. Therefore, each provincial chapter contains descriptions of individually created tasks that are unique to that province and explains how to achieve effective legal research outcomes for that jurisdiction.

As with federal research, understanding the research process in provinces and territories requires familiarity with the specific statutes and regulations that govern the process. For example, in Ontario, the *Interpretation Act*, the *Evidence Act*, and the *Legislation Act, 2006* are some of the essential sources of legislation that must be examined when developing an effective research protocol. Similar statutes and regulations govern the research process in other provinces and must be considered when developing legal research competence.

The Queen's Printer in each jurisdiction plays an essential role in disseminating legislation. Governed by statute and regulation, the Queen's Printer traditionally published official versions of legislation in print, and still does so in most provinces, but not all. For example, in New Brunswick, the Queen's Printer ceased publishing statutes in print in 2003, and the official version is now disseminated online.

Online dissemination of legislation plays an essential role in effective legal research across Canada. However, the version of legislation available on government websites is not necessarily the official version. Moreover, official status may be designated as of a specified date. For example, in Newfoundland and Labrador, legislation disseminated online on the provincial government website has been given official status. This is not the case in territories such as the Yukon and provinces such as Alberta, where only print sources of legislation are designated official. As well, while commercial publishers of legal information provide accessible and useful online and print versions of both legislation and case law that can be used in the research process, these versions are not official sources of law.

While researching legislation and bills online is possible in every jurisdiction, the information made available differs. Some provinces provide detailed historical information online, which assists with determining the legislative history of statutes, while others require a search of print sources to locate historical information. For example, in British Columbia, the government website provides *Debates* in the archived *Journals* available online, from 1851 on. Prince Edward Island recently placed online a full text of the *Journals of the Legislative Assembly of Prince Edward Island*, commencing March 1894. Note, however, the status given to this historical information. For example, the Northwest Territories designates its online version of *Hansard* to be for information purposes only, while the print version is considered to be the official version.

While government websites and commercial publishers of legal information provide many resources in an online platform, at this point, exclusive online research is not possible in any jurisdiction. Therefore, to demonstrate research competency in every province and territory, familiarity with the use of a combination of online and print research tools and methods is required.

Accurate citation of legislation sources is one of the requisite skills of legal research. In most jurisdictions, legislation exists that provides information about the recommended citation format for legislation created by that jurisdiction. Therefore, while the *Canadian Guide to Uniform Legal Citation*[1] provides general guidelines and recommendations for a standard format for citation for each jurisdiction, effective legal research requires an examination of the legislative requirements for citation to ensure that the McGill Guide recommendations accord with the jurisdiction's rules.

While a beginning law student may believe initially that competence entails an understanding of research methodology only for one's home province or territory, or the jurisdiction in which one intends to practise, one soon learns that a more inclusive understanding of provincial and territorial law is required. For example, a lawyer may be faced with a unique issue arising in his or her jurisdiction. Secondary source research may lead to case law from another jurisdiction that has judicially considered the problem. Competent legal research requires both an examination of the legislation underpinning these decisions, and a comparison of the legislation governing the matter to the legislation in the lawyer's jurisdiction. Therefore, having access to research protocols from other jurisdictions and learning how they operate ensures the development of overall research competence.

---

1   7th ed (Toronto: Carswell, 2010) [McGill Guide].

Locating and Working with Judicial Decisions

6

CONTENTS

LEARNING OUTCOMES

By the end of this chapter, you should be able to:

- Understand how judicial decisions formulate primary law
- Understand how judicial decisions are published and disseminated
- Distinguish among official, semi-official, and unofficial sources for judicial decisions
- Understand how case citations are used to locate both judicial decisions and administrative tribunal decisions, in print and online
- Understand why researching judicial decisions requires determining case history
- Understand the basic search paradigms used to locate judicial decisions

Research Tasks

Chapters 6 and 7 work sequentially to explain the essential nature of judicial decisions as primary law. Chapter 6 introduces judicial decisions, explains their creation, and describes how legal citations provide the foundation to locate judicial decisions online and in print. Chapter 7 builds on the information in this chapter, discussing how secondary sources are used to develop more complex topic searches of primary law, including both judicial decisions and legislation.

I.   Primary Law: The Interaction of Legislation and Judicial Decisions

Primary law consists of both legislation and judicial decisions; however, these differ in both form and function. Created by Parliament and the legislatures, legislation is a framework of rules that organizes legal relationships. By establishing legal obligations and identifying consequences for those who breach those obligations, legislation identifies both legal rights and responsibilities. Moreover, legislation contributes to dispute avoidance. As legislation is widely disseminated, individuals can determine whether their actions and those of others would result in a breach of a law.

In contrast, a judicial decision is a judge's ruling on the merit of one or more legal issues. In civil matters, a judge may be asked to decide the matter when parties are unable to resolve their disputes informally through negotiation or through an alternative dispute resolution method such as mediation. In criminal matters, where the state is one of the parties, a judge oversees proceedings until an accused is acquitted or convicted and sentenced, or until the charge is withdrawn. Occasionally, a reference case requires the Supreme Court of Canada to provide a legal analysis of a matter in an advisory capacity.

Since judicial decisions typically focus on dispute resolution, a judge must hear all parties' versions of the relevant facts, which are presented to the court as evidence, before considering the applicable law. The applicable law may derive from any combination of legislation; common-law principles; or existing judicial decisions, also known as case law. In addition, for novel legal issues, a judge may refer to policy documents, scholarly legal commentary, or even the law of a foreign jurisdiction. The parties' lawyers (or the parties themselves, if unrepresented by counsel) will help the judge understand their respective positions through legal argument. The judge will write his or her subsequent legal analysis, which becomes the judicial decision. This decision is then published, and added to the pre-existing body of primary case law.

A decision is final, unless one of the parties can successfully appeal the decision. Because courts of appeal, including the Supreme Court of Canada, exist to correct judicial errors of lower courts, an appellate court will affirm, reverse, or modify the original decision at trial.

II. Publication and Dissemination of Judicial Decisions: Official, Authoritative, and Unofficial Sources

A. Court File

Case law is published in both official and unofficial formats in a manner similar to that of legislation. Once the case is decided, the judicial decision is filed at the court registry office. Therefore most judicial decisions are available at the registry where the case was heard.

When presenting a judicial decision to a court as evidence of the law,[1] an official version should be provided, although for general research purposes, working with unofficial versions of cases is acceptable. Pursuant to the *Canada Evidence Act*,[2] a court will accept a judicial decision into evidence under seal of the court, or a copy that purports to be under the signature of a judge. Similarly, the Ontario *Evidence Act*[3] establishes that a judicial decision under seal or a copy of the decision under seal of a court will be accepted into evidence. Since decisions filed at the registry office include a seal or the deciding judge's signature, a copy obtained from the court file should be acceptable as evidence in a judicial proceeding.

Registry office contact information is usually available through the applicable court website.

B. Official Reporters Published by the Court

While all judicial decisions are first filed at the court registry office, noteworthy decisions that provide significant interpretations of legal principles are disseminated more widely in published case reporters. Official case reporters are those prepared by the court and published by the Queen's Printer.

Currently, the Canada Supreme Court Reports and the Federal Court Reports are the only case reporters with official status. The following table summarizes their status and availability.

---

1 While many legal issues are decided in court, others are decided by administrative bodies created pursuant to the governing statute. Decisions of these administrative bodies may be subject to judicial review or appeal by a court. The discussion in this chapter focuses on judicial proceedings only, unless otherwise indicated.

2 RSC 1985, c C-5, s 23(1).

3 RSO 1990, c E.23, s 38.

FIGURE 6.1   Official Reporters

Reporter	Authority	Availability—Print	Availability—Online
Canada Supreme Court Reports (SCR)	*Supreme Court Act*, RSC 1985, c S-26	Published in 3 stages, available at law libraries: 1. "Slips" of decisions are provided immediately after the decision. 2. Soft-bound sets, which contain a group of slips, are next provided. 3. Hard-bound sets, which contain all decisions for the year, are published.	Available on the Lexum website* as follows from 1876 to present as a scanned version of the actual SCR. Also available in the HeinOnline library, "Canada Supreme Court Reports"; scanned version of the official reporter from volume 1 (1876-1877) to present.
Federal Court Reports (FCR)	*Federal Courts Act*, RSC 1985, c F-7	Print volumes available in law libraries, but only those decisions considered significant are published.	Available on the Federal Court website** in 4 formats: 1990-1997: HTML version that does not include paragraph numbers or a seal. 1998-2007: HTML version that includes paragraph numbers but no seal. 2007-2009: HTML and PDF versions that include paragraph numbers but no seal. 2010 to present: HTML and PDF versions that include paragraph numbers and a seal.

   * Judgments of the Supreme Court of Canada, online: <http://scc.lexum.org/decisia-scc-csc/scc-csc/en/nav.do>.

 ** Decisions of the Federal Court, online: <http://decisions.fct-cf.gc.ca/en/index.html>. Decisions from 1992, 1993, and 1994 are currently not availabe.

C. Court and Tribunal Decisions Online—Authoritative

Some Canadian courts and tribunals maintain online databases of their judicial decisions, accessible at no cost. To determine the authority of a court or tribunal's online decisions, consult the Notices or Frequently Asked Questions section of the court website. For example:

> Ontario Court of Appeal:
> Coverage: 1998-present
>
> The official version of the Court of Appeal for Ontario reasons for judgment, endorsement and appeal book endorsement is the signed original in the court file. In the event that there is a question about the content, the original in the court file takes precedence. They may undergo editing changes after they have been released.[4]

Additionally, consult the legislation of the relevant jurisdiction to determine the governing evidentiary rules.

D. Publication by Law Societies—Semi-Official

Law reporters published under the auspices of some provincial law societies have been designated as semi-official by the publishers of the *Canadian Guide to Uniform Legal Citation*.[5] This status applies only to rules of citation; it does not convey official status for evidentiary purposes at court.

E. Commercial Print and Online; and Non-Commercial Online—Unofficial

Traditionally, commercial publishers of legal information prepared full texts of noteworthy judicial decisions and published them in case law reporters, also called primary law reporters. Although these sources are unofficial versions of judicial decisions, they remain an important source of legal information, particularly for research purposes.[6] There are numerous case reporters, organized by:

1. **court and jurisdiction**—e.g. the Ontario Reports, which include decisions released by courts in Ontario only, and the British Columbia Appeal Cases, which provide decisions from the British Columbia Court of Appeal only

2. **topic**—e.g. the Canadian Criminal Cases, which report select criminal cases only

---

4   Decisions of the Court of Appeal, online: <http://www.ontariocourts.ca/decisions_index/en/>.

5   7th ed (Toronto: Carswell, 2010) Appendix C-2 at A-28 [McGill Guide].

6   Commercial publishers of legal information provide organizational systems to assist with research, a process explained in Chapter 7.

3. **geographical region**—e.g. the Western Weekly Reports, which report significant cases from courts in western Canada only

4. **general**—e.g. the Dominion Law Reports, which report decisions on various legal topics from across Canada

Although judicial decisions and legislation were once available in print format only, commercial publishers of legal information now provide their versions online to paid subscribers, along with additional finding aids and tools. Print versions may also provide commentary to help with legal analysis. CanLII provides online access to judicial decisions and tribunal decisions at no cost to the user.

Online searching may be the preferred research method because of its speed and flexibility; however, sometimes print sources must be consulted, as explained later in this chapter.

F. Unreported Decisions

Not all judicial decisions are published in commercial reporters. Of the many hundreds of cases that are decided each year, many contain no distinguishing legal interpretations or factual circumstances that would differentiate them from existing case law. When research leads to an unreported decision, the case will be unavailable through an online or print commercial service.[7]

III. Judicial Decisions Citation Format

A legal citation is a unique code used to identify essential aspects of a case, including its location in print or online publications. The legal citation must be deciphered to locate a judicial decision. Although the McGill Guide provides recommendations for the comprehensive citation of judicial decisions, the information below supplements these general guidelines by explaining how to interpret a legal citation to locate a case.

A. Judicial Decision Citation Format: Original

Traditionally, citations for judicial decisions published in print reporters included:

- case name—names of the parties, also referred to as "style of cause"
- year of decision

---

7   *All-Canada Weekly Summaries* (ACWS) and *Weekly Criminal Bulletin* (WCB) are digests that provide the docket numbers of unreported decisions. The docket number provided by the court can be used to locate these cases at the court registry where the case was heard.

- reporter name, including its series, where applicable; volume number; and first page of the case

Using these elements in combination ensures that a specific case can be located. Reporter names are usually identified by acronym. To find the full name of a reporter, use one of the following sources, available in most law libraries:

- McGill Guide
- Mary Miles Prince, *Prince's Bieber Dictionary of Legal Abbreviations*[8]

The following source is available online:

- Cardiff Index to Legal Abbreviations <http://www.legalabbrevs.cardiff.ac.uk>

Several different formats are used to reference the year of decision:[9]

1. *Year of decision and part, or year of decision only.* Some reporter series use the year of the decision as the primary location information. In these situations, the importance of the year as location information is signified by enclosing the year in brackets, e.g. [1987]. Most of the decisions for that year are published in the same volume; however, decisions handed down near the end of one calendar year may not be reported until the next calendar year. In addition, if the number of the decisions or the length of each decision makes it impossible to publish all the cases in one annual volume of the reporter, the annual volume is published in separate parts for that year.

   The Supreme Court Reports (SCR) is one example of a case reporter that cites cases by year of decision and part, and also by year of decision only. The first citation example indicates that the case decided in 1990 was published in part 3 of the 1990 volume of the Supreme Court Reports at page 1273.

   > *Whitbread v Walley*, [1990] 3 SCR 1273

   The second citation example indicates a case cited by year of decision only.

   > *Filion v Magnan*, [1965] SCR 352

---

8 6th ed (New York: WS Hein, 2009).

9 This content is adapted with permission of the copyright holders of *The Bluebook: A Uniform System of Citation*. The copyright holders did not contribute to, review, approve, or endorse this text.

2. *Volume and series, or volume only.* Some reporter series do not use the year as the primary identifier. Instead, they organize their reporters by volume and series. A reporter series begins at volume 1 and progresses sequentially until a predetermined number is reached, e.g. 100, at which time the sequence begins again at volume 1 in a new series. Because the year that the case was decided is not the primary method used to locate cases, the year of the decision is enclosed in parentheses, e.g. (2004).

The Ontario Reports (OR) is an example of a case reporter that cites its cases by volume number and series. The following citation indicates that the case decided in 2001 was published in volume 55 of the third series of Ontario Reports at page 374.

R v Banks (2001), 55 OR (3d) 374

The following example indicates a case reporter that organizes its cases by volume only.

R v Wilkening (2009), 446 AR 102

3. *Year of decision and year of reporter.* Sometimes, a legal citation will include references to two different years in the same case citation, first in parentheses and then in brackets. This occurs only when a case that is published in a reporter organized by year was not included in the volume that matches the year of its decision. In the following example, the Supreme Court of Canada released its decision during 1966, but the case did not appear in the Supreme Court Reports until the 1967 volume was published.

Hamilton Street Railway v Northcott (1966), [1967] SCR 3

B.   Judicial Decision Citation Format Online: Neutral Citation

While the original citation format continues for sources in print reporters, a new citation structure has developed as more case law is published online. Cases are often made available online immediately following the decision (i.e. before they are available in print reporters). As a result, "neutral citations" have been developed to provide a standard citation using a specified format.[10] The neutral citation is added by the court immediately before the case is disseminated online.[11] This contrasts with the original citation format, which uses citations inserted by the publisher after the case is distributed and results in different citations for the same case.

While a neutral citation can be used to locate a judicial decision in most online databases, it cannot be used to find a court decision in a printed reporter. Therefore, case location requires an understanding of both methods of citation reference.

A neutral citation includes:

- case name
- year of decision
- acronym for the name of the court releasing the decision
- case number identifier

In neutral citation, there are no brackets or parentheses around the year of the decision. Because no reporter series are referenced, the acronyms that identify the court become the critical identifying information to locate the case. To find the full name of a court, or the appropriate acronym for a court, consult the McGill Guide.[12]

Wilson v Nova Scotia (AG), 2012 NSCA 14
This decision of the Nova Scotia Court of Appeal was the 14th decision of this court in 2012.

R v Boudreault, 2012 SCC 56
This decision of the Supreme Court of Canada was the 56th decision of this court in 2012.

---

10   For more information about the development of the neutral citation standard, see Canadian Citation Committee, "A Neutral Citation Standard for Case Law", online: <http://www.lexum.com/ccc-ccr/neutr/neutr.jur_en.html>.

11   Neutral citation is used in foreign jurisdictions as well.

12   *Supra* note 5, Appendix B-3 at A-15.

C. Judicial Citation Format: Commercial and Non-Commercial—Online

When searching online for judicial decisions, the most comprehensive research systems generally available to law students across Canada include CanLII, LexisNexis Quicklaw ("Quicklaw"), and Westlaw Canada ("Westlaw"). All three systems have adopted the same basic structure for case citation found in print reporters—i.e. case name, date, (e-)reporter name, and document number. The features that distinguish online systems from print reporters are either the manner that the year is referenced or the database identifier used in conjunction with the e-reporter name.

Both Quicklaw and Westlaw are subscription-based systems, while CanLII provides free access to those who wish to search its content.

1. CanLII

CanLII uses two distinctive citation formats. Originally, following the case name, CanLII referenced the year of decision without parentheses or brackets, followed by CanLII as its e-reporter name, and a unique case identification number. However, as Canadian courts and jurisdictions adopted neutral citation over the past decade, CanLII adopted the neutral citation format in its citation system, incorporating the jurisdiction and court into the citation reference, followed by "CanLII" in parentheses. The latter style is seen most frequently where the court or tribunal has adopted neutral citation. In the examples below, the first case is a 1997 decision of the Prince Edward Island Supreme Court—Trial Division; the second case is a decision of the Court of Appeal of Newfoundland and Labrador.

> *Davis v Walkup*, 1997 CanLII 4607 (PE SCTD)
>
> *R v Ryan*, 2007 NLCA 6 (CanLII)

2. Quicklaw

Quicklaw organizes its cases by year, and has adopted the convention of enclosing the year in brackets using the same convention as print reporters that organize their cases by year. Quicklaw databases use an acronym that identifies the jurisdiction and ends with the letter "J". Thus e.g. AJ signifies Alberta Judgments and NBJ signifies New Brunswick Judgments. The case number is a unique identifier preceded by "No". The example below is a 1990 decision of the Ontario Court of Appeal.

> *R v Westendorp*, [1990] OJ No 1109 (CA)

3. Westlaw

Westlaw uses neither parentheses nor brackets to enclose the year designation. The reporter name incorporates Carswell with identifying jurisdictional database information followed by a unique case number. The example below is a 2003 decision of the Manitoba Provincial Court.

> *R v Hiebert*, 2003 CarswellMan 117 (Prov Ct)

When directing the court or opposing counsel to a specific reference in a source, an accurate and specific page or paragraph number is required ("pinpoint"). Figure 6.2 highlights the rules for pinpointing to official sources such as the SCR and FCR.

FIGURE 6.2   Citation to Official Sources of Judicial Decisions

Reporter	Pinpointing to page number	Pinpointing to paragraph number	Neutral citation
SCR	Pinpoint to page number for decisions between 1876 and 1995.	Pinpoint to paragraph number for decisions from 1995 on.	Applied since 2000.
FCR	Pinpoint to page number for decisions between 1875* and 1998.	Pinpoint to paragraph number for decisions from 1998 on.	Applied since 2002.

* In 1971, the Federal Court of Canada was established and inherited the jurisdiction of the former Exchequer Court of Canada.

Figure 6.3 explains how pinpoint references are used in commercial print reporters as well as commercial and non-commercial online publications.

FIGURE 6.3   Citation to Unofficial Sources of Judicial Decisions

Reporter type	Pinpointing to page number	Pinpointing to paragraph number	Neutral citation
Commercial print	For most reporters, for decisions up to 2002, pinpoint to a page in the print version.	Since 2002, many courts and tribunals began including paragraph numbers in their decisions.* Pinpoints to paragraph numbers in print reporters should match the online version. For decisions before 2002, the online and print paragraph numbers should be cross-referenced.	Since 1999,** most courts and tribunals began to apply neutral citations to their judgments.†
Commercial†† and non-commercial# online publications	Page references for pre-2002 decisions should be made using a printed reporter.	Since 2002, paragraph references have been used; thus it is not necessary to verify with the printed reporter.	

* In 2002, the Canadian Judicial Council approved the "Canadian Guide to the Uniform Preparation of Judgments", online: <http://www.lexum.com/ccc-ccr/guide/guide.prep_en.html>.

** In 1999, the Canadian Judicial Council approved "A Neutral Citation Standard for Case Law", online: <http://www.lexum.com/ccc-ccr/neutr/neutr.jur_en.html>.

† The implementation date for neutral citation is not standard among all reporters. See the McGill Guide for a list of the abbreviations used in neutral citations and the commencement dates for the courts and tribunals.

†† E.g. Westlaw, Quicklaw, and CCH Online.

E.g. CanLII.

IV. Locating Judicial Decisions

A. Planning Considerations

Legal citations provide the code to locate cases, but the novice researcher may be unsure of the hierarchy of sources to consult to ensure both time- and cost-effective research. Intuitively, online searching may seem to be faster than print searching in a library, but if the researcher does not know the scope of the databases searched, or has ineffective search strategies, any potential time savings may be compromised through the recovery of insufficient or irrelevant information. Moreover, a particular decision may not be available in a particular database, leading to an erroneous conclusion that the case does not exist.

Additional issues to consider include:

- Are both print and online sources accessible? If so, what are these sources and are there restrictions? For example, sometimes cost considerations limit the use of subscription online services.
- Is cost efficiency a consideration? If so, it may be appropriate to begin the search with CanLII or the judicial decisions available on the court website. If cost is not a consideration, Quicklaw and Westlaw may be appropriate.
- Does a complete citation to a case exist, or is partial information available, including details of the case itself? All online sources allow searching by citation, but some also allow field searching using keywords, such as a judge's or lawyer's name.
- Is the case a recent or older decision? Although some older cases are available online, page references may not be available in online reporters before 2002. Therefore, although the case may be found online, a copy of the case from a printed reporter may be required to provide an accurate pinpoint citation to a specific page.
- Is the search restricted to judicial decisions or does it include decisions of administrative bodies? While both commercial and non-commercial providers of online legal information have comprehensive databases of both judicial and administrative law decisions, not every provider publishes every decision. Therefore, it may be necessary to consult more than one source.

Figure 6.4 identifies online search options for varying search tasks.

FIGURE 6.4   Online Search Options

	CanLII	Court / tribunal website	Quicklaw	Westlaw
Case citation provided; cost-effective method required	x	varies*		
Case citation provided; cost-effective method not required	x	varies*	x	x
Party name provided; partial or no citation provided	x	x	x	x
Judge's name, lawyer's name, the date, or the level of court provided; partial or no citation provided		varies	x	x
Case details and keywords; partial or no citation provided	x	varies	x	x
Tribunal decision; citation or partial reference provided	x	x	x	x
Functionality to filter, sort, or group results required	x		x	x

* Tribunal websites often organize their decisions by docket number and not necessarily by citation to a printed reporter.

B. Search Methods

1. Print Searches

TASK 6.1

Print Searches

- Using the case citation, determine the reporter(s) that have published the case.
- In a law library, use the library reference system to locate the call number of the reporter.
- Locate the reporter series, and find the case in the identified volume at the specified page.

2. Database Searches

For CanLII, Westlaw, and Quicklaw, the default database for case law searches is their largest collection of Canadian judicial decisions.

However, if the search is something within a specific jurisdiction or within a specific tribunal, you must choose the correct database before commencing the search, as the following examples illustrate.

TASK 6.2

CanLII Database Search

Go to Database Search. From the list of databases, choose the jurisdiction and the desired tribunal.

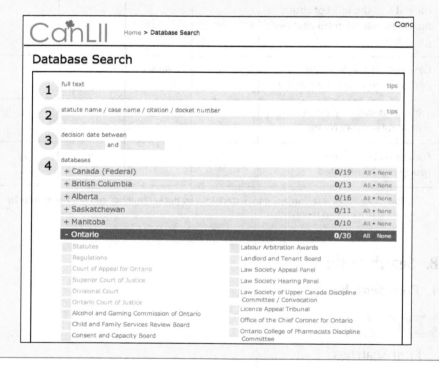

TASK 6.3

Quicklaw Source Directory

Go to Source Directory. Choose the jurisdiction. From the Cases folder, choose the tribunal.

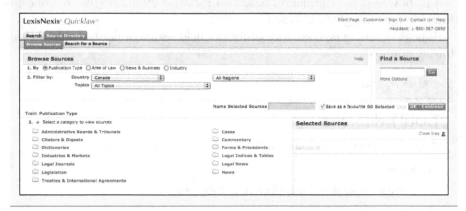

TASK 6.4

Westlaw Directory

From the Database Directory, choose the database and jurisdiction.

3. Field Searches

Every database online contains fields or descriptors that identify the information contained within the database.

Database fields that are used to describe court decisions include the party names, the case citation, the judges' names, the lawyers' names, and the year of the decision. Documents entered into the system are organized under these terms.

Therefore, if any of this information is known about a specific judicial decision, field searching can be used.

Accurately defining legal concept search terms is an essential search requirement. Review the list of terms and use a legal dictionary or thesaurus to find synonyms if required. For example, neither sexism nor racism are legal search terms; however, discrimination based on racial or ethnic origin are concepts found in human rights legislation.

If field searching is warranted, conduct a field search as illustrated in the following examples.

TASK 6.5

CanLII Field Search

CanLII provides three default searches using the following fields:

1. full text
2. statute name, case name, citation, or docket number
3. decision date

TASK 6.6

Westlaw Field Search

Available search fields in Westlaw are provided in a drop-down menu.

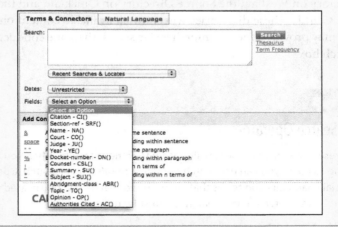

TASK 6.7

Quicklaw Field Search

Choose Quicklaw's source "All Canadian Court Cases", then select "Show document segments" to see all available search fields.

Although CanLII, Westlaw, and Quicklaw all provide options to quickly search for content on their systems, these search boxes do not necessarily search all content on these systems. For example, the "Find by Citation" box on Quicklaw does not search tribunal decisions. If your search is unsuccessful, recall the Database Directory on Westlaw, the Source Directory on Quicklaw, and the Database Search on CanLII. These directories will show all available content on their systems, and may provide a more comprehensive search than one conducted using a quick search box.

TASK 6.8

Using Search Operators

A legal research database uses an algorithm to retrieve results. When you are searching full text, you can use search operators to refine your search. Operators are special characters and terms that allow you to search in sophisticated ways, both within and between field searches. Consider using:

- **" "** Most legal databases allow a search for an exact phrase in quotation marks.

- **/n** Most legal research databases will allow a search for words located within a specific range of each other. E.g. "letter /5 credit" will find the word "letter" within five words of the word "credit".

- **/s** Most legal research databases allow a search for two words within the same sentence, or within a range of about ten words, regardless of which is first. E.g. "tax /s income" will find the words "tax" and "income" in the same sentence.

- **/p** Most legal research databases allow a search for two words within the same paragraph, or within a range of about 50 words, regardless of which word occurs first. E.g. "levy /p probate" will find the words "levy" and "probate" in the same paragraph.

The full range of operators available and their syntax may vary depending on the legal research database. CanLII's operators are shown here.

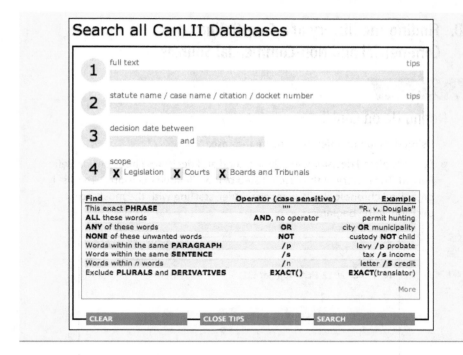

C. Case History: Noting Up

Almost every case has the potential to be appealed, and some administrative law decisions may be either appealed or judicially reviewed by a court. Therefore, determining the case history, or "noting up" a judicial decision, is an essential component of case law research.[13] While the McGill Guide[14] provides instructions to complete a case history citation, the information that follows describes research strategies to locate case history information.

---

13 An additional aspect of noting up involves determining the judicial treatment of a case, which traces subsequent courts' consideration of judicial decisions. This is discussed in Chapter 7.

14 *Supra* note 5 at ch 3.11.

D. Finding the History of a Case Online: Commercial and Non-Commercial Sources

Noting Up on CanLII

- Using the citation reference, locate the case.
- Select "Related decisions, legislation cited and decisions cited" beside Reflex Record. The history of the case is listed below "Related decisions". This list is organized chronologically in reverse order, starting with the most recent decision at the beginning.

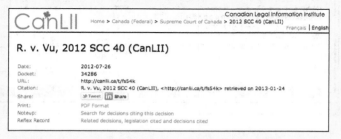

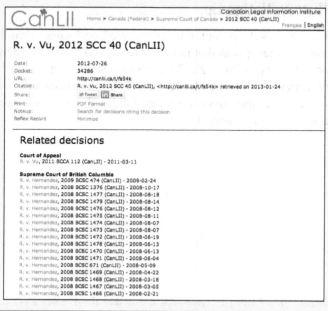

TASK 6.10

Noting Up on Westlaw

- Using the citation reference, locate the case.

- Select "Related Information Tab" and choose "Full History".

- The history of the case is listed, in chronological order, beginning with the trial level decision.

TASK 6.11

Noting Up on Quicklaw

- Using the citation reference, locate the case.

- Select "Note up with Quickcite".

- The history of the case is listed below the list of parallel citations. This list is organized chronologically in reverse order, starting with the most recent decision.

- Quicklaw provides an alert system, which can be configured to search on a daily, weekly, or monthly basis; results are sent by email.

Do not rely exclusively on commercial providers of legal information, even though they provide both print and online sources to gather information used when noting up.

E. Leave to Appeal

1. Supreme Court of Canada

For Supreme Court of Canada decisions, use the case history provided by the court itself to construct the case citation. The Supreme Court of Canada's website[15] provides essential information about all cases that have been appealed to that court, including:

- leave to appeal status
- hearing dates for cases that have been granted leave to appeal
- case information

---

15   <http://www.scc-csc.gc.ca>.

TASK 6.12

Locating Leave to Appeal Decisions on the SCC Website, CanLII, and Quicklaw

Leave to appeal decisions are available on:

- The SCC Judgments on Lexum—Select the Bulletin link, which provides a list, compiled weekly, of applications for leave to appeal and the judgments on applications. The database is searchable by party name.

- CanLII—On the left menu, go to the Canada (Federal) database. From the list of databases at the bottom of the screen, choose Supreme Court of Canada - Applications for Leave.

- Quicklaw—From the Source Directory, choose Supreme Court of Canada Rulings on Applications for Leave to Appeal and Other Motions.

To determine whether a case that has been granted leave to appeal has been scheduled for hearing, on the Supreme Court website, select "Cases" then "Appeals Ready for Hearing". If scheduled, the date of hearing will be provided.

Use the "SCC Case Information" link to find additional information about the case's preparation.

2. Other Court Databases

Consult other court databases to determine whether appeal information is provided. For example, on the Ontario Court of Appeal website,[16] go to Decisions of the Court and then choose "Motions for Leave to Appeal" to determine whether leave to appeal has been requested. If leave has been granted, go to Decisions of the Court and choose "Judgments" or "Judgments Released this Week" to see whether an appellate decision has been delivered.

Chapter 7 builds on the discussion of primary law research contained in earlier chapters to examine how secondary sources of law can be used to analyze complex research topics that include both legislation and judicial decisions.

---

16 <http://www.ontariocourts.on.ca/coa/en>.

Researching Secondary Sources of Law

7

LEARNING OUTCOMES

By the end of this chapter, you should be able to:

- Understand the relationship between primary and secondary sources of law
- Choose the appropriate print or online secondary source to locate and interpret primary law
- Structure a search of secondary sources to locate primary law using a fact and issue analysis
- Select appropriate research tools to note up or judicially consider primary law

Research Tasks

I. Relationship Between Primary and Secondary Source Law

As described in previous chapters, primary law includes legislation and judicial decisions. In an international context, primary law includes treaties and conventions through which governments regulate interactions among nations.

By default, legal information that is not primary law is secondary source law. One aspect of legal research competence is proficiency in the use of secondary sources of law to improve both the efficiency and comprehensiveness of primary law research.

While practising lawyers explore the legal issues presented when a client seeks legal advice, law students explore legal issues presented as legal hypotheticals. In both situations, the law that must be researched may not be immediately evident. The authors of secondary sources will have done much of the preliminary work for the researcher by analyzing the legal concepts, discovering nuances in the law, and identifying the relevant primary law.

There are two main categories of secondary sources: those that are used to locate primary law, and those that interpret its meaning or application. Some sources perform one function exclusively; others overlap.

To establish competence, a lawyer must be able to:

- use print and online sources that are appropriate to the research task, both general sources and those tailored to specific practice areas
- comparatively assess the strengths and limitations of sources, both commercially published sources and those in the public domain
- choose the source that best fits each step of the legal research process, considering both cost and time efficiencies

II. Generating a Topic Search Using Secondary Sources: Start with Facts, Issues, and Keywords

Consider the following situation.

TASK 7.1

Research Hypothetical Problem

Conrad Cash ("Cash"), 64 years old, was the sole owner of a lucrative business, Cash Computer Co., located in Blissville, Ontario. When Cash died on 1 May 2012, his net worth exceeded $100 million. In 2007, Cash revised his will. Beneficiaries of the estate included: Penny, spouse, age 58, $60 million; Farthing, daughter, age 32, $30 million; and the Blissville District School Board, remainder, to upgrade its computer technology systems and programs.

In 2011, Conrad and Penny Cash divorced after a bitter, year-long dispute. Later that year, Cash married the couple's dog walker, Yuro, 26. Unhappy with the remarriage, Farthing became estranged from her father.

In January 2012, Cash suffered a head injury in a motor vehicle accident. After his release from hospital in February 2012, Yuro told Farthing that she could not visit her father until he recovered. Farthing had no further contact with her father prior to his death.

Last month Farthing learned that her father had altered his will, leaving $80 million to Yuro, and the remainder to the Blissville Kennel Club. Farthing suspects that Yuro may have coerced or otherwise unduly influenced her father to change his will. She has sought legal advice to determine whether she can challenge the will's validity.

This hypothetical exemplifies the type of issue typically encountered by law students, articling students, or lawyers in practice, any of whom may be unfamiliar with the area of practice governing the client's concern. Because the governing primary law is not evident at this point, the researcher who is new to this area of law can use secondary sources first to gain an understanding of the principles of law at issue, to analyze the applicable law, and to identify the relevant primary law. The whole process—finding, analyzing, and noting up—is illustrated in Figure 7.1.

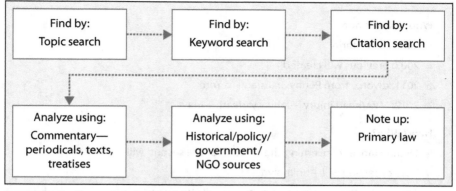

FIGURE 7.1   Secondary Source Options

Before selecting secondary sources to locate primary law, undertake a fact and issue analysis (as described in Chapter 2):

1. Sort and organize the facts under relevant headings.
2. Generate a legal keyword search list.
3. Frame the issue, incorporating one or more legal and fact words.
4. Use legal keywords to define the topic; choose one or more secondary sources to locate the controlling law.

TASK 7.2

Fact, Issue, and Keyword Summary

Who Are the Key Parties or Others with Information?

- Conrad Cash, creator of the will
- Farthing, daughter, beneficiary under the first will (client)
- Yuro, spouse, beneficiary under the second will
- Blissville Kennel Club, beneficiary under the second will
- Penny, former spouse, beneficiary under the first will
- Blissville District School Board, beneficiary under the first will

What Happened?

- Cash altered his will, disentitling former beneficiaries
- Cash did not inform his daughter about the change to his will following the accident

Where and When?

- Blissville, Ontario
- 2007: previous will created
- 2011: divorce from Penny; marriage to Yuro
- 2012: MVA/head injury—January; death—May

How? Why?

- Circumstances concerning the creation of the second will—unknown
- Date of second will—unknown
- Reasons for the creation of the second will—unknown

Additional Unknown/Assumed?

- Additional beneficiaries? Prior wills? Drafter of wills? Existence of relevant legislation, case law?

Legal Keywords

- will, beneficiary, validity, undue influence

Issue

Is Cash's second will valid?

NB: As research progresses, additional legal keywords may be suggested, more issues may become apparent, and other facts requiring scrutiny may be revealed. Revise the summary as required.

Because research tasks vary, no specific recommended research protocol can be applied uniformly to all research problems. Instead, you must consider what is already known and what remains to be discovered, and then decide which sources are most likely to provide relevant information. At this point, create a research plan; as the plan is executed, log information for further review and analysis. (See Chapter 9 to learn how to develop a research plan and log results.)

Figure 7.2 illustrates one approach to researching the fact hypothetical described in Task 7.1, using selected secondary sources to find and analyze primary law.

Although many secondary sources exist, if little is known about the issue and the governing primary law, consider a topic search using a legal encyclopedia.

In addition, take advantage of research learning opportunities provided through your law school, either through sessions offered by law or reference librarians or through training sessions provided by legal publishers.

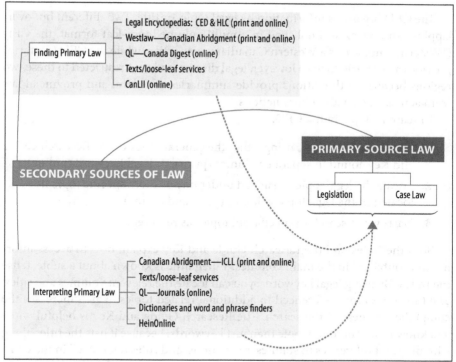

FIGURE 7.2   Mind Map: Using Secondary Sources to Locate and Analyze Primary Law

III. Locating Case Law by Topic: Print and Online

A. Legal Encyclopedias

1. Canadian Encyclopedic Digest

Available both in print and online, the *Canadian Encyclopedic Digest*[1] (CED), now in its fourth edition, is a comprehensive research tool useful for gaining a general understanding of the legal topic being researched. It references primary law (key cases and legislation) and may identify additional secondary sources that analyze primary law.

---

1   *Canadian Encyclopedic Digest*, 4th ed, loose-leaf (Toronto: Carswell, 2010) and online: <http://www.westlawcanada.com> (subscription required). The publisher provides e-learning tutorials for its products; see <http://www.westlawcanada.com/online-learning-centre/>.

The CED organizes information by legal topic, or title. Two different but over-lapping editions exist. Published in a multi-volume loose-leaf format, the CED (Western) emphasizes a Western Canadian perspective, while the CED (Ontario) provides an Ontario focus. However, legal discussion is not restricted to these two regions because both editions provide summaries of federal and provincial law from across all Canadian jurisdictions.

To search a topic in the CED:

1. Locate the legal topic using either the general Index or the Research Guide and Key, found in separate volumes (print), or legal keyword (online).

2. Locate the legal topic organized under one or more specific topic titles located in the legal topic volumes (print and online).

3. Narrow the search to specific subtopics as required.

Both the Index and the Research Guide and Key explain how to access information contained in the main volumes. When little is known about a subject, use the Index. By using legal keywords, you can locate the relevant volumes and titles. The topics are cross-referenced to additional related topics, which increases the comprehensiveness of the search. The Research Guide and Key is helpful when you know more about the topic than just keywords, because it lists the titles along with pinpoint references to statutes, regulations, and rules referenced in the CED.

Once you identify the relevant title using the Index, locate that title in the main volumes and search the title content. Each title divides the general topic into subtopics identified by numbered paragraphs (§§). A brief commentary supports the subtopics, accompanied by citation references to primary law. Supplements, placed at the beginning of each title with the same numbered paragraph system, update the law.

Titles are arranged by:

- title tab
- a grey-bordered supplement that updates the title content (if available)
- white pages (table of classification or contents)
- tables of cases, statutes, and rules and regulations (optional)
- paragraphs and
- an index to the title topic

The paragraphs within the title are organized into parts and then subdivided into numbered sections. Each part contains descriptions of different legal issues. Each section may then be further subdivided with additional information concerning cases and statutes. A "pending legislation" heading at the beginning of the update supplement reminds the researcher to check for amendments to legislation.

One must understand how to use both the print and online versions of the CED, because one or the other version may not always be accessible. However, assuming that neither availability nor is a factor, once you have established proficiency in both online and print-based research methods, you may choose the preferred version to locate primary law.

Using the hypothetical described in Task 7.1, consider the following steps, which illustrate the process of using the CED to find primary law.

TASK 7.3

Using the CED to Find Primary Law: Print

- Select the CED (Ontario) because the facts indicate that Ontario is the relevant jurisdiction.

- Select the Index volume and find the tabbed List of Titles. Record the Wills volume and title numbers (volume 53, title 161).

- Find "wills" in the Index. Examine the headings and record relevant subheadings. Note the subheading titled "Undue Influence". Other subheadings of interest might include "Requirements for a Valid Will" and "Suspicious Circumstances". Record both the descriptive phrase and corresponding paragraph reference (§) because CED topics are organized by volume, title, and paragraph number, not page number. Record all potentially relevant subtopics. Later, refine the search and exclude irrelevant subtopics.

- Knowing the currency of the material selected is critical. Record the currency date located at the bottom of the page—the Key and Index volumes were last updated in April 2012.

- Locate volume 53 and select title 161. Locate the table of contents. Select relevant topic headings and record the organizing classification code (III.i.1.d).

> III. Requirements for a Valid Will
> 1. Knowledge and approval
> (d) Undue Influence

- Subtopics related to the conditions under which a will can be created or revoked may also be of interest; they can be examined as the research continues. Examine cross-references to locate potential research leads.

- Within title 161, find the Title Index and scan the headings. On the basis of the facts of the problem you are researching, the heading "Undue Influence" at §75 seems relevant. Note the various subheadings under this subtopic.

Investigate such phrases as "general", "alleging", "presumptions", or "suspicious circumstances". The numbers following these phrases identify the numbered paragraphs that reference this subtopic.

■ Find §75. Notice the brief description "Undue Influence", followed by citation references and brief summaries of leading cases or references to legislation. Record the currency date for this title—September 2008.

■ Locate the identified judicial decisions and legislation by citation reference; review them to discern the underlying statutory scheme and the associated legal principles that apply to a claim of undue influence when a will's validity is being assessed.

■ Examine the supplement that updates the law, if available (grey-bordered pages). It provides recent additions to legislation and case law. Note the supplement's currency date—January 2012. Examine the supplement and locate the target paragraph (§75) reviewed earlier; record and review the updated information.

■ Using the CED, you have now located references to relevant primary law, which you can review to gain an understanding of how undue influence may affect a will's validity.

TASK 7.4

Using the CED to Find Primary Law: Online

Sign on to the Westlaw Canada website. Under the LawSource tab, locate Browse Tables of Contents and go to CED. Scan the list of titles, and open "Wills". (Although you can search the CED by keyword using the templates, at this point in the research this approach may be less efficient because you do not know enough about the topic to narrow the search sufficiently.)

TASK 7.5

CED Online: Subtopic Search

Drill down into the Wills topic and locate the subtopic "Undue Influence".
The classification code is the same as that for the print version; "Undue Influence"
is therefore a subtopic located under the broader topic "Requirements for a
Valid Will".

Record the currency date. Note that the classification code III.1.d is the same in
both the print and online versions of the CED.

TASK 7.6

Using the CED Online to Link to Primary Law

- Select the appropriate subtopic and maximize the screen to find the paragraph references, which are the same in print and online.
- Locate the relevant primary law by linking to the online version. For those cases not included in the CED online, locate the print version using its citation reference.
- No additional updating is required when using the online version, unlike the print version. Also, while the Ontario and Western print versions are published in separate sets, they are integrated in one platform online.

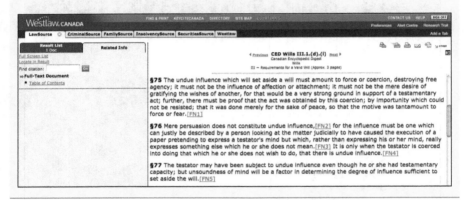

2. Halsbury's Laws of Canada

Halsbury's Laws of Canada[2] is a multi-volume encyclopedic-style reference similar to the CED in national scope and purpose. It organizes legal concepts by topic and subtopic, and is available in print and online.

HLC provides summary statements of the law supported by primary law references to judicial decisions and legislation, cross-referenced to related law. Each topic provides a table of contents, index, table of cases, and table of statutes. Topic titles are published in hardcover. HLC does not use a loose-leaf format; rather, annual cumulative supplements update the law.

To search an HLC topic:

1. Locate the legal topic using the Guide and Consolidated Index (print version only).

---

2 LexisNexis Canada, *Halsbury's Laws of Canada* (Toronto: LexisNexis Canada, 2006) print (supplemented publication) and online: <http://www.lexisnexis.com/ca/legal> (subscription required) [HLC].

2. Locate the legal topic in the main topic volumes; narrow the search to specific subtopics as required (print and online).

3. Update using the Cumulative Supplement if available (print version only).[3]

As with the CED, one must understand how to use both the print and online versions of HLC because one or the other version may not always be accessible. However, assuming that neither availability nor cost is a factor, once you have established proficiency in both online and print-based research methods, choose the preferred version to locate primary law.

TASK 7.7

Using HLC to Locate Primary Law: Print

■ Select the most recent softcover Guide and Consolidated Index of HLC. Using previously identified legal keywords, locate the Wills topic. Record relevant subtopic references (e.g. undue influence and suspicious circumstances), HWE-187, 188, 182.

■ Locate the Halsbury's Wills and Estates (HWE) volume and examine its organization. Find the Table of Cases and the Table of Statutes near the beginning of the volume. These tables identify the case law and legislation referenced in the volume. Locate and record the currency date (1 April 2012) found immediately before the Table of Cases.

■ Either the Table of Contents or the Index can be used to locate relevant information. Turn to the volume Index, and using the keyword "wills" note the cross-reference to "undue influence". Record and locate relevant paragraphs—HWE at paragraphs 187 and 188.

■ HLC and the CED use a similar paragraph referencing system. Turn to the relevant paragraphs. The organization of information is similar to that in the CED. Brief commentary, either of a general nature or specific to a province or territory, is followed by citation references to relevant case law and legislation.

■ If the cumulative supplement is available, locate the currency date, and note additional relevant information under the Wills and Estates topic.

---

3   In 2012, HLC was reissued, incorporating information previously published in the Cumulative Supplement in the main topic volumes.

TASK 7.8

Using HLC to Link to Primary Law: Online

- Sign in to the LexisNexis Quicklaw website. From the home page, select Halsbury's Laws of Canada. Choose Browse.

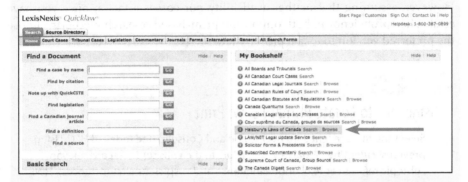

- Scan the alphabetized headings and select "Wills and Estates". Open the title, review the subtopics, and open "Contesting a Will". Note that the additional subtopics include "Undue Influence". Opening this link reveals an additional subtopic, "Burden of Proof", which leads to primary law.

- Note and record the alphanumeric code used by the publisher to organize the subject matter in the title. The relevant code for the subtopic of undue influence is considered under the broader topics of Wills is I.8(4). The CED used a similar style of alphanumeric code. Always record the code as part of a comprehensive search process.

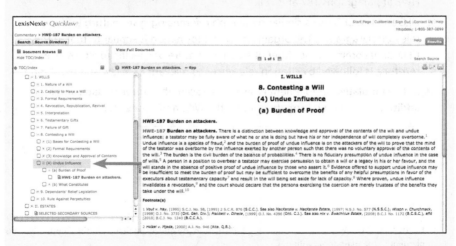

B. The Canadian Abridgment

The Canadian Abridgment[4] ("Abridgment") is a robust multi-function research resource available both in print and online. It is not an encyclopedia because it does not provide general summaries of research topics as do both the CED and HLC. However, it includes search features to locate primary law by:

- topic/case digest
- case name/citation/judicial consideration
- legislation name/citation/legislative consideration
- legal keyword

Furthermore, the Abridgment includes research tools to aid with primary law analysis, such as a periodical index that references legal commentary as well as specific case and legislative comments. It also includes a primary law note-up feature to determine the historical judicial treatment of both cases and legislation. The publisher of the Abridgment has compiled a concise reference tool, available in print and online, that summarizes its key features and provides guidelines for its use.[5]

Competent researchers must understand how to use both the print and online versions of the Abridgment because one or the other version may not always be accessible. However, assuming that neither availability nor cost is a factor, once you have established proficiency in both online and print-based research methods, you may choose the preferred version to locate primary law.

1. Finding Case Law by Topic Digest: Print

A successful topic search will reveal digests that lead to relevant judicial decisions. Digests are brief summaries, ranging from one to several paragraphs, that explain the court's decision of the legal issues. After reviewing the digests, organize the results of your research and select those decisions likely to be most relevant for further study.

A topic search to locate case digests requires the sequential review of:

- Key and Research Guide ("Guide") and/or the General Index ("Index")
- main volumes containing case digests
- annual and monthly case digest update supplements/Canadian Current Law

While the Guide and the Index are loose-leaf research tools, the main volumes containing the Digests are printed in hardcover volumes and softcover supplements.

---

4   *The Canadian Abridgment*, 3d ed (Toronto: Thomson Carswell) print (supplemental publication) and online: <http://www.westlawcanada.com>. Users of the Abridgment can find out proposed developments to the Abridgment along with research tips at <http://www.carswell.com/products/the-canadian-abridgment/>.

5   *A Short Guide to the Canadian Abridgment*, online: <http://www.carswell.com/DynamicData/AttachedDocs/TheCanadianAbridgment/CdnAbridg_ShortGuideDc488.pdf> [*Short Guide*].

TASK 7.9

Using Case Law Digests to Locate Judicial Decisions: Print

■ You can use either the General Index or the Key and Research Guide to locate relevant case digests; however, the search method used for each differs.

■ Begin with the Guide and Index. In the Guide, turn to the tab marked Key and find the "Subject Titles Table". If, as in this case, the keyword selected does not lead to the correct subject title (Wills), use the Index. Note that "will" is cross-referenced to the phrase "Estates & Trusts". Another strategy is to look for the word "wills" in the General Index, which is organized alphabetically.

■ In the General Index volume locate "Wills". Scan the subtopics; under the "Undue Influence" subtopic, record the reference to "Estates Issues, see Estates". Under "Estates", note the subheadings of "Will Challenges" and "Undue Influence".

■ Although using the General Index is efficient, you might find the Research Guide more effective because you are less likely to overlook relevant information.

■ In the Research Guide locate the "Estates and Trusts" title in the Contents Key. Note that you must examine volumes 32 through 35 to completely review this topic. Locate the subtopic "Undue Influence". Record the alphanumeric classification number. This number is an essential finding tool to locate relevant digests. On the basis of the facts, classification number I.7.b.iii.B may be of particular interest because this topic concerns undue influence by a family member. Record all the noteworthy classification numbers before beginning the case digest search. Note that many topics, including those under number I.7, are located in volume 33.

■ Before finding the relevant digests, review the Case Law Update volume, which will likely be shelved adjacent to the General Index and Guide. Use this search tool once you have identified the relevant classification numbers. In the Update volume under "Estates", look for classification number I.7.b.iii.B. Record any information you find, which can be used to locate digests in the supplements to the main volume.

■ The digests are located in the main volumes. Select the relevant hardcover volume (EST 33) and the softcover blue supplement to volume 33. Find the case digests that correspond to classification number I.7.b.iii.B, first in the hardcover volume and then in the supplement. Note and record the currency date on the cover of each volume.

■ Review the relevant digests concerning "Estates—Undue Influence" by looking at the Index volume or by scanning the volume to locate the relevant classification code.

- Note that the digests provide more detailed information about each case than do the CED and HLC. By scanning each digest, you can identify judicial decisions that warrant further examination. For example, by examining the citation reference, you can locate cases decided by a court of appeal and the Supreme Court of Canada. Depending on the cases you find, you might choose to examine cases decided by a court in the same jurisdiction, or you might select cases from various jurisdictions with similar facts.

- To update beyond the date covered by the supplement, locate the relevant softcover monthly supplements titled Canadian Current Law—Case Digests. You can examine each monthly supplement using both the same "Estates" topic and the same classification number (I.7.b.iii.B).

- However, you can shorten the search of the monthly supplements by recalling whether any relevant references were found in the Case Law Update and using that information to focus the search on the relevant monthly supplements.

- Because of the number of steps required in the case digest search, ensure that you record or log the steps as you complete them. This ensures efficiency and comprehensiveness in the event that your work is interrupted prior to completion.

2. Finding Case Law by Topic Digest: Online

TASK 7.10

Using the Abridgment to Link to Judicial Decisions: Online

- On the Westlaw Canada website under the LawSource tab, locate the "Browse Table of Contents" heading, link to the "Abridgment", scan the list of titles, and open "Estates and trusts". This link connects directly to the digests.

- The classification number (I.7.b.iii.B) is the same whether searching for digests in print or online.

- Select "+" and select "I. Estates", then "7. Will Challenges", then "b. Undue Influence", then "iii. Source of Influence", then "B. Family Member". Review the references found and link to the selected sources to review the primary law.

- Because judicial decisions are frequently added to the online databases, no additional steps are needed to update the law. However, be sure to always note the currency date of the research when using either the online or print version of the Abridgment, or any other research tool.

- As with the online versions of the CED and HLC, an additional benefit with online Abridgment searching is the increased functionality obtained through the provision of direct links to primary law. A further benefit is a cross-referencing feature that connects the CED and the Abridgment when conducting a search using either product.

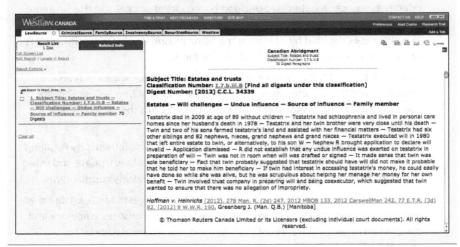

C. Canada Digest: Online

Quicklaw's *Canada Digest* (CD) service is comparable to the online version of the Abridgment. Unlike the Abridgment, however, there is no companion print service. The collection is extensive, with material dating from the 1800s, and includes federal and provincial judicial decisions, as well as decisions from some administrative boards and tribunals.

The CD uses a similar classification system to the Abridgment and can be browsed in a similar manner.

TASK 7.11

Using the Canada Digest to Conduct a
Case Digest Topic Search: Online

- Although LexisNexis Quicklaw provides a search template to locate primary law, when a broadly based topic search is required, browsing the *Canada Digest* is a sound option. From the home page, go to Search and locate "The Canada Digest". Select Browse.

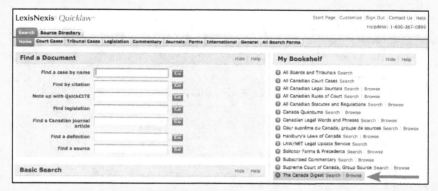

- Scan the titles and select the most appropriate topic according to previously identified keywords—in this case, "Canada Wills, Estates & Trusts Law Digest".

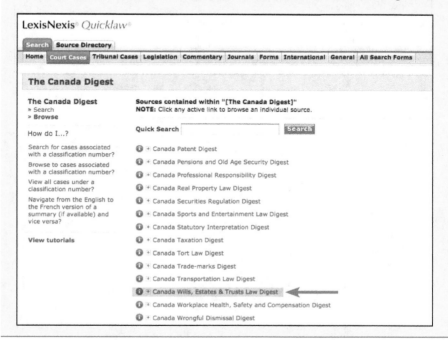

TASK 7.12

Using the Canada Digest to Locate Judicial Decisions: Online

From the LexisNexis Quicklaw home page, locate "The Canada Digest". Select
Browse. Locate and open the title "Canada Wills, Estates & Trusts Law Digest".
Browse the relevant subtopics. Record the classification number for "Undue
influence"—WIL520. Note the currency date by selecting the information icon.

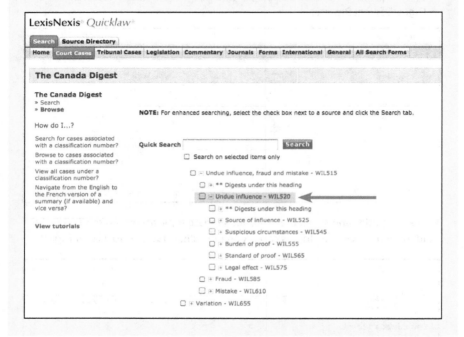

From the subtopic "Undue influence" review the case digests, select those that appear relevant, and link to the cases for a complete review.

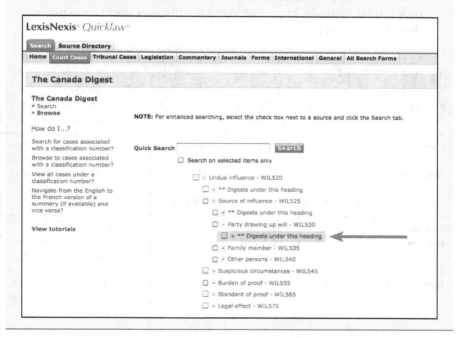

D. Comparative Advantages of Online and Print Topic Research

- It may be advisable for the novice researcher to start with a print text search because print indexes can be scanned more quickly than online indexes. However, online searching allows in-text word and phrase finding, while print searching requires a lengthier canvassing of indexes. Therefore, once you have established proficiency, you may prefer online searching for its convenience.

- Online searching frequently provides direct links to primary law. This saves the step of identifying primary law in another source.

- The online versions of the CED, HLC, and the Abridgment are updated more frequently than the print versions and do not require the researcher to scan supplements in order to update.

- Although law students are provided with free passwords to commercial online services while at school, they lose this benefit once they are in practice. The research cost must therefore be passed on to the client or subsumed by the lawyer. The cost of commercial online secondary sources may restrict its use once the lawyer enters practice, making the print version the only format available. Many university law libraries continue to maintain these products in print format.

	CED and Halsbury's		Abridgment— Case Digests		Canada Digest
	Print	Online	Print	Online	Online
Cost	Free (library)	Subscription	Free (library)	Subscription	Subscription
Updating	Update using supplements	Updated	Update using supplements	Updated	Updated
Search Method	Browse	Browse/ keyword search	Browse	Browse/ keyword search	Browse/ keyword search
Information	Topic overview Source citations	Same as print, links to sources	Case digests	Case digests, links to cases	Case digests, links to cases

FIGURE 7.3 Topic Search: Comparison of Print and Online Options

IV. Locating Primary Law by Name or Legal Citation

Understanding how to locate primary law using official sources is an essential competency. (Follow the steps described in Chapters 3, 4, and 5 to find official sources of legislation; follow the steps described in Chapter 6 to find judicial decisions.) However, you can use secondary sources to locate primary law if you know even part of the case or statute name.

TASK 7.13

Structuring a Search Using Primary Law Keywords or Citations

Returning to the issue of the validity of Conrad Cash's will, assume that you have not yet conducted a topic search. Instead, you have been requested to research the following:

■ Find *Vout*, a judicial decision about a will's validity. The jurisdiction, court level, and name of the other party are unknown. Note up *Vout*, determining both its history and its judicial treatment.

■ Locate Ontario legislation about succession, which includes information about wills.

Because research costs are usually a factor, consider lower-cost options before those that require a paid subscription.

A. CanLII: Online

CanLII[6] is a relatively recent addition to the domain of legal research resources. It began in 2000 under the auspices of the Federation of Law Societies of Canada, and provides free access to domestic primary law as well as links to foreign jurisdictions.

This resource is a sound option if a general keyword rather than a topic search is required. However, the prudent researcher should continue to undertake searches of commercial providers of legal information, particularly when searching for historical judicial decisions and secondary source commentary.

---

6   Canadian Legal Information Institute (CanLII), online: <http://www.canlii.org>.

TASK 7.14

CanLII: Locating Judicial Decisions by Keyword Search

On the CanLII home page, in the Search all CanLII Databases form, enter "Vout" in the "statute name / case name / citation / docket number" field. (Note that the search is case-insensitive.) Search. Two decisions in the case are found, from the Court of Appeal and the Supreme Court of Canada.

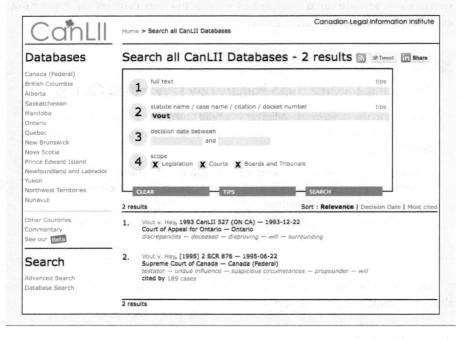

TASK 7.15

CanLII: Locating Legislation by Keyword Search

■ From the CanLII home page, go to Ontario to narrow the search by jurisdiction. Under the heading Legislation choose "Statutes and Regulations". In the search form, enter the keyword "succession" in the "title / citation" field, and then select the version and scope. Search. The *Succession Law Reform Act* is the first result.

■ CanLII's Statutes and Regulations of Ontario search page includes a link to the Ontario e-Laws website. However, CanLII provides added value through links to cases that have judicially considered the statute, which is not available through the government website. Judicial treatment of primary law is an essential aspect of legal research that will be discussed later in this chapter.

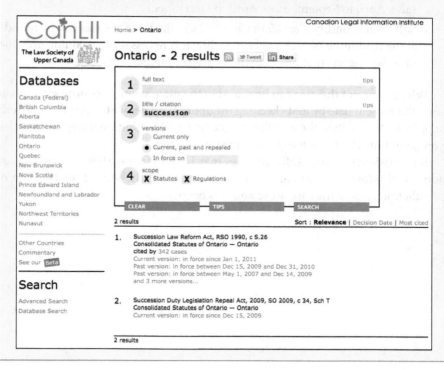

B. The Canadian Abridgment: Consolidated Table of Cases—Print

The Canadian Abridgment: Consolidated Table of Cases provides citation information for every level of court. However, as with any print service that frequently adds new information, updating is required. There may be as many as four different multiset series of volumes to review to complete a table of cases search, including:

- Set of 22 hardcover volumes, current to December 2011.
- Set of 22 softcover supplements, which post-date the hardcover volumes.
- Softcover volumes, quarterly supplements, which post-date the softcover volumes; these will not always be available, depending on the date of the search; however, if they are on the shelf, they will be dated from April to June, April to September, or April to December.
- Softcover monthly, *Canadian Current Law*; the table of cases can be found at the beginning of each paper monthly; it is necessary to examine only the monthly digests that postdate the quarterly supplements.

Whether or not the case can be found in the main volume, continue to update until the present date by first checking the annual supplements, then the quarterly supplements, and then the monthly supplements. This additional step ensures that you do not overlook a subsequent court proceeding.[7]

It is possible that two different cases may have the same style of cause, so use additional information to narrow the search, such as the year of the decision or jurisdiction (where the case arose and was heard).

---

7   For additional information regarding the sequence of volumes to consult, review the *Short Guide*, *supra* note 5.

TASK 7.16

Canadian Abridgment: Consolidated Table of Cases— Locating Judicial Decisions in Print

- Locate the *Consolidated Table of Cases* to find *Vout*. Information in the volumes is alphabetized. If the date of decision is unknown, select the main volume and search under the case name. Only one case has listed Vout as a party.

- Essential information provided by the citation includes the date the case was reported (1995), the jurisdiction, and the court level (Supreme Court of Canada). Locate the case using the citation information.

- Because the citation indicates that the case was decided by the Supreme Court of Canada, further review of the supplements is unlikely to provide additional information, but make a habit of checking the supplements to ensure that no additional information can be found. For the *Vout* decision, a further review of annual, quarterly, and monthly supplements yields no new information.

- Note the series of numbers and letters in bold. These can be used to locate the digest that presents a summary of the case.

- A case may contain judicial consideration of multiple legal issues. Because a separate digest is created for each legal issue discussed within the same case, the case may be digested under more than one legal topic. Therefore, there may be multiple digests, with different alphanumeric reference codes for each, as explained in Task 7.9.

C. Westlaw Canada and LexisNexis Quicklaw: Keyword Searching Online

When searching a topic, a general keyword search is not recommended because too many hits are provided, many of which will be irrelevant. However, when the keywords can be narrowed sufficiently, a keyword search for primary law can be undertaken using both Westlaw Canada and LexisNexis Quicklaw.

On the Westlaw home page, use the Custom Search Templates to search by case or legislation name, by words or phrases, or by legal commentary keyword found in law reports. On the Quicklaw home page, enter keywords in the Find a Document template or the Conduct a Basic Search template (found near the bottom of the page).

TASK 7.17

Westlaw: Locating Judicial Decisions Using a Keyword Search—Online

- A general search using the keyword phrase "undue influence" generates 10,000 documents.

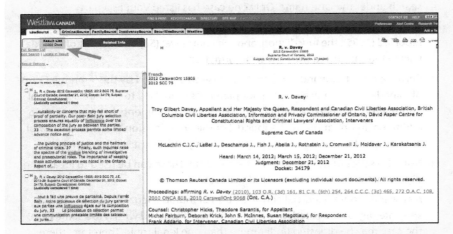

- A narrower search using the keyword phrases "undue influence" AND "contested will" generates 66 documents, with *Vout v Hay* being the first case.

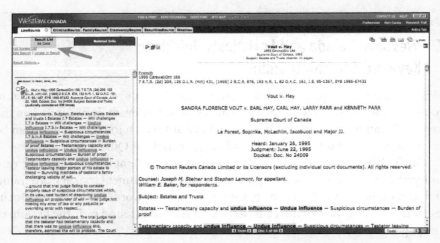

V. Noting Up Primary Law: Judicial Decisions—Print and Online

The previous discussion focused on using secondary sources of law to find primary law. However, before relying on a case as part of the analysis of a legal issue, the lawyer must first determine whether the case is authoritative, sometimes referred to as "good law". For example, a case decided in 1984 may be the leading case on a specific issue, having been referred to as authority by subsequent judges considering the same issue; on the other hand, it may have been overturned or further interpreted by a higher court, and will therefore no longer be authoritative.

Moreover, although the case may not have been appealed, and thus have no subsequent history, the legal issue may have been considered in one or more later cases. Decisions made by judges about the precedential value of a case can add or detract from the case's authority and weight. For example, judges may either endorse the reasoning of a prior case as a correct interpretation of the law, or decide that a different interpretation should be adopted. Furthermore, the case may be distinguished by a subsequent court as not applying closely enough to the underlying facts of the case. Therefore, determining the case history[8] and the subseqeunt judicial treatment of a case, also called "noting up", is an essential component of competent legal research.

This information can be found using both print and online sources.

A. The Canadian Abridgment: Canadian Case Citations—Print

The Abridgment provides both the case history and judicial treatment of decided case law. As with the Consolidated Table of Cases series, a search involves examining both hardcover texts and softcover supplements to ensure that the case is noted up to the most current date available.[9] The discussion that follows illustrates the noting-up process using the wills hypothetical and the *Vout* case.

---

8   See Chapter 6, sections IV.C and IV.D for an introduction to noting up case law.

9   *Short Guide, supra* note 5.

TASK 7.18

Noting Up Judicial Decisions Using Canadian Abridgment: Canadian Case Citations—Print

- Locate *The Canadian Abridgment: Canadian Case Citations* hardcover volumes. Cases are arranged in alphabetical order within the volume set. Locate the case name. *Vout* is found in volume R31. Record the volume's currency date— December 2006.

- Update to the softcover supplements—annual, quarterly, and monthly, if available. Record the currency dates to ensure that no gap in time occurs. The case citation information provides the necessary information to locate the case in print or online.

- Examine the information listed after the case, where available. The references identify the cases that have judicially considered the case, at each court level. The adjacent symbols indicate the judicial treatment given to the case. A symbol legend is provided at the bottom of each page for reference.

- To appreciate the importance of noting up and the value of this research tool, it is necessary to locate and brief the target case and consider its importance.

Vout v Hay: Case Brief

An 81-year-old man who was murdered left a major portion of his estate to a friend. Surviving family members challenged the will's validity. The trial judge admitted the will to probate because there was insufficient proof that the testator lacked mental capacity to create the will. The Court of Appeal set aside the decision and ordered a new trial on the grounds that the trial judge failed to properly consider the issue of suspicious circumstances.

The Supreme Court of Canada determined that suspicious circumstances may be raised by: (1) circumstances surrounding the preparation of the will; (2) circumstances tending to call into question the capacity of the testator; or (3) circumstances tending to show that the free will of the testator was overborne by acts of coercion or fraud.

In this case, the Supreme Court restored the decision at trial and held that the trial judge did not make any error of law or any palpable or overriding error with respect to facts.

...

- By using *Canadian Case Citations*, the researcher can discover the case history of *Vout*, which reached the Supreme Court of Canada, and locate cases that considered the legal test applied by the SCC in *Vout* when considering the issue of suspicious circumstances in the creation of a will.

B. Noting Up Cases: Westlaw Canada, LexisNexis Quicklaw, and CanLII—Online

Online noting-up functions are provided by both the commercial legal information services Westlaw Canada and LexisNexis Quicklaw and the free service CanLII. Because these services are updated frequently, there are no supplements to consult, and direct links to cases ensure more efficient searching. The additional cost of using commercial services must be considered when deciding which service to use.

TASK 7.19

Westlaw: Noting Up Cases Using KeyCite

Westlaw's noting-up feature is called KeyCite. Figure 7.4 explains Westlaw's noting-up symbols. Where available, the case history and judicial treatment are provided. Once you have located the case you wish to note up, go to the Related Info tab and select "Citing References".

Selecting the "Full History" link reveals the case history. Selecting the "Direct History (Graphical View)" link provides a schematic representation of the case history. By selecting both "Direct History (Graphical View)" and "Citing References", both case history and judicial treatment of the case can be determined.

While commercial sources of information such as Westlaw and Quicklaw, and free sources of information such as CanLII, provide helpful information to understand the disposition of the case at each level of court (i.e. the case history), you should ensure accuracy of this information by consulting the case itself. Sometimes, as in cases decided by the Supreme Court of Canada, the case history will be summarized in a paragraph prior to the reasons given by the court for its decision. Other courts hearing appeals may embed this information within the judicial reasoning itself.

TASK 7.20

Quicklaw: Noting Up Cases Using QuickCITE

Quicklaw's noting-up feature, called QuickCITE, can be accessed by clicking "Note up with QuickCITE" at the top left of each case. (Figure 7.4 explains Quicklaw's noting-up symbols.)

Where available, the case history and judicial treatment are provided.

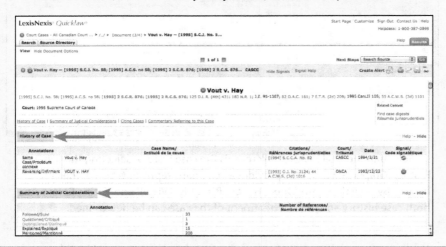

TASK 7.21

CanLII: Finding Judicial Treatment

CanLII's noting-up feature can be accessed at the beginning of each case.
Choose "Search for decisions citing this decision".

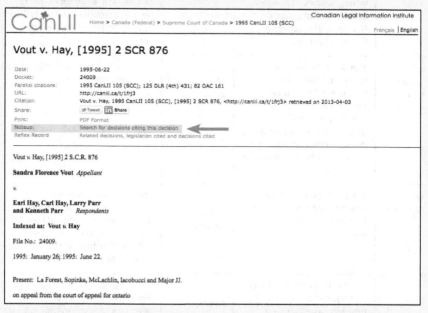

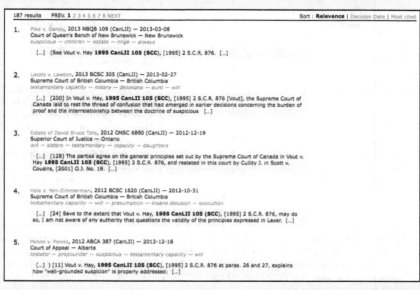

FIGURE 7.4 Comparison of Quicklaw and Westlaw Noting-Up Symbols

Westlaw	Meaning	Quicklaw	Meaning
⚑ Red flag	The case may not be good law, indicating that the decision has been reversed, or has not been followed within the same jurisdiction or by the Supreme Court of Canada.	⊗ Negative treatment	The case has negative history (judicial review allowed, reconsideration allowed, reversed, quashed, or varied by a higher court) or negative treatments (not followed or questioned by a subsequent court).
⚑ Yellow flag	The decision has some negative history or treatment, but has not been reversed or overruled. A yellow flag is also displayed if a treatment has been recently added, and has not yet been editorially analyzed.	⚠ Cautionary treatment	The case has been distinguished by a subsequent court.
H Blue H	The decision has some direct history but it is not known to be negative history.	⊕ Positive treatment	The case has positive history (affirmed, judicial review denied, or leave to appeal refused by a higher court) or positive treatments (followed or followed in a minority opinion of a subsequent court).
C Green C	The decision has no direct history, but there are treating cases or other citing references to the decision.	⬤ Neutral history or treatment	The case has neutral treatments (mentioned, explained, cited, or cited in a dissenting opinion) or the case has history (abandoned, abated, leave to appeal granted, reconsideration denied, related proceeding, same case, or supplementary reasons by a subsequent court), but the citing court does not comment on the case. This symbol is also attached to cases that have been added to Quicklaw within the past 3 business days, but have not yet been assigned a QuickCITE treatment.
		C Citator information	The case has no known history or treatments.

* Descriptors for these noting-up symbols taken from websites for Westlaw at <http://canada .westlaw.com/keycite/default.wl?rs=WLCA13.04&vr=2.0&rp=%2fkeycite%2fdefault.wl&sv =Split&fn=_top&mt=LawPro> and Quicklaw at <http://www.lexisnexis.com/help/global/ globalhelp_frameset.asp?locale=en_CA&lbu=CA&adaptation=legal&sPage=quickfindtips &fromHelp=trueQuicklaw>.

VI. Noting Up Primary Law: Legislation— Print and Online

Although noting up typically considers the judicial treatment and history of a case, there is an essential aspect of noting up that involves locating judicial decisions that consider legislation. When noting up legislation, the court's treatment of the legislation in a specific case can be determined.

A researcher may also be required to find cases that have judicially considered all versions of the legislation, even when the legislation has been subsequently repealed or amended.

These types of research tasks, which focus on discrete aspects of legislation, can be completed both in print and online, using both commercially available research products and those that are of no cost to the user.

A. The Canadian Abridgment: Canadian Statute Citations—Print

The Canadian Abridgment: Canadian Statute Citations is a comprehensive tool for locating cases that have judicially considered statutes, regulations, and rules.

TASK 7.22

Canadian Abridgment: Noting Up Legislation Using Canadian Statute Citations—Print

Locate the *Succession Law Reform Act*, RSO 1990, c S.26. Previous searches have indicated that this statute is relevant to the creation and interpretation of wills.

- Identify the title of the legislation (statute or regulation) to be examined for its judicial treatment. Determine the relevant sections to be considered. Examine its citation and determine the jurisdiction—federal or provincial.

- Locate *The Canadian Abridgment: Canadian Statute Citations*. Information is organized by jurisdiction. Judicial consideration of statutes is organized separately from regulations. Legislation within each jurisdiction is organized alphabetically.

- The system used is similar to other Abridgment products, with searches including hardcover volumes, updating to softcover supplements. If searching for legislation that has been in existence for some time, such as a revised statute, begin the search in the hardcover volume. Locate the statute by name and citation and find the specific sections to be considered.

- If they exist, previous versions of statutes are provided, facilitating searches of the judicial treatment of earlier versions of the statute.

- The judicial consideration of the statute is considered section by section, including sections that have been subsequently amended. Record the case citation information that has judicially considered the identified statute section(s).

- Note the currency date of the volume. Update with the annual and quarterly supplements. Record the case names found. Locate the case names using the accompanying citation information.

- The adjacent symbols indicate the judicial treatment of the legislation. A symbol legend is provided at the bottom of each page for reference, and is also reproduced in the *Short Guide*.

- If the statute being searched is more recent, it may be possible to begin the search with the supplement. Rely on the date of the citation to determine the period in time to begin the search.

- To note up regulations and rules, locate the relevant volumes and structure the search in a similar way.

B. Statute Citators: Print

The *Canada Statute Citator*, as well as the *Ontario Statute Citator* and the *British Columbia Statute Citator*,[10] reference important judicial decisions concerning current versions of legislation.

TASK 7.23

Canada Statute Citator and Ontario Statute Citator

- Locate the *Canada Statute Citator*. Federal statutes are organized alphabetically in a series of loose-leaf volumes.

- The short title, all amendments, and coming into force dates since the last statute revision (1985) are provided. Record the currency date, found at the bottom of each page. In addition, judicial decisions of note, with a brief explanation of relevance, are provided.

- Update the main entry by using the Weekly Bulletin Service (green pages) at the beginning of volume 1 of the Citator. Examine the green pages to determine whether there are bills in progress or consequential amendments.

- Although this service provides a brief summary of important aspects of a statute, it is not intended to be a comprehensive research tool. Thus, it does not include information about legislation prior to the last revision.

- The *Ontario Statute Citator* is available for Ontario research (1990 and on). It is organized in a similar manner to that of the *Canada Statute Citator* (with updates to pink, not green, pages).

For the *Succession Law Reform Act*, a Revised Statute of Ontario, no new information was located.

C. Legislation: Westlaw Canada, LexisNexis Quicklaw, and CanLII—Noting Up Online

Online noting-up functions are provided by both commercial legal information services such as Westlaw Canada and LexisNexis Quicklaw and the free service CanLII.

---

10 Loose-leaf (Aurora, ON: Canada Law Book, 2009). The citators consider legislation since the last revision for each jurisdiction.

TASK 7.24

Noting Up Statutes: Westlaw Canada—Online

The "Statutes Judicially Considered" feature has been integrated into the online version of the legislation found on Westlaw Canada.

■ On Westlaw Canada, under the LawSource tab, choose Legislation. Locate the jurisdiction and select the relevant statute from the alphabetical list. In the left menu go to the Related Info tab and choose "Citing References". Note the cases that have considered the statute. Select and link to particular cases.

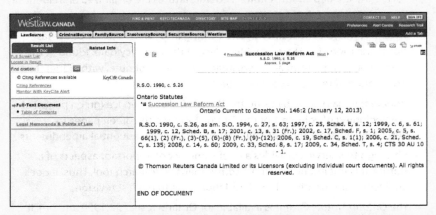

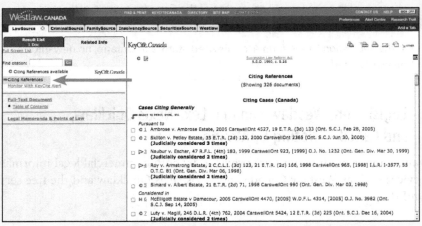

TASK 7.25

Noting Up Legislation: Westlaw Canada and LexisNexis Quicklaw—Online

Westlaw Canada provides "Regulations Judicially Considered" and "Rules Judicially Considered" features along with "Statutes Judicially Considered".

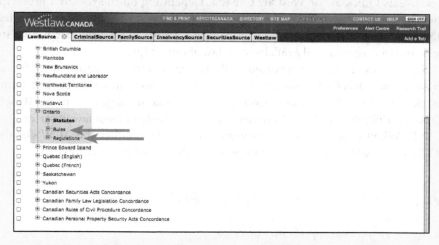

- The "Rules Judicially Considered" feature is useful when interpreting the rules of court on procedural matters. The steps provided in Task 7.24 can also be used on Westlaw to locate judicial consideration of rules of court as well as regulations. This service provides a direct link to case law that relates to specific rule interpretation for both federal and provincial law, as well as some international law.

LexisNexis Quicklaw uses a similar feature called "QuickCITE", which can be accessed at the top left of any individual statute section.

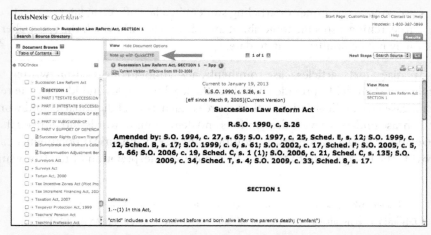

VII. Using Secondary Sources to Locate Unreported Judicial Decisions

Unreported decisions are those not published in a reporter series. However, many unreported decisions can be located using commercial online services such as LexisNexis Quicklaw or Westlaw Canada. Depending on the research problem, locating unreported decisions may be necessary—e.g. if you can find no reported decisions on point, or if you are completing a scholarly research paper and are required to investigate all available case law about a topic.

Summaries of older, unreported civil cases from across Canada can be found in *All-Canada Weekly Summaries* (ACWS).[11] Cases are organized by subject. Summaries of criminal judgments from across Canada are digested in the *Weekly Criminal Bulletin* (WCB).[12] Print versions are available in most law libraries.

NB: When providing a case citation, do not cite to either the ACWS or the WCB, because these sources do not provide full texts of the decisions.

VIII. Legal Commentary, Periodicals, Treatises, and Texts

To this point, the secondary sources discussed have been those that are used to find primary law. However, secondary sources are useful for analyzing both judicial decisions and legislation when:

- completing assigned course work in an academic setting,
- working as a research assistant for a professor engaged in legal scholarship, or
- working as a summer or articling student in a law office, or, later in practice, researching a specific topic about an area of law with which the researcher may not be familiar or up to date.

Treatises, texts, articles, case comments, and annotated legislation, written by experts in their fields, provide analysis of the legal principles and identify the relevant case law and legislation. Other sources, such as legal dictionaries and word and phrase finders, provide descriptions and definitions of words and phrases that have specific legal meanings. In addition, the use of historical documents can provide the background to the development and interpretation of the law, while

---

11 *All-Canada Weekly Summaries*, Third Series (Toronto: Canada Law Book, 2013).

12 Edward L Greenspan, ed, *Weekly Criminal Bulletin* (Toronto: Canada Law Book, 2013).

documents that assess current policy initiatives or position papers can help to interpret the law. An additional advantage is that many of these secondary sources provide citation references to legislation and case law.

Secondary source research can be undertaken through searches of:

- legal topics and terms
- authors
- primary law—judicial decisions and legislation

These resources are still often available only in print, but more and more are also available online. When conducting online research, ensure that the sources selected are authoritative and reliable.

A. Finding Commentary: Print

- Legal keywords can be used to find secondary sources as well as primary sources of law. Organize keywords, either alphabetically or in an order that will generate the greatest number of relevant articles. Maintain a consistent search pattern and record the results.
- Use periodical indexes to locate secondary sources. Periodical indexes contain citations, which enable you to locate articles, case and legislative comments, monographs, and book reviews. They differ only in the scope or jurisdiction of the journals indexed.
- Law journal articles have traditionally been published by law schools and other organizations in journal format. Many law libraries provide access to historical law journals in print. To find a law journal article requires a citation that includes the name of the author, the name of the article, and the journal title and year of publication.
- Most print indexes include a subject index (the largest index), an author index, a table of cases (with citation references), and a table of statutes.
- The search topic will dictate the starting place. If the topic is current, you may choose to start with the most recent paper part and work backward in time. If the topic has historical significance, begin at the time the topic was current and work forward in time.

Comprehensive print periodical indexes include:

- *The Canadian Abridgment: Index to Canadian Legal Literature* (ICLL)— indexes Canadian periodicals (Toronto: Carswell, 2011)
- *Current Law Index*—indexes international periodicals, including some Canadian sources (Los Altos, CA: Information Access Corporation, 1980) (supplemental publication)

Locating Commentary, Case, and Legislative Comments: Using the Canadian Abridgment—ICLL: Print

- Returning to the problem of the validity of Conrad Cash's will, select the search terms used for the primary law search, including "wills" and "undue influence". Because this topic concerns a testator who died in Ontario, begin the search with Canadian sources.

- Locate the ICLL, 1985–2000. The ICLL includes a 12-volume set of hardcover volumes, and softcover annual and monthly supplements. Volumes 1–7 are subject indexes, volumes 8–10 are author indexes, volume 11 provides tables of cases and statutes, and volume 12 contains book reviews.

- Determine whether to undertake a search by subject, author, or case or statute name. For this problem, conduct a search by topic/subject. The information is organized alphabetically by subject matter within each volume. Select the hardcover volume(s) containing information about undue influence and wills. Update with the annual and monthly supplements, noting the currency date for each and leaving no gap in time.

- Review the sources found and use the citation references to locate relevant material. Interlibrary loans can be arranged if required.

- If you are unsure of the full title of the journal to be searched, the periodical index lists the full name of the periodical linked to its acronym. The *Canadian Guide to Uniform Legal Citation*[13] provides a similar table in Appendix D.

Case and legislative comments provide analyses of cases or statutes. To find a case comment, determine the name of the case and its decision date.

- Select volume 11 and examine the alphabetized list of cases to determine whether a case comment exists. Update with the annual and monthly supplements.

- Case comments identify the court level in the case citation provided immediately after the case name. A case comment that referenced the Court of Appeal would discuss that court's decision; a case comment that referenced the Supreme Court of Canada would discuss that court's decision.

- The process for finding case comments and legislative comments is similar. Use the same books and the same processes used to find a case comment.

- In volume 11 of the ICLL, turn to the Table of Statutes. Federal legislation is organized alphabetically using the name of the statute. Provincial legislation is organized alphabetically by province. Non-Canadian legislation may also be the subject of legislative comment and is organized by country, followed by the title of the relevant legislation.

---

13   7th ed (Toronto: Carswell, 2010) [McGill Guide].

B. Finding Commentary: Online

Many online sources now provide online access to law journals; however, not all law journals are available online. Westlaw Canada and LexisNexis Quicklaw provide access to relatively recent law journal content. They both provide extensive databases of commentary on Canadian law, as well as on law from other countries. Sources found in online indexes will link to the full text of the article if available. HeinOnline is the only online source that currently provides comprehensive historical law journal content for Canada and the United States. HeinOnline scans the print version of journal articles and thus provides page numbers for legal citation purposes.

TASK 7.27

Using LexisNexis Quicklaw to Find Journal Articles and Case Commentary: Online

Use the words "wills" and "undue influence" as target search terms.

- On LexisNexis Quicklaw, choose "Source Directory" to see all available content. Choose the jurisdiction from the drop-down menus. Choose "Legal Journals".

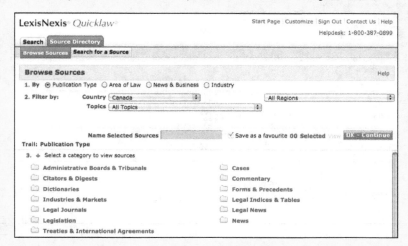

- A list of hundreds of journals and group sources is provided. For this question, choose the source "All Canadian Legal Journals". A search interface is provided that allows searching by keyword, author name, article title, year, and more.
- For a list of all fields used in this database, choose "Show Document Segments". For a list of search operators that can be used in preparing a search algorithm, click "View Connectors".
- To search for documents in which both the phrase "undue influence" and the word "wills" appears, use this search:
  - wills & "undue influence"

TASK 7.28

Using Westlaw to Find Journal Articles and Case Commentary: Online

On Westlaw Canada, search the ICLL database.

■ In the "Any Text" field, enter the following:
– wills and "undue influence"

■ To constrain the search, select "The results must contain: Terms in same paragraph". Law reports and articles can be searched using a similar strategy. Note that a search of the ICLL yields only a *citation* to a journal article, unless the full text of the article is available on Westlaw. Record all aspects of the citation, and then check Quicklaw, HeinOnline, or the print journal in the library to view the article.

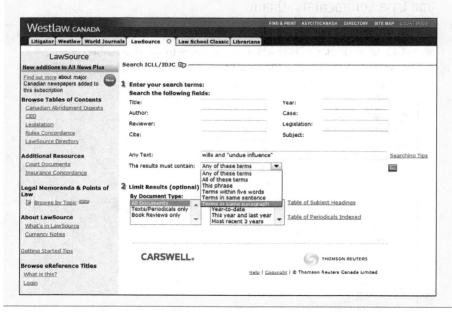

TASK 7.29

Using HeinOnline to Find Journal Articles

Many libraries subscribe to HeinOnline, which is a valuable resource for historical documents. HeinOnline's Law Journal Library, available in most large law libraries, provides full-text access to scanned content of law journals from Canada and the United States, with limited coverage of other jurisdictions. HeinOnline is the only online database that provides page numbers for law journals. Content is organized in alphabetical order by journal name for easy browsing; alternatively, the Search tab at the top left of the page provides a variety of searching options.

Browse View

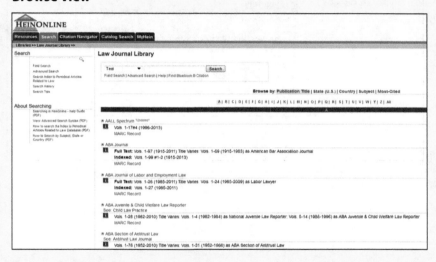

Field Search View

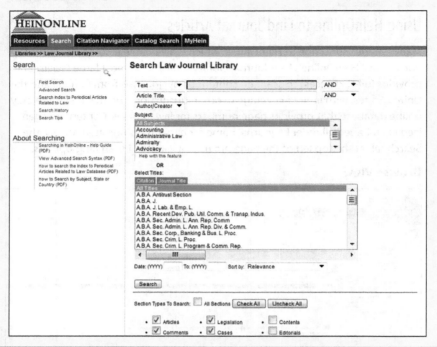

TASK 7.30

Using CanLII to Find Commentary

CanLII is not yet a rich source of commentary; however, it appears to be committed to improving this aspect of its legal source material.[14] Full-text searching is available as illustrated below.

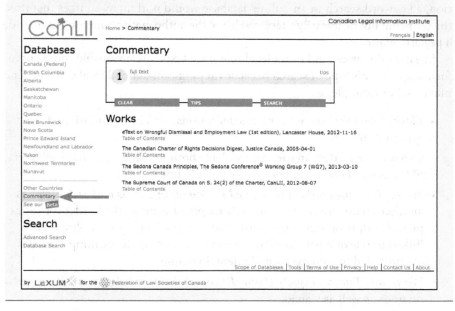

14   See *CanLII Strategic Priorities 2012-2014*, <http://www.canlii.org/en/info/CanLiiStratPlan _2012-14_EN.PDF> at 11.

C. Using Legal Dictionaries and Words and Phrases Judicially Considered

At times, researchers may be required to search, not by case or statute name or by legal topic, but by a legally defined term or phrase. For example, a topic search for the law that considers *parens patriae* jurisdiction would not yield results. In addition, a keyword search in an online database would find many sources that used the term, but not necessarily a targeted list of the authoritative sources that provide a precise definition.

Legal dictionaries (and other legal reference texts) are a valuable source of information for this type of search because they contain defined legal concepts and maxims. For example:

- *Black's Law Dictionary*[15] contains definitions from both English and American primary law.
- Canadian legal dictionaries are available both in print—e.g. *The Dictionary of Canadian Law*[16]—and online—e.g. Duhaime.[17]
- *Words & Phrases Judicially Defined in Canadian Courts and Tribunals*[18] is another volume in the *Canadian Abridgment* system. The hardcover series provides alphabetized legal words and phrases. The word or phrase is linked to relevant primary law source(s) explaining its meaning. Updates are provided in softcover supplemental volumes.
- *Words and Phrases Legally Defined*[19] contains information from other jurisdictions as well as Canada.
- *Canadian Legal Words and Phrases* is available on Quicklaw and provides direct links to cases.

---

15 *Black's Law Dictionary*, 9th ed. Available in print in most law libraries, and online via Westlaw.

16 Daphne Dukelow, *The Dictionary of Canadian Law*, 4th ed (Toronto: Thomson Carswell, 2011).

17 *Duhaime's Legal Dictionary*, online: <http://www.duhaime.org>.

18 Rae Blackburn and Cheryl Finch, eds, *Words & Phrases Judicially Defined in Canadian Courts and Tribunals* (Scarborough, ON: Carswell, 1993).

19 John B Saunders, ed, *Words and Phrases Legally Defined*, 4th ed (London: Butterworths, 2007).

D. Online Research

Become familiar with the sites listed below. Add to the list as you identify additional sources.

- Library and Archives Canada at <http://www.collectionscanada.gc.ca/index-e.html> is a rich source of historical information.
- Government agencies provide many of their policy documents online.
- Informit AGIS Plus Text and Gale Cengage Learning LegalTrac are two additional sources of law journal articles. Check with your law library to determine whether you have access to these websites.
- ProQuest Social Science Journals and Scholars Portal are two helpful resources for finding academic articles from various disciplines. These can be particularly useful when researching public policy. They are subscription-based; check with your law library to determine whether you have access.
- ProQuest Canadian Newsstand is another subscription-based resource that can be used to locate news articles from various newspapers. The databases are continuously updated to add both recent and historical articles.

Before researching online, pay particular attention to the source of the information to determine the validity and reliability of the information. Be prepared to verify the validity and reliability of any secondary source used.

E. Researching Primary Case Law and Secondary Source Law

You may find it helpful to create a comprehensive personalized resource for research planning, such as the one shown in Figure 7.5. This table can be modified to include call numbers to print sources and URLs to websites of frequently used sources.

FIGURE 7.5 Sample Comprehensive Personalized Resource for Research Planning

Publication—Encyclopedia	Call Number	Online (if applicable)
CED—Index		Westlaw Canada
CED—Research Guide		
Halsbury's Laws of Canada		LexisNexis Quicklaw
Other		
Publication—Finding Sources and Analyzing	**Call Number**	**Online (if applicable)**
Canadian Abridgment—Key and Research Guide		
Canadian Abridgment—Index		
Abridgment—Canadian Current Law—Case Digests		Westlaw Canada
Abridgment—Consolidated Table of Cases		
Abridgment—Canadian Case Citations		
Canadian Abridgment—Index to Canadian Legal Literature		Westlaw Canada
Current Law Index		
Treatises and monographs		
Annotated legislation		
Other		
Publication—Words and Phrases Defined	**Call Number**	**Online (if applicable)**
Canadian Abridgment—Words & Phrases Judicially Defined in Canadian Courts and Tribunals		Westlaw Canada
Canadian Legal Words and Phrases		LexisNexis Quicklaw

Introduction to International and Foreign Legal Research in a Canadian Context

8

CONTENTS

By the end of this chapter, you should be able to:

- Distinguish between public international, private international, and foreign law
- Locate foreign and international law
- Locate and determine the status of treaties
- Locate United Nations resolutions
- Use secondary sources to locate international law commentary

Research Tasks

The study of transnational law focuses on legal issues that transcend national borders. This chapter outlines research strategies to consider when presented with legal issues concerning foreign, private international, or public international law.

I. The Meaning of Foreign, Private International, and Public International Law

A. Foreign Law

Previous research chapters have focused on Canada's domestic legal system, which includes the law governing legal issues that arise and are resolved within Canada's borders. Most countries have similar domestic legal systems that establish both substantive and procedural legal rules governing their organizations, businesses, citizens, residents, and guests. Concepts of sovereignty and jurisdictional autonomy are foundational to a domestic legal system. This means that no foreign country's judiciary is obliged to decide a legal matter within its borders in the same manner as Canada would decide the matter; similarly, Canada's judiciary is not bound to apply the laws of a foreign jurisdiction to a domestic legal dispute.

However, not all legal disputes can be resolved by Canada's domestic legal system. Foreign domestic law becomes relevant in many situations, including:

- acquiring, disposing, or bequeathing real or personal property located in a foreign jurisdiction
- incorporating in, trading with, or conducting business in a foreign jurisdiction
- banking or investing in a foreign jurisdiction
- suing or enforcing a judgment against another's property located in a foreign jurisdiction
- resolving family issues such as custody of and access to minor children where one parent resides in a foreign jurisdiction

When researching a legal issue involving foreign law, the first step is to consider whether there is an international aspect to the situation. For example, there may be a treaty between the government of Canada and the foreign jurisdiction, which might govern some aspect of the dispute. We discuss this aspect of legal research below.

When researching foreign law, understanding the basic system of a foreign jurisdiction's legal rules is essential. From the view of practice, dispute resolution between parties with differing backgrounds requires a contextual understanding of the law of both jurisdictions, including the historical and cultural context in which the law was created and developed and is maintained. In addition, if the law of another country governs a Canadian client's matter the Canadian lawyer must consult with a lawyer licensed to practise in that jurisdiction, because lawyers licensed to practise solely in Canada cannot represent clients in a foreign jurisdiction without the permission of that jurisdiction.

Canadian courts can use the law of a foreign jurisdiction to interpret domestic law that is not yet settled. Although legislation and judicial decisions from foreign jurisdictions are not binding on Canadian courts, domestic law from Commonwealth countries such as the United Kingdom and Australia, and from common-law jurisdictions such as the United States, may be used to inform Canadian courts of the development of the law in countries with domestic legal systems that are similar to that of Canada.[1]

---

1   See e.g. *Purcell v Taylor* (1994), 120 DLR (4th) 161, 1994 CanLII 7514 (Ont Ct J (Gen Div)), where a Canadian court considered the law of several foreign jurisdictions as an aid to the statutory interpretation of the *Dog Owners' Liability Act*, RSO 1990, c D.16.

B. Private International Law: Conflict of Laws

Legal disputes may arise when one aspect of a legal relationship such as a contract is connected to Canada and another is connected to a foreign jurisdiction. Because both jurisdictions have equal status, a body of law termed "conflict of laws" has developed to resolve jurisdictional matters. This area of research considers issues such as:

- Which jurisdiction's court should resolve the dispute?
- Which jurisdiction's laws should apply?

C. Public International Law

Public international law is the law between and among nations. The primary sources of international law are treaties, which are similar to domestic statutes, and international judicial decisions, which may assist with treaty interpretation.

Lawyers may have to deal with public international law issues in the following situations:

- advocating a refugee matter in a Canadian court (Refugee Convention)
- enforcing a Canadian judgment against property held by another in a foreign jurisdiction (reciprocal enforcement of judgments treaties)
- arguing an international human rights violation
- representing a Canadian or foreign client before the Canadian International Trade Tribunal
- representing a client from another jurisdiction who is subject to an extradition order
- representing a corporate client in international banking, international investment, or international merger and acquisition matters

The *Statute of the International Court of Justice*[2] identifies the sources that apply in the adjudication of international legal disputes.

---

2 [1946] 3 Bevans 1179.

Article 38 of the Statute provides:

1. The Court, whose function is to decide in accordance with international law such disputes as are submitted to it, shall apply:
    a. international conventions (or treaties)
    b. international custom
    c. the general principles of law recognized by civilized nations
    d. judicial decisions and the teachings of the most highly qualified publicists

II. Researching Foreign Law

Increasingly, governments disseminate legal information through the Internet. However, online foreign law research may be impeded for the following reasons:

- Some governments lack the technological capability to publish information online.
- Legal resources are presented in the country's official language rather than in either of Canada's two official languages.
- Western search engines contain language barriers.

These problems are being addressed to some degree as librarians, organizations, and individuals worldwide commit to using technological resources to make legal resources available online.

When researching a legal issue with a foreign law aspect, consider the following sources and techniques.

A. Libraries of Foreign Jurisdictions

Law librarians employed in legislative and judicial libraries in many foreign countries have developed law guides, available online, that provide information about the jurisdiction's legal publishing system.[3] Use Google to find a law guide for the relevant jurisdiction.

---

3   Law and Technology Resources for Legal Professionals provides a number of legal research guides for other countries, online: LLRX.com <http://www.llrx.com/comparative_and_foreign_law.html>.

Finding Foreign Law Online

Although Google searches foreign websites, the site defaults to show results from Canada and the United States. To display results from other foreign websites:

- Go to Webopedia <http://www.webopedia.com/quick_ref/topleveldomains/countrycodeA-E.asp>, a country domain name directory, to find the domain extension for the jurisdiction being searched.

- Use Google's Advanced Search at <http://www.google.ca/advanced_search>. Enter the search terms in the appropriate box at the top of the page, and then enter the domain name in the site or domain box near the bottom of the page.

Find pages with...		To do this in the search box.
all these words:		Type the important words: `tri-colour rat terrier`
this exact word or phrase:		Put exact words in quotes: `"rat terrier"`
any of these words:		Type OR between all the words you want: `miniature OR standard`
none of these words:		Put a minus sign just before words that you don't want: `-rodent, -"Jack Russell"`
numbers ranging from:	to	Put two full stops between the numbers and add a unit of measurement: `10..35 kg, £300..£500, 2010..2011`

Then narrow your results by...		
language:	any language ▾	Find pages in the language that you select.
region:	any region ▾	Find pages published in a particular region.
last update:	anytime ▾	Find pages updated within the time that you specify.
site or domain:		Search one site (like `wikipedia.org`) or limit your results to a domain like `.edu`, `.org` or `.gov`
terms appearing:	anywhere in the page ▾	Search for terms in the whole page, page title or web address, or links to the page you're looking for.
SafeSearch:	Show most relevant results ▾	Tell SafeSearch whether to filter sexually explicit content.
reading level:	no reading level displayed ▾	Find pages at one reading level or just view the level info.
file type:	any format ▾	Find pages in the format that you prefer.
usage rights:	not filtered by licence ▾	Find pages that you are free to use yourself.

B. Canadian Law Libraries

Several of the largest law libraries in Canada and many of the largest law libraries in the United States include foreign and comparative law texts in their holdings. You may borrow these texts through your local law library's interlibrary loan system.

TASK 8.2

Using a Library Catalogue Online

One of the largest collections of foreign law texts resides at the Harvard Law School Library. The library's catalogue is available online at <http://hollis.harvard.edu>.

■ Use the "Advanced Search" and choose a title of interest, e.g. "Corporate Law in Germany". On the search results page, you can refine your search using a variety of category filters on the right side of the page, including publication date, author/creator, and subject. Select a subject filter, e.g. "Corporation law", for a further, shorter listing of works on that topic. Note that such texts are often in the language of origin.

C. Foreign Law Online

1. General Sources

There are a number of general sources for foreign law online:

- **World Legal Information Institute (WorldLII)** <http://www.worldlii.org> provides a thorough, up-to-date website offering a directory of legal information websites and government pages organized by country.

- **Guide to Law Online** <http://www.loc.gov/law/help/guide/nations.php>, prepared by the Law Library of Congress, is one of the most widely known and used foreign law compilation websites and includes links to government and country information.

- **Legislation Online** <http://legislationline.org>, prepared by the Organization for Security and Co-operation in Europe, provides full-text legislation in several subject areas. The site is limited to laws from Eastern and Western European countries, and the subject matter is limited to laws in areas such as elections, immigration, human rights, independence of the judiciary, policing, and prisons.

- **Worldwide Governments on the WWW** <http://www.gksoft.com/govt/en/world.html> provides a comprehensive directory of worldwide government ministry and agency websites.

2. Subject-Specific Metapages and Regional Sources

If you have not found the relevant legal information you need after searching the above sites, alter the search strategy. For example, a regional intergovernmental organization may track subject-specific legal material published by its members, while a non-governmental organization's website may compile laws of interest to its members and supporters.

3. Online Translators

As technology continues to develop, the following sources may assist with the interpretation of information available on foreign language websites:

- **FreeTranslation.com** <http://www.freetranslation.com> is an excellent website that allows you to enter specialized characters for more accurate results.
- **Babel Fish** <http://www.babelfish.com> is one of the oldest and most widely known online translators.
- **Word2Word.com** <http://www.word2word.com/dictionary.html> provides a comprehensive list of online dictionary links.
- **Inter-Active Terminology for Europe (IATE)** <http://iate.europa.eu/iatediff/SearchByQueryLoad.do> is a searchable EU inter-institutional terminology database administered by the Translation Centre for the Bodies of the European Union. It allows you to personalize the user settings to search for terms in the languages you use most often, narrowing your search to terms used in the domain of law.
- **Google Translate** <http://translate.google.com> is a simple, free service that provides fairly accurate translations.

III. Private International Law Research: Conflict of Laws

To locate general principles regarding jurisdictional differences, consider the following sources:

- J-G Castel & J Walker, *Canadian Conflict of Laws*[4] is a loose-leaf service available at many Canadian law libraries.

---

4   6th ed (Toronto: LexisNexis Canada, 2005) (loose-leaf).

- Legal encyclopedias such as the *Canadian Encyclopedic Digest*[5] and *Halsbury's Laws of Canada*[6] and digest services such as the *Canadian Abridgment* case digests[7] and *Quicklaw* digests[8] provide a summary of key legal principles from a Canadian perspective.[9]
- *Restatement of the Law (2d) of Conflict of Laws*,[10] available from Westlaw, provides the United States' approach to jurisdictional differences.

IV. Public International Law Research

Because one aspect of public international research requires interpreting international multilateral and bilateral agreements between and among governments of sovereign nations, this section focuses on treaty research. When searching for information about a country's obligations under customary international law, you can explore patterns of the country's past practice using these references:

- *Canadian Yearbook of International Law* (Vancouver: UBC Press). Available on HeinOnline and in law libraries.
- *British Yearbook of International Law* (Oxford: Oxford University Press). Available on HeinOnline and in law libraries.
- *Digest of United States Practice in International Law* (Washington, DC: Office of the Legal Advisor). Available on HeinOnline and in law libraries.

Additional sources for this type of analysis include international law texts and journal articles.

A. Locating Treaties

The Department of Foreign Affairs and International Trade's website[11] provides excellent search capabilities for locating international agreements to which Canada is a signatory. Although the website does not include the texts of treaties, it provides treaty location information along with a summary of the Canadian perspective on treaty practice and procedure.

---

5   4th ed (Toronto: Carswell, 2010).

6   (Toronto: LexisNexis Canada, 2006).

7   *The Canadian Abridgment: Canadian Current Law—Case Digests* (Toronto: Carswell, 2013).

8   *The Canada Digest*, online: LexisNexis *Quicklaw* <http://www.lexisnexis.ca>.

9   See Chapter 7 for instructions on the use of these print and online secondary sources of law.

10   American Law Institute, *Restatement of the Law (2d) of Conflict of Laws, with Appendices* (Philadelphia: American Law Institute, 2012).

11   Canada Treaty Information <http://www.treaty-accord.gc.ca>.

Locating Treaties to Which Canada Is a Signatory

For this example, assume that we want to find adoption treaties to which Canada is a signatory.

- Go to Canada Treaty Information <http://www.treaty-accord.gc.ca> and choose "All" from the Treaty List.

- Use the Detailed Search function to locate any existing treaties. The Keywords drop-down menu does not provide any keywords concerning adoption but the Subjects drop-down menu does. Select "Adoption" and then Search.

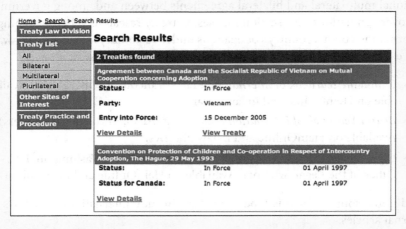

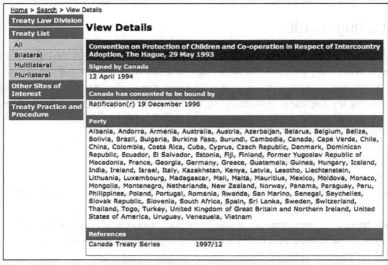

- The initial search result shows basic information. Assume that we want to know more about the *Convention on Protection of Children and Co-operation in respect of Intercountry Adoption.* Select "View Details" for more information.

The record provides:

- **Status:** In force 1 April 1997
- **Signed by Canada:** 12 April 1994
- **Ratified by Canada:** 19 December 1996
- **Parties to the treaty**
- **Citation:** Canada Treaty Series 1997/12

The citation provides the treaty's location in the Canada Treaty Series. This treaty is published in the Canada Treaty Series for 1997, document 12, and is available online[12] and in print at university libraries and law libraries.

Treaties and international agreements are registered and published by the UN Secretariat.[13]

The full text of treaties deposited with the UN are available online through the United Nations Treaty Collection.[14]

---

12 Hague Conference on Private International Law <http://www.hcch.net/upload/conventions/txt33en.pdf>.

13 E.g. *Charter of the United Nations,* 26 June 1945, Can TS 1945 No 7, Art 102 [entered into force 24 October 1945; ratification by Canada 9 November 1945].

14 <http://treaties.un.org>.

TASK 8.4

Using the United Nations Treaty Collection Advanced Search

Locate the *Convention on Protection of Children and Co-operation in respect of Inter-country Adoption*.

- On the United Nations Treaty Collection website <http://treaties.un.org>, select Advanced Search.

- Under "Search for", choose "Treaty". By default, "Show All Agreements" is chosen; this choice is appropriate for most searches. Under "Filter by", choose "English title". In the "Criteria for Selected Attribute" field, enter search keywords, e.g. "intercountry adoption". Click "Add to Search Criteria" and then click Search.

- On the results screen, select the Convention to view its details, then scroll down to "Volume In Pdf" and choose "v1870.pdf" to view a PDF of the Convention.

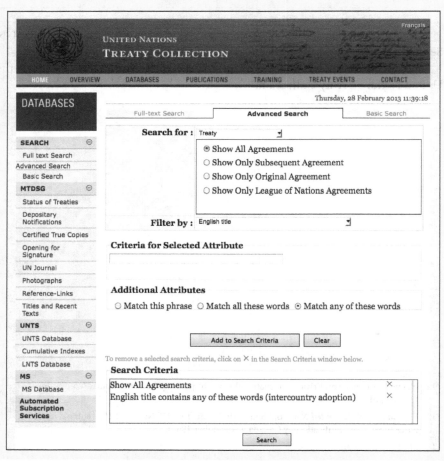

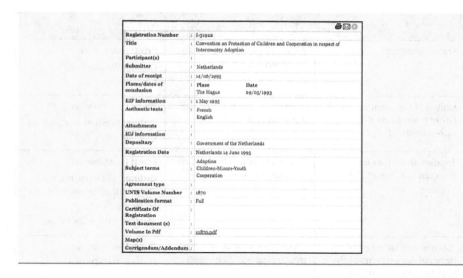

Registration Number	:	I-31922	
Title	:	Convention on Protection of Children and Cooperation in respect of Intercountry Adoption	
Participant(s)	:		
Submitter	:	Netherlands	
Date of receipt	:	14/06/1995	
Places/dates of conclusion	:	Place	Date
		The Hague	29/05/1993
EIF information	:	1 May 1995	
Authentic texts	:	French	
		English	
Attachments	:		
ICJ information	:		
Depositary	:	Government of the Netherlands	
Registration Date	:	Netherlands 14 June 1995	
Subject terms	:	Adoption	
		Children-Minors-Youth	
		Cooperation	
Agreement type	:		
UNTS Volume Number	:	1870	
Publication format	:	Full	
Certificate Of Registration	:		
Text document (s)	:		
Volume In Pdf	:	v1870.pdf	
Map(s)	:		
Corrigendum/Addendum	:		

B. Additional Sources for Locating Treaties

FIGURE 8.1   Treaty Sources

Source	Content	Location
United States of America		
Mary Miles Prince, *Prince's Bieber Dictionary of Legal Abbreviations: A Reference Guide for Attorneys, Legal Secretaries, Paralegals, and Law Students*, 6th ed (Buffalo, NY: WS Hein, 2009)	A comprehensive list of abbreviations used in legal reference works and useful for finding a treaty by citation	**Print:** Law libraries
USTREATIES database	Complete collections of all treaties to which the US is a signatory	**Online:** Westlaw <http://www.westlawcanada.com>
HeinOnline's Treaty and Agreements Library	Scanned versions of treaties as published, including Statutes at Large, UST,* TIAS,** and US Senate and State Department treaty sources	**Online:** HeinOnline <http://heinonline.org/HOL/Index?collection=ustreaties>
US Government Printing Office Senate treaty documents	Contains the text of treaties as submitted to the US Senate for ratification	**Online:** GPO <http://www.gpoaccess.gov/serialset/cdocuments/index.html>

Source	Content	Location
Statutes at Large	Treaties to which the US was a signatory until 1950	**Print:** Law libraries **Online:** Westlaw and HeinOnline
United States Treaties and Other International Agreements (UST)	Treaties to which the US was a signatory since 1950	**Print:** Law libraries **Online:** Westlaw and HeinOnline
Treaties and Other International Acts Series (TIAS)	Treaties to which the US was a signatory since 1945	**Print:** Law libraries **Online:** US Department of State <http://www.state.gov/s/l/treaty/tias> Westlaw and HeinOnline
Treaties and Other International Agreements of the United States of America	Comprehensive series of US treaties from 1776 to 1950	**Print:** Law libraries **Online:** HeinOnline
Europe		
European Treaty Series	European conventions and agreements between 1949 and 2003; from 2004, this series is continued by the Council of Europe Treaty Series	**Print:** Law libraries **Online:** Council of Europe <http://www.conventions.coe.int>
International Trade Treaties		
World Trade Organization, documents and resources	Foundational legal texts for WTO member countries	**Online:** <http://www.wto.org/english/res_e/res_e.htm> **Print:** Law libraries—Basic Instruments and Selected Documents
North American Trade Agreements		
NAFTA Secretariat	NAFTA agreements and documents	**Online:** <http://www.nafta-sec-alena.org> Westlaw Canada <http://www.westlawcanada.com>

* United States Treaties and Other International Agreements.

** Treaties and Other International Acts Series.

C. Status of Treaties

To determine Canada's treaty obligations in international law, you must locate both the treaty and its status information. Status is determined by answers to the following questions:

Is the treaty in force?	A treaty states coming into force information.[15] It is only in force for those countries that communicated their intention to be bound.
Has the treaty been signed?	A country can express its initial intention to be bound to a treaty in three main ways:
	1. *Signature:* A country's delegate, present at the date and time of the original completion of the treaty, can sign the treaty as an initial expression of the country's intention to be bound.
	2. *Accession:* A country that did not have a delegate present at the date and time of the original completion of the treaty can later express its intention to be bound to the treaty by acceding to the treaty. The treaty usually states the means of demonstrating accession.
	3. *Succession:* A newly formed country, with a delegate not present at the date and time of the original completion of the treaty, may assume the obligations of its predecessor state by succeeding to the treaty. The treaty usually states the means of demonstrating succession.

(Continued on the next page.)

---

15 See e.g. the *Rome Statute of the International Criminal Court*, 18 December 1998, Can TS 2002 No 13, Art 126, 2187 UNTS 3 (entered into force 1 July 2002; ratification by Canada 7 July 2000) article 126.

Has the treaty been ratified?	A country confirms its intent to be bound by a treaty in a written document called an instrument of ratification. Where the treaty provisions so require, a signatory country must deposit an instrument of ratification with the depository or registrar for the treaty. The depository or registrar for the treaty is usually specified in the treaty itself. The registrar is usually the United Nations; however, the treaty can specify any country. In Canada:
	Ratification processes are an internal constitutional matter for each country and they may frequently differ from one country to another. In Canada, ratification is part of the royal prerogative and is exercised by the Executive, in this case expressed by means of an Order in Council issued by the Governor General in Council, which authorizes the Minister of Foreign Affairs to sign an instrument of ratification. Ratification is then effected by delivery to the other party (in the case of a bilateral agreement) of an instrument of ratification signed by the Minister of Foreign Affairs.[16]
Has the treaty been implemented?	In Canada, most treaties must be implemented by our domestic legal system in order to take effect.[17] In other jurisdictions, such as the United States, the European Union, France, and Mexico, treaties take direct effect; such treaties are also known as self-executing treaties. The constitutions of these states "give treaties a status equivalent to ordinary statutes."[18]
Have reservations to the treaty been filed?	A reservation is a unilateral statement a state makes, when signing, ratifying, or acceding to a treaty, purporting to exclude or modify the legal effect of certain provisions of the treaty with respect to the state's own obligations. Unless the treaty specifically forbids it, other states may object to the reservations made by another nation.

---

16   Hugh M Kindred & Phillip M Saunders, *International Law: Chiefly as Interpreted and Applied in Canada*, 7th ed (Toronto: Emond Montgomery, 2006) at 120-21 [Kindred]. "International treaties and conventions are not part of Canadian law unless they have been implemented by statute": *Baker v Canada (Minister of Citizenship and Immigration)*, [1999] 2 SCR 817 at para 69, 174 DLR (4th) 193 [*Baker*], citing *Francis v The Queen*, [1956] SCR 618 at 621, 3 DLR (2d) 641 and *Capital Cities Communications Inc v Canadian Radio-Television Commission*, [1978] 2 SCR 141 at 172-73, 81 DLR (3d) 609.

17   Kindred, *supra* note 16 at 206.

18   *Ibid.*

Although most treaty status questions can be answered by viewing the Department of Foreign Affairs and International Trade website,[19] discussed above, take the following step to determine whether reservations have been filed.

TASK 8.5

Determining a Reservation to a Treaty

Q: Is the *Convention Relating to the Status of Refugees* in force? If so, is Botswana bound by it, and has Botswana filed any reservations to it?

■ On the United Nations Treaty Collection website, <http://treaties.un.org>, go to Databases and then, under MTDSG, select "Status of Treaties".

■ The Multilateral Treaties Deposited with the Secretary-General database provides information on multilateral treaties organized by topic, title, date of signature, party names, and ratification or accession dates, as well as the text of any reservations to a treaty. Although it does not include the full text of treaties, it is a reliable source to determine whether reservations to a multilateral treaty have been filed.

■ Select "CHAPTER V" on Refugees and Stateless Persons, then locate the Convention.

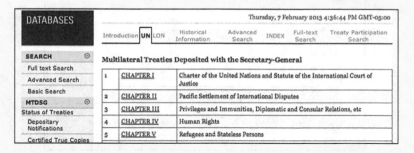

■ The treaty was completed at Geneva on 28 July 1951. It entered into force on 22 April 1954, in accordance with article 43. The text is located in United Nations, *Treaty Series*, vol 189, page 137. Its citation is 189 UNTS 137.

---

19   See Canada Treaty Information, *supra* note 11.

■ Locate Botswana in the list of participants. Although it acceded to the treaty on 6 January 1969, Botswana filed reservations to articles 7, 17, 26, 31, 32, and 34 and paragraph 1 of article 12.

CHAPTER V
REFUGEES AND STATELESS PERSONS

2 . Convention relating to the Status of Refugees
Geneva, 28 July 1951

Entry into force : 22 April 1954, in accordance with article 43.

Registration : 22 April 1954, No. 2545

Status : Signatories : 19. Parties : 145

Text : United Nations, *Treaty Series* , vol. 189, p. 137.

Note : The Convention was adopted by the United Nations Conference of Plenipotentiaries on the Status of Refugees and Stateless Persons, held at Geneva from 2 to 25 July 1951.
The Conference was convened pursuant to resolution 429 (V)¹, adopted by the General Assembly of the United Nations on 14 December 1950.

Participant	Signature	Accession(a), Succession(d), Ratification
Afghanistan		30 Aug 2005 a
Albania		18 Aug 1992 a
Algeria		21 Feb 1963 d
Angola		23 Jun 1981 a
Antigua and Barbuda		7 Sep 1995 a
Argentina		15 Nov 1961 a
Armenia		6 Jul 1993 a
Australia		22 Jan 1954 a
Austria	28 Jul 1951	1 Nov 1954
Azerbaijan		12 Feb 1993 a
Bahamas		15 Sep 1993 a
Belarus		23 Aug 2001 a
Belgium	28 Jul 1951	22 Jul 1953
Belize		27 Jun 1990 a
Benin		4 Apr 1962 d
Bolivia (Plurinational State of)		9 Feb 1982 a
Bosnia and Herzegovina ²		1 Sep 1993 d
Botswana		6 Jan 1969 a

Botswana
"Subject to the reservation of articles 7, 17, 26, 31, 32 and 34 and paragraph 1 of article 12 of the Convention."

A: The Convention is in force. Botswana is bound by the Convention, but has filed reservations to it.

D. Additional Sources for Treaty Status Research

See Figure 8.2 for additional sources for treaty status.

FIGURE 8.2   Additional Sources for Treaty Status

Source	Use	Availability
Canada		
CL Wiktor, *Canadian Treaty Calendar, 1928-1978* (Dobbs Ferry, NJ: Oceana, 1982)	Lists treaties in force for Canada by date of signature, with citations to the full text, where available	**Print:** Law libraries
CL Wiktor, *Index to Canadian Treaties, 1979-2003* (Halifax: Dalhousie Law School, 2003)	A supplement to the 1928-1978 version above	**Print:** Law libraries
"Canada-American Treaties"	Online database of bilateral treaties established between the United States and Canada from 1783 to 1997	**Online:** Minister of Foreign Affairs and International Trade, Library of International Relations
CL Wiktor, *Multilateral Treaty Calendar 1648-1995* (The Hague: Martinus Nijhoff Publishers, 1998)	Provides access to the title, party names, date, and place of signature, with citations to the full text of multilateral treaties signed since 1648 and ordered by date of signature	**Print:** Law libraries
MJ Bowman & DJ Harris, *Multilateral Treaties: Index and Current Status* (London: Butterworths, 1984)	Referred to as "Bowman and Harris", this source provides citations, party information, and signature dates for multilateral treaties published until about 1987	**Print:** Law libraries

Source	Use	Availability
United States		
"Treaty Actions"	A record of actions taken by the US with regard to international agreements (1997-2010)	**Online:** US Department of State <http://www.state.gov/s/l/treaty/c3428.htm>
"Treaties in Force"	An indexing tool for research on in-force treaties and agreements, published annually by the US Department of State since 1955, TIF summarizes treaties and other international agreements (both bilateral and multilateral) in force for the US as of January of the respective year; bilateral treaties are arranged by country and grouped by subject; multilateral treaties are grouped by subject	**Online:** US Department of State <http://www.state.gov/s/l/treaty/tif/index.htm>
Bilateral Treaties		
PH Rohn, *World Treaty Index* (Santa Barbara, CA: ABC-Clio, 1983-84)	Citations to bilateral treaties	**Print:** Law libraries **Online:** The current version is available for beta testing: World Treaty Index <http://worldtreatyindex.com>

E. International Law Research: Finding Judicial Decisions

When Canada ratifies an international treaty, it has, in essence, agreed to be bound by the treaty's terms. However, courts will approach the enforcement of a treaty differently depending on whether its provisions are specifically incorporated into domestic legislation. Where a treaty has been incorporated into domestic legislation, it becomes enforceable in the same manner as any other legislative provision enforced. In the absence of implementation, a treaty serves only as a guiding document for courts when they consider questions that give rise to matters having a connection to the treaty content.

One such example arose in the Supreme Court of Canada decision in *Baker*,[20] an immigration case dealing with the issue of whether a mother of four Canadian

---

20 *Supra* note 16.

children, subject to a deportation order, qualified for an exemption to the rule that an application for permanent residence must be made outside Canada.

In *Baker*, the Supreme Court considered how the fact that Canada is a signatory to the *Convention on the Rights of the Child*[21] applied to the relevant legislation governing the mother's application. The Supreme Court confirmed that the provisions of the Convention, not having been incorporated into domestic law, had no direct application within Canadian law. However, in the view of the majority of the Court, the values reflected in this and other international treaties helped to inform the statutory interpretation process.

When searching for judicial decisions that involve international law decided by a Canadian court, follow the search strategies described in Chapters 6 and 7. However, when searching for judicial decisions decided by international courts, consider the additional sources in Figure 8.3.

FIGURE 8.3   Sources for Judicial Decisions

Source	Content	Availability
Permanent Court of International Justice (PCIJ)		
International Court of Justice	Most PCIJ decisions are available for free	**Online:** <http://www.icj-cij.org>
WorldCourts	Most PCIJ decisions	**Online:** <http://www.worldcourts.com>
Permanent Court of International Justice, *The Case Law of the International Court* (Leiden: AW Sijthoff, 1952-1976)	Significant PCIJ decisions	**Print:** Law libraries
International Court of Justice (ICJ)		
International Court of Justice, *Reports of Judgments, Advisory Opinions and Orders* (Leiden: AW Sijthoffs)	Significant cases reported	**Print:** Law libraries
International Court of Justice	Most ICJ decisions	**Online:** <http://www.icj-cij.org>

---

21   *Baker, supra* note 16 at paras 69-71. November 1989, Can TS 1992 No 3, 1577 UNTS 3 (entered into force 2 September 1990), online: <http://www.ohchr.org/EN/ProfessionalInterest/Pages/CRC.aspx>.

Source	Content	Availability
Westlaw Canada, International Court of Justice database (INT-ICJ)	All ICJ decisions (full text with some summaries) from 2000 onward	**Online:** <http://canada.westlaw.com>
Project on International Courts and Tribunals (PICT)	Most ICJ decisions	**Online:** <http://www.pict-pcti.org>
Pleadings		
International Court of Justice, *Pleadings, Oral Arguments, Documents* (Leiden: AW Sijthoffs)	Select pleadings from significant cases	**Print:** Law libraries
International Court of Justice	Pleadings before the ICJ	**Online:** <http://www.icj-cij.org>
International Criminal Tribunal for Rwanda (ICTR)		
Genocide, War Crimes, and Crimes Against Humanity: A Digest of the Case Law of the International Criminal Tribunal for Rwanda (New York: NY Human Rights Watch, 2010)	Topical digests from the ICTR	**Print:** Law libraries **Online:** <http://www.unhcr.org/refworld/docid/4b5438802.html>
Annotated Leading Cases of International Criminal Tribunals (Cambridge, UK: Intersentia)	Full-text decisions	**Print:** Law libraries
International Criminal Tribunal for the Former Yugoslavia (ICTY)		
Judicial Reports, 1994-1995, 2 vols (Leiden: Martinus Nijhoff, 1999)	Significant decisions from the tribunal from 1994-1995	**Print:** Law libraries
Annotated Leading Cases of International Criminal Tribunals (Cambridge, UK: Intersentia)	Significant decisions from several criminal tribunals	**Print:** Law libraries
ICTY website	Full text of ICTY legal texts and judgments	**Online:** <http://www.un.org/icty>
International Criminal Court (ICC)		
ICC website	Current investigations and hearings, founding documents of the court and case law	**Online:** <http://www.icc-cpi.int>
Coalition for the International Criminal Court	Primary documents from before the court's inception	**Online:** <http://www.iccnow.org>

Source	Content	Availability
European Court of Human Rights		
European Court of Human Rights website	Full-text case law—judgments, decisions, resolutions, and reports	**Online:** <http://www.echr.coe.int/echr>
Westlaw Canada	Full-text decisions	**Online:** <http://canada.westlaw.com>

F. Finding Journal Articles and Commentary Using Secondary Sources

See Figure 8.4 for some secondary sources of international law.

FIGURE 8.4   Secondary Sources of International Law

Source	Content	Location
Westlaw WORLD-JLR	Full-text law journals from the US, Canada, and Europe; also contains an index to legal literature from the US, Canada, Great Britain, New Zealand, and Australia	**Online:** <http://directory.westlaw.com> Visit the Directory
Quicklaw For US law reviews, use "Law Reviews, CLE, Legal Journals & Periodicals, Combined"	Collection of select international law journals	**Online:** <http://www.lexisnexis.ca> Use the Quicklaw source directory
HeinOnline	Historical international journal content	**Online:** <http://heinonline.org>
European Research Papers Archive	Free, searchable database of European journal articles	**Online:** <http://eiop.or.at/erpa>
Directory of Open Access Journals	Directory of free, open-access journal articles	**Online:** <http://doaj.org>

G. Citations

1. Locating Citation Elements for Treaties, United Nations General Assembly Resolutions, and United Nations Security Council Resolutions[22]

FIGURE 8.5   Locating Citation Elements

Source	Content	Location
Canada Treaty Information	Date of signature, citation to Canada Treaty Series, date of entry into force, and date of ratification for Canada	**Online:** <http://www.treaty-accord.gc.ca>
United Nations Multilateral Treaties Deposited with the Secretary-General	Similar to Canada Treaty Information, but provides citations to United Nations Treaty Series	**Online:** <http://treaties.un.org/pages/ParticipationStatus.aspx>
CL Wiktor, *Multilateral Treaty Calendar 1648-1995* (The Hague: Martinus Nijhoff, 1998)	Parallel citations for multilateral treaties from 1648 to 1995; organized chronologically by date of signature	**Print:** Law libraries
United Nations General Assembly	Resolution title, resolution number, session, and year	**Online:** <http://www.un.org/documents/resga.htm>
United Nations Official Document System, "Resolutions and Decisions Adopted by the General Assembly During its [relevant] Session"	Supplement number, document number, and page number	**Online:** <http://documents.un.org>
United Nations Official Document System	Session, document number, and page number	**Online:** <http://documents.un.org>
United Nations Security Council	Resolution title, resolution number, and year	**Online:** <http://www.un.org/Docs/sc/unsc_resolutions.html>

---

22 For citation style of international materials, see *Canadian Guide to Uniform Legal Citation*, 7th ed (Toronto: Carswell, 2010) ch 5 [McGill Guide].

When citing to UN documents:

- The UN document number provided is usually the resolution number, not the document number for the supplement. Both the document and the resolution number are required. However, the supplement number may not be provided.
- A citation that includes the acronym UN GAOR is a citation reference to the official record. Do not use UN GAOR as part of the citation if you have not located the supplement itself.

2. Treaty Citation

To create a citation, follow McGill Guide format. In addition to the treaty's name, include both the Canada Treaty Series number and the United Nations Treaty Series number, as well as the date in force and the date of ratification.

Convention on Protection of Children and Co-operation in respect of Intercountry Adoption, 12 April 1994, Can TS 1997 No 12, 1870 UNTS 167 (entered into force 1 April 1997; ratified by Canada 19 December 1996)

3. Foreign Law Legal Citation

Consult the following resources:

- Columbia Law Review et al, *The Bluebook: A Uniform System of Citation*, 19th ed (Cambridge, MA: Harvard Law Review Association, 2010).
- Association of Legal Writing Directors, *ALWD Citation Manual: A Professional System of Citation*, 4th ed (New York: Aspen, 2010).

Legal Research: Creating a Plan and Maintaining a Record

9

I. The Role of Legal Research in Law School and in Professional Practice

The Federation of Law Societies of Canada has identified the selection of sources and methods to conduct relevant Canadian legal research as an essential research competency. (See Chapter 1 to review required competencies.) Implicit in that statement are several considerations including:

- Research selection includes decisions about efficient methods and comprehensive sources.
- Canadian legal research is not restricted to domestic law, but can include foreign law, public and private law, and international law.
- In practice, conducting research takes time; its financial cost must be borne by the client or subsumed by the client's legal representative.
- Competent legal research requires speed and accuracy to ensure that a client's legal issues are resolved in a timely and cost-efficient manner.

A. Competent Legal Research: Ethical and Professional Obligations

All lawyers are governed by and must comply with the rules of professional conduct in the jurisdiction of their practice.[1] These rules, which establish the professional obligations required of lawyers in their daily work, are situated in a broader ethical context of the overall standards of the profession.

In Ontario, compliance with Rule 2.01, Competence, ensures that lawyers recognize their professional obligation to first obtain and then maintain the necessary knowledge and requisite skills to serve their clients competently. Although the rule purports to list the skills that competent lawyers are expected to demonstrate, the stated list only identifies broad skill categories rather than the skills themselves. Each skill category contains a myriad of discrete skills, each of which includes a unique set of tasks to master, synthesize, and apply.

Within the identified list of skills categories, legal research is mentioned first, conveying the message that accurate legal research provides the foundation for developing competence in the remainder of the skills listed. Law students can establish that they have acquired competency in the research skills required of lawyers by both planning a sound research path and recording or logging their research findings. The systematic collection of research not only facilitates communication with the client about the course of the matter for which the client has retained the lawyer, but, should a question be raised about the management of a matter, also provides a comprehensive record of the manner in which the work was undertaken.

Below are the relevant sections of the Law Society of Upper Canada's *Rules of Professional Conduct* pertaining to the ethical and professional obligations underlying competent legal research.[2]

1.03 INTERPRETATION

Standards of the Legal Profession

1.03(1) These rules shall be interpreted in a way that recognizes that

(a) *a lawyer has a duty to carry on the practice of law and discharge all responsibilities* to clients, tribunals, the public, and other legal practitioners *honourably and with integrity,*

---

1 Although the discussion in this chapter focuses on the Rules of Professional Conduct for lawyers practising in Ontario, similar expectations are held for lawyers practising in other jurisdictions. Consult the law society in the jurisdiction of practice to review specific rules.

2 Online: The Law Society of Upper Canada <http://www.lsuc.on.ca/with.aspx?id=671>.

(b) a lawyer has special responsibilities by virtue of the privileges afforded the legal profession and the important role it plays in a free and democratic society and in the administration of justice, including a special responsibility to recognize the diversity of the Ontario community, to protect the dignity of individuals, and to respect human rights laws in force in Ontario, …

(d) the rules are intended to express to the profession and to the public the high ethical ideals of the legal profession, …

2.01 COMPETENCE

Definitions

2.01(1) In this rule

"competent lawyer" means a lawyer who has and applies relevant skills, attributes, and values in a manner appropriate to each matter undertaken on behalf of a client including

(a) knowing general legal principles and procedures and the substantive law and procedure for the areas of law in which the lawyer practises,

(b) investigating facts, identifying issues, ascertaining client objectives, considering possible options, and developing and advising the client on appropriate courses of action,

(c) implementing, as each matter requires, the chosen course of action through the application of appropriate skills, including,

    (i) legal research,

    (ii) analysis,

    (iii) application of the law to the relevant facts,

    (iv) writing and drafting,

    (v) negotiation,

    (vi) alternative dispute resolution,

    (vii) advocacy, and

    (viii) problem-solving ability,

(d) communicating at all stages of a matter in a timely and effective manner that is appropriate to the age and abilities of the client,

(e) performing all functions conscientiously, diligently, and in a timely and cost-effective manner,

(f) applying intellectual capacity, judgment, and deliberation to all functions, …

(j) pursuing appropriate professional development to maintain and enhance legal knowledge and skills, and

(k) adapting to changing professional requirements, standards, techniques, and practices.

B. Creating a Research Plan and Recording the Results: Some Factors to Consider

Legal research planning requires the consideration of many factors. Some of these are listed below:

- Research may involve both domestic and, sometimes, international law.
- Domestic research may require investigation of both federal and provincial or territorial jurisdictions.
- Research typically involves both primary and secondary sources of law.
- Researching legislation is one aspect of primary law research; researching judicial decisions is another. These two aspects of primary law research overlap. When researching legislation, researchers must also consider the binding and persuasive judicial decisions that have considered the legislation under analysis.
- Secondary sources include both research tools to help locate the law and commentary to help interpret the law.
- As challenging as this may be to accept in the 21st century, not all legal research can be completed online; competent legal research requires the considered use of both print and online sources.
- Successful development of research competence requires, first, understanding the methodology of the research process, and then systematically applying the methodology to fact-specific events.

FIGURE 9.1 Incorporating the Research Plan with the Research Log

A **research plan** sets out the necessary research and identifies research tools to accomplish the plan, while a **research log** records the research results. Developing a research plan and maintaining a research log ensures that research progresses in a systematic and organized manner.

Planning research establishes:

- that the lawyer understood the legal issues before beginning the work
- that the lawyer made appropriate choices regarding which resources to select and which methods to use

Recording research establishes:

- that the lawyer has undertaken thorough and accurate research
- that the lawyer has accounted for changes to the research plan that may occur during the research process

To develop sound research plans and research logs, law students must be able to:

- Select and use available print and online sources according to the requirements of each task, whether the sources are of a general nature or tailored to specific practice areas.
- Assess the comparative strengths and limitations of every source, whether commercially published or in the public domain.
- Choose the source that best fits each step of the legal research process, considering both cost and time efficiencies.
- Systematically record research findings.

C. Transitioning from Law School: Legal Research Within the Context of Legal Practice

Although most law students learn the basics of legal research at law school, students who are hired by a law firm or a legal department for a summer term or an articling position find that applying legal research in practice must take into account the additional consideration of law as a business. Thus, at the planning stage of a legal research task, a guiding question is: "What is the most time-efficient and cost-effective way to conduct this research?"

Law students should be aware of cost issues when choosing a research strategy. That does not mean that the most inexpensive search process is the preferred route, because the time taken to conduct research must always be factored into cost calculations, and the least expensive method may not be sufficiently comprehensive. It does mean, however, that you should become aware of and use reliable legal resources that are in the public domain.

In law school, inadequate legal research may result in a poor grade on an assignment. In legal practice, inadequate research could affect the client's interests and the professional reputation of those acting for the client. In extreme situations, it might lead to claims of negligent or unprofessional conduct, and could result in sanctions by the lawyer's governing body.

Below are some facts that summer or articling students should note when planning a research task:

- Larger firms may have a law library on site, and a librarian who might supervise or otherwise guide legal research activities, including legal research training for lawyers and students.
- A firm, clinic, or legal department will have access to the Internet, which can be used to access official sources of statutes where available through government websites and CanLII.

- A firm or legal department may subscribe to online legal research services such as LexisNexis Quicklaw, and Westlaw Canada. Always ask your employer for the pricing model—including the fees per search, per hour, or for unlimited access. The pricing model may restrict online searching, including the particular databases to which the firm subscribes.

- For a firm or legal department that does not subscribe to these services, access the courthouse library or the nearest university law library.

- If access to a university law library is not available, locate the nearest university library as larger ones include historical statutes and government publications in their holdings.

- Research assistance may be available through the governing law society.[3]

When logging research results, note the following:

- Large firms and departments may have an information technology (IT) department and dedicated networks to ensure that research results are saved, while smaller firms may use an external hard drive.

- Large firms and departments may have a document management system.

- Quicklaw and Westlaw provide features to track research and assign results to client files for billing purposes.

Combining research methods and resources will likely provide the most efficient search strategy. For example:

- Locate the information that is available online. Determine whether the source is subscription-based, which may increase the research cost, or is free to the user.

- Determine whether the online source is official. If it is not, supplement the research with text-based official sources.

- Use text-based research to find information that is not included in online products.

- Every step of the research process requires that you note the currency of your sources, because legal matters usually have an associated time frame. Examine each source, whether print or online, determine its currency, and record that information.

---

3   See e.g. the Great Library, online: The Law Society of Upper Canada <http://rc.lsuc.on.ca/library/home.htm>.

D. Research Plan and Research Log Protocol

Thorough planning requires knowing more than topical substantive law. Depending on the legal matter, specific procedural rules, remedies, forms, precedents, or public records may apply. Therefore, when planning research, consider the following:

- What is the controlling area of law that governs each issue?
- Which jurisdiction governs—e.g. federal, provincial, municipal, international, or foreign?
- What type of primary law applies—e.g. statute, common, or civil law?
- Is there another type of information necessary to answer the legal issue?

TASK 9.1

Research Plan and Research Log Protocol

1. **Fact and issue analysis**
   - Arises from client interview in practice, or legal hypothetical in law school.
   - Sort and organize facts—who, what, where, when, how, why, assumed, and unknown.
   - Determine the topic of law—identify legal keywords.
   - Identify material facts and connect them to legal concepts to create the legal issues to be answered.

2. **Determine research parameters**
   - Public law or private law?
   - Jurisdiction: domestic federal, provincial, municipal, or international or foreign?
   - Is the law governed by a statutory scheme, civil law, or the common law?

3. **Create a research plan template for each issue**
   - Where useful, consult secondary sources to gain an understanding of the legal concepts at issue and to identify the relevant primary law: legislation and judicial decisions (Chapter 7).
   - Locate primary law: federal legislation (see Chapters 3 and 4); provincial legislation (see Chapter 5); judicial decisions (see Chapter 6); and international and foreign law (see Chapter 8).
   - Interpret primary law (see Chapters 3, 4, 6, and 7 for federal law; Chapters 5, 6, and 7 for provincial law; and Chapters 7 and 8 for international and foreign law).

4. **Complete the research plan first**
   - Identify the sources likely to provide information to answer each issue.
   - Review the methodology to use for each source (see respective chapters and Appendix A for a sample research plan).

5. **Execute the plan and log the results**
   - Record and date the work undertaken.
   - Sort and organize the information collected.
   - Determine whether supplementary issues have arisen that require amending the plan.
   - Append relevant results to the document.

6. **Review information obtained**
   - Complete the analysis (see Chapters 10 and 11).
   - Communicate the results to identified audiences (Chapters 12, 13, and 14).

FIGURE 9.2   Research Synopsis: Chapter Location

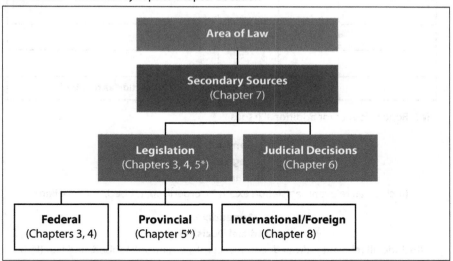

* Including specific provincial research chapters.

TASK 9.2

Research Plan and Log: Format

General area/topic of law:

Common law? _____ Civil law? _____ Public? _____ Private? _____

Jurisdiction: Federal? _____ Provincial? _____ Municipal? _____
                International/foreign? _____

Issue 1:

Legislation? _____ Judicial decisions? _____ Unknown? _____

PLAN		LOG	
Legal information required	Sources to check	Checked on date?	Findings (append results to document) (If additional questions are raised in the course of research, add them to column 1)
			Enlarge this section as required

NB: Repeat format for additional issues.

Appendix A:
Legislation
Statutes and Regulations
(Include all relevant legislation excerpts, organized, tabbed, and labelled)

Appendix B:
Judicial Decisions
(Include all relevant judicial decision excerpts, organized, tabbed, and labelled)

Appendix C:
Secondary Sources
(Include all relevant secondary sources, organized, tabbed, and labelled)

Appendix D:
Other

E. Completing the Research Plan and Research Log

1. Factual Analysis

Whereas law students analyze legal hypotheticals presented to them in law school, in legal practice lawyers frequently conduct research after meeting with and being retained by the client. After the client interview and a preliminary assessment of the facts followed by issue drafting, the lawyer's next step is to locate the controlling law. Creating a chart can assist the planning process by linking the facts to the law to be researched.

FIGURE 9.3   Link Facts and Law: Research Planning Tool—Example

Facts	Evidence of the facts	Law	Evidence of the law
Arising from client's statement	E.g. documents, records, witness statements	• Legislation	• Official version of a statute (consolidated version or version as enacted) • Bills • Regulations • Executive orders, statutory orders, statutory instruments • Judicial interpretation of a statute
Arising from client's statement	E.g. documents, records, witness statements	• Judicial decisions • Treaties • Laws from other jurisdictions • Rules of court • Forms and precedents	• Official or semi-official versions, where available • Administrative tribunal decisions • Case history • Judicial consideration of cases

2. *Determine the Controlling Area of Law*

- Once you have assessed the facts and identified the issues, use secondary sources of law to determine controlling areas of law such as contract, tort, criminal, family, property, wills, corporate, immigration, tax, employment, and public law.
- Review textbooks, loose-leaf services, and encyclopedia entries such as those found in the *Canadian Encyclopedic Digest* or *Halsbury's Laws of Canada*. Encyclopedias provide a summary of discrete points of law. Textbooks and loose-leaf services provide detail about a particular area of law. Use these sources as a springboard for further research by reviewing the footnotes to find citations to relevant primary law.

3. *Locate Primary Law*

Locating relevant primary law requires, at a minimum:

- determining jurisdiction: federal, provincial, municipal, international, or the domestic law of a foreign country
- locating the relevant statute(s) that govern the legal issue(s)
- locating regulations made pursuant to the statute that govern the legal issue(s)
- locating judicial decisions pursuant to the legislation
- for common-law matters not based in statute, locating judicial decisions that interpret the common law

Depending on the complexity of the research problem, additional research may be necessary, including:

- examining the legislative history of the statute to determine how and when the statute was created and whether changes or amendments have been made to the statute between the time it was first introduced and its current version
- reviewing the legislative debates that were held as the statute, while in bill form, proceeded through Parliament and the Senate (or provincial legislature)
- determining the coming into force of the enacted version of a statute
- determining whether bills in progress may amend the statute in the future
- discovering whether there has been judicial consideration of the statute

- interpreting the meaning and effect of the legislation (both statutes and regulations) or other subordinate legislation
- determining whether the research requires the use of official versions of the statute or whether unofficial print or online versions will suffice
- examining the case history and judicial treatment of relevant judicial decisions

Because each one of these processes requires a number of separate steps, using a research plan to organize the tasks to be completed, and then logging the results, will ensure that you take a comprehensive approach to every task, thus building research competence.

PART III
Legal Analysis

Foundations of Statutory and Case Analysis

10

CONTENTS

LEARNING OUTCOMES

By the end of this chapter, you should be able to:

- Understand how the rules of statutory interpretation are used to determine the meaning of legislation
- Understand the concepts of precedent and *stare decisis*
- Identify the essential components of judicial decisions used in legal reasoning
- Understand how policy informs legal analysis
- Understand how critical legal theory provides a contextual perspective for legal analysis
- Create a case brief

Analytical Tasks

I. Legal Analysis: Overview

Once a lawyer determines the legal issues raised by the facts of the client's problem, and undertakes the research necessary to determine the applicable legislation and case law, the next step is to analyze the findings. The relevant legal principles are then synthesized, and through this process the connections among relevant principles are determined. Next, techniques of inductive and deductive reasoning are used to develop and assess the legal arguments that both support and challenge the client's legal position. During the process, the lawyer may need to consider broader policy factors that may affect the analysis. Once complete, the analysis becomes a legal opinion. Reduced to writing, this opinion can be communicated to different audiences in formats appropriate for them—e.g. a letter of opinion to a client or a memorandum of law to a lawyer. Moreover, the opinion forms the basis of additional advocacy work—e.g. demand letters, courtroom advocacy, or alternative dispute resolution measures such as settlement negotiations or mediation.

Legal analysis focuses on the interpretation of the primary law. As illustrated in Figure 10.1, this analysis involves a non-linear process. Depending on the legal issues raised by the unique facts of a case, a lawyer may be required to consider the purpose and meaning of legislation as first enacted, judicial interpretations of that legislation, and the common law, all of which may be shaped by policy and can be interpreted through legal theory.

In the discussion that follows, we review the process of statutory interpretation, followed by strategies to analyze case law, including case briefing, and then consider policy issues, followed by an introduction to legal theory. Chapter 11 builds on this discussion, explaining the development of legal argument through the application of the tools of inductive and deductive reasoning. We illustrate the use of these tools by providing examples of the application of legal argument to the facts of specific cases.

II. Analysis of Legislation

There are several excellent sources that you can use to help you understand statutory interpretation.[1] In addition, the Department of Justice has published a series of online articles.[2] According to the website, both the English Legislative Language Committee and the English Legislative Language Working Group "have been working to improve the readability of legislation drafted in English. The work of these committees and groups is gathered in this text, *Legistics*. … The articles in *Legistics* have been formally accepted by management of the Branch and reflect Branch drafting policy." See Figure 10.2 on p. 10:10 to view the table of contents.

A. Elements of a Statute

The first task in the legal analysis of a client's issue is to determine, through the research process, whether statutory and regulatory provisions apply.

Statutes as enacted, which first appear in bill form, may be created for several reasons, including creating the law—e.g. *National Flag of Canada Act*;[3] amending an existing statute—e.g. *Accepting Schools Act, 2012*,[4] which amended education legislation to address bullying; or meeting a perceived need in relation to the government's agenda—e.g. *Safe Streets Act, 1999*,[5] which targeted aggressive solicitation

---

1   E.g. Donald J Gifford, Kenneth H Gifford & Michael I Jeffery, *How to Understand Statutes and By-Laws* (Scarborough, ON: Carswell, 1996); Ruth Sullivan, *Sullivan on the Construction of Statutes*, 5th ed (Markham, ON: LexisNexis, 2008) [Sullivan]; Randal N Graham, *Statutory Interpretation: Theory and Practice* (Toronto: Emond Montgomery, 2001) [Graham].

2   As of June 2013, *Legistics* is unavailable on the Justice Laws website. References to *Legistics* are based on the articles prior to June 2013 at <http://laws-lois.justice.gc.ca/eng/RelatedResources>.

3   SC 2012, c 12. The bill that created it is Bill C-288, 1st Sess, 41st Parl, 2012, *An Act respecting the National Flag of Canada* (assented to 28 June 2012), SC 2012, c 12.

4   SO 2012, c 5. The bill that created it is Bill 13, *An Act to amend the Education Act with respect to bullying and other matters*, 1st Sess, 40th Parl, 2012 (assented to 19 June 2012), SO 2012, c 5.

5   SO 1999, c 8. The bill that created it is *An Act to promote safety in Ontario by prohibiting aggressive solicitation, solicitation of persons in certain places and disposal of dangerous things in certain places, and to amend the Highway Traffic Act to regulate certain activities on roadways*, 3rd Sess, 36th Parl, 1999 (assented to 14 December 1999), SO 1999, c 8.

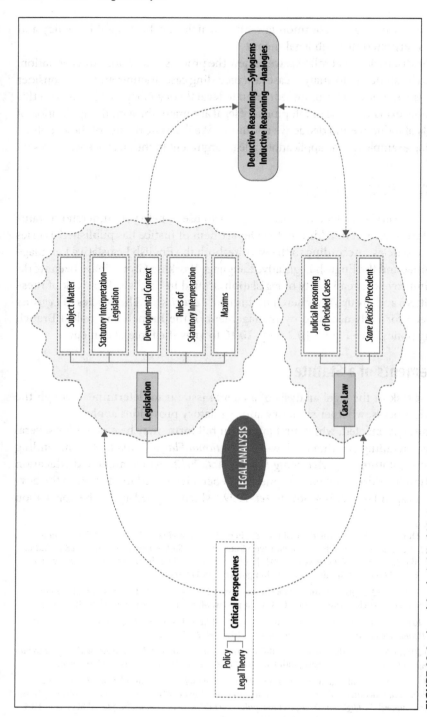

FIGURE 10.1 Legal Analysis Mind Map

or panhandling. (Chapters 3 and 5 discuss the federal and provincial law-making process.)

Statutes are formatted in a specific manner and with particular elements. Noteworthy elements include:

Legal citation. A legal citation follows the name of the statute. The citation identifies the legislature that created the statute, its year of enactment, and its unique chapter reference.

Long title. A statute may be given a long title that describes the scope of the Act. Although helpful in terms of providing a sense of the Act's overall purpose and resolving ambiguity about its meaning, the long title is unwieldy and is frequently replaced with a short title.

Short title. Statutes are often given a short title, which provides an efficient, official term of reference. Where available, a short title is used in place of the long title in legal citation.

Words of enactment. Enacting words are not found in every statute of Parliament or a legislature; however, when they are used, they are found immediately after the long title.

Preamble. The preamble is a short descriptive statement explaining the statute's context, which can be used as an interpretive guide to resolve ambiguity about the meaning of a section of the statute.

Purpose. Some statutes have a purpose section, which can help with a statute's interpretation because it articulates the specific purpose(s) for which the statute was created.

Parts, sections, subsections, paragraphs, and clauses. The substance of the legislation is often organized into large groupings (parts), then into sections, subsections, paragraphs, and clauses. Within this framework can be found the statutory scheme to achieve the legislative purpose. The statute may identify certain activities that are either mandated or prohibited, while an accompanying regulation may provide interpretive detail. Determining the organization of the statute helps with its interpretation. For example, definitions may be located in more than one place in a statute. Definitions that appear at the beginning of the statute may apply generally to the statute as a whole, while definitions that appear in only one part and not another apply to that part only.

Marginal notes. Marginal notes provide an interpretive aid by indicating the general subject matter covered by each section.

B. Word Meaning in Context: Parts of Speech, Grammar, Punctuation, Sentences, and Paragraphs

Statutory interpretation requires close attention to word choices, parts of speech, punctuation, and sentence and paragraph organization. A few of the more critical word choice distinctions are the following, as illustrated in Task 10.1:

- *May/shall.* The consequences of a provision that says a court "may" consider parties' income can differ from one that says a court "shall" consider parties' income. "May" indicates that a court has discretion to consider income. "Shall" indicates that a court must consider income; failure by a court to consider parties' income will constitute a legal error, which may provide grounds for one of the parties to appeal the decision.
- *Or/and.* The use of the conjunction "or" within a list of items provides a greater range of possibilities than the conjunction "and". Failure to recognize this difference can lead to an inaccurate assessment of a party's rights and responsibilities.
- *Notwithstanding.* Generally, "notwithstanding" means that the rights or obligations set out thereafter will, in specified circumstances, trump other rights and obligations established within the statute.

TASK 10.1

Applying Rules of Statutory Interpretation

Consider sections 5(1), 17(6.1), and 17(6.4) of the *Divorce Act*, RSC 1985, c 3 (2d Supp):

5(1) A court in a province has jurisdiction to hear and determine a variation proceeding **if**
(a) **either** former spouse is ordinarily resident in the province at the commencement of the proceeding; **or**
(b) **both** former spouses accept the jurisdiction of the court.
...

17(6.1) A court making a variation order in respect of a child support order **shall** do so in accordance with the applicable guidelines.
...

17(6.4) **Notwithstanding** subsection (6.1), a court **may** award an amount that is different from the amount that would be determined in accordance with the applicable guidelines on the consent of both spouses **if** it is satisfied that reasonable arrangements have been made for the support of the child to whom the order relates.

- First, note that paragraphs (a) and (b) of section 5(1) are prefaced by "if" and separated by "or". This means that the court has jurisdiction to hear the proceeding if either of the circumstances in paragraph (a) or (b) exists.

- Second, note that section 17(6.1) provides that a court shall determine child support obligations in accordance with prescribed guidelines. Therefore, in most cases the court is obliged to apply these guidelines. Section 17(6.4), however, carves out an exception to this mandatory application in situations where spouses have not followed the guidelines but have consented to other reasonable arrangements. In this case, use of the word "may" provides a judge with discretion to consider a child support award that departs from the guidelines "notwithstanding" the earlier statutory provision. However, a judge may still resort to the guidelines in making the support order even if spouses had consented to other reasonable arrangements.

Consult additional print or online sources to delve more deeply into the statutory interpretation of the above-noted sections.[6] For example, the table of contents on the *Legistics* website[7] (see Figure 10.2) provides separate article links for the words "notwithstanding" and "if", as well as for terms found under "Expressing Possibility", such as "may". Additional article links are provided for use of conjunctions (such as "and" and "or") under "Conjunctions between paragraphs". These articles explain not only the intent of the framers of the legislation but also how these words and phrases have been judicially considered.

Therefore, when interpreting statutes, not only must you examine the structure and organization of the statute, along with governing legislation that aids with statutory interpretation,[8] but you must also be mindful of the judicial decisions that have interpreted the legal meaning of the specific words and phrases used within a statute. Moreover, when courts determine the judicial meaning of these words and phrases, they do so not in isolation but in the context of their use within each sentence, applying accepted rules of grammar and punctuation.

However, when a statute's meaning remains unclear, courts rely on additional rules of interpretation.

---

6 *Supra* notes 1 and 2.

7 *Supra* note 2.

8 See e.g. *Interpretation Act*, RSC 1985, c I-21.

FIGURE 10.2 Department of Justice: Legistics—Table of Contents

Part 1—Words and Expressions	
Attributing meaning to terms	However
Body Corporate and Corporation	If, where and when
But	Members of Parliament
Comprise	Notwithstanding, alternatives to
Consider	One (pronominal use)
Days After	Possessives
Deem	Pursuant to
Definitions	References to Text in Columns
Everyone and Anyone	Restrictive elements
Expiry, expiration and end	Rounding of numbers
Expressing Obligations and Prohibitions	Series of Nouns
Expressing Permission, Powers or Rights	Such
Expressing Possibility	Terms and conditions
Expressing Universality	Themselves (singular)
First Nation(s)—Aboriginal	There—words
Formula Descriptions	They (singular)
Geographical names	Time periods
Gender-neutral Language	Triad separators in metric measurements
Hereby	

Part 2—Sentences	
Cross-references	Present indicative
More than one sentence in a section or subsection	Sentence structure: Complexity and organization

Part 3—Paragraphing	
What is paragraphing?	Conjunctions between paragraphs
Why paragraph?	Punctuation of paragraphs
How do you paragraph?	When should you paragraph?
The logical relationship among paragraphed elements	Table of factors and examples

Part 4—Punctuation	
Compounds and hyphenation	Em dashes

References	
Printed reference material	On-line reference material

Source: Department of Justice, online: <http://laws-lois.justice.gc.ca/eng/RelatedResources/> (and see note 2 above).

C. Rules of Statutory Interpretation and Maxims

In addition to considering statutory elements and the use of particular statutory language, courts apply further rules of interpretation. Analysis of these rules forms the basis for an entire law school course; the following discussion simply provides a brief starting point for the interpretive process.[9]

In the modern approach to interpretation:

> The words of an Act are to be read in their entire context and in their grammatical and ordinary sense harmoniously with the scheme of the Act, the object of the Act, and the intention of Parliament.[10]

1. The Three Rules of Statutory Interpretation

> [O]ur law recognizes three main approaches to all statutes: their usual names are (1) the "literal (plain meaning) rule"; (2) the "golden rule"; (3) the "mischief (*Heydon's Case*) rule." Any one of these three approaches may legitimately be adopted by your court in the interpretation of any statute: …[11]

Willis's summary of the three rules of interpretation remains a good account of the approaches taken by courts to resolve ambiguity in those situations where the intent of the drafters of the legislation is not obvious.

a. THE LITERAL, PLAIN MEANING, OR ORDINARY RULE

This rule requires the court to interpret the legislation in the context of accepted rules of grammar as commonly understood. Evolution of this rule now also allows a court to consider the "ordinary" meaning of legislative language and the broader purpose of the legislation.[12] The Supreme Court of Canada has confirmed that the "modern" approach to the interpretation of both common-law statutes and the Quebec *Civil Code* should be applied.[13] As a result, the backdating process, which was discussed in Chapter 4, may become relevant when attempting to interpret the meaning of the legislation.[14]

---

9   For a comprehensive discussion of rules of statutory interpretation, including the historical development of these rules, see Sullivan, *supra* note 1.

10   Elmer A Driedger, *Construction of Statutes*, 2d ed (Toronto: Butterworths, 1983) at 87.

11   John Willis, "Statute Interpretation in a Nutshell" (1938) 16 Can Bar Rev 1 at 9-10.

12   *2747-3174 Québec Inc v Quebec (Régie des permis d'alcool)*, [1996] 3 SCR 919 at para 150.

13   See *Rizzo & Rizzo Shoes Ltd (Re)*, [1998] 1 SCR 27; and *Épiciers Unis Métro-Richelieu Inc, division "Éconogros" v Collin*, 2004 SCC 59, [2004] 3 SCR 257.

14   For a discussion of the development of the rules of statutory interpretation, see Sullivan, *supra* note 1.

b. THE GOLDEN RULE

A court may modify the plain meaning of the statute if a literal interpretation would lead to an "absurd" result. Although the application of this rule can be challenging, the underlying assumption is that because Parliament or the legislature would not intend for legislation to have an absurd result, a court can examine the statute for both logical consistency and broader considerations, such as a just and reasonable outcome.[15]

c. MISCHIEF RULE

A court may examine the state of the law as it existed before the legislation, and consider the drafters' purpose in creating the law and the "mischief" they sought to correct through the remedy of legislation. Courts continue to consider the purpose of the legislation in their statutory interpretation.

2. Maxims

In addition to the three rules of statutory interpretation, courts may consider specific maxims when interpreting a statute's meaning. There are many maxims; a few of the most commonly applied are described below.[16]

- *Noscitur a sociis* means "know the thing by its associates", and *ejusdem generis* means "of the same class or group". These maxims are applicable when a list of specific items is followed by a more general term. The rule implied in the maxims is that the more general term can be interpreted with reference to the specific items.

- *Expressio unius est exclusio alterius* means "the expression of one thing means the exclusion of the other". This maxim is applicable when specific items are stated in a list of items and others are omitted. The rule implied in the maxim is that the omission was intended; otherwise, the language would have been expressly inclusive.

Although interpretive principles such as maxims can help a court determine a statute's meaning, they do not trump other interpretive aids. The overarching rule of statutory interpretation requires the court to determine the intention of the legislature, which "takes precedence over all maxims or canons or aids relating to statutory interpretation".[17]

---

15   See also Graham, *supra* note 1, for a discussion of the rules and maxims of statutory interpretation.

16   For an example of the *noscitur a sociis* maxim, see *R v Daoust*, 2004 SCC 6, [2004] 1 SCR 217 at para 51; for an example of the *ejusdem generis* maxim, see *Walker v Ritchie*, 2006 SCC 45, [2006] 2 SCR 428 at paras 24-25; and for an example of the *expressio unius est exclusio alterius* maxim, see *R v Multiform Manufacturing*, [1990] 2 SCR 624 at 631.

17   See *Century Services Inc v Canada (Attorney General)*, 2010 SCC 60, [2010] 3 SCR 379 at para 127, Abella J dissenting, citing *Ottawa Senators Hockey Club Corp (Re)* (2005), 73 OR (3d) 737 at para 42, 193 OAC 95 (CA).

D. Bilingual Legislation

Unique interpretive questions can arise within a legal system where legislation is drafted in more than one language. This is the case in Canada, where federal legislation, and that of a number of provinces, is drafted in both English and French. When legislation is enacted in both languages, both the English and French versions of a statute or regulation are official. In cases where the versions seem to have different meanings, a court must interpret the legislation to resolve the apparent discrepancy.

Often, a meaning that is common to both languages is identified and adopted. For example, in a case that dealt with whether imported rock lobsters should be categorized as "crustaceans/crustacés" or as "lobsters/homards", the Federal Court of Appeal reasoned that although an English interpretation of "lobster" could support clawless crustaceans, the same was not true of the French word "homard".[18] It was appropriate to use the shared "ordinary" meaning of "lobster/homard", which required the crustacean to have claws. As a result, the imported goods fell within the "crustaceans/crustacés" category.

TASK 10.2

Developing a Systematic Approach to Statutory Interpretation

■ Begin by reading the statute itself. Examine guidelines to meaning provided in the long title, preamble, and/or purpose sections.

■ Read individual sections to determine the steps taken to achieve the statute's purpose, including obligations, prohibitions, sanctions, and remedies.

■ Backdate the statute if necessary. Useful inferences about the purpose of the statute may be drawn from a study of the discussions held when the statute was in bill form.

■ Examine relevant federal or provincial interpretation statutes that provide general principles for the interpretation of all statutes for that jurisdiction.

■ Consider interpretive rules and maxims that may have been used by a court to resolve ambiguity; look for language in the judicial reasons that indicates which specific rules and maxims were applied by the court.

■ Explore the meaning of a court's analysis by referring to texts and websites that explain how these rules and maxims are applied.

---

18 *Deltonic Trading Corp v Deputy Minister of National Revenue, Customs & Excise* (1990), 113 NR 7, 3 TTR 242 (FCA).

III. Case Analysis

The next step in legal analysis is selecting and interpreting relevant judicial decisions. (This discussion builds on Chapter 6, which explains how to locate judicial decisions.) Relevancy is determined by choosing cases whose legal principles would apply to the client's facts and issues. Cases may include those that interpret relevant statutory or regulatory provisions or, in the absence of a statutory framework, that focus on common-law principles.

In interpreting the case before it, a court typically:

- reviews the principles of law that guide its decisions
- undertakes statutory interpretation or, if the case derives from the common law, addresses common-law principles
- provides support for those principles by citing specific legal authorities
- states whether it is bound by decided cases
- if it is not bound by decided cases, refers to cases that have considered similar issues and identifies persuasive aspects of the decisions, or perhaps distinguishes those that are not applicable
- if there is no Canadian law on point, considers law from foreign jurisdictions to determine whether similar issues have been considered outside Canada

Overall, this discussion forms the judicial reasoning of the case, and provides the basis for the conclusions that the court then draws to clarify the meaning and applicability of existing legal principles, which can then be applied to new facts and issues. This information, in summary form, is contained in case briefs. Cases that do not provide this type of reasoning process typically have little weight.

As you begin to assess judicial reasons arising from decided law and to summarize the principles in a case brief format, it becomes possible to examine trends and to synthesize legal principles, all of which is a precursor to developing a legal argument. However, before selecting a case to analyze, you must assess the weight of each case in the context of precedent and *stare decisis*.

A. Precedent and Stare Decisis

A significant premise of legal analysis in common-law jurisdictions is that similar cases should be treated alike.

This involves understanding the doctrines of precedent and *stare decisis*. The doctrine of precedent "consists of the rules which prescribe how prior cases must, may and can be used".[19]

---

19 William Twining & David Miers, *How to Do Things with Rules*, 5th ed (New York: Cambridge University Press, 2010) at 277.

The doctrine of precedent involves considering decided cases that have applied a legal principle to facts and issues similar to those of the client. The client's facts and issues are compared with those of decided cases, similarities and differences between the cases are identified, and then the judicial reasoning in the decided cases is considered.

The concept of *stare decisis*, however, means that "judges in a common law system are bound to follow precedent cases, decided by judges of higher courts, given a similar fact situation in the precedent case and the case at hand".[20]

The reasons given by a court to support its decision in one case compel similar rulings in similar situations in future cases. Where a higher court has rendered a decision on the basis of facts and issues that are sufficiently similar to a case being adjudicated by a lower court within the same jurisdiction, the lower court must follow the reasoning—the *binding authority*—expressed in the higher court's decision. The lower court must apply the principle established by the higher court within its jurisdiction, unless it can distinguish the earlier decision, either on its facts or on its issues.

Even if a lower court is not bound by another court's decision, it may follow or adopt the reasoning of a court of another jurisdiction, or a court of the same level of authority within the jurisdiction, as *persuasive authority*. This occurs when one court finds another court's reasoning about a similar issue sufficiently compelling to incorporate the reasoning into its decision. A court may also choose not to follow a non-binding decision, sometimes distinguishing it as sufficiently different on facts or issues, or even rejecting the reasoning of the court.

Under the doctrine of *stare decisis*, the Supreme Court of Canada is now the only court in Canada whose decisions have the potential to bind all other courts in Canada. A Court of Appeal decision in a province will be binding on all lower courts within that province only. Federal Court decisions constitute persuasive authority for provincial courts. Decisions from courts in other provinces and from jurisdictions outside Canada may be persuasive authority only; they cannot bind other courts.

B. Case Briefing Format

A case brief provides a summary of a judge's written decision. It is an organizational tool; as such, it may use any one of several different formats including IRAC (issue, rule, analysis, conclusion). Law students prepare case briefs to summarize the legal reasoning and legal principles of the cases discussed in their classes. Case briefs are beneficial for several reasons.

> First, the act of preparing and writing a summary of a case tends to fix it more firmly in the mind. Second, brief and accurate notes are helpful for

---

20   Gerald L Gall, *The Canadian Legal System*, 5th ed (Toronto: Thomson Carswell, 2004) at 31.

review. Third, and more importantly, making a summary of the significant facts of the case requires skill and judgment. The process of picking out the significant facts from a mass of those that are insignificant is one of the lawyer's most important skills, and the best way to learn to do it is by practice.[21]

No single approach is universally applicable; the choice of format for a case brief is an individual preference.

Typically, a reported judicial decision includes the court's judgment and a number of standard and optional elements. Standard elements are:

- the case name, also referred to as the "style of cause", followed by the case citation, which is used to locate the case in print and online
- the court level, jurisdiction, and name of the presiding judge(s)
- the date of hearing and the date the decision was released

The following may also be provided:

- subject keywords from the case, used to organize the case in research subject indexes
- a headnote, which is a case summary provided by editorial staff of the case publisher

    NB: A headnote is not primary law, and should not be cited as legal authority when briefing cases or constructing legal argument.
- cases, legislation, and secondary sources referred to by the court in its decision; cases on appeal may include details of the appeal history, followed by the names of counsel appearing for the respective parties in this case

The judgment itself is then set out.

- The judgment begins after the judge's surname appears. In an appeal, where more than one judge must decide the case, concurring judges' names, in parentheses, follow the name of the judge writing the majority decision. If the court has not reached a unanimous decision, the justice writing the minority decision will be listed, followed by the names, if any, of those who agree with the minority decision. With a unanimous decision, the names

---

21   Stephen Waddams, *Introduction to the Study of Law*, 6th ed (Toronto: Carswell, 2004) at 22. See also Tracy Turner, "Finding Consensus in Legal Writing Discourse Regarding Organizational Structure: A Review and Analysis of the use of IRAC and Its Progenies" (2012) 9 JAWLD 351. This article identifies many variations of the IRAC structure used in legal writing and identifies core principles of effective organization for legal analysis.

of the justice writing the decision may not be provided, and the phrase "For the Court" may replace the justices' names.

- The judgment typically provides a synopsis of the relevant facts of the case, the legal issues, the decision, and the reasons for decision. The narrative style ranges from informal to formal. Lengthy and more complex cases may include organizational devices such as subheadings or, in rare cases, a table of contents.[22]

Given the variety of formats available for a case brief, a good approach is to summarize the case with a series of questions in mind. The "who, what, when, where, how, and why" analysis described in Chapter 2, modified slightly, provides the necessary framework to prepare a case brief.

TASK 10.3

Case Briefing Tips

- Read the entire case at least once before beginning to prepare a case brief.
  Visual learners might consider developing a colour-coded system to make case brief preparation easier: use different coloured highlighters to highlight particular aspects of the text—e.g. green for facts, red for legal issues, yellow for *ratio decidendi*, blue for judicial reasons, and pink for dissent.

- Construct a complete legal citation, including court level and page numbers, to ensure future access to essential information.

- Write the facts section after completing all other portions of the case brief, because legally relevant or outcome-determinative facts are more easily ascertained at that point.

- Develop shorthand notations and be consistent in their use—e.g. P for plaintiff and D for defendant.

- Add supplementary information obtained from class discussion as required.

C. Applying Case Briefing Skills

1. *Read the Decision*

Locate the following decision in print or online: *Rowe v Canning*, 1994 CanLII 4474, 117 Nfld & PEIR 353, 4 MVR (3d) 269 (Nfld SCTD). Read the case, and try to answer the questions "who, what, when, where, how, and why".

---

22   E.g. *Carter v Canada (Attorney General)*, 2012 BCSC 886, 261 CRR (2d) 1.

2. Create a Case Brief

Once you have read the court's decision, you can prepare a case brief, which is a summary of the judge's written decision. You may wish to choose the IRAC format as discussed earlier in this chapter, or a different organizational tool. Include the style of cause, year of decision, court level, relevant facts, legal issues, and the court's decision at a minimum, as illustrated by the following example of a case brief synopsis.

CASE BRIEF: SYNOPSIS

Case Name and Citation
Rowe v Canning (1994), 117 Nfld & PEIR 353, 1994 CanLII 4474 (Nfld SC (TD)).

Relevant Facts
Rowe lost control of the motorcycle he was operating after it was hit by a small horse/pony and crashed. Rowe and his passenger, Furey, sued the Cannings (father and son) for damages, claiming that, by allowing the horse to roam, they were negligent. Initially, the Cannings denied liability, claiming that it was not their horse that had struck the motorcycle. Upon a finding by the court that the Cannings' horse had struck Rowe's motorcycle, the Cannings argued, in the alternative, that Rowe was contributorily negligent because he did not keep a proper lookout while driving. The accident occurred in the town of Conception Bay, Newfoundland.

Legal Issues
1. Did the Cannings own the horse involved in the accident?
2. If the Cannings owned the horse, were they negligent under either:
   (a) a breach of a duty created by municipal regulations, or
   (b) a breach of a duty at common law?
3. Was Rowe contributorily negligent for failing to keep a proper lookout?

Result
The trial judge found as fact that the Cannings were the owners of the horse that hit Rowe's motorcycle. Further, they breached their legal duty as animal owners to prevent their animals from roaming at large. This duty arose both at common law and under a Conception Bay South municipal regulation: the judge found liability pursuant to the regulation. Thus, they were liable to Rowe and Furey for damages. Rowe was not contributorily negligent because the judge found that he had kept a proper lookout.

Law students can use case brief synopses as an effective tool to prepare for class discussion. Frequently, beginning law students are provided with casebooks that include excerpts of cases that explain relevant legal principles. These excerpts often form the basis for class discussion. Using a case brief synopsis can help a student distill the essential factual elements and legal principles from the case; where appropriate, additional information can be added following class discussion. These case brief synopses are also useful for exam preparation purposes in that they provide a succinct statement of the relevant legal principles that may be tested during a law school examination.

The case brief synopsis is a condensed version of the case brief, which proves a more detailed case summation. This more expansive case brief as demonstrated in the next example may be appropriate when summarizing the law prior to completing complex legal documents such as memoranda, or facta, or in preparation for oral argument at a moot court competition, or even during trial preparation.

CASE BRIEF

Case Name and Citation
Rowe v Canning (1994), 117 Nfld & PEIR 353, 1994 CanLII 4474 (Nfld SC (TD)).

Relevant Facts
Rowe lost control of the motorcycle he was operating after it was hit by a small horse/pony and crashed. Rowe and his passenger, Furey, sued the Cannings (father and son) for damages, claiming that, by allowing the horse to roam, they were negligent. Initially, the Cannings denied liability, claiming that it was not their horse that had struck the motorcycle. Earlier that day, Canning (son) had tethered the horse to a steel peg, but at some point it had escaped its tether. It was found not far from the accident location near the time of the accident.

Upon a finding by the court that the Cannings' horse had struck Rowe's motorcycle, the Cannings argued, in the alternative, that Rowe was contributorily negligent because he did not keep a proper lookout while driving. The accident occurred in the town of Conception Bay South, Newfoundland.

Legal Issues
1. Did the Cannings own the horse involved in the accident?
2. If the Cannings owned the horse, were they negligent under either:
   (a) a breach of a duty created by municipal regulations, or
   (b) a breach of a duty at common law?
3. Was Rowe contributorily negligent for failing to keep a proper lookout?

Holding
Yes, the Cannings are the owners of the horse involved in the accident.

The Cannings are liable in negligence for damages to Rowe and Furey. First, they breached a duty created by the municipal regulation. Second, even if the regulation had not been in effect, the court would have found a breach of duty under the common law.

Rowe was not contributorily negligent because the judge found that he did keep a proper lookout.

Legal and Factual Basis for Holding

The trial judge found as a fact that the Cannings were the owners of the horse that struck the motorcycle.

There are two distinct bases to find liability in negligence. First, in Conception Bay South, municipal regulations require animal owners to restrain their animals from roaming at large. Although the *Livestock Act*, RSN 1990, c L-20 may apply in some circumstances, on the facts of this case it did not because the horse did not fall within the class of animals prohibited from running at large by the Act, nor was there a ministerial order in place.

The court found that the Cannings were liable pursuant to the regulation.

Second, there is a common-law duty on owners to prevent their animals from roaming at large where the volume of traffic means an accident would be likely. The judge applied the decision of *Fleming v Atkinson*, [1959] SCR 513, 1959 CanLII 10. The Supreme Court decided that ordinary rules of negligence apply to straying animals, considering all the surrounding circumstances, including the nature of the highway and the amount and nature of the traffic. Therefore, more generally, for jurisdictions where municipal regulations have not been created, there is a common-law duty on owners to prevent their animals from roaming at large. Had the Cannings not been found liable pursuant to the municipal regulation, they would have been found liable in breach of a common-law duty.

Finally, based on the facts, the judge found that Rowe was keeping a proper lookout on the road and, therefore, was not contributorily negligent.

IV. Policy, Legislation, and Case Law

A. Examining Underlying Policy

In the course of legal analysis of a client's issue, the solution can sometimes be determined from an analysis of existing legislation and case law. This occurs when the legal issue either has been contemplated by the drafters of governing legislation or has been the subject of judicial interpretation by a binding court of law.

> **Policy:** The general principles by which a government is guided in its management of public affairs, or the legislature in its measures.
>
> —*Black's Law Dictionary*, 6th ed

However, many legal issues cannot be determined solely through an examination of existing legislation or case law. For example, sometimes the legal question will have arisen because of changes in underlying societal structures or values. Sometimes legislation has been created in the context of competing policy interests— e.g. balancing the costs of implementing a social program, such as universal child care, with prospective future benefits. Frequently, these types of legal problems, which require a balancing of legal interests rather than a clearly delineated application of a legal principle, occur in the context of constitutional or human rights litigation. In these cases, consider whether an examination of underlying policy will provide relevant information to help with a legal analysis.

Policy is not law; however, policy guides the interpretation of law. Therefore, when a novel legal issue that the courts have not yet considered is brought forward, knowledge of underlying policy initiatives or directives allows for the development of a legal argument supported by policy considerations. For example, a government body may be asked to interpret its legislation in a way that is consistent with the underlying policy that led to the creation of the statute.

Public Policy: The principle of law which holds that no subject can lawfully do that which has a tendency to be injurious to the public or against the public good. ... The term "policy" as applied to a statute, regulation, rule of law, course of action, or the like, refers to its probable effect, tendency, or object, considered with reference to the social or political well-being of the state. Thus, certain classes of acts are said to be "against public policy," when the law refuses to enforce or recognize them, on the grounds that they have a mischievous tendency, so as to be injurious to the interests of the state, apart from illegality or immorality.

—*Black's Law Dictionary*, 6th ed

Sources of policy information include:

- *Existing legislation.* Consult the legislative debates and committee reports that considered the legislation or its amendments while in bill form.[23] Also, consult government websites, which frequently include policy statements about the development and application of their legislation.

- *Existing case law.* Review the sources considered by the court to determine whether policy factors were considered in the judgment.

- *Authored works.* Review articles and treatises for analysis of legal developments that may have influenced case law or legislation.

- *Non-governmental and professional organizations.* Search the websites of organizations that interact with government for collected policy information relevant to their work.

- *Law reform organizations.* Look for posted information, often commissioned, critiquing government policy.

---

23   Review Chapter 3 for the process for locating federal debates; see specific provincial chapters for provincial processes. In addition, review the discussion in Chapter 7 about locating commentary.

When determining whether research should include an examination of policy, consider whether the law is well settled or in a stage of review or reform, or whether the dispute a court must settle requires a balancing of competing interests. In such situations, examine how policy information can be integrated into legal argument. (This topic is discussed in Chapter 11.)

V. Critical Perspectives on Case Law and Legislation

Critical reading, or making analytical judgments of the text, is essential to legal analysis. Understanding the meaning within the text is part of the first stage of legal analysis. Consequently, when analyzing legislation, judicial decisions, or secondary sources of law, law students and lawyers should keep in mind:

- What is the context of the text?
- What purpose does the material serve—why does it exist?
- What is the source of the material?
- Who created the material?

When you read cases and review legislation, awareness of the theoretical rationale(s) underpinning the legal rule allows you to consider the law's development at a deeper level. Consider the assumptions inherent in the law; such understanding is a powerful tool for law reform. For example, one decision-maker might decide that a contract should be enforced because it was entered into by two autonomous individuals who freely consented to the agreement. This decision would reflect a liberal emphasis on individual autonomy. Another decision-maker might decide that the apparent autonomy of these individuals must be assessed within the context of the inequalities generated by the gender or race dynamics at play. This approach could reflect feminist legal theory or critical race theory.

Although it is impossible to capture the rich array of legal theory discourse in existence, a brief introduction is provided below.

A. Naturalism, Positivism, Realism, and Critical Legal Studies

Legal philosophers argue incessantly about the nature of law itself, and the relationship between law and morals. The most common debates revolve around naturalism, positivism, and realism, with the latter being a relative newcomer to the conversation.[24]

---

24 Much of the information in this section is derived from the following sources: Richard F Devlin, "Jurisprudence for Judges: Why Legal Theory Matters for Social Context Education" (2001) 27

Naturalism finds its roots in writings as far back as the 11th century. Essentially, naturalists claim that law is universal, objective, and able to transcend political or historical contexts. Naturalists assume that there is a relationship between law and morality, and they understand the law as being derived from a source distinct from, and superior to, humans. Naturalists argue that law consists of a series of propositions derived from nature through the process of reasoning.[25]

A reaction to naturalism can be found in *positivism*, which became popular in the 19th century. Positivism questions the connection between law and morals claimed by naturalists. Positivists take the position that what the law is and what it should be entail different inquiries. While most positivist thinkers would agree that it is important to consider what the law should be, their position is that this should be done separately from the determination of the existence and content of the law itself. Positivism still influences much legal thought, though its emphasis on the formal validity of law has been criticized as leading to unjust outcomes.[26]

In the 1920s and 1930s, both naturalism and positivism were challenged by *realism*. Legal realists understand law as indeterminate and always changing, and they reject the proposition that rules determine the outcome of cases. In the 1970s, a broad umbrella movement known as *critical legal studies* emerged, with features that are distinct from the realist movement.

Critical legal theorists challenge the alleged existence of a universal, rational foundation of law. Critical legal theory does not view law as a distinctive and discrete discipline, and its proponents take the position that law can never exist independently from politics and morality. Specifically, adherents of critical legal theory assert that the law reproduces society's economic and political power.[27]

Of growing importance to lawyers and courts is the development of critical jurisprudence that focuses on how the law affects particular groups. Given that, until recently, the law was predominantly articulated and enforced by white, heterosexual males, it is not surprising that critical legal theorists find room to critique various aspects of the law from these perspectives.

Queen's LJ 161; Raymond Wacks, *Philosophy of Law: A Very Short Introduction* (Oxford: Oxford University Press, 2006); Dorothy Brown, "Fighting Racism in the Twenty-First Century" (2004) 61 Wash & Lee Law Rev 1485; Brenda Cossman, "Sexuality, Queer Theory, and 'Feminism After': Reading and Rereading the Sexual Subject" (2004) 49 McGill LJ 847, *McGill Law Journal* online: <http://lawjournal.mcgill.ca/documents/Cossman.pdf>.

25   Devlin, *supra* note 24 at 171; Wacks, *supra* note 24 at 3.

26   Devlin, *supra* note 24 at 175-176.

27   Wacks, *supra* note 24 at 92-93.

B. Feminist Legal Theory

Feminist legal theory has evolved into several branches. Among the best known are *liberal feminist theory* and *radical feminist theory*.

Liberal feminist theory's roots lie with principles of liberalism. The liberal mindset is dominant within the current Canadian legal system. Liberals assume the importance of individual autonomy, and take the position that law, and the state generally, should function to provide each citizen with sufficient opportunities to pursue his or her own rational choices, to the extent that this pursuit does not infringe on the liberty of others. Liberal feminists argue that because men and women are equally rational, their opportunities to exercise rational choices should also be equal.[28] This approach might be understood as the quest for "formal" equality under the law. Early advances in women's legal rights, such as the right for married women to own property and the right for women to vote, were prompted by formal equality arguments.

In contrast, radical feminists argue that simply incorporating women within existing legal structures is insufficient, because law is not neutral, and as such its application to women will still often lead to unjust results.[29] They advocate for "substantive equality", which might require, in the light of women's unequal social status, that women be treated differently in order to achieve actual equality. Radical feminists strive to change the patriarchal system that subjugates women. One key approach to this endeavour is to articulate the gender implications of rules and practices that may initially seem neutral. Another is to challenge the legitimacy of norms that claim to be representative of the community, and, where necessary, to recognize gender-specific legal norms. One example of such recognition is found in the decision of *R v Lavallee*,[30] in which the Supreme Court of Canada held that expert evidence of "battered woman syndrome" could be accepted in support of a self-defence claim.[31]

C. Critical Race Theory

Critical race theory began to gather strength in the mid-1970s, and has continued to criticize the law's slow rate of progress in promoting and protecting racial equality. It examines the impact that the law and legal traditions have had on people of colour as members of a group rather than as individuals, and seeks to

---

28   *Ibid* at 102.

29   Cossman, *supra* note 24 at footnote 51.

30   [1990] 1 SCR 852.

31   Devlin, *supra* note 24 at 186. Devlin also discusses "integrative" feminism as a branch of feminism that highlights the limitations of a gender-neutral perspective.

expose the ways in which the law is neither neutral nor objective, but rather designed to support the subordination of people of colour.[32]

Much of the work in critical race theory has exposed problems within the criminal justice system, but its scope encompasses other areas as well. In *Van de Perre v Edwards*,[33] a Supreme Court of Canada case dealing with a custody dispute between a Caucasian mother and an African-American father, a number of parties intervened to provide the court with perspectives on the importance of making a decision that properly took into account the need for children of colour to be exposed to their cultural heritage. The Court held, contrary to the intervenors' argument, that although race is always an important consideration in custody issues involving mixed-race parentages, where it had not been presented as a key issue by the parties themselves, it should not be entertained as a key factor within the decision. The fact that the Supreme Court of Canada was told that the parties had been reluctant to raise the race issue because of its political sensitivity[34] illustrates the ongoing relevance of critical race theory.

D. First Nations Jurisprudence

In recent years, *First Nations jurisprudence* has developed in reaction to the assumption that white legal structures are and should be determinative of both our common-law and civil-law regimes.[35]

A great deal of First Nations jurisprudence aims to reveal coercive aspects of the law. Examples of coercion include the establishment of reserves, which have served to disenfranchise and marginalize Aboriginal people, and the establishment of residential schools, in which thousands of Aboriginal children were separated from their families and suffered abuse at the hands of institutional personnel.[36]

Over time, the scope of critique has broadened to encompass scrutiny of the criminal justice system and its discriminatory approaches to First Nations people.[37] One specific aspect of the criminal law system that has been called into question is sentencing practices, which, by calling on neutral factors such as prior criminal records and employment history, can result in systemic discrimination. Such criticism influenced 1996 amendments to the *Criminal Code* to introduce restorative

---

32   Brown, *supra* note 24 at 1485-1486.

33   2001 SCC 60, [2001] 2 SCR 1014.

34   *Ibid* at para 45.

35   Devlin, *supra* note 24 at 190.

36   See JR Miller, "Troubled Legacy: A History of Native Residential Schools" (2003) 66 Sask L Rev 357.

37   PA Monture-Okanee & ME Turpel, "Aboriginal Peoples and Canadian Criminal Law: Rethinking Justice" (1992) 26 UBC L Rev 239.

justice principles into sentencing.[38] Restorative justice focuses on harm done to both victims and the community, and on restoring victims and communities through a process whereby all of the parties who are affected by the offence come together to determine how to deal with the results of the offence.[39]

Some Aboriginal theorists believe that it is not possible to incorporate the perspectives of First Nations people into the existing legal structures, and that separate criminal justice systems are required. Others suggest that it may be possible for non-Aboriginal judges and First Nations communities to bridge the divide in perspectives if judges are willing to rely on First Nations narratives[40] to improve their understanding of First Nations perspectives.

E. Gay/Lesbian Theory and Queer Theory

During the past decade in Canada, the work of *gay/lesbian legal theorists* and activists has led to significant changes to the legal landscape. Much of this work has focused on challenges to discriminatory laws that violate the equality guarantees under section 15 of the *Canadian Charter of Rights and Freedoms*. In 2004, the Supreme Court of Canada was called upon in *Reference re Same-Sex Marriage*[41] to assess the constitutionality of proposed federal legislation aimed at legalizing same-sex marriages in Canada. The legislation was drafted after a number of courts across the country had declared unconstitutional the common-law principle that the definition of marriage consisted of "one man and one woman".[42]

Critics suggest that the fact that progress has been made toward formal equality does not mean that the legal system neither discriminates against nor holds stereotypes about gays and lesbians. One author has argued that lesbian and gay parents risk negative outcomes in custody cases if they do not conform to beliefs about acceptable gay sexual conduct, which means quiet and apolitical behaviour.[43]

---

38 *Criminal Code*, RSC 1985, c C-46, Part XXIII.

39 Megan Stephens, "Lessons from the Front Lines in Canada's Restorative Justice Experiment: The Experience of Sentencing Judges" (2007) 33 Queen's LJ 19.

40 Devlin, *supra* note 24 at 191-192.

41 2004 SCC 79, [2004] 3 SCR 698.

42 The legislation in question was subsequently enacted as the *Civil Marriage Act*, SC 2005, c 33.

43 Shelley Gavigan, "Mothers, Other Mothers, and Others: The Legal Challenges and Contradictions of Lesbian Parents" in Dorothy Chunn & Dany Lacombe, eds, *Law as a Gendering Practice* (Toronto: Oxford University Press, 2000) 101.

VI. Conclusion

The information in this chapter has introduced the foundations for the development of thorough legal analysis. Chapter 11 builds on this information by explaining how to synthesize legal principles derived from the analysis of primary law, considering policy and theory where appropriate, and then explaining how to develop legal arguments that bring facts and law together.

Developing Legal Arguments   11

CONTENTS

LEARNING OUTCOMES

By the end of this chapter, you should be able to:

- Identify the purpose and structure of a legal argument
- Use inductive and deductive reasoning to formulate legal arguments
- Predict the outcome by summarizing the legal argument conclusions
- Consider the distinction between sound legal argument and fallacious argument

Writing Tasks

I. Purpose of a Legal Argument

To provide sound legal advice, a lawyer must know both the strengths and weaknesses of the client's claim and, to the extent possible, the strengths and weaknesses of the claims of the other parties to the dispute. This understanding is accomplished through the construction of *legal arguments*. First, the lawyer identifies the relevant legal principles that support the client's position. Next, the lawyer tests the strength and validity of the client's arguments by formulating *counterarguments*, taking the position of the other side to the dispute and searching for weaknesses in the client's position. By considering not only the strengths but also the limitations of the client's position, the lawyer can anticipate the arguments that the client will face from well-prepared opposing counsel should the matter go to court. The process of examining both sides to the dispute also provides an opportunity to refute the counterargument, thereby strengthening the client's overall position.

Once the points of argument have been fully explored, the lawyer can provide the client with a legal opinion, which is an informed prediction of the likely outcome of the dispute. The development of a sound legal opinion is predicated on comprehensive legal research, because the applicable statutory and case law form the legal basis of the argument. Once the relevant law has been determined, the facts of the case are applied to the law, and then the strongest arguments to be made on behalf of the client are identified. At this point, the lawyer and the client can begin to explore options for resolving the outstanding legal issues, and determine whether the dispute is destined for a formal dispute resolution process such as a trial or hearing, an alternative dispute resolution process, or an informal resolution between the parties.

The sections that follow explain the process by which legal arguments are developed through *inductive reasoning*, using analogies, and through *deductive reasoning*, using syllogisms.

II. Developing Arguments Through Inductive and Deductive Reasoning: An Introduction

A. Inductive Reasoning: Begin with an Analogy

An analogy is a comparison between two objects, situations, or ideas that enables one to classify the similarities and differences between the two. It then becomes possible to create a class or set of similar items with associated qualities, and exclude or distinguish others that do not belong to that set. For example, one might compare a violin and a clarinet and put them together in the class of "musical instruments". Examining both the similarities and differences between the two objects, one could then reason that an oboe, but not a lamp, would belong to the same class.

In law, analogical reasoning is used to predict an outcome by analyzing previously decided cases. Although the facts of different cases are rarely the same, a court will compare the facts and issues of the case before it with the facts and issues of earlier cases. If the facts and issues are similar, and if the reasoning of the previous decision is sound, the court may adopt a similar approach, and reach a similar conclusion. Cases that differ on their facts and issues will be distinguished. The reasoning in the decided case may be either persuasive or binding, depending on the court that heard the earlier case. (See Chapter 10 on the difference between persuasive and binding authorities.) Precedent cases are those cases that contain the basic legal analysis on which other courts choose to anchor their decisions when faced with a similar issue; however, precedent cases do not have to be binding. The law thus develops through judicial interpretation of individual cases.

When a client seeks legal advice, the lawyer first locates the relevant law and analyzes it, and then assesses the similarities and differences between previously decided cases and the client's situation. The lawyer can predict a likely outcome by determining whether the client's case is more congruent with one line of decisions and less so with another. If the case brings forward a novel point of law not previously considered, the lawyer can argue that, on the basis of decided law, a court should adopt a specific approach that has greater commonality to the client's situation.

Inductive reasoning builds on analogical reasoning. By examining the facts and issues of specific cases, assessing their similarities and differences, noting the result, and then classifying the outcomes, the lawyer can identify a specific inclusory or exclusory rule that can be used to predict the likely outcome of future cases.

Figure 11.1 represents a prediction of the outcome of cases 2 and 3 based on the knowledge of the outcome of case 1. If the facts of case 2 are identical to those of case 1, then the outcome is predictable with a high degree of certainty because of the application of *stare decisis*. However, if the factors are only partially congruent, the outcome is less certain, leading to the question, "How will case 3 be decided?"

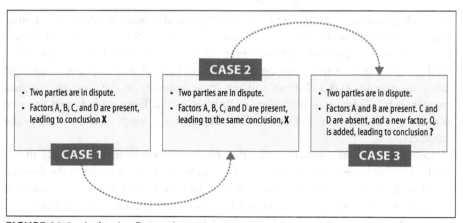

FIGURE 11.1 Inductive Reasoning

One lawyer may attempt to argue that case 3 is similar enough to cases 1 and 2 to warrant the same conclusion because all three cases contain factors A and B, and downplay the absence in case 3 of factors C and D and the presence of new factor Q. Another lawyer may attempt to distinguish case 3, highlighting the absence of factors C and D and the presence of new factor Q.

As cases are decided about the same legal issue, one or more rules will ultimately emerge that can be applied to predict future case outcomes. Rarely if ever will one case be so similar to another on the facts that its outcome can be predicted by direct reference to the decision making of the decided case. However, a court's analysis of the similarities and differences between previously decided cases and the case before it will provide the judicial reasoning for the court to either apply or distinguish decided case law.

A comprehensive legal research process will lead you to existing cases that may be relevant to your legal issue. Once you have identified cases that might be relevant, a two-step analytical process, described below, provides the basis of inductive reasoning.

1. Categorize Case Information

The research process provides you with cases to review to determine their relevance and weight. First, read the whole case, not just the headnote. Determine the legal issues before the court. Identify the factual basis the court considered in determining each issue. Examine the legal basis for the decision—i.e. the primary law the court considered for each issue. Determine the outcome and the judicial reasons on which the decision for each issue was based. Once you have gathered this information from each case, the next stage is to prepare a comparative analysis to determine case relevance and weight.

2. Prepare a Comparative Analysis of Similarities and Differences Between and Among Cases

The process of inductive reasoning includes examining the similarities and differences between and among case facts and issues. This process may be called synthesis, fusion, or amalgamation. By noting distinctive similarities and differences between and among cases, the lawyer can predict whether the rules arising from the cases are either applicable or distinguishable from the client's legal issue. In some situations, it may be difficult to determine whether the case is similar enough for the rule to apply, or whether the differences require the case to be distinguished. If the case is favourable to the client, the lawyer will have to argue why the rule should be followed; if the case is unfavourable to the client, the lawyer will have to argue why the case should be distinguished.

Prediction of an outcome on the basis of inductive reasoning, which predicts a future outcome based on past similar events, is explained in the next section. However, inductive reasoning is only one method used to formulate arguments. A lawyer must also be able to create an argument using deductive reasoning, which is explained later in this chapter.

B. Using Inductive Reasoning to Develop a Legal Argument

Consider the following fact hypothetical.[1]

Inductive and Deductive Reasoning Hypothetical

Consider the following fact hypothetical:

Amir Shybani and Rita Haddad

Amir Shybani ("Amir") and Rita Haddad ("Rita") became engaged three months ago. Because some family members did not approve of their relationship, they decided to get married without informing their families. At 6:00 a.m. on 13 July 2xxx, they left their home in Mendossa on Amir's motorcycle for the two-hour drive to Kinnton, where they planned to be married by a justice of the peace.

As they rode along, the early morning fog lifted, the sun rose, and the day became warmer. The couple became uncomfortable in their leather motorcycle suits and helmets. However, both knew that this gear provided the best protection in case of an accident.

At about 7:30 a.m. Rita, who was the passenger, saw a dog dart from the side of the road and run toward the motorcycle. She cried out a warning and squeezed Amir's arm to get his attention. Amir swerved sharply. Rita was thrown from the motorcycle. She slid across the road, injuring her hand when her glove came off. Although Amir was uninjured, his motorcycle was damaged when it fell onto the road. The couple saw the dog, trailing its leash, as it disappeared into the brush on the other side of the road.

On the same morning as Amir and Rita's accident, Cramwell Brook, the owner of the Cramwell's Kennel, left his house at 7:00 a.m. to take his dog Stormy, a Pomeranian, for a walk. Because Stormy was not yet following basic commands, Cramwell was providing additional obedience training. Just as Cramwell was leaving with Stormy, a client drove up to the kennel gate. When Cramwell opened the gate to let the client enter, Stormy broke free and disappeared into the adjacent field. Cramwell called the Animal Control bylaw officer to inform her of Stormy's disappearance and set out to look for Stormy. The officer found Stormy at

---

1 The authors gratefully acknowledge permission from Shelley Kierstead, Suzanne Gordon, and Sherifa Elkhadem, authors of *The Law Workbook: Developing Skills for Legal Research and Writing*, 2d ed (Toronto: Emond Montgomery, 2011), to adapt the legal reasoning and fact hypothetical based on "Romeo and Juliet" for discussion in this text.

9:00 a.m. in a nearby field. Stormy did not appear to be injured. In addition, one witness to the accident, who was travelling in a hot air balloon at the time, came forward and informed police that he had seen a dog run across the road in front of the motorcycle around the time of the accident. The hot air balloonist could not determine whether the dog had hit the motorcycle.

The doctor who treated Rita told her that her motorcycle suit and helmet had saved her from serious injury. However, because she is a cashier in a grocery store, the injury to her hand will prevent her from working for the next few months. Rita needs money to meet her short-term expenses, which include her rent and therapy for the injury to her hand. Amir, a self-employed writer, would like his motorcycle repaired.

1. Identify the Relevant Facts

- Undertake a factual analysis—who, what, when, where, how, and why
- List the key people involved and provide a short description of each
- Identify the key events, including time and location, and describe how they unfolded
- Identify any unknown or assumed facts that might be relevant

NB: At this point, legally relevant material facts that will determine the outcome may be difficult to assess with certainty. Be prepared to revise the relevant facts as the legal analysis develops.

2. Assess the Significance of the Events

- Determine the complaint or claim that Shybani and Haddad might make against Brook—i.e. how were they affected?
- List the facts or evidence that Shybani or Haddad might use to support these claims.
- List the facts or evidence that Brook might rely on to justify or excuse the claim against him.

Focusing solely on the material facts may exclude contextual information required to appreciate the circumstances of a particular problem or dispute. Therefore, you should try to identify additional facts that help to explain the events and circumstances. Frequently, you can discover such facts by asking the question "why". Include these facts in your analysis when they tie in to the legal issues—e.g. because they describe a pattern of behaviour, the predisposition of one of the parties, or a relevant post-event occurrence.

3. *Identify the Relevant Primary Law*

As discussed in previous chapters, you may prefer to search for legislation first and then locate case law. Alternatively, you could use secondary sources to identify cases that explain relevant legal principles as well as applicable legislation.

For the hypothetical problem discussed in this section, a topic search was completed first. Although analysis of legislation would typically be undertaken before a review of case law, the fact hypothetical does not identify the jurisdiction where the accident occurred. Therefore, the jurisprudence was reviewed first. Cases selected included a case decided by the Supreme Court of Canada, as well as four cases from lower courts of different jurisdictions.[2] Legislation discussed in these cases was then reviewed, and, ultimately, legislation that was considered in each case was identified and incorporated in the overall analysis.

Case law considered for this hypothetical includes:

Cases

Rowe v Canning (1994), 117 Nfld & PEIR 353, 1994 CanLII 4474 (Nfld SC (TD))
Fleming v Atkinson, [1959] SCR 513, 1959 CanLII 10
Spanton v Laviolette (1977), 19 OR (2d) 21, 83 DLR (3d) 740 (Sm Cl Ct)
Bujold v Dempsey (1996), 181 NBR (2d) 111 (QB)
Ruckheim v Robinson, [1995] 4 WWR 284, 1 BCLR (3d) 46 (CA)

In each case:

- An animal strayed onto a highway, causing the driver of a vehicle to lose control, with resulting injuries or damage.
- The drivers' actions as contributors to the accident were assessed.

---

2   Note that legislation is binding only on individuals who are within the legislative body's jurisdiction.

4. Brief the Cases: Compare Similarities and Differences in Facts and Questions of Law

TASK 11.2

Case Brief: Rowe v Canning

Case Name and Citation

Rowe v Canning (1994), 117 Nfld & PEIR 353, 1994 CanLII 4474 (Nfld SC (TD)).

Relevant Facts

Rowe lost control of the motorcycle he was operating after it was hit by a small horse and crashed. Rowe and his passenger Furey sued the Cannings (father and son) for damages, claiming that, by allowing the horse to roam, they were negligent. Initially, the Cannings denied liability, claiming that it was not their horse that had struck the motorcycle. Earlier that day Canning (son) had tethered the horse to a steel peg, but at some point, it had escaped its tether. It was found not far from the accident location near the time of the accident.

Upon a finding by the court that the Cannings' horse had struck Rowe's motorcycle, the Cannings argued, in the alternative, that Rowe was contributorily negligent because he did not keep a proper lookout while driving. The accident occurred in the town of Conception Bay South, Newfoundland.

Legal Issues

1. Did the Cannings own the horse involved in the accident?

2. If the Cannings owned the horse, were they negligent under either:

   a. a breach of a duty created by municipal regulations, or

   b. a breach of a duty at common law?

3. Was Rowe contributorily negligent for failing to keep a proper lookout?

Holding

Yes, the Cannings were the owners of the horse involved in the accident.

The Cannings were liable in negligence for damages to Rowe and Furey. First, they breached a duty created by the municipal regulation. Second, even if the regulation had not been in effect, the court would have found a breach of duty under the common law.

Rowe was not contributorily negligent because the judge found that he did keep a proper lookout.

Legal and Factual Basis for Holding

The trial judge found as a fact that the Cannings were the owners of the horse that struck the motorcycle.

There are two distinct bases to find liability in negligence. First, in Conception Bay South, municipal regulations require animal owners to restrain their animals from roaming at large. Although the *Livestock Act*, RSN 1990, c L-20 may apply in some circumstances, on the facts of this case it did not because the horse did not fall within the class of animals prohibited from running at large by the Act, nor was there a ministerial order in place.

The court found that the Cannings were liable pursuant to the regulation.

Second, there is a common-law duty on owners to prevent their animals from roaming at large where the volume of traffic means an accident would be likely. The judge applied the decision of *Fleming v Atkinson*, [1959] SCR 513, 1959 CanLII 10. The Supreme Court decided that ordinary rules of negligence apply to straying animals, considering all the surrounding circumstances, including the nature of the highway and the amount and nature of the traffic. Therefore, more generally, for jurisdictions where municipal regulations have not been created, there is a common-law duty on owners to prevent their animals from roaming at large. Had the Cannings not been found liable pursuant to the municipal regulation, they would have been found liable in breach of a common-law duty.

Finally, based on the facts, the judge found that Rowe was keeping a proper lookout on the road and, therefore, was not contributorily negligent.

FACTUAL SIMILARITIES

Shybani and Haddad v Brook	*Rowe v Canning*
An animal ran out across the highway into the path of an oncoming motorcycle.	An animal ran out across the highway into the path of an oncoming motorcycle.
The passenger saw the animal approaching and alerted the driver to the danger.	The passenger saw the animal approaching and alerted the driver to the danger.
The motorcycle driver lost control; both driver and passenger fell from the motorcycle.	The motorcycle driver lost control; both driver and passenger fell from the motorcycle.

FACTUAL DIFFERENCES

Shybani and Haddad v Brook	Rowe v Canning
An animal—dog (Pomeranian).	An animal—horse.
The driver lost control of his motorcycle when he swerved to avoid hitting the dog.	The driver lost control of his motorcycle when the horse struck the motorcycle.
The passenger's injuries required medical treatment, and may affect her income in the short term.	The driver's and passenger's injuries were minor; the plaintiffs walked away from the accident.
A witness confirmed that a dog trailing a leash ran in front of the motorcycle, but could not confirm whether the motorcycle hit the dog.	Independent witnesses could not confirm that a horse running free at the time of the accident belonged to the Cannings.
As the dog ran away, the driver and passenger observed that the dog had a leash and collar.	The driver and passenger saw Canning lead a horse away.

Next, compare the legal issues raised in the problem and the court's treatment of similar legal issues in the comparison case by determining whether the court's conclusions in the decided case could resolve the legal issues in the client's situation.

When comparing cases, note the difference between *questions of fact* and *questions of law*. Questions of fact concern the factual details of the case before the court. To resolve a question of fact, a judge considers the parties' evidence to support their respective claims—e.g. determination of identities, conditions, dates, and times. Questions of law concern the court's analysis of the relevant legal principles arising from the facts.

Findings of fact are restricted to the case being heard; each judge (or jury) must make their own findings of fact to which the law is then applied. However, the similarity between case facts can be compared, and the legal findings that result can be examined to predict outcomes if the case facts are similar, or to distinguish cases if the facts are dissimilar.

COMPARISON: QUESTIONS OF LAW AND FACT

Legal Questions in *Shybani and Haddad v Brook*	Answers to Similar Legal Questions in *Rowe v Canning*
Did Brook's dog Stormy run into Shybani's path, causing him to lose control of his motorcycle?	This is a *question of fact*, not law; the court considering Shybani and Haddad's claim must hear evidence to decide whether the dog in that case belonged to Brook.
Is an owner of an animal that roams at large liable for damage caused by that animal?	There are two distinct bases to find liability. First, in Conception Bay South, municipal regulations require animal owners to restrain their animals from roaming at large. Although the *Livestock Act*, RSNL 1990, c L-20 may apply in some circumstances, on the facts of the case it did not because the horse did not fall within the class of animals prohibited from running at large by the Act, nor was there a ministerial order in place. Second, there is a common-law duty on owners to prevent their animals from roaming at large where the volume of traffic means an accident would be likely.
Can a driver of a vehicle be found contributorily negligent in a claim for damages caused by an animal that roams?	Ordinary rules of negligence apply to straying animals.
Was Shybani contributorily negligent?	This is a *question of fact*, not law; the court deciding Shybani and Haddad's claim must hear evidence to decide whether Shybani was driving in a way that contributed to the accident.
	Ratio/**applicable legal principle:** There may be a statutory or regulatory duty depending on the jurisdiction and type of animal. If neither a statute nor a regulation applies, at common law animal owners are responsible for damages caused by their roaming animals.
	Decision: The defendant was negligent and 100% liable for the plaintiff's damages.

TASK 11.3

Case Brief: Fleming v Atkinson

Case Name and Citation
Fleming v Atkinson, [1959] SCR 513, 159 CanLII 10.

Procedural History
SCC majority upheld the decision of both the trial court and the Ontario Court of Appeal, awarding the plaintiff damages for the defendant's breach of duty in allowing cattle to roam a highway.

Relevant Facts
The driver of a motor vehicle struck three cows and killed two. They were part of the defendant's larger herd grazing on the side of the road. The cattle, in the ordinary course of feeding during the day, were "running on the roads", according to the defendant's employee. The driver, accompanied by two passengers, applied the brakes and skidded to a stop; however, the driver suffered personal injuries.

Legal Issues
Is an owner of cattle roaming a highway liable for damages caused by those animals?

Holding
Majority: the defendant was negligent and liable for 100% of damages.

Legal and Factual Basis for Holding
Applying the ordinary rules of negligence, when cattle cause damages by straying onto the road, their owner will be liable for those damages.

The trial judge found that the cattle trespassed on the highway. By contrast, the Court of Appeal held that though the presence of the cattle on the highway was not unlawful, the cattle owner should have foreseen that their presence on the road might result in their being struck by vehicles whose drivers were unaware of their presence.

On appeal, the Supreme Court of Canada rejected the common-law rule arising from a line of cases in England that "there is no duty on an owner of land adjoining a highway toward a person driving a vehicle on the highway to maintain fences" and keep his cattle off the highway. Instead the majority decided that "there can be no difficulty in the application of the **ordinary rules of negligence** to the facts in this type of case and the matter should be left to the tribunal of fact to determine, with **due regard to all the circumstances, including the nature of the highway and the amount and nature of the traffic that might reasonably be expected to be upon it, whether or not it would be negligent to allow a domestic animal to be at large**" (emphasis added).

Although contributory negligence was argued, the majority did not consider this issue on appeal. However, the trial court found the driver contributorily negligent at 40% because he was not keeping a lookout and did not have his vehicle under such control that he could stop if his way was impeded.

FACTUAL SIMILARITIES

Shybani and Haddad v Brook	Fleming v Atkinson
The case involved a highway vehicle accident caused by an animal in the roadway, resulting in personal injuries.	Same.
The driver was aware of the danger and took steps to avoid hitting the animal.	Same.

FACTUAL DIFFERENCES

Shybani and Haddad v Brook	Fleming v Atkinson
The accident involved a dog.	The accident involved cattle.
The accident involved a motorcycle.	The accident involved a car.
The dog owner took steps to secure the dog.	The cattle owner allowed the cattle freedom to roam the road.

COMPARISON: QUESTIONS OF LAW AND FACT

Legal Questions in Shybani and Haddad v Brook	Answers to Similar Legal Questions in Fleming v Atkinson
Is Brook's dog Stormy the dog that ran out onto the highway and caused Shybani to lose control of his motorcycle?	Question of fact; no similar factual issue raised. It was conceded that the cattle belonged to the defendant.
Is an owner of an animal that roams at large liable for damage caused by that animal?	**Ratio:** According to ordinary rules of negligence, owners of cattle owe a duty of care and are responsible for damages caused when their animals roam free on a road.
	Decision: For the plaintiff. The defendant cattle owner was 60% negligent. The plaintiff driver was 40% contributorily negligent.

TASK 11.4

Case Brief: Bujold v Dempsey

Case Name and Citation

Bujold v Dempsey (1996), 181 NBR (2d) 111 (QB).

Relevant Facts

The plaintiffs, Bujold and Dobson, were walking their dogs off leash along a rural highway. The defendant, Dempsey, struck the plaintiffs when she swerved to avoid hitting the dogs. The plaintiffs sued for damages.

Legal Issues

1. Did the dogs cause the accident?

2. If the dogs caused the accident, were their owners negligent by failing to restrain their dogs while walking on the highway?

3. Was the defendant driving in a negligent manner?

Holding

The plaintiffs succeeded at trial.

Legal and Factual Basis for Holding

There is a duty on the operator of a motor vehicle to exercise reasonable skill or reasonable self-possession, whether in emergencies or in ordinary circumstances.

There are two distinct bases to find liability. First, under the *Municipalities Act*, RSNB 1973, c M-22, no person who owns a dog shall permit it to run at large. Second, aside from a statutory duty, the owner of a domesticated animal that is allowed to create a hazard on a highway can be found liable in negligence where the hazard causes or contributes to damages that result.

FACTUAL SIMILARITIES

Shybani and Haddad v Brook	Bujold v Dempsey
The case involved an accident caused when a driver swerved to avoid hitting a dog roaming on a road.	Same.

FACTUAL DIFFERENCES

Shybani and Haddad v Brook	Bujold v Dempsey
Passenger warned the driver.	No warning.
Vehicle—motorcycle.	Vehicle—car.
Animal owner sued by driver.	Animal owners sued driver.

COMPARISON: QUESTIONS OF LAW AND FACT

Legal Questions in Shybani and Haddad v Brook	Answers to Similar Legal Questions in Bujold v Dempsey
Is Brook's dog Stormy the dog that ran out onto the highway and caused Shybani to lose control of his motorcycle?	Question of fact—dogs owned by plaintiffs.
Is an owner of an animal that roams at large liable for damage caused by that animal?	There are two distinct bases to find liability. First, under the *Municipalities Act*, RSNB 1973, c M-22, no person who owns a dog shall permit it to run at large. Second, aside from a statutory duty, the owner of a domesticated animal that is allowed to create a hazard on a highway can be found liable in negligence where the hazard causes or contributes to damages that result.
Can a driver of a vehicle be found contributorily negligent in a claim for damages caused by an animal that roams?	There is a duty on the operator of a motor vehicle to exercise reasonable skill or reasonable self-possession, whether in emergencies or in ordinary circumstances.
Was Shybani contributorily negligent?	Question of fact—driving too fast for road conditions.
	Decision: For the plaintiffs. The defendant driver was 75% negligent. The plaintiff dog owners were 25% contributorily negligent.

TASK 11.5

Case Brief: Spanton v Laviolette

Case Name and Citation
Spanton v Laviolette (1977), 19 OR (2d) 21, 83 DLR (3d) 740 (Sm Cl Ct).

Relevant Facts
The plaintiff, driving in a car at noon in a city on a four-lane divided roadway at the posted speed limit (30 mph), struck a large dog that ran into the car's path from an adjacent park where it had been exercising, off leash, with its owner's sister. The plaintiff had seen the dog approaching when he was still five car-lengths from the dog. He applied the brake and slowed the vehicle. The dog reversed direction twice; at the point that the driver thought the dog was returning to its owner, the driver removed his foot from the brake and coasted, and hit the dog at approximately 25 mph. The dog, which had not had obedience training, was not seriously injured. The driver was not injured, but the car sustained damage to the bumper, fender, grille, and headlamp. Driving conditions were good at the time.

Legal Issues
1. Was the dog owner liable in negligence for damage to the car?
2. Was the driver contributorily negligent for damage to his car?

Holding
(1) Yes, the dog owner was 25% negligent. (2) Yes, the car driver was 75% contributorily negligent.

Legal and Factual Basis for Holding
There is a positive duty for owners to take reasonable care to control the movement of their animals onto public highways. However, dog owners who allow their animals to stray into traffic have not *de facto* breached that duty; it is still open to the dog owners to show that they had taken reasonable (albeit unsuccessful) steps to prevent the accident.

The Supreme Court of Canada in *Fleming v Atkinson*, [1959] SCR 513 held that the ordinary rules of negligence are applicable in determining the liability of an owner of adjacent lands for domestic animals that escape to or stray onto an adjoining highway. However, only three of the six SCC justices found a positive duty to take reasonable care to control the movement of their animals onto public highways. In *Spanton*, the court stated:

> [e]ven this somewhat weakened decision, when taken together with the rules governing persons who conduct animals to or near highways indicates that the case before me should be analyzed upon the basis that the dog's owner owed such a duty of reasonable care to users of the road.
>
> What is "reasonable care" in such circumstances? If the concept is to be meaningful at all, one must resist the temptation to find that there has been an absence of

reasonable care *de facto* on every occasion on which a dog is allowed to stray into traffic. To do otherwise would be to convert a principle of negligence into a rule of strict liability. In my opinion, it would, therefore, be wrong for the law to make it extremely difficult or impossible (*de facto*) for the owner of a dog straying into traffic to escape liability by showing that reasonable (albeit unsuccessful) steps had been taken to prevent such an occurrence.

FACTUAL SIMILARITIES

Shybani and Haddad v Brook	*Spanton v Laviolette*
The case involved a roadway vehicle accident caused by a dog running free on the highway.	Same.
The driver attempted to avoid hitting the dog.	Same.

FACTUAL DIFFERENCES

Shybani and Haddad v Brook	*Spanton v Laviolette*
The passenger warned the driver about the danger.	The driver saw the approaching dog and braked.
The accident involved a motorcycle.	The accident involved a car.
The driver is suing the animal owner for the injuries sustained by his passenger, and damage to his motorcycle.	The driver sued the animal owner for the damage sustained to his car.

COMPARISON: QUESTIONS OF LAW AND FACT

Legal Questions in *Shybani and Haddad v Brook*	Answers to Similar Legal Questions in *Spanton v Laviolette*
Is Brook's dog Stormy the dog that ran out onto the highway and caused Shybani to lose control of his motorcycle?	Question of fact; no similar factual issue raised. It was conceded that the dog in the accident belonged to the defendant.
Is an owner of an animal that roams at large liable for damage caused by that animal?	According to the common-law duty of reasonable care, owners of animals (or stray dogs) are responsible for damages caused when their animals roam free or stray.
Can a driver of a vehicle be found contributorily negligent in a claim for damages caused by an animal that roams?	Contributory negligence results when a driver who sees an approaching animal fails to take possible steps to reduce the severity of the impact because the driver has a duty to avoid hitting the animal if possible.
Was Shybani contributorily negligent?	Question of fact; in *Spanton*, the court found that the driver could have reduced the severity of the impact by continuing to brake rather than coasting.
	Decision: The defendant dog owner was 25% negligent. The plaintiff driver was 75% contributorily negligent. *Negligence Act*, RSO 1970, c 296.

TASK 11.6

Case Brief: Ruckheim v Robinson

Case Name and Citation
Ruckheim v Robinson, [1995] 4 WWR 284, 1 BCLR (3d) 46 (CA).

Relevant Facts
The defendant's dog escaped its pen and collided with a motorcycle, causing the driver to be thrown off the motorcycle and injured.

Legal Issue

1. When risk is foreseeable, does a dog owner have a duty to keep the dog under control?

Holding
The plaintiff was awarded damages, which included compensation for injury, wage loss, and future income loss. The defendants were 100% liable for damages caused by the injuries.

Legal and Factual Basis for Holding
In this case the defendant was negligent because it was reasonably foreseeable that the dog could escape from the pen.

FACTUAL SIMILARITIES

Shybani and Haddad v Brook	*Ruckheim v Robinson*
The case involved a motorcycle accident caused when a dog ran into the path of a motorcycle.	Same.
A person sustained injuries that would affect their work.	Same.

FACTUAL DIFFERENCES

Shybani and Haddad v Brook	*Ruckheim v Robinson*
The passenger warned the driver.	The driver was not warned.
The driver swerved to avoid the dog.	The dog struck the motorcycle.

COMPARISON: QUESTIONS OF LAW AND FACT

Legal Questions in *Shybani and Haddad v Brook*	Answers to Similar Legal Questions in *Ruckheim v Robinson*
Is Brook's dog Stormy the dog that ran out onto the highway and caused Shybani to lose control of his motorcycle?	Question of fact—the defendants were the dog owners.
Is an owner of an animal that roams at large liable for damage caused by that animal?	Animal owners have a duty to ensure that their animals are under control; it is reasonably foreseeable that a roaming animal may cause damage.
Can a driver of a vehicle be found contributorily negligent in a claim for damages caused by an animal that roams?	
Was Shybani contributorily negligent?	There was no issue of contributory negligence.
	Decision: The defendant dog owner was liable.

5. Create a Table to Compare Findings

Once the cases have been briefed and analyzed, the applicable legislation and case law can be summarized to determine those cases that are most likely to be predictive in the client's case.[3] When you are required to integrate the law from several cases, you may find it helpful to summarize the essential elements in table form in order to compare:

- the controlling legal principles derived from case law
- the binding or persuasive nature of the case
- the potential applicability of legislation
- the analogous and distinguishing features of each case

---

3 Commercial sources of legal information and CanLII provide noting-up features, which can assist in determining whether legal principles have been applied or distinguished in subsequent judicial decisions.

TASK 11.7

Creating a Comparison Table

Case	Issues	Answer	
Rowe v Canning	1. Do animal owners have a common-law or statutory duty to secure their animals?	Yes: common-law duty; statute or municipal regulations may apply.	
	2. Can a driver be found contributorily negligent?	Yes.	
Fleming v Atkinson	1. Is an owner of cattle roaming a highway liable for damages?	Yes: common-law duty.	
Bujold v Dempsey	1. Were dog owners negligent while walking dogs on the highway?	Yes: common-law duty; statute or municipal regulations may apply.	
	2. Was the defendant driving in a negligent manner?	Yes.	
Spanton v Laviolette	1. Was the dog owner liable in negligence for damage?	Yes: common-law duty.	
	2. Was the driver contributorily negligent?	Yes: negligence legislation applies.	
Ruckheim v Robinson	1. When the risk is foreseeable, does the dog owner have a duty to keep the dog under control?	Yes: common-law duty.	

Holding	Applicable?	Distinguishable?
Owners are required to prevent their animals from roaming at large where an accident would be likely.	Common-law rule applies but statutory duty applies only within the statute's or regulation's jurisdiction: non-binding.	• Type of animal.
Drivers have a duty to keep a proper lookout.	Statutory or common-law rules of contributory negligence apply.	Decided on the facts of each case.
Ordinary rules of negligence apply when roaming domestic animals cause damages.	Common-law rule applies: binding.	• Type of animal. • Type of vehicle. • Owner permitted animals to roam.
The owner of a domesticated animal that creates a hazard on a highway can be found liable in negligence for damages.	Common-law and statutory rules apply: non-binding.	• Type of vehicle. • Dog walked off leash.
Drivers are required to exercise reasonable skill in all circumstances.	Statutory or common-law rules of contributory negligence apply.	Decided on the facts of each case.
A dog owner owes a duty of reasonable care to users of the road, but can escape liability by showing that reasonable (albeit unsuccessful) steps had been taken.	Common law applies: *Negligence Act* applies within the statute's jurisdiction.	• Type of vehicle. • Dog exercised off leash.
	Common law applies: non-binding. *Negligence Act* applies within the statute's jurisdiciton.	• The driver saw the dog but did not take evasive action.
Animal owners have a duty to ensure that their animals are under control; it is reasonably foreseeable that a roaming animal may cause damage.	Common law applies: non-binding.	• Dog escaped from pen.

6. Create a Statement of the Law of Both General and Specific Applicability

a. Rowe v Canning

Legal Principle of General Applicability

There are two distinct bases to find liability in negligence. First, in Conception Bay South, municipal regulations require animal owners to restrain their animals from roaming at large. Although the *Livestock Act*, RSN 1990, c L-20 may apply in some circumstances, on the facts of this case it did not because the horse did not fall within the class of animals prohibited from running at large by the Act, nor was there a ministerial order in place.

Second, there is a common-law duty on owners to prevent their animals from roaming at large where the volume of traffic means an accident would be likely. The judge applied the decision of *Fleming v Atkinson*, [1959] SCR 513, 1959 CanLII 10. The Supreme Court decided that ordinary rules of negligence apply to straying animals, considering all the surrounding circumstances, including the nature of the highway and the amount and nature of the traffic. Therefore, more generally, for jurisdictions where municipal regulations have not been created, there is a common-law duty on owners to prevent their animals from roaming at large. Had the Cannings not been found liable pursuant to the municipal regulation, they would have been found liable in breach of a common-law duty.

Specific Applicability to the Facts of Shybani and Haddad

Although similarities exist between the facts of Shybani and Haddad's case and the *Rowe* case concerning the cause of the accident, the distinguishing features would likely preclude any further application of *Rowe* to Shybani and Haddad's case. The precursor legislation was restricted to livestock and did not govern dogs. Moreover, *Rowe* was decided under legislation that was subsequently repealed in 2010. The replacement legislation governs companion animals, including dogs; however, it is significantly different from the precursor legislation and requires its own judicial consideration.

Because *Rowe* is not an appellate decision, if *Rowe* were applied to the facts of a case from the same jurisdiction, it might be persuasive but would not bind another court.

b. Fleming v Atkinson

Legal Principle of General Applicability

In Canada at common law, ordinary rules of negligence apply when straying domestic animals cause damage.

Specific Applicability to the Facts of Shybani and Haddad

Although there are several distinguishing features in *Fleming* (the type of animal, the type of vehicle, animals having been permitted to roam rather than having escaped), it is likely that this general principle will apply, and, moreover, be binding. However, as the Supreme Court of Canada found, at common law, rather than under specific legislation, a lawyer from any jurisdiction would still be required to complete further research to determine whether legislation had been created that modified or superseded the common-law rule established in this case. Moreover, noting up of this case would reveal whether lower courts had applied this decision or distinguished it.

c. *Bujold v Dempsey*

Legal Principle of General Applicability

Although animal owners have a duty to control their animals and prevent them from causing harm, drivers have a corresponding duty to exercise reasonable skill in all circumstances.

Specific Applicability to the Facts of Shybani and Haddad

Although there are distinguishing factors in this case (the plaintiffs were the injured dog walkers; dogs were on the roadway with the permission of their owners), the basic principle will likely apply. Whether the dogs were on the roadway with their owners' approval or had strayed there without their owners' knowledge does not appear to be determinative in finding liability. However, the driver's responsibility in taking steps to avoid the accident will be factored into a damage award.

There are many unknown facts that must be determined to fully assess the likelihood of Shybani's contributory negligence. The fact that Haddad was clothed properly to withstand a more serious injury would reduce a claim of contributory negligence, as would the fact that Shybani had little warning time to avoid the dog. However, the speed limit and the distance travelled from the time Shybani and Haddad set out on their journey until the time of the accident must be determined to discover whether Shybani had been speeding. The witness must be interviewed to determine whether he saw Shybani driving erratically. Accident reconstruction procedures may provide additional information about the accident details.

Because *Bujold* is a trial decision from New Brunswick, it is not binding in any jurisdiction, but may provide persuasive authority.

d. *Spanton v Laviolette*

Legal Principle of General Applicability

There is a positive duty for dog owners to take reasonable care to control the movement of their animals onto public highways; however, dog owners can establish that they have not breached their duty by showing that they had taken reasonable (albeit unsuccessful) steps to prevent the accident. In each case, the facts will be considered to determine whether, pursuant to legislation, a driver is contributorily negligent.

Specific Applicability to the Facts of Shybani and Haddad

The general principle will likely apply, although this case opens a potential argument for Brook that the steps he took, which included leashing the dog and keeping it penned, may be considered reasonable if unsuccessful steps to prevent the accident.

If the court is persuaded by this argument, Shybani could argue that the steps taken by Brook were insufficient, because he should have ensured that Stormy's leash was secured before he opened the gate to allow the car to enter the grounds. (However, different facts—e.g. an intruder entering the kennel to steal a dog and leaving the gate unlatched, allowing Stormy to roam free, all of which was unknown to Brook—might raise an argument about whether his liability may be reduced.)

In *Spanton*, the court found both the driver and the dog owner to be liable, with the driver bearing the higher degree of responsibility for failing to take necessary steps to avoid the accident.

Because *Spanton* is a trial decision from Ontario, it is not binding in any jurisdiction but may provide persuasive authority. Therefore, regardless of the jurisdiction, existing legislation must be examined to look for legislation that governs the legal issues of the case, such as legislation that governs negligence and animals roaming at large.

e. *Ruckheim v Robinson*

Legal Principle of General Applicability

Animal owners have a duty to ensure that their animals are under control and cannot injure other persons, because it is reasonably foreseeable that an escaped animal may cause damage.

Specific Applicability to the Facts of Shybani and Haddad

The facts of *Ruckheim* are the most similar to the facts of Shybani and Haddad's case, so it is likely that a court will consider *Ruckheim* to determine the respective responsibilities of Shybani and Brook. In both cases, the owner took steps to keep the dog secured, yet the dog escaped and caused injury to a motorcycle rider. The distinguishing factor, swerving to avoid or striking the dog, is not likely to be determinative of the outcome. The legislation considered is not relevant to the analysis of liability.

7. Summarize the Findings

Identify the characteristics from the cases that are similar and those that are different. The similarities lead to the creation of a general legal rule that can be applied to future cases. Differences may occur because the case is distinguishable on its facts and issues, or because there are two distinct lines of reasoning that are developing in the trial courts. In this event, ultimately, one of the cases will be appealed, and an appeal court will decide the direction that the law should take.

1. Owners of animals have a common-law duty in negligence for damages caused when their animals roam at large.

2. In some jurisdictions, a corresponding statutory duty may have been created. Therefore, it is necessary to review existing legislation to determine whether it either supersedes or modifies the common-law rule.

3. Contributory negligence will be assessed on the facts to determine whether the driver was keeping a proper lookout or ought to have anticipated the dangerous situation.

It may appear that the finding in favour of the animal owners and against the driver in *Bujold* is inconsistent with the remainder of the cases; however, the court in *Bujold* found that the driver lost control because she was driving too fast when she swerved to miss the dogs. Recall that the court decided that the presence of the dogs on the road was not sufficient to explain the extent to which the driver lost control of her car.[4] This is a similar result to the *Spanton* case, where the court found that the driver had anticipated the accident and could have taken additional action.

8. Apply the Legal Principles to the Facts of the Client's Case

After you have completed the preceding, consider how these principles would be applied to the facts of your client's situation.

- State the answer or conclusion to the particular or general legal question, predicting how the court is likely to rule.

- Support the conclusion with the general legal rule that will apply to the facts of the client's problem.

- Provide specific examples from analogous and distinguishable cases to demonstrate how the courts have previously applied the legal principles.

---

4   Notice in the summary above that the verbs chosen differ when describing the actions of judges and lawyers in a case. Judges decide, conclude, reason, determine, find, and hold, while lawyers argue, posit, claim, counter, and present.

- Emphasize the strengths and weaknesses of the predictions in a final summary of the analytical findings.

Note that, in inductive reasoning, when the legal synthesis of the law is entirely or mostly favourable to the client's issue, or entirely or mostly opposed to the client's issue, it is feasible to predict a probable outcome with a high degree of certainty. However, when the decisions result in differing outcomes, or a sufficient number of decisions have not yet been delivered to allow for a full comparison of similarities and differences, the legal opinion will be qualified. Inductive reasoning is one method to analyze primary law. Deductive reasoning is also used to analyze primary law with the aim of predicting a probable result for your client's legal issue.

C. Developing an Argument Through Deductive Reasoning: Formulate Legal Syllogisms

> **Syllogism.** In logic, the full logical form of a single argument. It consists of three propositions (two premises and the conclusion), and these contain three terms, of which the two occurring in the conclusion are brought together in the premises by being referred to a common class.
>
> *Black's Law Dictionary*, 7th ed

In the example in Figure 11.2, the major premise is a general statement—in this case, about a specific class of objects, focusing on a specific characteristic of all

Consider the following syllogism:

1. "All cats have whiskers"	☑	(Major premise)
2. "Puff is a cat"	☑	(Minor premise)
3. "Therefore, Puff has whiskers"	☑	(Conclusion)

However:

1. "All cats have webbed feet"	☒	(Major premise)
2. "Puff is a cat"	☑	(Minor Premise)
3. "Therefore, Puff has webbed feet"	?	(Conclusion)

Or:

1. "All cats have whiskers"	☑	(Major premise)
2. "Puff has whiskers"	☑	(Minor premise)
3. "Therefore, Puff is a cat"	?	(Conclusion)

FIGURE 11.2 Deductive Reasoning: Syllogisms

members of the class. The minor premise identifies one member of that specific class. Assuming that the statement about all the members of the general class is true (major premise), and the statement about the individual member of the class is true (minor premise), then the conclusion will also be true.

Deducing the correctness of the conclusion to the argument depends on the certainty of the correctness of the major and minor premises. If either premise is incorrect, as shown in the second example, then the correctness of the conclusion cannot be determined. In the third example, although the major and minor premises might be accurate statements, because the minor premise focuses on a characteristic of the class that could be shared by other classes—e.g. walruses—the accuracy of the conclusion cannot be determined.

When using deductive reasoning to draft a legal argument, *legal syllogisms* are used to formulate both the legal argument and the counterargument.[5] The following apply when making a legal argument:

1. The *major premise* in the legal argument is a statement about the law— e.g. legal rule or legal principle. The major premise may be derived from a section of a statute or regulation, a *ratio* from a precedent case, or a general legal principle arising from the process of inductive reasoning.

2. The *minor premise* in the legal argument is the position taken by the client about the major premise, based on facts arising from the client's legal problem—e.g. the client has or has not followed or breached a specified legal rule. Evidence is required to establish the fact(s) claimed in the minor premise of the argument.

3. The minor premise in the *counterargument* is the negative or opposite of the position taken by the client. Evidence is required to establish the fact(s) claimed in the minor premise of the counterargument.

4. The *conclusion* is unknown until the facts are assessed and the weight of the evidence for both sides to the dispute tips the balance of the argument in favour of one party or the other, leading to the predictive conclusion or likely outcome.

In deductive reasoning, a syllogism is required to analyze each legal point for which an argument will be made. This process of developing argument and counterargument is repeated for as many major premises as can be identified. However, even though the syllogism format is used to develop the argument, the terms

---

5 Eveline T Feteris, *Fundamentals of Legal Argumentation* (London: Kluwer Academic Publishers, 1999) at 29.

"syllogism", "proposition", and "premise" do not appear in the argument discussion. Instead, syllogisms are the framework for the arguments created that will ultimately delineate the strength of the client's position.

If you experience difficulty when constructing a syllogism, using "if/then" conditional statements may help.[6] The "if" clause sets out the legal rule or principle that applies, typically found in the major premise, while the "then" clause establishes the result or consequence typically found in the conclusion. The middle term, or minor premise, contains the client's position. The facts of the case can be considered to determine whether the evidence supports the client's position or that of the other party to the dispute.

Whether you attempt to formulate an argument through inductive reasoning or through deductive reasoning, you must analyze the legislation and brief the cases as discussed in Chapter 10 and demonstrated in the previous section on inductive reasoning. When employing deductive reasoning, continue the analysis with the following steps:

- Determine whether legislation exists that governs the client's legal issue.
- If legislation does exist, determine whether the relevant sections of the legislation have been judicially considered. If so, select relevant cases and analyze them as described in the discussion of inductive reasoning.
- If no legislation is found, determine whether the common law applies and has been judicially considered.
- Once you have identified the controlling law, and determined the legal rule, formulate an if/then statement that sets out the legal rule and the outcome for a breach or omission of the rule.
- Create as many legal syllogisms as necessary to fully evaluate the client's legal situation.
- Apply the law to the facts; examine both sides of the issue; determine a likely conclusion for each argument; and, within this framework, distinguish cases where appropriate.
- Provide a concluding statement that summarizes the argument results.

Note that in deductive reasoning, the strength of the conclusion depends on knowing the facts in support of the parties to the dispute. Therefore, when facts are unknown or open to different interpretation, the predictive outcome will be less certain, leading to a qualified legal opinion.

---

6 *Ibid.*

D. Using Deductive Reasoning to Develop a Legal Argument

The preliminary steps of deductive reasoning and inductive reasoning are the same—fact assessment, issue drafting, and research to locate the relevant primary law. Relevant legislation is reviewed, including judicial treatment of the relevant legislation, or, if the client's issue matter is governed by the common law, relevant cases are located and then briefed to ascertain relevant legal principles.

Let's use the case of Shybani and Haddad to demonstrate how deductive reasoning can be used to develop legal argument.

1. State the Legal Issues

1. By allowing Stormy to break free, was Brook negligent and thus liable for damages to Shybani and Haddad?
2. Was Shybani contributorily negligent and thus liable for damages?

2. Identify the Applicable Legal Rule(s)

The inductive reasoning analysis completed above identified two general principles of the law: (1) animal owners have a duty of care to control their animals; and (2) drivers of vehicles have a duty to keep a proper lookout. Both these duties arise at common law and in some jurisdictions by statute.

In deductive reasoning, you must identify and cite the legal authority for the legal principle or rule. It could come from binding case law, or persuasive case law from the same jurisdiction, or persuasive case law from other jurisdictions, or from legislation.

> Owners of animals have a legal duty in negligence for damages caused when their animals run free.
>
> Contributory negligence will be assessed on the facts to determine whether the driver was keeping a proper lookout or ought to have anticipated the dangerous situation developing.

In this situation, for both legal rules, legal authority comes from a general legal principle derived from a review of binding and persuasive sources. For the second legal rule, assume that the jurisdiction is Ontario. Therefore, not only would the legal principle arise from case law, but legislation would also apply.

> *Negligence Act*, RSO 1990, c N.1
>   3. In any action for damages that is founded upon the fault or negligence of the defendant if fault or negligence is found on the part of the plaintiff that contributed to the damages, the court shall apportion the damages to the degree of fault or negligence found against the parties respectively.

3. Transpose the Legal Rule into a Conditional If/Then Statement

Creating an if/then statement clarifies the conditions that will result in the legal consequence.

For the first legal rule, two conditions must be met. The animal must be running free *and* the animal must have caused damage. Unless both conditions occurred sequentially, the animal owner will not be liable under this legal principle.[7] For the second principle, once evidence is found that the plaintiff is at fault, then the court shall apportion the damages proportionately between the plaintiff and the defendant.

> **If** a person allows his or her animal to run free, **and** the animal causes damage, **then** the person is negligent and liable for damages caused.
>
> **If** a person entitled to receive damages in a claim of negligence contributed to the damages caused, **then** the person is contributorily negligent, and the court shall apportion damages accordingly.

4. Create a Legal Syllogism That Reflects the Legal Rule or Principle

First, identify the major premise, which is the applicable legal rule, then identify the minor premise that is the client's position in respect of the major premise, along with the minor premise that will be claimed by the other party to the dispute. Then state the evidence in support of the respective positions. Include unknowns and assumptions that may affect the overall conclusion. Identify case law that supports one or the other side to the dispute. Finally, weigh the strength of the respective positions and state the likely conclusion, qualified if necessary.

---

7   For a discussion about rule structure, see Margaret E McCallum, Deborah A Schmedemann & Christina L Kunz, *Synthesis: Legal Reading, Reasoning and Writing in Canada*, 2d ed (Toronto: CCH Canadian, 2008) at 9-16. This is an example of conjunctive rule structure, signified by the use of the word "and", where more than one condition must be met to result in the legal consequence.

TASK 11.8

Legal Syllogism Format: Issue 1

Major Premise: Governing Legal Rule
A person whose dog runs free is liable in negligence for damages caused (*Fleming v Atkinson*).

Minor Premise: Client's Position/Other Side's Counterposition with Respect to the Major Premise	
Shybani/Haddad's Position	**Brook's Position**
Brook *negligently allowed* his dog to run free and is thus liable to Haddad for damages.	Brook did *not negligently allow* his dog to run free and is therefore not liable for damages claimed by Haddad and Shybani.
Evidence in Support of Shybani/Haddad's Position	**Evidence in Support of Brook's Position**
• Stormy is Brook's dog. • Stormy was running loose on the morning of the motorcycle accident. • His escape was foreseeable; his leash should have been secured before the car was allowed into the kennel because Brook knew the dog was not obedient. • Haddad saw the dog, who darted in front of the motorcycle on which she was a passenger, and warned Shybani. He did not have enough time to brake or slow the motorcycle. • The witness will likely confirm that a dog trailing a leash ran in front of a motorcycle.	• Stormy was leashed prior to the incident. • His escape was not foreseeable. • Brook took immediate steps to locate the dog, both searching and calling Animal Control.
Identify Assumed or Unknown Facts • It is assumed that Shybani was driving safely for the road conditions—i.e. dry roads, sun not in eyes, not speeding. • It is assumed that the road is a well-travelled thoroughfare and not a rural road. • Police accident report. • Distance travelled/time taken.	*Identify Assumed or Unknown Facts* • Road conditions. • Driver's speed. • Whether the driver was driving appropriately for road and weather conditions.

Conclusion
Assuming that no additional facts are discovered that would negate the known evidence, it is likely that Brook will be found negligent and liable for damages caused by Stormy running in front of Shybani.

TASK 11.9

Legal Syllogism Format: Issue 2

Major Premise: Governing Legal Rule	
Persons who are entitled to receive damages in a claim of negligence shall have the damage claim reduced in proportion to the degree that they were contributorily negligent (*Negligence Act*, RSO 1970, c 296).	
Minor Premise: Client's Position/Other Side's Counterposition with Respect to the Major Premise	
Shybani/Haddad's Position	**Brook's Position**
Shybani/Haddad *did not negligently* contribute to the damages.	Shybani/Haddad *did negligently* contribute to Haddad's injury.
Evidence in Support of Shybani's Position	**Evidence in Support of Brook's Position**
• Both the driver and the passenger were attired to reduce impact injury in the event of a fall from the motorcycle. • Shybani did not have enough time to brake or slow the motorcycle following Haddad's warning. • Swerving to avoid the dog was preferable to hitting the dog, which could have injured the driver, the passenger, and the dog. • The witness will likely support Shybani's assertion that a dog ran in front of the motorcycle.	• Rely on *Bujold/Spanton*, where the drivers' actions contributed to the damages. • The witness's perspective does not allow him to testify to events that occurred at ground level.
Unknown/Assumed Facts • It is assumed that Shybani was driving safely for the road and weather conditions—i.e. dry roads, sun not in eyes, not speeding. • Police accident report. • Distance travelled/time taken.	*Unknown/Assumed Facts* • Shybani was driving in an unsafe manner for the road and weather conditions—i.e. speeding, sun in eyes. • Shybani received a warning from Haddad that should have allowed him enough time to brake and slow the motorcycle.
Conclusion	
Brook's argument would be strengthened by information from the police report about speeding or driving in an unsafe manner, which might be determined by accident reconstruction. However, without that evidence, Shybani is unlikely to be found contributorily negligent for both his and Haddad's damages.	

Unlike inductive reasoning, which examines trends in case law and predicts a future outcome on the basis of similar past events, deductive reasoning allows for a more precise analysis of the argument to be made on the facts of the client's issues. Both types of reasoning are used in predictive writing, such as legal memoranda, or persuasive writing, such as facta, both of which are discussed in Part IV of this text.

E. Predicting the Outcome by Summarizing the Legal Argument Conclusions

Summarizing the results of the legal analysis in written form is required before communicating the results to the client. The law is applied to the facts of the case, and predictions are made and qualified, if necessary, about the likely outcome if the matter reaches court. Headings are used to organize the component parts of the discussion, and subheadings provide the reader with the primary legal conclusion.[8]

1. Summary of the Law

a. ANIMAL OWNERS' LIABILITY IN NEGLIGENCE FOR THEIR ROAMING ANIMALS

Repeatedly, Canadian courts have found that animal owners have a duty to prevent their animals from roaming free and are therefore liable for the damages caused when they fail to secure their animals. In *Fleming v Atkinson*,[9] the Supreme Court of Canada found that at common law, ordinary rules of negligence apply in these cases, while in *Ruckheim v Robinson*[10] the court found that animal owners have a duty to ensure that their animals are under control; it is reasonably foreseeable that a roaming animal may cause damage. In *Bujold v Dempsey*,[11] the court found that the owner of a domesticated animal that creates a hazard on a highway can be found liable in negligence for damages. In some jurisdictions, legislation states this rule explicitly.[12]

---

8   See Chapter 12 on plain language writing, which discusses the use of headings and subheadings to bring clarity to legal writing.

9   [1959] SCR 513, 1959 CanLII 10.

10   [1995] 4 WWR 284, 1 BCLR (3d) 46 (CA).

11   (1996), 181 NBR (2d) 111 (QB).

12   See e.g. Newfoundland and Labrador's *Animal Health and Protection Act*, SNL 2010, c A-9.1, ss 31-34.

b. DRIVERS MUST KEEP A PROPER LOOKOUT TO AVOID BEING HELD CONTRIBUTORILY NEGLIGENT

In all circumstances, drivers have a duty to exercise reasonable care: failure to do so will result in a finding of contributory negligence if damages result. Generally, the courts have found that drivers have fulfilled this duty as long as they drive in an alert manner and do not exceed the speed limit.

In *Ruckheim*,[13] contributory negligence was not an issue before the court. In *Fleming*,[14] *Bujold*,[15] and *Spanton v Laviolette*,[16] the court found that the drivers' actions contributed significantly to the damages, and reduced the damage award accordingly. Some jurisdictions have legislation that governs the determination of contributory negligence.[17]

2. Application of the Law to the Facts of This Case

a. BROOK NEGLIGENTLY ALLOWED HIS DOG TO ROAM

If Shybani and Haddad proceed to trial, a court would likely conclude that Brook negligently allowed his dog to escape onto the road, causing Shybani to lose control of his motorcycle, thus making Brook liable in damages.

Haddad can argue that, based on the binding authority of *Fleming* and the persuasive authority of *Ruckheim*, *Bujold*, and *Spanton*, dog owners are liable for damages when their animals roam and damages result. The evidence indicates that Stormy was running free when it darted into the path of Shybani's motorcycle.

Brook is unlikely to succeed if he attempts to counter Haddad's argument by claiming that he took reasonable steps to secure the dog. The intent of the owner to secure an animal will not release an owner from liability of a roaming animal; even the owner of a dog that had been penned, but escaped, was found liable (*Ruckheim*). Therefore, unless additional facts are uncovered that would undermine the claim, Brook will be liable for damages to Haddad and Shybani.

b. SHYBANI AND HADDAD ARE NOT CONTRIBUTORILY NEGLIGENT

Assuming that a court finds Brook negligent, a finding of contributory negligence is unlikely. To find contributory negligence a court must be satisfied that the driver could have avoided the accident or reduced its impact, as found in *Fleming*, *Bujold*,

---

13 *Supra* note 10.

14 *Supra* note 9.

15 *Supra* note 11.

16 (1977), 19 OR (2d) 21, 83 DLR (3d) 740 (Sm Cl Ct).

17 See e.g. Ontario's *Negligence Act*, RSO 1990, c N.1, ss 3-4.

and *Spanton*. To reduce his damages, Brook will require additional evidence to support his claim of contributory negligence. For example, if the distance travelled in the time of the journey indicated that Shybani was speeding, or if evidence is found that Shybani saw the dog before Haddad's warning, Brook's claim would be strengthened. However, based on the known facts, including Haddad's attire, which prevented further injury, Brook is unlikely to succeed with his argument of contributory negligence.

3. Result

Brook will likely be liable for damages caused when Shybani swerved to avoid hitting Stormy, which had escaped onto the highway. Assuming that a court finds that Shybani was exercising due care when driving, therefore the court is unlikely to assess contributory negligence on Shybani's part.[18]

F. Recognizing Logical Fallacies

Recognizing the difference between a sound legal argument and a false argument is important for two reasons. First, if a legal argument is not properly constructed, the other party to the dispute can successfully challenge the claim by identifying the gaps or errors. Second, if you cannot recognize your opponent's faulty reasoning, you will not be able to successfully challenge opposing counsel.

A false argument is a series of statements that purports to be an argument but is fundamentally flawed. Examples of false arguments include *ad hominem* attacks, in which an argument is challenged not on the basis of its soundness but on the basis of who makes it, and a *slippery slope claim*, in which an act is claimed, without proof, to be the first step in a series of consequences resulting in a negative outcome.

Many websites and texts provide descriptions and exercises designed to help the reader recognize logical fallacies and false arguments. For example:

- Foundation for Critical Thinking, <http://www.criticalthinking.org/ctmodel/logic-model1.htm>
- University of North Carolina at Chapel Hill's Writing Center, <http://writingcenter.unc.edu/handouts/fallacies>

---

18   Although the format described here will help you to structure the argument and report conclusions of a complex legal argument, do not sacrifice substance for form—i.e. do not follow the format so rigidly that the writing loses its narrative flow. Once you can follow the format with sufficient precision to ensure that you have included the necessary content, you can work on reclaiming your writer's voice to present the work in your preferred style.

- Bruce N Waller, *Critical Thinking: Consider the Verdict*, 6th ed (Upper Saddle River, NJ: Pearson, 2011)

False arguments do not advance the position of one's client in court.[19] It is therefore advisable to study the structure of the various types of false arguments so that you can successfully challenge them if they are advanced.

G. Creating a Legal Argument: Overview

1. **Identify the Relevant Facts**
2. **Identify the Legal Issue(s)**
3. **Research the Legal Issue(s) and Categorize Case Information**
4. **Apply the Analytical Tools of Inductive Reasoning**
   - Write a case brief for each relevant case you located.
   - Prepare a comparative analysis by making a chart that compares similarities and differences between and among cases.
   - Provide a supporting statement of the general legal rule that will apply to the facts of the problem at hand.
   - Provide specific examples from *analogous* and *distinguishable* cases to demonstrate how courts have previously applied the law in question.
   - Provide a concluding statement that summarizes the applicable law and the likely outcome when it is applied to your client's problem.
5. **Apply the Analytical Tools of Deductive Reasoning**
   - Follow the process for inductive reasoning as described above.
   - For each argument, construct a legal syllogism—major premise, minor premise for each side to the dispute, facts or evidence in support of each side, and conclusion.
   - Summarize the argument results.
6. **Communicate the Results**

---

19 These types of fallacious arguments may be seen at times in the political arena, especially in election campaigns, or sometimes during Question Period.

PART IV
Communication: Legal Writing

Legal Writing: Organizing Principles

12

I. Overview: Therapeutic Considerations of Audience, Purpose, and Tone

In addition to mastering the technical format required in a legal document, you should also take into account a number of other considerations. The first of these considerations is the document's purpose. For example, the document may be intended to provide an objective account of a legal situation, to predict a likely outcome, or to persuade a decision-maker to adopt a particular interpretation of the law. Another important consideration is the capacity of the intended audience to understand the document's message. Each of these considerations affects a writer's choice and arrangement of words.

A document's *purpose*, *audience*, and *tone* are fundamental considerations. Plain language principles and citation rules complement the organizing principles that are foundational to competent legal writing. These issues are discussed in this chapter and further in Chapter 13, where vehicles of legal communication, including the memorandum of law, the opinion letter, and the factum, are described.

Next, two related concepts are introduced: writing as an expression of professional identity and writing as a potentially therapeutic agent. Both concepts have implications for the interpretation of purpose, audience, and tone.

A. Professional Identity

A lawyer's work encompasses service to clients, protection and promotion of the public interest, and the creation of a practice that is consistent with the lawyer's personal values. While it is natural to focus primarily on clients' legal interests, advancing other important interests is also integral to the lawyer's role.

A legal document reflects the professional identity of the lawyer who created it. In a recent study of the development of legal writing expertise, one senior lawyer noted: "[T]hat is your image, and it's the image you project either to the profession, the world or whatever. And it's either one of crispness or intellectual sloppiness".[1]

Codes of professional conduct help to define boundaries for professional work. For example, the Law Society of Upper Canada's *Rules of Professional Conduct* provide that, in offering legal services, a lawyer should not use means that are false or misleading; that amount to coercion, duress, or harassment; or that take advantage of a person who is vulnerable or who has not yet recovered from a traumatic experience.[2]

Additionally, the rules provide that lawyers should conduct themselves in a manner that maintains the integrity of their profession.

Rule 4.01(2) provides:

When acting as an advocate, a lawyer shall not ...

(e) knowingly attempt to deceive a tribunal or influence the course of justice by ... misstating facts or law ...

(f) knowingly misstate the contents of a document ...

(h) deliberately refrain from informing the tribunal of any binding authority that the lawyer considers to be directly on point and that has not been mentioned by an opponent.

Rule 6.03(5) provides:

A lawyer shall not in the course of professional practice send correspondence or otherwise communicate to a client, another legal practitioner, or any other person in a manner that is abusive, offensive, or otherwise inconsistent with the proper tone of a professional communication from a lawyer.

---

1   Erika Abner & Shelley Kierstead, "A Preliminary Exploration of the Elements of Expert Performance in Legal Writing" (2010) 16 J Legal Writing Inst 363 at 389.

2   Law Society of Upper Canada, *Rules of Professional Conduct* (Toronto: LSUC, 2000), r 3.01(2).

While these rules clarify the need to communicate in an honest and respectful manner, they are not focused on the aspects of effective legal writing that accommodate the writer's voice. Traditionally, the voice of the law, as it resounds in legal documents, has been characterized as impersonal, general, and formal.[3] Increasingly, however, a different view of writing is emerging—one that perceives legal writing as representative of the writer, with all of his or her experiences, interacting with the conventions of legal discourse and with particular patterns of speech. Within this process, writing epitomizes the writer's professional identity.

One method of humanizing written communication (and hence enhancing the writer's voice) in documents such as memoranda, opinion letters, and litigation documents is to consider the non-legal implications of the messages that they convey. The approach described below is consistent with the *Rules of Professional Conduct* and provides additional benefits for both the writer and the reader. For example, the writer may feel less alienated from his or her documents.[4] Benefits for readers are explored below.

B. Legal Writers as Therapeutic Agents

Legal writing is not therapy. However, it is possible for the legal writer to take into account therapeutic (non-legal) considerations, such as a client's psychological well-being; it is also possible to maximize this well-being in some instances. Therapeutic jurisprudence is an emerging area of research and writing that explores these issues.[5]

The judicial role in formulating decisions that respond to litigants' emotional needs has been explored in previous academic writing.[6] An example of therapeutic jurisprudence is provided in the passage below. The excerpted paragraphs are from a recent child protection decision[7] involving a parent who was unsuccessful in retaining parenting rights to her child.

---

3 J Christopher Rideout, "Voice, Self, and Persona in Legal Writing" (2009) 15 J Legal Writing Inst 67.

4 For a discussion of the experience of alienation, see Douglas Litowitz, "Legal Writing: Its Nature, Limits and Dangers" (1998) 49 Mercer L Rev 709.

5 For a general overview of therapeutic jurisprudence, see David Wexler & Bruce Winick, *Law in a Therapeutic Key: Developments in Therapeutic Jurisprudence* (Durham, NC: Carolina Academic Press, 1996).

6 See e.g. Nathalie Des Rosiers, "From Telling to Listening: A Therapeutic Analysis of the Role of Courts in Minority-Majority Conflicts" (2000) 37 Court Review 54, and Amy D Ronner & Bruce Winick, "Silencing the Appellant's Voice: The Antitherapeutic Per Curiam Affirmance" (2000) 24 Seattle U Law R 499.

7 *Catholic Children's Aid Society of Toronto v SS*, 2010 ONCJ 700 at paras 161-163 (emphasis added and internal citations omitted).

Conclusion

161 An order will go that:

   (a) [RS] be made a Crown ward without access for the purpose of adoption.

   (b) That the mother will have no access to [AS] for the purpose of adoption.

162 *I recognize that this will be a very difficult outcome for the mother. She demonstrated her love for the children and did the very best she could.* It appears that she will likely have an open adoption arrangement for [AS]. The mother is a good candidate for an open adoption arrangement for [RS] as well. The mother has demonstrated that she is willing to work co-operatively with the children's caregivers and is unlikely to undermine any future placement.

163 This order does not preclude the society, in its capacity as custodial parent of Crown wards, from permitting the mother to visit the children prior to an adoption. The society will have full control over any contact that the mother has with them.

While not alleviating the trauma that the mother is likely to experience, the wording of the judgment recognizes how difficult the decision will be for her, and articulates the efforts that she has made. It provides some hope for possible continued contact with her children. The judgment may have the additional benefit in years to come of informing the children why they did not grow up with their mother. It may help to clarify that their adoption was not the result of their mother not wanting to parent them, but rather the result of the fact that she could not parent them. In crafting this decision, the judge paid careful attention to the audience that was most likely to be affected by it, its purpose (to convey the result in the least emotionally damaging manner), and the tone that was most likely to achieve this purpose.

Lawyers also have the capacity to consider audience, purpose, and tone in a manner that lightens an emotionally difficult message. Without sacrificing sound legal analysis, fearless advocacy, or strong arguments, lawyers can produce legal documents whose tone recognizes legal system participants as the intended audience and gives voice to the interests of clients without destroying the integrity of opposing parties.

The approach to writing presented in this chapter is consistent with the concept of preventive lawyering,[8] which examines ways to prevent legal risks from becoming legal problems. The approach also resonates with the concept of client-centred lawyering. One of the justifications for client-centred lawyering is that clients view solutions generated within the lawyer–client relationship as successful when and

---

8   For a discussion of preventive lawyering, see Susan Daicoff, *Comprehensive Law Practice: Law as a Healing Profession* (Durham, NC: Carolina Academic Press, 2011).

to the extent that these solutions respond to their concerns about non-legal consequences.[9] In addition, studies suggest that if clients believe that they have been heard and understood, they tend to believe that the legal system has been responsive to their situation, regardless of their actual level of success.[10] By producing writing that is keenly attuned to the potential reactions of their readers, lawyers are likely to persuade their readers both of the soundness of their legal analysis and of their respect for the human circumstances that underlie many legal problems. This approach may, in turn, improve both individual and public confidence in the work of lawyers generally.

C. Applying More Nuanced Considerations of Audience, Purpose, and Tone

Relatively minor changes to legal documents may positively affect a reader's response to them. The first example below focuses on an opinion letter that is aimed at providing clients with an objective opinion concerning their legal situation. The second example, an excerpt from a statement of claim, illustrates the potential for setting out a legal claim without evoking instant hostility from the opposing party.

1. Example: Opinion Letter

In an opinion letter, it is critical to integrate legally relevant facts with facts that are important to the client. Further, a compassionate recitation of facts may assist clients in feeling that their situation has truly been understood and that the opinion responds to their needs at both the legal and the human level. Compare the following two paragraphs:

1. You indicated that you have developed an attachment to the matrimonial home and the neighbourhood in which it is located. However, given that your children are independent adults, there is virtually no prospect of you successfully obtaining exclusive possession of the matrimonial home.
2. We discussed at length your fondness for the matrimonial home—which you have lived in for 20 years—and for the neighbourhood generally. Unfortunately, given that your children are now living on their own, my research suggests that a claim for exclusive possession of the matrimonial home would very likely be unsuccessful.

---

9   *Ibid* at 5.

10   Ronner & Winick, *supra* note 6. See especially the sources listed at note 13 therein.

The first paragraph provides an accurate description of the facts that the clients presented to the lawyer and a clear articulation of the lawyer's opinion. However, the information is presented in a fairly formal and impersonal manner. The second paragraph pays closer attention to the needs of the readers (the disappointed clients), adopting a less formal and more empathetic tone, which is likely to resonate more positively with the clients.

TASK 12.1

Opinion Letter: Consider the Audience

Consider the passages below from an opinion letter sent to individuals who were seeking to avoid paying an international education program fee for a child who had been in their care for a number of years, but for whom they did not act as "guardian".[11] How do the passages reflect the lawyer's empathy for the clients' position while providing solid legal advice?

Because you and your wife are ordinarily resident in [province] and have been raising [child] as your own daughter here for the past five years, and because [child] is now a Canadian citizen, it naturally does not seem right to you that you should have to pay for [child]'s schooling. However, [child]'s application to the board shows her as having a [country of origin of child] address, and the board's acceptance letter shows you as having been appointed as [child]'s custodian, not her guardian.

...

As you can see, there are a number of things to think about and to discuss before you can proceed. While some of what I have said in this letter may be disappointing to you, I hope that you and your wife will understand that the research and analysis outlined above has saved you from making a court application that would almost certainly have failed because it would have lacked the proper motivation and focus. If you now decide to apply for guardianship, you will be in a much better position to make an application that has a good chance of success.

---

11   The sample was kindly provided by a lawyer who removed all identifying information from the letter. A copy is on file with co-author Shelley Kierstead.

2. Example: Statement of Claim

Although an opinion letter has a specific audience—the party to whom it is directed—pleadings and facta are examples of legal documents that are viewed by a broader audience. Judges, for example, are part of the audience for these documents, and, as a result, the professional responsibility requirements associated with acting in a credible manner come sharply into focus. Opposing parties also read these documents, and it is relevant to recall that inflammatory language can be harmful both to the opposing party and to your client. Needlessly escalating the hostility associated with a legal proceeding through the use of inflammatory legal documents is likely to exacerbate litigation-related stress, which has been identified as harmful.[12]

Pleadings often contain "boilerplate" clauses—standard clauses intended to cover a broad range of possible circumstances. Consider the following excerpt from a standard motor vehicle accident claim:[13]

> [Para]   The particulars of the negligence of the Defendant are as follows:
>
> ...
>
>   (k) at the time being her faculties of observance, perception, judgment and self-control were impaired, and due to her physical and mental condition, she was incompetent to operate a motor vehicle with normal and reasonable care and attention;
>
>   (l) her ability to operate a motor vehicle was impaired by reason of consumption of alcohol and drugs;
>
> ...

While lawyers justify pleadings of this nature on the basis that they can encompass all possible situations, it may be useful to consider the likely response of a defendant who has never used drugs and who abhors drinking and driving. Reading this claim is likely to anger the defendant and inspire a hostile response. Such a reaction has the potential to escalate the defendant's litigiousness. In light of the current permissiveness of procedural rules that allow for the amendment of documents, it seems likely that certain boilerplate standards can be safely deleted in many cases, resulting in a more realistic set of allegations that delineate all plausible claims while remaining respectful of the opposing party.

---

12   For an account of this stress in the family litigation context, see MK Pruett and TD Jackson, "Perspectives on the Divorce Process: Parental Perceptions of the Legal System and Its Impact on Family Relations" (2001) 29 J Am Acad Psychiatry 18.

13   The statement of claim from which these paragraphs were excerpted was kindly provided by a lawyer who removed all identifying information. The document is on file with co-author Shelley Kierstead.

TASK 12.2

Factum Drafting: Consider the Tone

Examine the following factum paragraphs and consider how they could be rewritten. Keep in mind that one of the purposes of a factum is to persuade a decision-maker of the strength of a client's position while representing facts and legal principles accurately. Consider the challenge of presenting the client's case in the most persuasive manner while not disparaging the other party. The factum from which the following excerpts are derived was written to support a motion by the defendant to have the plaintiff's claim dismissed because it was commenced after the expiry of the relevant limitation period.

[Para]   Section 5(1)(b) of the *Limitations Act* provides that the limitation period is to run from "the day on which a reasonable person with the abilities and in the circumstances of the person with the claim first ought to have known of the matters referred to" in the claim.

   [Sources omitted]

[Para]   Case law has established factors that might delay the commencement of a limitation period. It is obvious that none of these factors exists in this case to provide a justification for Ms. Smill's blatant failure to commence this action within the two-year limitation period prescribed by the Act.

[Para]   The full extent of a medical injury need not be known in order to have reasonable awareness that a claim is emergent. The source of this claim is the riding accident that allegedly occurred on September 22, 20XX. The plaintiff claims to have experienced intense pain after the riding fall. She sought medical attention within a day of the accident. If there was any basis whatsoever for this highly questionable claim, the plaintiff would or should have known in September 20XX that the accident was its source.

   [Sources omitted]

II. Plain Language

A. Traditional Legal Writing

> We Lawyers do not write plain English. We use eight words to say what could be said in two. We use arcane phrases to express common-place ideas. Seeking to be precise, we become redundant. Seeking to be cautious, we become verbose. Our sentences twist on, phrase within clause within clause, glazing the eyes and numbing the minds of our readers.[14]

Clear communication is a professional obligation. Yet too often legal documents are inaccessible to their audience. In response to complaints by clients that legal documents were too difficult to understand, the plain language movement began to focus on the needs of the reader. The term "plain language" is often used interchangeably with the term "plain English" in the academic literature on this topic.[15]

Drafting documents in plain language traverses both national geographical boundaries and disciplines of study.[16] The Canadian Bar Association prepared a resolution on plain language documentation more than 20 years ago,[17] recommending, among other things, that

> Canadian law schools and Bar Admissions courses should be urged to include a plain language drafting course in their curriculum in an effort to instruct law students on how to write better, more plainly, and more clearly.

B. Incorporating Plain Language Principles in Legal Writing

Whether or not you have had an opportunity to take a course or attend a conference on plain language drafting, there are a number of steps that you can take to improve the clarity of your writing.

---

14 Richard C Wydick, *Plain English for Lawyers*, 4th ed (Durham, NC: Carolina Academic Press, 1988) at 3.

15 Christine Mowat, *A Plain Language Handbook for Legal Writers* (Scarborough, ON: Carswell, 1998) at 3-4.

16 See the Plain Language Association International website at <http://www.plainlanguagenetwork.org> for links to information about plain language drafting, including research, conference information, and sources that can be used to develop legal literacy.

17 See the Plain Language Association International website, *ibid*, for a copy of the proposed resolution. The Canadian Bar Association provides links to plain language sources through its website at <http://www.cba.org>.

1. Become Aware of Plain Language Principles

The term "plain language" can be misconstrued without a thorough investigation of its meaning.

Michèle M. Asprey explains it as follows:[18]

> Some people think that because plain language is simple, it must be simplistic—a kind of baby-talk. That is also wrong. Simple in this sense doesn't mean simplistic. It means straightforward, clear, precise. It can be elegant and dramatic. It can even be beautiful.

Plain language drafting focuses on increasing the audience's understanding of complex information. Not only does it focus on technical aspects of writing, such as sentence length, it also focuses on information organization, such as the use of headings, subheadings, and even the ratio of text to blank space on a page.

2. Assess Your Strengths and Weaknesses

Developing skill in plain language drafting requires an understanding of the rules of grammar, punctuation, capitalization, and sentence and paragraph organization. You need to understand these rules to be able to apply them when editing both your own work and the work of others.

Many students entering law school find it useful to refresh their skills.[19] For example, applying the plain language recommendation "prefer the active voice," which is discussed later in this chapter, presumes an understanding of the difference between the active voice and the present tense, two concepts that are frequently confused.[20]

Therefore, it is important to assess your skill level objectively at the beginning of your legal studies. Do not rely solely on computer spell-checkers and grammar-checkers when proofreading. These programs identify some but not all errors.

---

18   Michèle M Asprey, *Plain Language for Lawyers*, 4th ed (Annandale, AU: Federation Press, 2010) at 12. See also the Plain Language Association International website for further comments on plain language in the legal writing context, *supra* note 16.

19   Many universities provide academic writing centres, which frequently make their resources available online.

20   As identified by co-author Moira McCarney in the writing quiz that she provides to her students during the first week of classes.

3. Adopt Five Conventions to Improve Clarity[21]

a. SENTENCE LENGTH AND ORGANIZATION

Become aware of sentence length. Most sentences should contain fewer than 25 words; however, a variation in sentence length enhances narrative flow. Avoid extremely long sentences. When writing a conditional sentence ("If ... then/unless/except"), place the clause containing the condition where it will help the reader. Generally, a conditional clause that is longer than the main part of the sentence is placed at the end of the sentence, while a short conditional clause is placed at the beginning. For example, "Unless *mens rea* can be established, the accused will be acquitted of the first degree murder charge that he is facing".

Each sentence should contain one main thought. When sentences are connected by a conjunction ("and", "or", "but"), ensure that the ideas are connected. Maintain parallel structure within a sentence. Do not write in sentence fragments (subordinate clauses or phrases standing alone). For example, "Whether the accused will plead guilty".

Place the subject near the beginning of a sentence and modifying words close to the words that they modify. Avoid negative sentence construction when possible; if one of your sentences contains a double or triple negative construction, start over unless you are consciously producing a particular effect. For example, "The accused did not plead not guilty".

Software applications allow you to check average sentence length. For example, the average sentence length in this chapter is 18.2 words.

b. ACTIVE VOICE

Generally, it is preferable to use the active voice in legal writing, although there are situations in which the passive voice is a better choice.

When a sentence is written in the active voice, the subject of the sentence is the person or object that performs the action.

On Friday, Jones assaulted Smith.

---

21 This section highlights some techniques to improve the clarity of your writing. However, there are many other excellent sources, some which contain general information to improve writing skills, some which provide tips to create specific documents, and others which supply practice exercise assignments. See e.g. the links provided in the Literacy Resources section of the Plain Language Association International website, *supra* note 16, and Christine Mowat's text, *supra* note 15, as well as sources listed at the end of this section.

When a sentence is written in the passive voice, the subject of the sentence is the person or object that is acted upon.

> On Friday, Smith was assaulted by Jones.
>
> On Friday, Smith was assaulted.

In the last example, the sentence is properly constructed because it has a subject, "Smith," and a verb, "was assaulted," even though the reader does not know who committed the assault.

However, passive voice sentence construction can lead to ambiguity when the actor is hidden, as in the last example. It may also result in sentences that are longer than those constructed in the active voice, as can be seen in the examples above.

The use of the passive voice is appropriate in certain circumstances—when, for example, the actor is unknown or the focus of the sentence is on the act rather than the actor. Consider the following example in which a company's press release might intentionally hide the actor.

> Letters of termination were issued to 20 employees on Friday.

Now consider how that same idea might be communicated in the active voice by the union representing the terminated employees:

> On Friday, Nancy Berrie, CEO of the profitable Berries to You food-processing company, fired 20 employees.

In this example, the active voice is effective in identifying the actor and the action taken.

To determine if the passive voice is being used, look for adverbs such as "by" coupled with various tenses of the verb "to be" (e.g. "is", "was/were", "will"). These words are often a sign of a passive voice construction. Some word-processing programs have a grammar feature that locates the passive voice and suggests alternatives. However, the alternatives are not always phrased appropriately, so you must be able to invent a desirable substitute.

c. NOMINALIZATION

Nominalization occurs when a verb is converted into a noun. For example, "agree" becomes "agreement", "settle" becomes "settlement", "avoid" becomes "avoidance", and "disturb" becomes "disturbance".

Although the occasional use of nominalization is acceptable, excessive use is undesirable. Nominalization, the passive voice, and wordy sentences are often associated. For example, compare the following:

> An agreement to settle the dispute was reached by the parties.
>
> The parties agreed to settle the dispute.

The first sentence contains 11 words, while the second sentence contains 7. The first sentence uses passive voice construction, while the second sentence uses the active voice. The first sentence nominalizes the verb "agree," while the second sentence uses the verb itself.

Reducing nominalization and passive voice sentence construction improves the clarity of the message.

d. WORD CHOICE

Words should be chosen with care as you strive to make your point accurately and briefly. Developing a robust vocabulary and selecting strong nouns and verbs that are the most appropriate words to describe an object or event decrease the use of adjectives and adverbs and reduce the overall word count.

Remove unnecessary words or phrases. The removal of "very" is a good example of this rule: rather than describing something as "very small", substitute the word "tiny". Phrases such as "it is clear that" and "it goes without saying that" bloat a sentence and add no usable information; they should be omitted. There is some disagreement whether legal redundancies such as "force and effect", "null and void", and "cease and desist" can be avoided. Although in each instance the second word duplicates the meaning of the first, sometimes these phrases have been the subject of judicial interpretation and therefore should not be altered.

While words with a specific legal meaning are part of a lawyer's working vocabulary, there are other words, called "legalese" or "legalisms", that may sound lawyerly but are archaic; these include "said", "aforesaid", and "aforementioned". They can be removed without loss of meaning. When using standard and necessary legal terms, consider your audience. For example, when writing to a client who is unfamiliar with the law, avoid legal terms or explain them in plain language.

Avoid varying a word or term that refers to a particular object or event within a single document because this practice can lead to confusion. For example, consider a document that contains the sentence "Smith shot Jones with a gun". Throughout the document, the word "gun" should be used when referring to the weapon that shot Jones; the words "pistol" or "revolver" should not appear in this context.

e. AUDIENCE

Those who write in plain language consider their audience and vary the structure of a document to accommodate the audience's needs. Since their audience is frequently a judge or another lawyer and the document may become public, the tone is usually formal. Therefore, avoid the use of contractions, slang and informal phrasing, and colourful euphemisms. Gender-neutral language is the norm, unless you are discussing the facts of a specific case.

Avoid the use of exclamation points, emoticons, or typographical techniques such as boldfacing, underlining, highlighting, or italicizing words or phrases. Rhetorical questions should be used sparingly, if at all. While these techniques are often adopted by a writer to draw certain points to a reader's attention, they are usually not appropriate in formal legal writing.

One technique that is particularly helpful to most readers, and that is frequently overlooked by writers, is the use of informational headings and subheadings to organize text. In lengthy documents, these headings and subheadings can be compiled into a table of contents to help the reader navigate the document. They are being used increasingly by the judiciary in written judgments.

Finally, recognize that plain language focuses not merely subjectively on the information to be conveyed by the writer but also objectively on the ease with which this information is received by the reader. Therefore, you should take all the time you need, not only to proofread but also to edit your work as often as necessary, before arriving at a final draft.

FIGURE 12.1   Plain Language Sources

Author(s)	Title	Journal	Year
US Journal Articles			
Abner, Erika & Shelley Kierstead	A Preliminary Exploration of the Elements of Expert Performance in Legal Writing	Legal Writing: The Journal of the Legal Writing Institute	2010
Bierig, Steven M	Lawyers Etc.: An Arbitrator's Perspective on Writing	Chicago Bar Association Record	2000
Bingler, Richard	The Politics of Legal Writing: Now Comes the Unbending Boss	The Scribes Journal of Legal Writing	1998-2000
Cohen, Debra R	Competent Legal Writing— A Lawyer's Professional Responsibility	University of Cincinnati Law Review	1999

Author(s)	Title	Journal	Year
Cooney, Mark	Plain Language: Are You a Hyphen-Happy Lawyer?	Michigan Bar Journal	2011
Eagleson, Robert	Plain Language: Changing the Lawyer's Image and Goals	The Scribes Journal of Legal Writing	1998-2000
Eagleson, Robert	Plain Language: Ensnaring Perceptions on Communication: Underlying Obstacles to Lawyers' Writing Plainly	Michigan Bar Journal	2010
Flammer, Sean	Persuading Judges: An Empirical Analysis of Writing Style, Persuasion and the Use of Plain English	Legal Writing: The Journal of the Legal Writing Institute	2010
Garner, Bryan A	Plain Language: Set the Right Hedonic Tone to Keep Readers' Interest	Michigan Bar Journal	2010
Haggard, Thomas	The "Best Of" Series: Good Writing as a Professional Responsibility	The Scribes Journal of Legal Writing	2001-2
Haggard, Thomas	Plain Language: The Ambiguous And and Or	Michigan Bar Journal	2001
Haggard, Thomas	Plain Language: Definitions	Michigan Bar Journal	2001
Kimble, Joseph	Answering the Critics of Plain Language	The Scribes Journal of Legal Writing	1994-95
Kimble, Joseph	Plain Language: The Great Myth That Plain Language Is Not Precise	Michigan Bar Journal	1998-2000
Kimble, Joseph	Plain Language: A Modest Wish List for Legal Writing	Michigan Bar Journal	2000
Kimble, Joseph	Plain Language: Plain Words (Part 1)	Michigan Bar Journal	2001
Kimble, Joseph	Plain Language: Plain Words (Part 2)	Michigan Bar Journal	2001
Kimble, Joseph	Writing for Dollars, Writing to Please	The Scribes Journal of Legal Writing	1996-97
Mooney, Clark J	Plain Language: To Mrs. Finklebean: The Truth About Conjunctions as Sentence-Starters	Michigan Bar Journal	2010

Author(s)	Title	Journal	Year
Narko, Kathleen Dillon	Nota Bene: Lifting the Fog of Legalese Targets Wide Audience: Plain Language for Everyone	Chicago Bar Association Record	2006
Oettle, Kenneth F	Plain Language: Don't Give Your Adversaries Free Airtime	Michigan Bar Journal	2008
Oettle, Kenneth F	Plain Language: Eschew Exaggerations, Disparagements, and Other Intensifiers	Michigan Bar Journal	2008
Oettle, Kenneth F	Plain Language: Give a Quotation a Good Introduction	Michigan Bar Journal	2008
Painter, Mark P	Plain Language: Writing Smaller	Michigan Bar Journal	2010
Pinckert, Eric	Plain English, Plain Sense	Michigan Bar Journal	2000
Rohe, John F	Plain Language: The Arrows in Our Quiver	Michigan Bar Journal	2000
Schiess, Wayne	What Plain English Really Is	The Scribes Journal of Legal Writing	2003-4
Siegel, Jane M	Plain Language: The Politics and Power of Plain Language	Michigan Bar Journal	2011
Wydick, Richard C	Review Essay [review of the book Legal Language by Peter M Tiersma]	The Scribes Journal of Legal Writing	1998-2000
Younger, Irving	The "Best Of" Series: Symptoms of Bad Writing	The Scribes Journal of Legal Writing	2001-2
Canadian Journal Articles*			
Laskin, John I, JA	Forget the Windup and Make the Pitch: Some Suggestions for Writing More Persuasive Factums	The Advocates' Society Journal	1999
McLachlin, Beverley, CJC	Legal Writing: Some Tools	Alberta Law Review	2001

* In addition to the two articles listed here, the CBA provides links to many articles about plain language writing. See <http://www.cba.org/cba/home/includes/SearchPage.aspx ?txtSearch=plain>.

III. Applying Citation Rules

Whatever citation method one chooses, overarching principles and conventions must be understood and followed where appropriate to ensure a consistent format. In Canada, the most widely used publication of recommended citation rules is the *Canadian Guide to Uniform Legal Citation*.[22] In the commentary that follows, we highlight some of the features that should be noted when learning legal citation.

In legal documents, variations of citation rules apply within the document itself and the end of the document in a table that summarizes the references used as discussed below.

A. What to Cite: Print and Online

- primary sources of law: legislation and case law
- secondary sources of law (books, periodical articles, *Hansard*, government documents, newspaper articles, policy manuals, website information)
- e-communication sources (email messages, text messages, phone calls, social media)
- cites to any reference (including paraphrases, borrowed ideas to any source of information not originally your own)
- quotations: direct or indirect (paraphrases of direct quotations)

B. When and How to Cite

1. Footnotes

- When citing any of the material noted above, provide an authority and footnote it appropriately.
- A footnote number follows the last word of the thought to which the footnote refers; the number need not appear at the end of a sentence. More than one footnote number may appear in the same sentence. If the word to which the footnote number is appended is followed by a punctuation mark, the footnote number follows immediately after the punctuation.
- The footnote itself begins with a number that refers the reader to a specific part of the text. Each footnote ends with a period.

---

22 7th ed (Toronto: Carswell, 2010) [McGill Guide].

- Note the different conventions when providing a short-form identifier for legal documents and for factual references. In a memorandum of law, places, people, and events should be given a short-form identifier in the text. Use parentheses and quotation marks to identify them: e.g. Marcus McCord ("McCord") attended the Danville Fair ("Fair") on 12 October 20XX. Then, for the remainder of the paper, use the short-form identifier and not the full name.

- In contrast, cases, statutes, and other primary and secondary legal sources may be given a short-form title only in a footnote: e.g. if referring to the *Criminal Code* in the text, the citation includes a short form [*Code*] at the end of the footnote followed by a period. Once the short-form identifier is given in the footnote, the full title is not used again in the body of the text.

- Strive to make a memorandum of law easy to read by placing relevant identifying information in the footnote, rather than in the body of the memorandum.

2. *Case Citations*

- A complete citation is used the first time a case is mentioned, whether in the text or in a footnote.

- Once a case has received a short title, do not refer to the case by the full title again in the document.

- Chapter 3 of the McGill Guide suggests several conventions to adopt when selecting reporters to use and their placement within a case citation.

- A pinpoint identifies specific words and phrases in primary law that are used to support a point in a legal argument; they are also used when identifying secondary sources that support some aspect of a legal argument.

- Accurate pinpointing requires that you identify the reporter you are using; if referencing more than one reporter, you must identify the particular reporter you are citing.

- A pinpoint reference must refer to the actual text. When citing to a case, never provide a pinpoint reference to a headnote, which is the creation of a publisher and not a court.

- Footnotes for legal memoranda are placed at the bottom of the page. Traditionally, citations for facta are placed within the text itself or following a numbered paragraph. It has become more common in recent years for facta citation references to be put into footnotes.

- If the style of cause is given in the text, do not include it in the footnote. Instead, begin the citation with the year. If the court provided a neutral citation, place that first. Otherwise, begin the citation with the year either in parentheses, e.g. (1992), or brackets, e.g. [1993], depending on the style used in the reporter.

3. Citation of Legislation

- A statute title that is contained in the text is not reproduced in the footnote citation. The citation begins with the statute volume: e.g. RSC 1985 or RSO 1990. However, if the name of the statute is not included in the text, include the statute title in the footnote.
- Use the official short title, when available, to reference statutes.
- If a statute section has been renumbered and the renumbering is relevant to your discussion, indicate the renumbering by placing the information in square brackets in the text: e.g. "section 25 of the *Code* [formerly section 22]". Ensure that the reference is to the same statute consolidation by consulting the tables of concordance, if necessary.
- When referring to legislation, the word "section" is written in full in the body of the text, while the abbreviation "s" is used in footnotes. If a section number is mentioned in the text, do not repeat it in the footnote. If it is omitted from the text, pinpoint it in the footnote.

4. Subsequent References

- *Supra* directs the reader to the original footnote. It is always italicized, and it is capitalized if it is the first word in the citation. *Supra* is followed immediately by the word "note" and the number of the footnote that contains the complete citation. A pinpoint reference is usually required.

Supra note 4 at 7.

- When an original reference is not in close proximity to a subsequent reference that needs a footnote, include a short title followed by a comma in the subsequent footnote.

Jones, supra note 4 at 7.

- *Ibid*, which means "the same as", is a cross-referencing signal used to refer the reader back to the preceding footnote. It is italicized and capitalized if it is the first word in the citation.
- A pinpoint reference is often required with *ibid*: e.g. *Ibid* at 10.

- For books and articles, use either a short form of the title or the author's name. Assume, for example, that footnote 8 reads as follows:

> 8. J Berryman et al, *Remedies: Cases and Materials*, 6th ed (Toronto: Emond Montgomery, 2012) [*Remedies*].

A subsequent reference to this footnote in footnote 10 could be either of the following:

> 10. *Remedies, supra* note 8 at 36.
> 10. Berryman, *supra* note 8 at 36.

5. Tables of Authorities

- A writer's sources are summarized at the end of documents such as memoranda and facta. The McGill Guide provides an example of a suggested style to organize primary law and secondary law sources, which can be adapted as required.

6. Quotations

- A quotation must be an exact reproduction of the original source.
- Paraphrases are not included in quotation marks but must be pinpoint referenced.

Finally, examine your work from the point of view of your reader. If your reader might be in doubt about the source to which you are referring, insert a footnote.

Vehicles of Legal Communication

13

By the end of this chapter, you should be able to:

- Distinguish between objective and persuasive legal writing
- Identify the purpose, structure, and audience of a memorandum of law
- Identify the purpose, structure, and audience of a letter of opinion
- Identify the purpose, structure, and audience of an affidavit
- Identify the purpose, structure, and audience of a factum
- Identify the purpose, structure, and audience of a motion
- Identify the purpose, structure, and audience of both a case comment and a legislative comment

Writing Tasks

I. Overview: Contrasting Objective Writing with Persuasive Writing

Chapter 12 discussed the importance of determining the audience, purpose, and tone of various legal documents and the need to convey your message clearly. There is another dimension that you now must consider: whether you have created the document merely to inform your readers, or both to inform and to persuade them to adopt a specific point of view.

This chapter explains how to create both types of legal documents: those that are used primarily to inform (such as letters of opinion, affidavits, and memoranda of law) and those that are used for the dual purpose of informing and advocating (such as facta and motions). In addition, the chapter reviews another form of legal writing, the case or legislative comment, which incorporates the critical analysis found in a legal essay within a discussion of the development of a specific area of the law.

Most law students are expected to prepare at least some of these documents at law school and, depending on their type of legal practice, after their call to the bar.

II. Memorandum of Law

A. Structure

Audience: Other lawyers, the judiciary, and possibly the client. Typically, a memorandum of law is prepared for a supervising lawyer with primary carriage of the file.

Purpose: To analyze and synthesize the law that applies to legal issues. A memorandum that is created to address a specific client's situation includes legal argument and can serve as a source document for many other legal documents, including letters and facta.

Tone: Objective, neutral, and formal.

The legal advice that a lawyer gives to a client is only as sound as the lawyer's knowledge of the law and its application to the facts provided by the client. Because the law changes over time, the results of the legal research undertaken on behalf of a client must reflect the state of the law at the time the client seeks legal advice.

A memorandum of law is usually an internal document within a firm or department that assists a lawyer in understanding the law that applies to a specific issue. Sometimes, legal memoranda focus on a general discussion of the law. Legal memoranda may be completed for the judiciary by law clerks. However, when they are created to answer a client's specific legal needs, they also include relevant facts, a summary of the applicable law, legal arguments for both sides of the dispute, and remedies potentially available to the client. While a memorandum of law examines the advocacy that may be undertaken on behalf of the client, it is considered to be objective legal writing because it analyzes both sides of a dispute, identifying the strengths and weaknesses of the parties' claims.

Although the format of a memorandum of law may vary among law offices, the type of information to be included is similar in most instances. The discussion that follows describes this information.[1]

---

1   The discussion about document preparation described in this chapter is necessarily generic. Once you begin to work or volunteer in a legal setting, ask to see the precedent file and adapt the information in this chapter accordingly.

Essential Components of a Memorandum of Law

Thoroughly prepared legal memoranda have several features in common, including:

- effective organization and clear, reader-friendly plain language writing
- accurate identification of legal issues
- thorough analysis of relevant legislation and case law
- accurate citation of sources
- if the memorandum is addressing a client's issue:
  - a summary of facts that are relevant to both sides of the dispute (see Chapter 2)
  - a summary of potential legal arguments and counterarguments for both sides of the dispute (see Chapter 11)
  - a conclusion that predicts the likely outcome of the dispute (qualified if necessary) and recommendations when required
  - potential remedies available to the client
- if the predicted outcome must be qualified, an explanation of why the qualification is needed (e.g. additional facts must be ascertained, law is unsettled)
- if the issue involves developing law, statutory interpretation, or a potential constitutional challenge, a complete legislative history, underlying policy considerations, and a summary of the law from other jurisdictions
- table of authorities; table of contents
- appendixes containing relevant excerpts from sources

B. Organization

Memoranda of law can range in length from a few pages to 20 pages or more. Legal memoranda that exceed 5 pages can be easily navigated if they are prefaced by a title page and, on a subsequent page, a table of contents, which lists sections by heading and subheading and assigns them a page number. Within the body of the document are: the facts, the legal issues, a brief answer, an analysis (with issues and subissues numbered and lettered), a conclusion, and a table of authorities.

The section entitled "Facts" describes the facts that relate to the client's problem. It is followed by a section entitled "Legal Issues", which identifies the relevant issues that arise from these facts. The next section is the "Brief Answer", which is a summary of your legal opinion about the merit of the client's position. The brief answer summarizes the salient points that are reviewed in depth in the "Discussion", which follows. The discussion provides an analysis of the law, including relevant primary law (legislation and judicial decisions) and secondary sources if applicable. Synthesize this information to provide a framework for an analysis of the client's factual situation. The law as it existed at the time the problem arose is then applied to the facts. Once you have thoroughly analyzed and synthesized the law, examine the strengths and the weaknesses of the client's position by assessing both the legal arguments favourable to the client and the counterarguments (the legal arguments that support the position of the other side to the dispute).

Once each legal issue has been analyzed and the client's legal position has been determined, summarize the client's overall legal position in a section entitled "Conclusion". A conclusion may contain recommendations when appropriate. If it does, call the section "Conclusion and Recommendations". The document is supported by citations throughout. A "Table of Authorities", similar to a bibliography, is placed at the end of the memorandum, and the document concludes with "Appendixes", which includes excerpts of the soruces relied on in the analysis.

This analytical format can be applied to Shybani and Haddad's legal problem, which was described in Chapter 11. Review the information and decide how each aspect of the legal analysis would be organized in a memorandum of law. For example, Figure 13.1 illustrates how the discussion section would include a legal analysis and a summary of the law derived from reviewing the legislation and cases and applying the techniques of inductive reasoning. It would also include the application of the facts to the law, which involves a deductive reasoning analysis.

1. Facts

Facts are presented sometimes in narrative paragraphs and sometimes in numbered statements; determine the style that your law firm or school prefers.

When preparing the facts section:

- Identify the client and the other parties; briefly summarize the basis of the dispute.
- Answer the questions who, where, what, when, how, and why.
- Determine the order of presentation, either chronological or otherwise.
- Include all legally relevant facts, which include both facts that support your client's position and those that undermine it.
- Include connector facts, which, although not determinative of the legal outcome, are necessary to understand the relevant facts, including facts that are contrary.
- Omit irrelevant facts.
- Present the facts accurately.
- Present the facts objectively.

FIGURE 13.1 Memorandum of Law Format: Shybani and Haddad v Brook

---

(Title Page)

Memorandum of Law

TO: Person who commissioned the memorandum   (professor/lawyer/judge)

FROM: Writer's name

DATE: December 1, 20XX   (date of submission of final draft)

CLIENT: Shybani and Haddad # RJ 20XX–543   (client's name and file number)

RE: 1. Liability—Negligence—Animal running free

            2. Contributory negligence   (identification of legal issues)

****

(First Page)

Table of Contents

Facts   (Page numbers)

Legal Issues

   1. Is Brook liable to Shybani and Haddad for damages by negligently allowing his dog
to run free?

   2. Are Shybani and Haddad contributorily negligent?

Brief Answer   (Similar to a headnote in a case, a brief answer in a memorandum
                 provides the legal and factual basis to answer the issue.)

Discussion

                (Use headings and subheadings to organize content)

   **1. Is Brook liable to Shybani and Haddad for damages for negligently allowing his
dog to run free?**

      a. Legal Analysis
         i. Legislation
         ii. Case Law

(Add additional headings if needed: e.g. secondary sources of law, policy information.
       Alternatively, incorporate this type of information under the
              headings of Legislation or Case Law, if preferred.)

      b. Summary of Law

Animal owners are liable for damages caused when animals roam free.

      c. Application of Law to Facts (Legal Arguments)

*Brook negligently allowed his dog to run free and is liable for resulting damages to
Shybani and Haddad.*

   2. Are Shybani and Haddad contributorily negligent?

      a. Legal Analysis
         i. Legislation
         ii. Case Law

      b. Summary of Law

Drivers must keep a proper lookout to avoid being held contributorily negligent.

      c. Application of Law to Facts (Legal Arguments)

Shybani and Haddad are not contributorily negligent.

Conclusion and Recommendations

Table of Authorities

Appendixes (primary and secondary sources of law, other sources)

- Omit conclusions and arguments.
- Identify assumed and unknown facts.
- Ensure that all facts relied on in the discussion section are included in the facts section.

2. Legal Issues

- Number the issues; use letters for any subissues.
- Ensure that each issue is relevant to the legal problem.
- Frame each issue broadly enough to encompass a full discussion of the law.

Present the issues and subissues as questions to be answered by the legal analysis found later in the memorandum.

3. Brief Answer

- The brief answer introduces the Discussion section, which provides in-depth legal analysis and argument summary to support the analysis. The brief answer summarizes the factual and legal basis to answer the issues.
- The brief answer provides a balanced account of both the strengths and the weaknesses of the client's case.
- State your conclusions about each issue and subissue clearly and concisely, supporting them with brief (but thorough) factual and legal reasons; most issues can be addressed in one paragraph.
- Ensure that you state the likely outcome.
- Omit statements requiring citations to legal authority.
- Provide a balanced account of both the strengths and the weaknesses of the client's case.

4. Discussion

In a memorandum that addresses many issues, consider each issue separately. Analyze the law, apply the law to the client's facts, and provide a legal opinion about the likely outcome. Restate the issue. Include subheadings to organize the discussion of legislation and case law as follows:

a. Legislation

- Discuss the relevant legislation if it exists. Consider whether both statutes and regulations are relevant. Some memoranda require a more comprehensive analysis, including creating legislative histories and locating bills in progress.
- Analyze the relevant legislation before discussing case law because case law often judicially considers legislation.

b. Case Law

- Discuss the relevant cases in the Case Law section using the steps as explained in Chapters 10 and 11.
- If a case is analogous to the client's fact pattern, describe the facts, the court's holding, and the court's reasoning.

c. Summary of Legal Principles

- Summarize the relevant legal principles derived from both case law and legislation to provide a general statement of the law, which, in the next section, will then be applied to the facts of the case.

d. Application of Law to Facts (Legal Arguments)

- Include legal arguments on the client's position; review the process of argument creation described in Chapter 11.
- Apply the relevant law to the client's facts in a logical order: conclusion, law, application of law to facts, transition to next argument.
- Determine the jurisdiction of the court hearing the matter. If facts are in dispute, a formal argument may be necessary.
- Use scholarly analysis from secondary sources such as treatises and monographs, if it supports your legal argument, to help you interpret the law.

e. Policy

- If the law is either unsettled, subject to judicial interpretation, or subject to a constitutional challenge, consider whether a policy discussion should be used to develop your legal discussion. (Chapter 10 reviews the way in which policy can expand a legal argument.)
- Do not confuse a policy issue analysis with a legal essay. A policy issue analysis is directly focused on the client's circumstances and follows the same format as a legal issue analysis. A legal essay is a more broadly based commentary.
- If the matter reaches court, integrate the policy argument into the trial submissions. If the decision at trial is appealed, include the policy considerations in the legal argument in the factum.

5. Conclusion

- Provide a summary of the client's position concerning the identified legal issues.
- Summarize the analysis of each issue by explaining the relationship of the law to the facts of the client's case.

- Predict an outcome arising from the legal analysis, qualified to the extent necessary on the basis of the state of the law and the certainty of the facts.
- Ensure the conclusion is objective and realistic.
- Avoid raising new issues, unless they have arisen in the process of the analysis and take the form of a recommendation for follow-up research and analysis.
- Include recommendations when appropriate (typically these recommendations focus on determining unknown or assumed material facts, which may either support or undermine the client's argument).
- Format the conclusion in numbered paragraphs unless otherwise instructed.

6. Table of Authorities

- Follow the recommendations in Chapter 1 of the McGill Guide under the heading "Bibliographies".
- Add subheadings under the headings "Legislation", "Jurisprudence" or "Case Law", and "Secondary Sources" if required: e.g. subdivide "Legislation" into "Statutes" and "Regulations" if listing numerous sources.
- Subdivide secondary sources into monographs, treatises, and law review articles if using many sources.

7. Appendixes

- Provide as many appendixes as necessary (e.g. one each for legislation, jurisprudence, and secondary sources).

8. Document Preparation

TASK 13.2

Organizational Checklist

All documents discussed in this chapter have specific preparation rules; therefore, learn the rules before beginning to plan your document. Rules applicable to documents to be filed with a court may be found in statutory regulations (e.g. *Rules of Civil Procedure* and *Rules of Criminal Procedure*). Other courts and tribunals have their own rules for document preparation and submission; therefore, locate this information early in the document preparation process. Documents prepared for law schools and law offices, including legal memoranda, are also governed by their own rules. The following list, while not exhaustive, identifies many of the factors to consider before submitting a document.

1. Is the document correctly formatted in accordance with the relevant document preparation rules?
   - Pagination and page limit
   - Font style, point size, margins, line spacing, and indentation
2. Has the document been proofread to ensure that it conforms with plain language guidelines, and that it is grammatical, correctly punctuated, and free of spelling errors?
3. Have the rules of citation for footnotes, the table of authorities, and quotations been applied accurately?
4. Have appendixes been included when appropriate?
5. Has the primary law been updated to reflect the current state of the law?
6. If forms are required, have the correct forms been selected, and have they been completed accurately?
7. Have duplicate copies of the document been prepared in the event of a hard drive crash, external drive loss or corruption, or laptop theft? (If you are a student, email work in progress to yourself frequently; law firms typically have their own systems to ensure the preservation of documents.)
8. Has the document been completed ahead of schedule to allow time to edit the final draft?

NB: Documents prepared in a law school setting can be used as templates for future documents and as samples of your work for employment purposes.

III. Letter of Opinion

A. Structure

Audience: Usually the client, although a letter of opinion might be prepared for client-related purposes, such as seeking legal assistance on behalf of the client.

Purpose: To answer the client's legal issue and describe the options that are available to resolve the client's issue as of the date of the letter. Typically, a letter of opinion is created after some work has been done on the client's behalf, and after there has been communication between the lawyer and client about the strengths and weaknesses of the case.

Tone: Objective, neutral, and formal. It should not seek to persuade a client to choose a particular course of action. Rather, it should outline the legal and factual basis for the options that it sets out and describe the legal and factual consequences that may flow from these options. However, as discussed in Chapter 12, the lawyer should be mindful of how the letter will be received by the client, especially if it contains unwelcome information; therefore, choose words and phrases with care.

Lawyers are required to draft many letters on behalf of their clients. An "opening letter" confirms the details of the retainer with new clients. A "reporting letter" advises the client about the progress being made with the legal issue. Sometimes these types of letters are combined. A "closing letter", which is sent when the matter is concluded, summarizes the work completed on the client's behalf and informs the client that the lawyer's work is finished.

If the client is involved in a dispute, the lawyer must communicate with legal counsel for the other represented parties. Sometimes this communication is for the purposes of obtaining additional information from one of the parties. A "demand letter", by contrast, directs the party to do or stop doing something.

When a person retains a lawyer for assistance with a complex legal matter, the lawyer often needs to advise the client about the options available to resolve the matter. This letter forms a permanent record of the discussion between the lawyer and the client. It also confirms to the client the progress of the work undertaken by the lawyer. In the event of a misunderstanding between the lawyer and the client, the correspondence provides a written summary of the basis for the lawyer's actions.

Chapter 12 provided information about the potential consequences of failing to consider how a reader may receive the content of a document as a result of its wording and tone. The manner in which information is communicated in a letter of opinion must be unequivocal, especially when the lawyer's opinion does not support the client's aspirations.

B. Organization

Effective communication with clients is a professional obligation.[2] One aspect of effective communication is providing clients with clearly written correspondence in a timely fashion. The information that follows provides general guidelines for creating letters that communicate a legal opinion; it should be adapted as required.

Because a lawyer is accountable for a legal opinion given to a client, it is essential that the opinion is correct. Often law clerks, law students, articling students, or junior lawyers undertake much of the legal research and communicate their findings in a memorandum of law to the lawyer who has carriage of the file. A letter of opinion is drafted after factual and legal research is complete. Because a letter of opinion attempts to answer a client's questions, its language should reflect the level of legal knowledge possessed by the client.

---

2   Law Society of Upper Canada, *Rules of Professional Conduct* (Toronto: LSUC, 2000), r 2.01(1)(d).

The client must be able to rely on the fact that the opinion is accurate as of the date that the letter is signed and sent. The date on the letter above the salutation indicates the date that the letter was prepared for signature. The law should be accurate. The letter should be signed and mailed or emailed without delay.

The introductory paragraph should confirm the date that the client sought a legal opinion. This paragraph or the second paragraph should also summarize the legally significant facts provided by the client. There are two important reasons for this. A summary gives the client an opportunity to review and correct any errors or omissions that might change the legal opinion. The summary also establishes the basis for the lawyer's opinion. This written record can be important if a difference of opinion later arises between the lawyer and the client concerning the factual basis of the client's issue.

The letter should also contain a statement about the legal issues that have been researched. This statement is not as detailed or specific as the legal issues section of a memorandum of law. Rather, it is a summary—e.g.: "We have researched the legal grounds that permit termination of employment for cause". The general issue statement may appear in the introductory paragraph or at the beginning of the discussion of the legal issue, depending on the construction of the letter.

Clients must know about the progress of their case so that they can make informed decisions. A thoroughly prepared letter of opinion should include a brief summary of the law as it has been applied to the facts of the case and should address both the strengths and the weaknesses of the client's position.

Since the purpose of an opinion letter is to inform rather than persuade, the lawyer should identify options and consequences without encouraging the client to take a particular course of action—that is the client's decision. Similarly, attempting to predict the outcome of a legal proceeding may mislead the client. However, a general discussion that outlines the available remedies should be included.

Recall from the factual analysis in Chapter 2 how unknown or assumed facts must be identified. Review the letter to determine whether information is missing or whether the letter contains assumptions that, if altered, might change the legal opinion. If material facts are unknown or ambiguous, give a qualified opinion on the basis of the information provided, stating that your opinion is subject to change in the event that additional legally relevant facts are forthcoming.

In the concluding paragraph, state the next steps to be taken. Does the client need to contact the lawyer by a specific date to give instructions? Is there anything else to be done, or does the closing letter terminate the relationship with the client? Does the lawyer need to file a court document or consult someone else? Set deadlines, and follow them up to ensure that the work is completed.

Plain language principles apply. Use the active voice wherever possible. When several people have worked on a file, it is acceptable to use the first person plural: e.g. "in our opinion" rather than "in my opinion". The style of the letter will vary in accordance with the preferences of the law firm and the type of law relevant to the case. Frequently, precedent letters are available and should be followed for style and format.

TASK 13.3

Letter of Opinion Checklist: Content and Form

Once a letter of opinion has been drafted, put yourself in the position of the recipient of the letter. Use the following checklist to consider how the letter may be received by the client, editing the document as required.

- Are the relevant dates included: e.g. the date that the letter was composed, the date(s) that the client was seen, the dates that activities were undertaken or that future activities will occur?

- Are the relevant facts included? Are they accurately and clearly summarized? Are they presented in a neutral tone?

- Are the reasons the client sought legal advice and the general legal issue clearly and accurately stated at the beginning of the letter?

- Is the general legal issue answered and is the legal opinion briefly stated in a manner that is neither too simplistic nor overly technical? Have you omitted references to legal authorities that might confuse the reader yet still explained the legal and factual reasons that support the opinion?

- After reading the letter, do questions remain? Should they have been answered in the letter? Does the letter include any assumptions, unknown facts, or other details that require clarification or qualify the opinion?

- Will the reader understand what happens next: who is supposed to take the next step—the client or the lawyer? Is the client required to provide further information? Is the matter resolved?

- Is the tone of the letter appropriate? Does the letter use language appropriate to the audience? Does the letter strive for a neutral tone? Does the letter inform the client but avoid encouraging a particular course of action?

- How might the client react to the letter? Can you convey in a word or phrase that you have heard and appreciate the client's situation beyond its mere legalities? Empathy may be expressed in phrases such as "I recognize that you may be concerned/disappointed/uncertain that" or "Recognizing that your goal may be difficult to achieve because ...".

- Does the letter make sense? Is the message clear? If not, where might the problem lie: in technical concerns, such as sentence or paragraph structure; in an incomplete legal or factual basis for the opinion; in plain language problems?

- Does the letter look professional from the point of view of its overall appearance, font, spacing, salutation, address, margins, signature, length, and so on?

IV. Affidavit

A. Structure

Audience: Court, quasi-judicial, government, or administrative body that requires a sworn version of facts.

Purpose: To establish the factual record of a person who may have information relevant to a dispute but who is not a party. An affidavit contains no legal argument. Some affidavits are procedural: e.g. establishing that a document was served on a party in accordance with procedural rules.[3]

Tone: Objective, neutral, and formal; an affidavit should not seek to persuade, but merely inform. The facts must be clearly and accurately stated. The person making the affidavit can be examined and cross-examined on an affidavit's contents in a legal proceeding.

Affidavit: A written or printed declaration or statement of facts, made voluntarily, and confirmed by the oath or affirmation of the party making it, taken before a person having authority to administer such oath or affirmation.[4]

Statements of fact can be provided either orally or in written form. At a trial or hearing, a person who has factual information about a matter before the court or tribunal swears an oath (or affirms) to tell the truth. Witnesses give evidence about facts in their oral testimony. Lawyers then examine and cross-examine the witnesses about their evidence. Following this test of the witness's recollection of the facts, a judge or jury decides the weight to give the evidence.

Facts can also be presented to a court, tribunal, or other administrative body in written form using an affidavit. Barristers and solicitors who are entitled to practise law may also be commissioners for taking affidavits[5] and are thus permitted to administer an oath or affirmation to the person making the affidavit (the "affiant").[6]

Typically, affidavits are used when it is either unnecessary or impractical to orally examine a person who may have relevant factual information. The affiant is required to swear to (or affirm) the truth of the statements of fact contained in the affidavit.

---

3   This summary provides you with general concepts related to the preparation of affidavits for the purpose of a legal writing assignment. It does not purport to provide a definitive review of procedural or substantive law concerning affidavits. See the rules of civil procedure and evidence in your jurisdiction for additional information.

4   *Black's Law Dictionary*, 6th ed, *sub verbo* "affidavit".

5   See e.g. *Commissioners for Taking Affidavits Act*, RSO 1990, c C.17, s 1.

6   *Supra* note 4, *sub verbo* "affiant".

Affidavits can be used for many purposes, including:

- to summarize a professional's findings (e.g. in medical reports or psychological evaluations)
- to summarize assets to show that a sponsor can financially support a potential immigrant
- to establish a person's identity when documents have been lost or stolen

B. Organization

Specific rules concerning the format of an affidavit and the information that it contains are functions of the legal purpose of the affidavit and the court or administrative body that will consider the affidavit evidence. Determine the jurisdiction and the court or other body that requires the affidavit, secure the appropriate forms, and comply with the relevant procedural rules.

TASK 13.4

Preparing Affidavits: Checklist

When preparing an affidavit, consider the following:

- The information should be presented in numbered paragraphs.
- The first paragraph should contain the name of the affiant.
- Information establishing the identity and credentials of the affiant should be contained in the first or second paragraph.
- Typically, affidavits contain information about the direct knowledge of an affiant: what the affiant saw, heard, or experienced. Statements of this nature are considered to be within the actual knowledge of the affiant. These statements must be separated from information that is based on an affiant's belief. For example, a family physician might have prescribed a course of treatment for a patient on the basis of a specialist's report. The physician will have knowledge of certain aspects of the patient's condition only indirectly through the specialist, a third party. The affidavit would therefore state that the family physician prescribed the treatment after receiving information contained in the report from the specialist, which she "believed was an accurate statement of facts".
- The affiant should state the purpose for which the affidavit was created. Usually this statement of purpose is found near the beginning of the affidavit, or at the end, immediately before the affiant's signature.
- The information should be organized logically.

- Each paragraph should include only one core fact or piece of information. Each paragraph generally contains only one sentence, although more than one sentence can be included if the additional sentences explain the point being made in the first sentence.

- The discussion of facts should proceed logically. Subheadings can be used to organize the information if the affidavit is lengthy and the facts address more than one topic.

- Facts are neutral and must not be presented as argument. There must be no attempt to conceal, distort, omit, or shade the facts to the benefit or detriment of the affiant or the parties.

- Plain language should be used to ensure clarity.

The information in this chapter is intended as an introductory guide. Review samples of affidavits to better understand their structure and use in court proceedings; many examples can be found appended to court documents online.

V. Case and Legislative Comments

A. Structure

Audience: Practising members of the bar and judiciary, legal scholars, students, and the public.

Purpose: To disseminate information about the development of the law by providing an analysis of a case law or legislation.

Tone: Case and legislative comments incorporate aspects of both objective and persuasive writing. While a comment must include a balanced discussion of the various issues, the writer is expected to express a point of view. The writing style may adopt a more conversational tone than that found in a memorandum of law or a legal essay. The conventions of plain language and legal citation are applied.

Earlier chapters introduced primary and secondary sources of law. Primary law consists of legislation and cases. Secondary sources of law include commentary about primary law, such as scholarly analysis found in legal treatises, journal articles, and analytical commentary about specific cases, called "case comments". Legislative comments are similar; however, they may focus on the development of legislation and how it has been interpreted by the judiciary in the past or may be interpreted in the future.

B. Organization

Both case and legislative comments critically analyze primary law.

Cases that involve novel legal issues, competing policy interests, and developing law are more likely to be appealed than cases that involve the application of well-settled law. Contentious leading cases are often the subject matter of case comments.

The writer of a case comment moves beyond the facts of the case to provide a critical analysis of the judicial reasoning and an opinion about the effect of the decision on the development of a specific point of law. Case comments may consider legal issues or public policy considerations that were not expressly addressed by the court.

A case comment does not always adopt a neutral tone. Although the writer of a case comment should maintain a balanced and even-handed approach when discussing the facts and issues, typically the writer also expresses a point of view. By doing so, the writer attempts to elucidate some aspect of the broader legal debate. In an effort to provide balance, publishers often publish case comments in tandem. For example, after a controversial labour law decision, a case comment written by a lawyer representing management might be followed by a comment written by a lawyer representing the union involved. When reading a case comment, it is therefore imperative to determine the interests of the writer and assess how they might affect the writer's perspective.

The writer of a legislative comment usually addresses an interpretation issue (e.g. the constitutionality of a law). Legislative comments look at the history of the legislation and examine how it has been judicially considered. Typically, a writer does not consider an entire statute or regulation. Rather, a contentious section is usually the focus of the comment, albeit within the context of the statute as a whole.

Writing a case or legislative comment may be an assignment in law school, during articles, or when in practice. Increasingly, lawyers prepare case or legislative comments that appear on law firm websites; law students frequently assist with this work. When preparing to write a case or legislative comment, read and critique case and legislative comments written by others.[7] Analyze the comments for both content and style. Which comments are clear and persuasive? What has the writer done to achieve this?[8]

---

7 Recall from Chapter 7 that *The Canadian Abridgment* indexes case and legislative commentary separately in the *Index to Canadian Legal Literature* (both in print and online).

8 When writing a case or legislative comment, use these summaries as guides rather than templates.

TASK 13.5

Case Comment Analysis

Whether reading or writing a case comment, look for a neutral and even-handed account of the following:

- a brief review of the legally significant facts and issues before the court
- a brief judicial history of the case at each level of court
- a summary of the judicial reasoning of the case (including dissents)
- a critical analysis of the decision, which may include a discussion concerning the development of the law before the decision
- the legal principles adopted by the court
- the effect the decision may have on future decisions
- an alternative analysis to that given by the court
- policy considerations
- an opinion concerning the soundness of the judicial analysis and disposition of the case
- a conclusion that considers the evolution of the law and the prospective effect of the decision

TASK 13.6

Legislative Comment Analysis

Whether reading or writing a legislative comment, look for a neutral and even-handed discussion of the historical development of the legislation, including

- an identification of the specific sections of legislation being scrutinized
- the reasons that these sections may be noteworthy or problematic
- the consequences that might flow from various interpretations
- a discussion of the legislative treatment of the identified sections by the judiciary
- possible policy reasons why the legislation was drafted in its present form
- an opinion concerning the soundness of the legislative structure, supported by the author's reason for the opinion
- a conclusion that considers the evolution of the law and the prospective effect of the legislation under scrutiny

VI. Factum

A. Structure

Audience: The judiciary, parties to the case, and their counsel.

Purpose: To assist all parties and the judiciary in appreciating the respective legal positions of the appellant, the respondent, and the intervenors before, during, and after the oral argument. Following a decision at trial, all parties examine the reasons given for the decision. The unsuccessful party reviews the decision to determine if the trial judge may have committed a reversible legal error that would result in a successful appeal. The successful party reviews the decision to determine the response to an appeal. The factum is the principal document used during the appeal process to communicate with both the court and the other parties to the dispute.[9]

Tone: Persuasive and formal. The factum delineates the arguments which support a party's position that will be elaborated orally during the appeal itself.

A trial or hearing is conducted when a civil dispute between two or more parties cannot be resolved, or when a person who is charged with a crime or an offence defends the charge in court. If the dispute proceeds to trial, the adversarial legal system requires legal counsel to present arguments in favour of their client's position.

A judgment may be appealed. An appeal of the trial judgment will succeed if the appellant is able to persuade an appeal court that a reversible legal error has been committed. The respondent will attempt to persuade the appeal court that the judgment of the lower court was correctly decided and should be upheld, or that any errors committed were not reversible legal errors.

B. Using Legal Argument to Persuade

Appellate advocacy provides lawyers with two distinct, albeit interrelated, opportunities to use legal argument to persuade a court of their client's position. The first is through a carefully crafted and well-written factum. The second is through oral argument that uses the factum as a foundation. The oral argument allows lawyers to interact with judges: the lawyers are given the opportunity to build on their written submission, and the judges have the opportunity to question the lawyers about the arguments outlined in the facta of both parties. Through this

---

9   In administrative law, you may also need to create facta for an appeal or judicial review of administrative action. As noted below, facta may be used in lower courts as well (e.g. parties may prepare facta for pre-trial motions).

interactive process, lawyers can reinforce the strengths of their clients' positions and draw attention to flaws in the arguments of the opposing side.

Whether writing a factum or preparing an oral argument, a lawyer's task is to persuade. Judges are persuaded by sound legal argument, not by rhetoric. Review the standard format for a sound legal argument.[10]

C. Developing an Overview

A factum presents a court with a synopsis of the arguments that the appellant, respondent, and intervenor intend to make. The appellant sets out the basis for the appeal, followed by an argument supported by facts and law. The respondent replies with an argument that counters the appellant's position and provides the court with the respondent's position. With leave of the court, intervenors, who provide a specific point of view related to but distinct from that of either of the parties, may then be asked to outline their arguments in a factum. The appellate judges review the facta before hearing counsels' oral argument.

It is necessary to consult the official rules of the court to ensure that the documents presented to the court comply with the required format.[11]

Before beginning to construct a factum, counsel must think about a number of organizing questions, including the following:

- What error of law, or error of mixed fact and law, may have been committed by the trial court?
- What arguments must be made by the appellant and respondent to support their respective positions?
- What arguments will be required to reply to opposing counsel?
- What facts are relevant?
- What law is relevant?
- How can arguments be constructed persuasively?
- How can opposing counsel's position be challenged?

Answering these questions provides the framework that becomes the basis for the written argument and ultimately the oral argument before the court.

Presenting persuasive arguments in a factum requires skill, knowledge, and practice. Those with little competitive mooting or appellate experience may wish to adopt the following approach to factum development.

---

10 See Chapter 11.

11 See e.g. Ontario, *Rules of Civil Procedure*, RRO 1990, Reg 194, rule 61, and Canada, *Rules of the Supreme Court of Canada*, SOR/2002-156, rule 42.

D. Unifying the Submission by Developing the Theory of the Case

A case theory explains how the law should apply to the facts of the case in a way that is favourable to your client. The theme provides a cohesive structure to both the written and the oral argument; it helps the judge or jury make sense of the facts and the law.

Typically, both the theory and the theme are determined before trial. On appeal, they may be revised to reflect some aspect of the trial decision. However, if a factum is being written by law students for a moot court competition, the mooters will not have had the benefit of preparing the case from its inception and reading the transcript of the original decision, including the opening and closing statements of counsel, which integrate the facts and law. Therefore, before proceeding to construct their arguments, law students must tentatively establish their theory and theme. Note that the words "theory" and "theme" never appear in a factum; they are merely organizational devices used to develop a framework for the argument.

TASK 13.7

Theory and Theme: Building the Foundation for Legal Argument

A strong theory

- is consistent with facts that are not in dispute
- relies on legal principles that are central to the dispute
- addresses and accounts for unfavourable and disputed facts
- is concise and logical and makes sense

When developing your theory and theme, consider:

- How do you want the court to view the case (what is your theory)?
- What theory is the other side likely to adopt?
- Which theory is more persuasive and why?
- How can this information be reduced to an overall theme?

Developing your theory and the theme takes time and reflection. Once you have established both the theory and theme of the case, review the rules for the formal construction of the document.

Facts

- Provide all the facts necessary to develop the case theory. Remember that the facts come from both the events that led to the dispute and the decision of the court or tribunal that made the original finding (adjudicative facts). If undertaking a constitutional challenge or participating in an appeal that requires the interpretation of legislation, you must also consider legislative facts (i.e. those that are derived from the legislative history obtained through the backdating process).

- Organize the facts, using subheadings if necessary. Do not include argument in the facts section. In particular, do not try to shape the facts to reflect the client's position. Facts are neutral. The interpretation of the facts must be left to the argument section of the factum.

Argument

- When structuring legal arguments, recall that the purpose of the written and oral argument is not merely to inform. Rather, the objective is to persuade the appellate judges of the merits of your case. Presentation of arguments in a persuasive and compelling manner is essential. In each argument, ensure that the law and facts are integrated and clearly identified, using persuasive subheadings. Use information obtained from secondary sources, when appropriate, to support the argument.

- The art of persuasion develops over time with practice. For tips on developing appellate advocacy skills, consult print and online sources such as the *Advocates' Quarterly* or the *Advocates' Society Journal*.

- In the final edit, ensure that you have complied with citation requirements. In order to persuade, both the oral and the written argument must be clearly articulated.

E. Organization

1. Format

The overall format of the factum is similar in many ways to a memorandum of law. First, summarize the material facts; then identify the legal issues. In the appellant's factum, the issues relate to the error of law on which the appeal is based; they may include the matters that the court should address to resolve the legal error. The respondent's factum advances the respondent's position.

Next, present the argument, focusing on your client's position. The counter-argument will be presented by the other party to the dispute; each party should prepare to refute the other party's arguments during oral submissions. When making an argument, weave the law and the facts together to support the client's claim. You may choose to include a policy discussion to support the legal analysis, depending on the issue before the court. A conclusion directs the court's attention to the remedy that is being sought. Follow document preparation rules for supporting documents that should be included, as well as the acceptable citation methods for citing authorities. Add a cover and backing page before the document is assembled in its final form, following the rules of the court for document preparation.

2. Argument

The argument is key to the persuasive value of the factum. The following format provides the framework of the argument.

a. ESTABLISH THE GOVERNING LAW

- Every legal argument must centre on relevant statutory and/or case law. Therefore, first identify the law that governs your case.

- Provide authority through legal citation of relevant statute and case law principles. Both sources are relevant when, for example, a statutory provision has been judicially interpreted.

b. ESTABLISH THE FACTUAL AND LEGAL BASIS FOR THE ARGUMENT

- Determine the facts on which the parties agree and the facts that are in dispute. The agreed facts can support either side's argument, but counsel must be prepared to justify their respective interpretations of any disputed facts.

- Find additional facts in the trial record and the decision of the lower court judge. Look for statements made by the judge during the course of the trial.

- Determine whether the lower court judge interpreted the law correctly. Look for omissions: did the judge fail to consider a relevant point of law?

- Connect the facts previously outlined in the facts section to each legal point.

c. CREATE A SUBMISSION

- Finally, create a submission by stating the client's position with respect to the interpretation of the law based on the facts of the case.

- A submission is a summary statement of the legal position that counsel wants the court to adopt when applying the law to the facts of the case. This statement is connected to the error of law cited by the appellant and refuted by the respondent. The appellant might state, "The trial judge erred by …", while the respondent might respond with, "The trial judge correctly concluded that …".

d. GO BEYOND THE FACTS AND THE LAW OF THE CASE UNDER APPEAL

- Cases that are appealed frequently address a point of law that will affect other cases. Therefore, look for an opportunity to go beyond the facts of the case under appeal to examine whether there are broader considerations that must be addressed.

- When both sides have merit and the law is undecided, an examination of underlying policy considerations can broaden the context of the argument.

- Policy considerations are not the law and do not replace legal argument; instead, they provide context. Anticipate policy arguments that may support the other side in order to prepare a response to questions from the appellate court.

- If the government is one of the parties, typically, policy plays an important part in the legal submissions. You can appreciate the interaction of law and policy by examining facta that have been used in constitutional challenges, including the facta of intervenors. Facta are available online—e.g. on the Supreme Court of Canada website.

- Intervenors have been given permission by the court to file supporting information and to make arguments. They may expand on a party's position, or they may present a perspective not contemplated by either of the parties. Intervenors have expert knowledge in specific policy areas, which counsel brings before the court in the factum.

- When examining a factum written on behalf of a party or an intervenor, identify the following components and consider them when incorporating policy into your legal argument:
  - the legal position taken by the party or intervenor
  - the evidence that was relied on to support the legal position
  - the law that was used to support the legal position and the context in which the law was created
  - the use of secondary sources, such as treatises, to provide evidence to support the party or intervenor's claims
  - the use of binding and non-binding jurisprudence to support the legal position
  - the integration of this information to create a policy argument in support of a legal position

e. REVIEW AND REDRAFT

Once you have completed the preliminary draft, review the document. Make alterations to improve the narrative flow and make your factum more persuasive. For example:

- Add persuasive subheadings to identify the significant points in the submission (a persuasive subheading incorporates a party's perspective). Persuasive subheadings can be used as an introduction to most paragraphs in a factum. They can then be reproduced in the index page of the factum, where they can summarize and preview counsel's argument. In a section 6(1) *Charter* challenge regarding the denial of a Canadian passport, an example of a persuasive subheading could be: "A passport is the manifestation of the rights granted pursuant to s 6(1) of the *Charter*".

- Reorganize your paragraphs if necessary. While separate paragraphs should be used while structuring each part of the argument, it may become apparent that the overall argument would be more effective if several points of law were discussed in succession before the facts were introduced.

- Consider beginning the submission with a conclusion before discussing the law.

- Consider emphasizing a particular fact to provide the context for a legal point.

- Review the facta of the opposing parties. By identifying weaknesses or gaps in their argument construction, you may be able to strengthen your argument by advising the court of gaps in the argument of opposing counsel during oral submission.

NB: This suggested format is a guide; adapt it as required.

VII. Motion

A. Structure

Audience: Judges, masters, parties to the case, and their counsel.

Purpose: To resolve legal issues that are identified before or during the trial and which, if left unresolved, would affect the trial process. A decision on a motion results in a court order, which is subject to appeal.

Tone: Persuasive and formal. The motion records of both parties provide the framework for the argument, which is supported by affidavit evidence.

Like other court procedures, motions are governed by the jurisdiction and court in which the motion is heard. It is therefore necessary to comply with the relevant rules. Motions are used in many contexts, which are too numerous to mention here. Law students who work in clinics may be required to prepare motion documents and argue a motion. The material that follows identifies some of the features of a motion and suggests sources that can help in their preparation.

B. Organization

Motions can be brought by any party. In civil matters, a party who brings a motion, whether the plaintiff or defendant at trial, is the moving party; the other party is the responding party.

Supporting documents in a motions record include an affidavit and perhaps a factum. A factum in support of a motion is less detailed than a factum in support of an appeal because it focuses on a narrow point of law preliminary to the determination of the case on its merits.

If you are asked to prepare a motion, find out whether the bar associations, law societies, or courts in your jurisdiction have material to assist you. For example, "How to Prepare Motion Materials", written under the auspices of the Law Society of Upper Canada, contains comprehensive instructions for motion preparation and is available online.[12] Additional how-to guides provided at the same website may help you to prepare for procedural matters relevant to specific areas of practice, including

- administrative law
- business law
- civil litigation
- criminal law
- family law
- legal research
- practice management
- real estate law

Other jurisdictions and organizations provide similar services. For example, "How to Prepare and File a Notice of Motion, Affidavit and Memorandum of Argument" can be found online at the Alberta Courts website.[13] Law*Central* Canada, which provides links to a wide array of legal information, includes guidance about court procedures in a number of jurisdictions across Canada.[14]

---

12   <http://rc.lsuc.on.ca/jsp/ht/prepareMotionMaterials.jsp>.

13   <http://www.albertacourts.ab.ca/ca/publication/noticeofmotionselfrepresentedpackage.pdf>.

14   <http://www.lawcentralcanada.ca/LawCentralCanada/default.aspx>.

PART V

Applying Legal Skills to Legal Practice

CHAPTER 14   Transitioning from Classroom to Courtroom

Transitioning from Classroom to Courtroom*

14

---

* The two primary authors of this chapter, Moira McCarney and Rose Faddoul, wish to acknowledge the guidance provided by Rose Voyvodic. We met Rose in her capacity as executive director of Legal Assistance of Windsor (LAW) when we were students, and she became our teacher, colleague, mentor, and friend. In her work at LAW and later as academic director of the clinic programs at the University of Windsor's Faculty of Law, Rose exemplified client-centred lawyering in theory and in practice before her untimely death in 2007. Some of the material in this chapter is based on our collaborative work with Rose, and we are grateful for her influence.

I. Legal Clinics at Law Schools

A. Scope of Practice

In Canada and the United States, legal clinics provide a range of services to clients, including those who cannot afford the cost of retaining a lawyer in private practice. Many legal clinics confine their areas of practice to matters that disproportionately affect those in financial need (e.g. landlord–tenant, employment, and access to benefits such as social assistance or other forms of income replacement).[1] However, each clinic's scope of practice varies and may focus on specific areas of law or client groups.

Legal clinics provide one of the first opportunities for law students to observe lawyers in practice. Although not all clinics provide volunteer or employment opportunities for students, legal clinics associated with law schools offer students opportunities to enhance their legal education by working directly with clients under the supervision of practising lawyers.[2]

---

1   Lenny Abramowicz, "The Critical Characteristics of Community Legal Aid Clinics in Ontario" (2004) 19 J L & Soc Pol'y 70. This article examines the unique characteristics of the community clinic model in Ontario that have led to its success and that differentiate it from other types of legal services.

2   Consult law school websites and legal aid services in your community to find clinic volunteer opportunities.

Most lawyers who work in clinics focus on providing both direct and indirect client services, including individual client advocacy, community legal education, and law reform initiatives. Clinics associated with law schools have the companion objective of student education, providing volunteer law students with opportunities to develop their legal skills and knowledge in an environment where, under supervision, they can receive both direction and critical feedback about their professional growth.

The value that law schools and clinic lawyers place on a vigorous, comprehensive education is evident from their efforts to develop and enhance legal education within these clinics. For example, many lawyers belong to professional organizations such as the Clinical Legal Education Association,[3] whose mission is (in part) to "advocate for clinical legal education as fundamental to the education of lawyers". In Canada, the Association for Canadian Clinical Legal Education[4] identifies its unifying purposes as follows:

- provide a forum for legal educators across Canada to share best practices, pedagogies, and other information related to clinical legal education
- encourage the promotion and improvement of clinical legal education in Canadian law schools
- promote clinical pedagogy and research
- facilitate the dissemination of information pertaining to clinical legal education to clinicians in Canada
- promote or organize conferences or other activities to facilitate the purposes of the association

B. Preparing for Practice

Law students, clinic staff, and law school administration share the responsibility of ensuring that students' volunteer efforts result not only in beneficial outcomes for clients but also in progressive educational experiences for students. Typically, a law school administration focuses on administrative functions, including resource allocation in concert with their funding partners. Lawyers who work in clinics not only determine how best to provide services to their clients but also how best to offer learning opportunities for students to observe and model practising lawyers.

---

3   See <http://cleaweb.org>. While this organization focuses on issues of concern to American educators and those practising in the United States, it also invites participation from the international community of lawyers and educators.

4   <http://accle.ca>. Law students may join this organization.

No matter how diligently law students work to acquire the foundational skills of legal research, analysis, and writing while at law school, a successful transition to practice involves acquiring additional skills and knowledge that are not always stressed in traditional law school curricula. As a result, some students entering clinical placements or externships may have difficulty transitioning from law school into practice.[5] Those who supervise students in their placements sometimes question whether students' experiences in law school were sufficiently devoted to the acquisition of foundational lawyering skills.[6]

Part of the challenge that transitioning students experience can be traced to the "transfer of learning", a term that refers to the difficulty of transferring knowledge acquired in one setting and applying it to another. In a clinic setting, transfer of learning issues may arise not because students lack knowledge but because they have difficulty recognizing how they should apply or modify the knowledge that they acquired in the classroom when they begin to work in a law office.

While educators, including practising lawyers, bear the primary responsibility for assisting students in linking their classroom learning to a law clinic or other legal setting,[7] students can help to prepare themselves for the advanced learning opportunities available in a clinic setting by anticipating the additional expectations in the new environment. Some of these opportunities may include demonstrating professionalism, facilitating supervision, and providing client services, both directly (interviewing, advising, and resolving issues) and indirectly (participating in community legal education and law reform initiatives). Figure 14.1 illustrates the learning opportunities frequently available in clinical placements.

---

5   Carolyn R Young & Barbara A Blanco, "What Students Don't Know *Will* Hurt Them: A Frank View from the Field on How to Better Prepare Our Clinic and Externship Students" (2007) 14 Clinical L Rev. These authors asked a selection of practising lawyers who supervised externships two questions: "What is your assessment of students' preparedness when they first arrive at your placement, and, assuming the answer reveals the need for improvement, how would you suggest we go about it?" The article focuses on observations of students in externship placements and suggests improvements to programs to help students transition from law school into an externship or clinical placement.

6   See Tonya Kowalski, "Toward a Pedagogy for Teaching Legal Writing in Law School Clinics" (2010) 17:1 Clinical L Rev 285 at 288ff, who identifies this phenomenon as "collective amnesia". This article considers factors that may assist students in transferring their learning to new experiences. These types of observations are not restricted to the United States: see also Moira McCarney, Catherine Cotter, Shaunna Mireau, Karen Sawatzky & Pamela V Lysaght, *The LRW Rubik's Cube©: Towards a Standardized Approach to Building Lawyering Skills*, presented to the 2010 conference of the Canadian Association of Law Libraries. This panel discussion included speakers involved in legal education in both the university setting and in practice. Those in practice noted the difficulty that students experience in applying skills that were taught in their law school curriculum.

7   Examples of transfer of learning opportunities include bar admission programs created under the auspices of law societies and orientation programs provided by law firms or legal clinics for their summer and articling students.

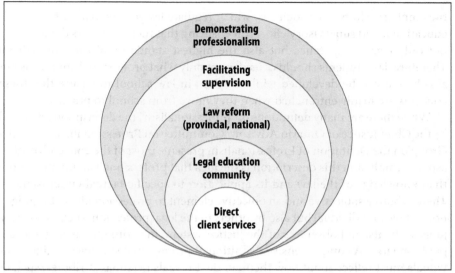

FIGURE 14.1   Clinical Placement Learning Opportunities

C. Demonstrating Professionalism

Professionalism as a personal characteristic is revealed in an attitude and approach to an occupation that is commonly characterized by intelligence, integrity, maturity, and thoughtfulness. The expectation among lawyers, whose occupation is defined as a profession, and in the public, who receive legal services, is that professionalism will inform a lawyer's work and conduct.

• • •

A lawyer should recognize ethical practice and conduct as a key component of professionalism, but in addition to their obligations to observe ethical standards established by their governing body, lawyers are expected to exhibit professional self-discipline and high standards of character.

> Chief Justice of Ontario Advisory Committee on Professionalism, Working Group on the Definition of Professionalism, "Elements of Professionalism", October 2001 (revised December 2001 and June 2002)

At law school, the traditional methods of recording students' academic achievement, including the assignment of grades, often focus on an assessment of the students' assimilation of legal principles acquired during their course of studies. However, while a pattern of grades may reveal the relative ease or difficulty that a student experienced when acquiring knowledge, following transition to practice the emphasis shifts. Law societies, which regulate lawyers' activities, focus their educational and supervisory efforts on ensuring that their members demonstrate not only legal competence but also the highest standards of professionalism. Therefore, law students should consider not only what professionalism means but also how it can be developed while they are in law school to ensure that these concepts are firmly entrenched when they move from school to practice.

While there are many definitions of "professionalism", the description advanced by the Chief Justice of Ontario Advisory Committee on Professionalism, Working Group on the Definition of Professionalism presents most of the concept's critical aspects. Implicit in this description is the idea that professionalism involves more than knowledge of the law and its application to specific factual circumstances. There is both a subjective and an objective element to professionalism; it is judged not just by an individual but also by others in the legal profession, such as lawyers, judges, clients, and observers of the justice system, including the media and the public at large. A comprehensive definition of professionalism suggests that individuals must reflect about how their conduct reveals personal attributes, such as honour and truthfulness.

While the law society of the jurisdiction in which you practise has the formal authority to discipline lawyers whose behaviour falls below acceptable standards of conduct, lawyers' work is judged informally by others, both within and outside the profession. It is these judgments that contribute to a lawyer's reputation.

> Reputation is only a candle, of wavering and uncertain flame, and easily blown out, but it is the light by which the world looks for and finds merit.
>
> Attributed to James Russell Lowell

> Character is like a tree and reputation its shadow. The shadow is what we think it is; the tree is the real thing.
>
> Attributed to Abraham Lincoln

Your professional reputation has numerous facets. Three of the foundational ones are listed below.

- Knowledge and skills: What you know and can do.
- Values and habits: How core ethical principles guide your customary behaviour.
- Judgment and conduct: How you approach decision making, especially in unanticipated circumstances, and how you act and react, both as an individual and as a member of a group.

1. Knowledge and Skills

Previous chapters have discussed the development of the core skills of a lawyer, including research, analysis, and writing. These skills are an extension of the legal knowledge that you obtained in law school courses. Supervising lawyers expect student volunteers to apply these skills and knowledge to their work with clients.

Therefore, before accepting a clinical placement, participate thoughtfully in all law school classes to develop your mastery of legal concepts, and thoroughly review the skills and techniques described in Chapters 2 to 12, which provide much of the essential information about research, writing, and analysis.

Note that problem-based learning in law schools, which is founded on hypothetical situations, no matter how comprehensive, does not entirely prepare you for interviewing and advising your clients. While these skills are best taught in a clinic setting, the framework for developing these skills within a client-centred legal practice is discussed later in this chapter.

2. Values and Habits

While skills can be learned and practised, an assessment of values requires you to examine your personal beliefs about standards, ethics, and morals. Although values can be examined, challenged, and tested in healthy debates within the law school curriculum, you acquire your personal values and habits before you enter law school; therefore, they are not subject to the same type of learning as are skills.[8]

Moreover, in legal practice, your consideration of values moves from theory to application. If values are culturally based, differing viewpoints may arise from time to time between lawyers and law students; culturally based values may also affect a client's receptivity to advice.

Habits too are conditioned by early learning. Before volunteering at a clinic, students should examine those of their habits that either facilitate or impede the achievement of desired outcomes. For example, in law school, a student who experiences time management issues may procrastinate, with the result that an assignment is incomplete at the due date. Even if the student is penalized for the late submission, the only person affected is the student. However, if the same student's habit of procrastination leads to the late filing of a court document, the student may compromise a client's legal interests and affect the reputation of the clinic and the supervising lawyer as well as his or her own reputation. In these situations, the student's error cannot be easily rectified.

---

8   See Rose Voyvodic, "Lawyers Meet the Social Context: Understanding Cultural Competence" (2006) 84 Can Bar Rev 563. This article discusses in part how clinic legal education programs can teach aspects of cultural competence and legal ethics.

Self-reflection is a fruitful process for evaluating how your values and habits may affect your professional reputation.[9] Therefore, while in law school:

- Critically assess your core values and habits.
- Seek advice from respected members of the profession about habits that can facilitate or undermine your professional reputation.
- Open yourself to mentoring relationships, both as a mentee and later as a mentor.
- Become aware of perspectives that guide decision making on the basis of core values rather than situational ethics.
- Critically analyze situations in which the decisions of others have violated professional standards or ethical conduct, determine the choices that led to these decisions, and consider how different choices could have resulted in a better outcome.
- Become aware of the daily decisions that reflect your personal values and habits, and question whether they are consistent with professional standards.

While assessing skills and knowledge is appropriate in a classroom setting, a consideration of values and habits is particularly amenable to self-reflection, which may involve keeping a journal. In addition, the supervision offered in a clinic can provide valuable feedback about your judgment and conduct.

D. Preparing for Supervision

Law students are supervised in legal clinics by lawyers who are licensed to practise law by the law society of the jurisdiction in which they are situated. Lawyers are governed by the rules of professional conduct of these societies and are subject to disciplinary procedures if they fail to uphold their professional obligations. Supervising lawyers expect law students to respond conscientiously to their supervision in an effort to acquire skills and knowledge, and to demonstrate the attitudes and conduct that will support their developing professional reputation as well as the reputation of the clinic, the law school, and the bar.

Before articling, law students may choose to work in supervised settings, either in clinics or as paid part-time employees of law offices. If you are a beginning law

---

9   See Roy Stuckey, *Best Practices for Legal Education: A Vision and a Road Map* (Columbia, SC: Clinical Legal Education Association, 2007) for a discussion of why self-reflection and journaling should be part of a student's law school experience. An electronic version of this document is available on the website of the Clinical Legal Education Association, <http://cleaweb.org>. See also Appendix B, Academic Success, for a discussion of how developing appropriate habits can enhance your law school experience.

student, regular supervisory meetings to discuss cases are mandatory. After your call to the bar, direct supervision is not required; however, mentoring (both receiving and providing support to others) and collegial discussions with other lawyers can assist you with practice-based advice that comes from direct experience. Articling is a transition phase, requiring supervision, but also providing opportunities to exercise independent judgment.

In a supervised clinic setting, students have the opportunity not only to observe lawyers at work but also to participate in many of the activities undertaken by lawyers. Students can expect guidance about how to perform specific tasks as well as critical assessments of their conduct and judgment.

Consider the following organizing questions, which may help you to prepare for supervision:

- What is the purpose and objective of any specific activity, such as conducting an interview or undertaking a plea negotiation with an assistant Crown attorney? How does it advance the client's interests?

- What information is available to accomplish a task (e.g. facts obtained from interviews, documentary or other evidence, or knowledge of legal principles)? What knowledge is missing? How can the information gap be closed (e.g. legal research, re-interviewing the client, consulting others with direct experience)?

- What conclusion can be reached (e.g. can you recommend a specific course of action)? What inferences can you draw, and what assumptions are you relying on to reach your conclusion? What are the consequences of these conclusions? Is there another way to interpret the information that might lead to a different conclusion? Have you examined the situation from the perspectives of all parties, including the decision-maker?

- How do you receive critical feedback? How do the opinions of others, including the critical feedback of supervisors and colleagues, enhance your learning?

- How would you alter your approach the next time you are faced with a similar task? How do you approach decision making?

- How do you react to the uncivil or unprofessional conduct of others? Do you escalate the issue by reacting similarly, or do you circumvent confrontation?

- Can you differentiate between assertive, firm, and forceful behaviour that advances a cause and aggressive, antagonistic behaviour that invites retaliation?

- When undertaking any activity in a public or private legal forum (e.g. court or office), are you reliable? Do you keep your promises and fulfill your undertakings?

II. Preparing for Practice

Essential skills for clinic work include client interviewing and counselling.

A. Interviewing the Client: Structuring the Meeting[10]

Figure 14.2 illustrates a method for structuring a meeting with a client.

1. Purpose

While law students focus on learning legal principles, in practice, cases are usually resolved on the basis of their facts. The client interview establishes the factual foundation of every case. The objective of the interview is to understand the factual basis of the client's legal issues, which will lead to determining the appropriate remedy or relief.

As the facts are revealed, first through the client interview and then through additional procedures, such as interviewing witnesses or other parties to the dispute or obtaining relevant documents, determine the legal issues and identify the legal implications of the client's situation. Without a comprehensive interview that allows a client to reveal his or her story, your assessment of the governing law may be compromised and you may give the client erroneous advice. Therefore, developing sound interviewing techniques is one step in the process of becoming a competent lawyer.

Becoming a skilled interviewer takes study and practice because interviewing involves a number of discrete skills, including interpersonal communication, task organization, active listening, fact gathering, and assessment. While the information that follows summarizes general considerations for structuring a client interview, you can enhance your skills by participating in interviewing training sessions that include mock interviews and feedback.

2. Preparation for the Interview

Most law offices do not offer walk-in appointments. Before an interview is scheduled, preliminary information is usually provided by telephone or in an email. Review this information before the interview to determine if you need to do preliminary research to understand the legal problem.

Follow the workplace protocol for client interviews, which may include gathering the necessary forms (e.g. retainers or consents to obtain/transmit information).

---

10 This discussion about interviewing clients is based on and adapted from David Binder & Susan Price, *Legal Interviewing and Counseling* (St. Paul, MN: West Publishing, 1977).

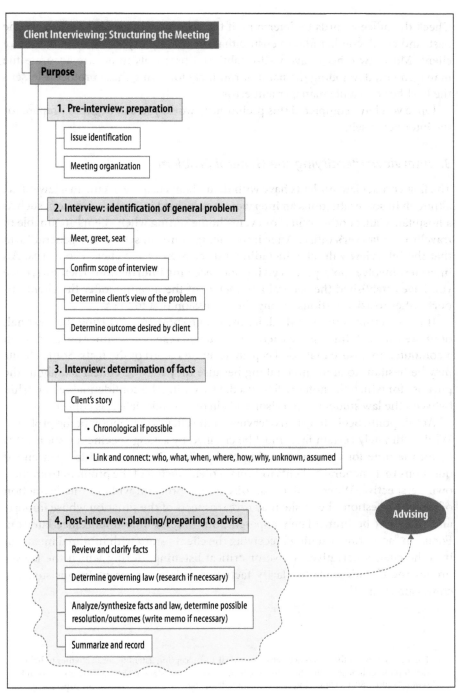

FIGURE 14.2   Client Interview Structure

Check the office records to determine if the client has sought legal advice in the past, and check conflict files to ensure that the other party to the dispute is not a client. Most law offices have well-established protocols to ensure accurate file management; developing the habit of routinely following these protocols lessens the likelihood of a file management error.

Once you have completed this preliminary work, you can begin to prepare for the interview itself.

3. Interview: Identifying the General Problem

The first contact law students have with their clients usually occurs in a law office, although in some situations an interview may be held in another location, such as a hospital, a jail, another office, or even a home setting when clients are unable to travel to the lawyer's office. After introducing yourself, set out the general form that the interview will take, including a discussion of the client's concerns. An interview involves both parties giving and receiving information. Therefore, once you have established the general parameters of the meeting, offer the client opportunities to ask questions during the discussion that follows.

If the meeting is time-limited, let the client know (e.g. "During the next half hour, we can …"). Inform the client that you will take notes, either by hand or on a computer, to ensure that you keep an accurate record of the facts. Some clients may be hesitant to allow note taking because they may be concerned about the purpose for which the notes will be used. Discussing the confidential relationship between the law student/supervisor and client may alleviate this concern.

At this point, begin to get an overview of the client's perception of the problem. While ultimately certain facts must be clarified by asking specific questions, this is not the time for close questioning of the client. Rather, provide open-ended questions that encourage clients to explain their version of the problem from their own perspective. When a client can discuss the problem without the distraction of probing questions, he or she may reveal aspects of the situation whose importance may not be immediately apparent, but may assume importance later on. Focus on "accepting listening", receiving the client's story with minimal intrusion into the client's narrative. Active or critical listening, during which the lawyer probes the client's story to clarify factual details or apparent inconsistencies, comes afterward.[11]

---

11   For a discussion of the difference between critical and accepting listening, and activities to help develop the skill of accepting listening, see Jean Koh Peters & Mark Weisberg, "Experiments in Listening" (2004) NYLS Clinical Research Institute Paper No. 04/05-5, online: <http://papers.ssrn.com/sol3/papers.cfm?abstract_id=601182>.

Once you have obtained a general overview of the client's perception of the problem, ascertain the general outcomes or remedies that the client wants. Even if you suspect that the client is unlikely to obtain these outcomes, or remedies, simply receive the information at this stage. After you have obtained the complete story, finish your research and analysis, discuss the case with your supervisor, clarify the client's options, and then speak to the client about his or her potential remedies during an advising session.

4. Determining the Facts

Once you have obtained a general view of the client's perception of the problem and learned what the client hopes to achieve, focus on the details of the client's story.[12] The organizing words who, what, when, where, how, and why, discussed in Chapter 2, may help to reveal information that explains the client's situation. Record the relevant events chronologically. As you learn about the sequence of events, consider the involvement of other parties, the reasons for their actions, and the detail surrounding the event's occurrence. Information that may be relevant but has not yet been ascertained, along with information yet to be confirmed, is included in the category of unkown or assumed facts, which will require further investigation.

It may not always be possible to obtain a chronological summary of the facts from your client. Some clients, particularly those with cognitive, emotional, or physical conditions and those who have experienced traumatic events, may have difficulty ordering information in sequence. In these cases, be flexible: record the information that the client can provide, attempt to organize the information chronologically, and determine whether the confidential relationship you have with the client allows you to seek out others who may be able to confirm or amplify the client's account.[13]

As the interview ends, review your notes. Consider the next steps from the clinic's perspective (e.g. obtaining a retainer to open the file, undertaking work on the client's behalf, obtaining consents to speak to other parties, reviewing the file with your supervisor, and arranging a subsequent meeting with the client to discuss options). Review and record any steps that the client must take (e.g. submitting a document). Determine when and how the next contact will be made (e.g. by letter, telephone call, email, or in person). Avoid making promises or predictions about the outcome of the case.

---

12   Review Chapter 2, which provides a fact assessment protocol.

13   Some community agencies partner with those in the legal field to provide support for clients with specific legal needs. See e.g. Mental Health Services in Windsor Essex, *Navigating the Criminal Justice System*, <http://www.cmha-wecb.on.ca/docs/home/justice_book.pdf>.

5. Post-Interview: Planning and Preparing to Offer Advice

At this stage, complete accurate and thorough file notes. Files may be transferred to others in an office; therefore, the information obtained at the interview must be comprehensible to someone who was not there. In preparation for meeting with your supervisor, it may be appropriate to undertake legal research; however, you may also do your research after the supervisory meeting. Depending on the complexity of the file, you may need to write a memorandum of law.

Consider all options. For example, on the basis of the facts and the law, is this a case that

- may be settled informally through negotiation?
- may be settled through an alternative dispute resolution process, such as mediation?
- may be settled through a formal dispute resolution process, such as a trial or hearing?
- may be appropriately referred to another legal or non-legal service provider?
- reveals no legal issue and requires no further work?

Once you have discussed and confirmed your ideas with your supervisor, the next stage is advising the client of his or her options, determining the client's wishes, and deciding if and how the case can be moved forward.

B. Advising the Client: Structuring the Meeting

Figure 14.3 shows a method of structuring a meeting during which you provide advice.

> Of all the skills that good lawyers must possess, the ability to counsel clients effectively may be the most critical. To counsel clients about their legal problems, lawyers must be knowledgeable about substantive and procedural law. They must be able to engage in strategic planning. They must have well-developed interpersonal skills. They must be able to predict with some degree of certainty the likelihood of certain results occurring as a result of particular action(s) or failure(s) to act. They must effectively communicate to the client the many nuances of their craft in understandable and non-technical language. They must have a breadth of vision that enables them to present to clients a wide range of alternatives and options to consider and weigh.
>
> Robert D Dinerstein[14]

---

14   Robert D Dinerstein, "Client-Centered Counseling: Reappraisal and Refinement" (1990) 32 Ariz L Rev 501.

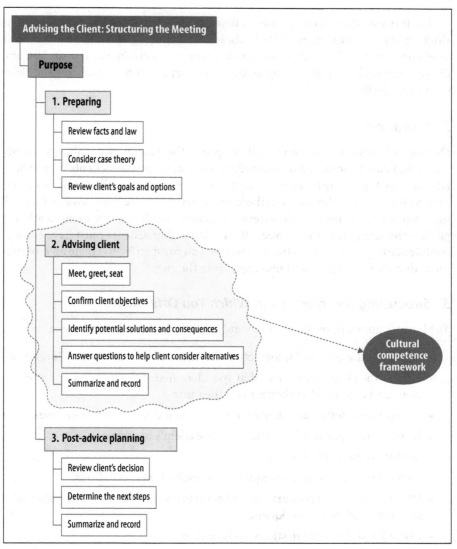

FIGURE 14.3   Advising Clients

1. Purpose

Students advise clients after conducting the initial interview and discussing the client's problems with their supervisor. Counselling clients about their legal options requires many skills that are not typically addressed in a traditional law school curriculum. To prepare for a counselling session, review the notes from the interview, focusing specifically on the client's objectives, do any necessary research, and carefully consider the options available to the client.

The process of counselling assists clients in learning about their options, considering the consequences of their choice, and making a decision from their available options. After a client has made his or her decision, the law student and the supervising lawyer then consider their next steps in either advancing the claim or closing the file.

2. Preparing

During an interview, ascertain the client's goals. The client may not always identify a goal that can be achieved through the legal system. Instead, clients may articulate their goals in a way that focuses on personal matters that affect various aspects of their life. You may be required therefore to articulate the legal remedy that will most likely achieve the client's preferred outcome. Implicit in the identification of goals is the strength of the lawyer–client relationship. Clients must have enough confidence in you to discuss their concerns; you must strive to create an environment that elicits candour and openness from the client.

3. Structuring the Interview in Which You Offer Advice

The basic framework of the interview might include the following steps:

- Highlight the essential information discussed at the preliminary interview.
- Review the client's objectives that you identified at the preliminary interview, and confirm that they remain the same.
- Determine whether any new events have altered the client's objectives.
- Identify the legal and factual basis of the client's concerns.
- Identify the potential solutions.
- Examine the potential consequences of each of these solutions.
- Discuss the client's concerns and observations about each of the potential solutions and their consequences.
- Consider additional questions and concerns.
- Prioritize the client's wishes about the desired objectives.
- Identify the next steps that each of the solutions requires.
- Confirm the next steps for both you and the client.

When a client must choose among options, one of the questions that he or she may ask you is, "What would you advise?" Avoid answering this question directly. A student cannot know all the issues that affect a client's life; the choice of options belongs to the client, not to the student. However, you can help the client reach a decision by reviewing the options and their potential consequences. Recognize that the client may not be ready to make a decision at this time and may want more time to consider the options or discuss them with a friend or family member.

To help the client sort out the information, consider using visual aids, such as the chart as shown in Figure 14.4.

Alternative	Explanation	Pro	Con	Rank order	Follow-up/ other
1					
2					
3					

FIGURE 14.4   Considering Alternative Choices

When the client comes to a decision, summarize and determine the next steps, and conclude the interview.

4. Post-Advice Planning

Review the client's decision with your supervising lawyer, including the reasons that the client chose a particular option and rejected the others. Summarize your notes to ensure that an accurate record is compiled, and take the next steps in the case plan. Examples of specific work that you might undertake on behalf of a client are provided later in the chapter.

C. Legal Education and Law Reform

As well as providing direct service to clients, a clinic setting offers other opportunities to enhance a student's knowledge about the law. Legal education can take many forms: e.g. creating documents that communicate with clients about legal services, sponsoring workshops that address needs within a community, and addressing situations that arise because of a crisis or event. The skills involved in participating in community legal education are similar to those that have been discussed in earlier chapters (research, analysis, problem solving, advising, and communicating). However, the people with whom you work may not be seeking a specific legal remedy but rather may be seeking general legal information to deal with a community problem. Frequently, opportunities exist to partner with other community members, such as the police, community health officials, social workers and counsellors, and financial services staff.

Law reform initiatives tend to have a broader perspective and focus on issues that affect the development of the law itself. To participate in law reform, you will need to be able to research law and policy, both domestic and international. Law reform initiatives often involve writing policy papers and addressing lawmakers, such as municipal councils and provincial or federal parliamentary committees.

D. Communication

No matter what tasks confront you in a clinical setting, you will need strong research, writing, and analysis skills. Focus on plain language writing, as discussed in Chapter 12, when creating documents that summarize legal argument, participating in community legal education, or drafting policy documents.[15]

III. Overview of the Client's Legal Issue

The rest of this chapter describes the process of bringing a civil matter to trial for clients Amir Shybani and Rita Haddad, who were introduced in Chapter 11.

Because Rita's legal matter involves a personal injury claim, it is unlikely that a legal clinic would accept her case. Personal injury cases frequently involve catastrophic loss and have life-altering consequences. Expert medical witnesses are usually required, damages must be calculated to take into account present and future losses, insurance companies are often parties to the litigation, and the costs of advancing a claim are substantial.

However, assume that a clinic has decided to accept both Rita and Amir as clients for the following reasons:

- Amir was uninsured at the time of the accident; as a result, he has been charged with a provincial offence, which is a matter typically within the clinic's mandate.
- Amir is currently unemployed.
- The motorcycle was the couple's only mode of transportation, and they cannot drive it now because of damage caused by the accident.
- Rita does not want to sue Amir personally because of their personal relationship.
- Rita was unable to work temporarily because of her injuries but is recovering; she has no future claims for damages other than those previously described in Chapter 11.

---

15   See e.g. Christine Mowat, *A Plain Language Handbook for Legal Writers* (Scarborough, ON: Carswell, 1998), which provides samples of documents used in a variety of legal settings.

- Both Rita's and Amir's claims for damages are quantifiable and fall within the monetary jurisdiction of the Small Claims Court. Although Small Claims Courts are structured to allow plaintiffs to bring claims without retaining counsel, Rita and Amir do not feel capable of bringing a claim against the dog owner, Cramwell Brook, because it is anticipated that, as owner of Cramwell's Kennel, he has the financial resources to retain counsel if he chooses.

The following information illustrates selected steps taken during the civil process in the hope of assisting Rita and Amir recoup some of their losses.

IV. Learning Outcomes for Student Volunteers at a Legal Clinic

The following learning outcomes[16] explore the legal skills that can be developed as a student volunteer at a legal clinic; they will vary according to the type of clinic work that you are involved in.

1. Engage in client-centred legal practice by
- establishing client rapport
- maintaining communication with the client during the course of the retainer
- working with clients to resolve legal issues
- working with community partners to assess and serve community needs

2. Demonstrate requisite legal skills by
- eliciting relevant facts during interviews
- identifying legal issues
- developing action plans to address the client's legal issues
- undertaking legal research as required
- drafting legal documents, such as memoranda, correspondence, and pleadings

---

16   The following suggestions for clinic learning outcomes have been adapted from those developed by Rose Faddoul while she was a student in the MEd program at the University of Windsor.

- participating in negotiation and settlement discussions
- engaging in legal analysis and the assessment of evidence
- advising clients competently
- determining the court or tribunal of competent jurisdiction together with its rules of practice for every matter
- preparing effectively for each phase of a trial or hearing
- preparing effective questions for witnesses
- making effective opening and closing submissions
- marshalling evidence
- challenging opponent's evidence by making appropriate objections and conducting effective cross-examination

3. Demonstrate ethical and professional conduct in the workplace by
- adhering to clinic rules of practice and procedure
- demonstrating civility in relationships with others
- determining how the rules of professional conduct apply to daily tasks
- identifying and considering ethical issues in day-to-day legal practice

4. Participate in requisite supervision by
- engaging in self-reflection of performance
- modifying work and performance in accordance with assessment
- identifying performance strengths, weaknesses, and other issues that may require attention

5. Follow office management procedures by
- establishing and adhering to a bring-forward system, which includes a record of limitation periods
- managing and maintaining legal files in good order
- recording all communications, documents, and appearances, in accordance with clinic procedure
- securing evidence

V. Work Plan Overview: Civil File

A work plan overview is provided in Figure 14.5.

A. Gathering Facts

1. Initial Interview

When a prospective client schedules an appointment, where possible, the person making the appointment should ensure that the client's problem falls within the clinic's case selection criteria. Although initially Rita and Amir's legal issue was thought to fall outside the clinic's mandate, further exploration during the interview revealed that Rita and Amir were eligible to receive the clinic's services.

The following questions might be included in an interview; they can be adapted as required.

a. INTRODUCTION

Begin with a greeting, recognizing that the same form of welcome for all clients is unlikely to be appropriate. For example, in Western culture, a handshake is often an appropriate greeting for two same-sex or opposite-sex people who meet for the first time; however, this form of greeting may be inappropriate in certain cultures. In this case, offering to shake Rita's hand is inappropriate because she has hand injuries. Alter your greeting to fit the circumstances. For example:

> Good morning/afternoon. My name is XXXX, and I am a student at the Legal Aid Clinic.

Because information about a clinic is often available in a brochure or on a website, the client may already be aware of following information.

> At this clinic, students, supervised by lawyers, provide legal services to members of the community who qualify for our services. [Explain the clinic's qualifying or restricting conditions, such as those that apply to financial condition, geographical location, or legal matter. Also review the meaning of a retainer and confidentiality.] My supervisor will review the information we have discussed and decide whether we can open a file to assist you with this matter.

When clients do not qualify, try to refer them to other community services rather than sending them out to search for help on their own. If the client is eligible, continue with the interview, following clinic guidelines to ensure that you gather the essential information.

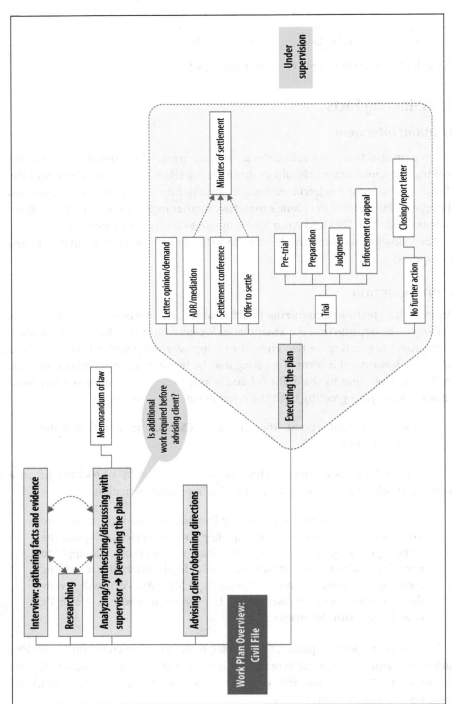

FIGURE 14.5 Civil File: Work Plan Overview

b. FACT ASSESSMENT

Begin with general questions to encourage the client to reveal his or her problem without constraints or restrictions.

> What brings you here today?
>
> What can you tell me about why you are here today?
>
> I understand that you have some issues that you want to discuss.

Encourage the client to talk about the circumstances that may have a direct or indirect effect on the legal issue. For example, in this case, Amir disclosed that he was unemployed and could not afford his insurance premium. This information can lead to more specific questions.[17]

> When did you become aware that you were uninsured?
>
> Were you aware that you were uninsured on the day of the accident?
>
> Did you receive a notice of termination for your insurance coverage?
>
> How long were you carrying insurance before it was terminated?

To gain a general understanding of the broader scope of the problem, consider asking questions that are not directly relevant to the legal issue, but that may be helpful in other ways (e.g. assisting you in referring the client to a social agency that may benefit him or her).

> Do you have any other source of income, apart from your wages as a cashier?

c. EVIDENCE COLLECTION

As the interview continues, consider how you would prove the facts of the case, if it went to a trial or a hearing, i.e. through witness testimony or through documents or other evidence.

> After I copy these documents, I will give you back the original.
>
> I am going to keep some of the documents to ensure they are available for trial, and I will give you a copy for your records.

Some of the questions asked of Rita and Amir might include:

> Do you have any documents, pictures, or any other evidence with you today?

---

17 Chapter 2 provides suggestions about fact assessment.

Did you see anyone who may have witnessed the accident? Did you happen to get their names and contact information?

Did the police arrive at the scene, and did they provide you with a report?

Were pictures taken of the accident site, the motorcycle, or the injuries? Do you have a picture of the motorcycle before the accident? Who took the pictures? Do you have the photographer's contact information?

Do you have medical reports from any doctor who treated you for the injuries that you sustained in the accident?

d. WRAP-UP

Before concluding the interview, summarize the results of the discussion, including the client's general objective, and discuss the next steps, including who will take them.

> Once I complete additional research, I will discuss the results with my supervisor; we will send you a letter that summarizes our legal opinion about the issues that we have discussed today. In the meantime, please provide the contact information for the witness who observed the accident and the photographs taken by the police officer. Please make sure to get receipts for the costs of medical treatment or care, including travel expenses, and bring them to our next meeting.

NB: Note limitation periods. For example, if the client has been served with a statement of claim, determine when it was issued and served because there is only a short time to file a defence in response to a claim.

Help the client review the retainer before he or she signs it. Obtain release-of-information forms, which allow you to contact others who may have informaiton, such as the police or doctor, and any other documents that may be necessary to assist with the collection of evidence. The clinic cannot gather information without the client's written consent.

e. FOLLOW-UP

Follow the clinic protocol for file management, which may include some of the following steps:

- Make a diary entry for important dates required by the clinic.
- Complete file notes that summarize the interview.
- Draft an opening letter, which includes a detailed summary of the facts reported by your client. In the event of an error or omission, the client will be able to correct the factual record.
- Draft additional letters as required.
- Submit the file for review by the supervising lawyer.

B. Researching the Law

Legal advice must be based on a sound understanding of the law that applies to the facts obtained during the interview.[18] Research is frequently required:

- Review Chapter 9, which explains how to create a research plan and log the results as you complete the research.
- Execute the plan, applying the information provided in Chapters 3 and 4, if the applicable legislation is federal, or Chapter 5, if the applicable legislation is provincial.
- Locate judicial decisions, as explained in Chapter 6.
- Use secondary sources of law to assist with the research process, either as a starting point to identify governing legislation and critical cases, or to help you understand the legal issues at hand, as discussed in Chapter 7.
- Analyze the results, as described in Chapters 10 and 11.

Taking these steps will provide the legal foundation necessary to proceed with the case. In Rita and Amir's case, research revealed one applicable statute and one municipal bylaw:

- *Negligence Act*, RSO 1990, c N.1
- A Bylaw for the Care and Control of Animals in the Municipality of Kinnton

Locating the judicial decisions that interpret the relevant sections is the next step, followed by a legal analysis applied to the facts of the case summary.

C. Planning

Typically, the planning phase involves a discussion between the student and the supervising lawyer about the facts and evidence, the governing law, and (considering the client's objectives) the options and possible outcomes. In complex situations, such as Rita and Amir's, you may need to write a memorandum of law before the planning meeting to determine the legal and factual basis for each option that is available to each client.

The student and the supervising lawyer usually discuss the case after the initial client interview. The student explains the facts and proposes a plan of action. The

---

18   Jurisdiction is an essential consideration when you are conducting research into a matter that will be decided by a court, since the court proceedings are governed by specific rules. This example describes a procedure in Ontario and therefore follows Ontario law, including rules of civil procedure. However, it can be adapted to accommodate the laws and bylaws of other jurisdictions, because all other jurisdictions in Canada have enacted legislation that governs negligence.

student must resist the urge to act immediately and first think about what needs to be done.

Create a "to do" list and accomplish these tasks before settling on a plan of action. For example:

Collect Evidence

- Determine which witnesses must be interviewed. For example, the balloon operator may have witnessed the accident; the bylaw officer may have information about the dog; the police may have an accident report; the treating physician may have information about the injuries; and the garage mechanic may have information about the cost of repairing the motorcycle.

Research:[19]

- Think more broadly about the problem and consider whether other legislation may apply, e.g. the *Insurance Act*.

Remedy: Damages

- Are the injuries permanent? Confirm, from the evidence gathered, that the injuries are temporary.
- Obtain receipts to prove out-of-pocket costs of therapy, medical equipment, and medication.
- Obtain a statement of wages for Rita.
- Obtain an invoice for repairs to the motorcycle.

A discussion about the initial plan of action with the supervising lawyer is essential because the lawyer's feedback will ensure that you are taking the right course of action. Once you have identified the issues and researched the law, a further discussion with the supervising lawyer is necessary to determine whether to

- change the plan of action on the basis of your research findings
- undertake further research and/or collect additional evidence or information

Ensure that you have enough information to draft a memorandum of law[20] that outlines all aspects of the case, including costs. A cost–benefit analysis may be necessary to determine that the cost of litigation will not exceed the amount

---

19 Review Chapter 7 to determine the secondary sources available to help you locate relevant legislation and case law.

20 Review Chapter 13 to examine the structure of a memorandum of law.

claimed. After completing the memorandum, you may be ready to draft a letter of opinion to the client and seek instructions about how to proceed.

D. Advising the Client

As discussed previously in this chapter, advising the client after exploring the options is a critical phase in the management of a civil file. Unless the client has the information necessary to make an informed decision and the time to consider both the positive and the negative consequences of every option, problems may emerge. If the client later asserts "You didn't tell me that" or "If I had known, I would never have …", the records of your discussion about the client's options must be unambiguous.

The most appropriate method of advising the client is through a letter of opinion, which can respond to the client's questions and explain his or her legal position. It is a crucial document on which the client will rely in making decisions. An inaccurate or incomplete letter of opinion may lead to choices that have negative consequences for the client, which in turn may result in a complaint or claim against both you and your supervising lawyer.

A letter of opinion generally includes

- a summary of the facts
- a list of the legal issues
- a plain language review of the law as it relates to the facts
- an application of the law to the facts
- a discussion of the strengths and weaknesses of the claim
- a list of options, which may include an analysis of the advantages and disadvantages of each option
- a summary of the next steps to be taken on the file

The letter concludes with a request for instructions by a specified date.

If the client believes that he or she has received incomplete or inaccurate advice, you must attempt to restore a positive relationship by determining how the miscommunication may have occurred and discussing steps to avoid the problem in the future. If a significant error or omission is identified, immediately inform your supervising lawyer, who will determine whether the law society and the lawyer's insurer for errors and omissions must be notified.

In Rita and Amir's case, the dog's owner, Cramwell Brook, denied any responsibility, claiming that the damages and injuries were entirely Amir's fault.

Amir and Rita would have welcomed an opportunity to negotiate or mediate the dispute, but the dog's owner refused. Because the only remaining options were either to abandon the claim or to sue for damages in Small Claims Court, reluctantly Amir and Rita decided to sue.

E. Executing the Plan

A trial is never the preferred option to settle a dispute; it is time-consuming, uncertain in outcome, and expensive. Examination and cross-examination is an uncomfortable process for witnesses. Experienced lawyers always explore settlement options before they consider going to trial.[21] However, if a matter cannot be resolved in any other way, sometimes a trial is necessary. If a matter goes to trial, ensure that the implementation of any plan approved by the supervising lawyer and the client proceeds in an orderly fashion, and record all steps taken.

1. Trial

a. STATEMENT OF CLAIM

The trial process begins with a statement of claim,[22] which provides a brief summary of the material facts and law that frames the dispute. The claim answers the questions typically asked when fact gathering:

- What happened?
- To whom did it happen?
- Where and when did it happen?
- What legal claim is being made?
- What outcome does the client request?

Amir and Rita's statement of claim is reproduced in Figure 14.6.

b. STATEMENT OF DEFENCE

A statement of defence is a response to a statement of claim. There are strict time limits for filing this statement in court. If a statement of defence is not filed after a claim is made against a party, the plaintiff can take the next steps to enforce the claim. In Brook's statement of defence, reproduced in Figure 14.7, note the blanket assertions that claim Rita's and Amir's negligence and contributory negligence caused their damages and injuries.

---

21 Increasingly, law schools offer instruction in alternative dispute resolution. Explore these options with your career advisers when selecting courses, especially if you believe that a career in litigation is in your future.

22 When preparing documents and filing and serving claims, comply with the rules of the court that will decide the claim.

FIGURE 14.6   Sample Statement of Claim

SC-13-00001

ONTARIO SUPERIOR COURT OF JUSTICE
KINNTON SMALL CLAIMS COURT

B E T W E E N:

AMIR SHYBANI and RITA HADDAD

PLAINTIFFS

V

CRAMWELL BROOK

DEFENDANT

STATEMENT OF CLAIM

1. The plaintiffs claim
   a. damages in the amount of $25,000;
   b. special damages in an amount to be determined;
   c. prejudgment and post-judgment interest on these amounts in accordance with the *Courts of Justice Act*, RSO 1990, c C.43; and
   d. costs of this action together with the applicable harmonized sales tax.
2. The plaintiff, Amir Shybani, is a writer residing in the city of Mendossa, county of Humblin, province of Ontario.
3. The plaintiff, Rita Haddad, is a cashier residing in the city of Mendossa, county of Humblin, province of Ontario.
4. The defendant is the owner of a dog kennel, Cramwell's Kennel, a sole proprietorship within the town of Kinnton, county of Humblin, province of Ontario. At all material times, he was the owner and possessor of a Pomeranian dog named Stormy.
5. On or about July 13, 20XX at approximately 8:00 a.m., the plaintiffs were riding on a motorcycle owned by Amir Shybani. Amir was the operator; Rita was the passenger. They were eastbound on Highway 18, in the town of Kinnton, proceeding at a rate of speed of approximately 70 kilometres per hour when a dog ran in front of the motorcycle, causing Amir to swerve to avoid hitting the dog. The dog was later identified as the Pomeranian named Stormy.
6. As a result of these events, Rita was thrown from the motorcycle and suffered the following injuries:
   a. a fracture of her right thumb and index finger; and
   b. several abrasions, cuts, and bruises on both hands.
7. The driver, Amir, suffered no injuries; however, his motorcycle required a new tailpipe, dual seat, kickstand, tires, headlight, mirrors, chain, and fresh paint because of the damages to the motorcycle.
8. The defendant and/or his agents, servants, or employees were negligent as owners and possessors of Stormy and breached their duty of care by
   a. permitting Stormy to run at large without supervision;
   b. permitting Stormy to run at the plaintiffs while they were on a motorcycle;

(Figure 14.6 is continued on the next page.)

    c. permitting Stormy to behave in a manner that posed a menace to the safety of the plaintiffs and their property;

    d. failing to exercise reasonable precautions to prevent Stormy from

      i. charging the plaintiffs; and

      ii. behaving in a manner that posed a menace to the safety of the plaintiffs;

    e. failing to take the necessary measures to control Stormy in the interests of public safety, such as

      i. failing to confine Stormy to the defendant's property;

      ii. failing to restrain Stormy by means of a leash or any other reasonable means;

      iii. failing to consider Stormy's past and present temperament and behaviour;

      iv. failing to consider the probability that Stormy could wander off, given his past and present behaviour;

      v. failing to consider Stormy's propensity to dash out into the road;

      vi. failing to consider Stormy's propensity to run after a moving vehicle; and

      vii. failing to take precautions to prevent Stormy from charging the plaintiffs while they were on the motorcycle.

9. As a result of the negligent conduct of the defendant, his servants, agents, or employees, the plaintiff Rita has suffered

    a. temporary pain in her right hand;

    b. temporary damage to her right hand, restricting its use;

    c. 10 physical therapy sessions between September 1, 20XX and November 15, 20XX.

10. The plaintiff Amir determined after the accident that his contract for insurance had lapsed and his motorcycle was not insured at the time of the accident.

11. As a result of the damages that he has suffered, the plaintiff Amir claims pecuniary damages in the amount of $5,000 for the repair of his motorcycle.

12. As a result of the damages that she has suffered, the plaintiff Rita claims pecuniary damages in the amount of $12,000 and non-pecuniary damages in the amount of $8,000.

13. The plaintiffs plead and rely on provisions of the *Negligence Act*, RSO 1990, c N.1, as amended, and A Bylaw for the Care and Control of Animals in the Municipality of Kinnton, in addition to the common law.

14. The plaintiffs propose that the action be tried in the city of Mendossa.

Date of issue: January 5, 20XX

"Name of Lawyer"
LEGAL AID CLINIC
Barristers and Solicitors
2121 Avenue Road
Mendossa, Ontario
N9A 1B2

FIGURE 14.7   Sample Statement of Defence

SC-13-00001

ONTARIO SUPERIOR COURT OF JUSTICE
KINNTON SMALL CLAIMS COURT

BETWEEN:

AMIR SHYBANI and RITA HADDAD

PLAINTIFFS

V

CRAMWELL BROOK

DEFENDANT

STATEMENT OF DEFENCE

1. The defendant admits the allegations in paragraphs 2 and 3 of the plaintiffs' statement of claim.
2. The defendant denies the allegations in paragraphs 1, 4, 5, 6, 7, 8, 9, 11, 12, and 13.
3. The defendant has no knowledge of the allegations set out in paragraph 10.
4. The defendant expressly denies the allegations of negligence made against him and his servants, agents, or employees.
5. The defendant states that he took all reasonable measures to control the dog Stormy.
6. Further, the defendant denies that he caused or contributed to the negligence claimed by the plaintiffs in paragraph 8 of their statement of claim or that he caused or contributed to the damages alleged.
7. The defendant states that the collision that occurred on July 13, 20XX was caused either by the negligence or by the contributory negligence of the plaintiffs in that Rita Haddad
   a. failed to keep a proper lookout;
   b. failed to wear proper protective clothing and a helmet and/or failed to secure her helmet;
   c. created a situation of danger and emergency on the highway; and
   d. failed to meet the required and applicable standard of care.
8. The defendant states that the collision that occurred on July 13, 20XX was caused either by the negligence or by the contributory negligence of the plaintiffs in that Amir Shybani
   a. failed to safely and reasonably swerve or to take reasonable evasive action to avoid injuries and/or damages to the plaintiffs or to the motorcycle;
   b. drove at an excessive rate of speed;
   c. failed to consider the road conditions that resulted from the severe weather conditions on the previous evening;
   d. failed to keep proper control of the motorcycle;

(Figure 14.7 is concluded on the next page.)

    e. drove erratically or carelessly;

    f. created a situation of danger and emergency on the highway;

    g. failed to keep a proper lookout;

    h. failed to wear proper protective clothing and a helmet and/or failed to secure his helmet;

    i. was impaired by alcohol, drugs, sleeplessness, poor health, or by a combination thereof, which impaired his ability to drive the motorcycle;

    j. was incompetent as a driver and lacked the reasonable skill and self-command to operate a motorcycle;

    k. was in poor health and operated a motor vehicle while he knew or ought to have known that his ability to operate a motor vehicle was impaired;

    l. misapplied the throttle and/or brakes of the motorcycle, thereby creating a situation of danger and emergency; and

    m. failed to meet the required and applicable standard of care.

9. The defendant denies that the plaintiffs have sustained the injuries, damages, and losses as alleged, or at all, and put the plaintiffs to the strict proof thereof.

10. In addition or in the alternative, the defendant states that any injuries, losses, and damages are excessive, indirect, and remote and that the plaintiffs have failed to mitigate these injuries, losses, and damages.

11. The defendant pleads and relies on the provisions of the *Highway Traffic Act*, RSO 1990, c H.8, as amended, and the *Negligence Act*, RSO 1990, c N.1.

12. The defendant submits that the action should be dismissed with costs.

Date of issue: January 15, 20XX

"Name of Lawyer"
Barristers and Solicitors
333 Ford Road
Kinnton, Ontario
N9B 2A3

Telephone: 519-555-2222
Fax: 519-555-3333
Lawyers for the Defendant

"Name of Lawyer"
LEGAL AID CLINIC
Barristers and Solicitors
2121 Avenue Road
Mendossa, Ontario
N9A 1B2

Telephone: 519-555-5555
Fax: 519-555-6666
Lawyers for the Plaintiffs

Statements of claim and defence are merely the assertions of the plaintiffs and defendants about the cause of their damages and injuries; these assertions will be proven or disproven in court. At trial, through a series of questions, the relevant facts will be revealed, the law will be considered, and a decision will be rendered.

c. PREPARATION

Successful trial preparation does not begin at the last minute. From the earliest signs that the case may not settle and therefore may be destined for trial, begin to consider how the facts can be proven in evidence.

In law school, the facts of a case are provided in hypothetical problems; in the practice of law, the only facts that will form the basis of a judgment are those that are accepted by a court. Most facts are brought before a court as evidence adduced through the testimony of witnesses by means of a process of questioning by the lawyers representing the plaintiff and the defendant.

TASK 14.1

Preparing for a Trial or Hearing: Planning Checklist

The following checklist can be used to organize your preparation for trials and hearings.

Do you know the law?

- Do you know the substantive law (i.e. the elements that you must establish to succeed with the client's claim)?
- Do you know the procedural law that governs the case (i.e. the rules of civil procedure, the Small Claims Court rules, the rules that apply generally to administrative tribunals, or the rules and regulations made under the governing statute)?

Do you know the facts of the case?

- Have you reviewed the file notes? Do you have a broad view of the facts? Do you understand the chronology of the events? Can you diagram or chart them? Do you understand the facts from your opponent's point of view?
- Do you know which facts must be proven in evidence?
- Have you considered all of the factors that might affect the interpretation of the facts (e.g. cultural competency issues)?

Have you formulated an effective case by integrating the facts and the law?

- Have you developed a sound theory of the case? Does your theory rely on accurate facts that lead to a logical conclusion? Is it consistent with the known facts? Does it explain the unfavourable facts?

- Have you anticipated the strengths and weaknesses of your opponent's case theory?

- Have you diagrammed your arguments? Have you completed the process of inductive and deductive reasoning? Have you analyzed the facts that prove your argument, as well as the argument that supports your opponent's position?

- Have you assembled the evidence that you need to prove your arguments?

Have you organized the evidence?

- Do you know the rules of evidence that apply?

- Do you know how to introduce documents in evidence?

- Do you know how to prepare your witnesses to give evidence during their examination-in-chief?

- Do you know how to prepare your witnesses to withstand cross-examination?

- Do you know how to make objections to your opponent's examinations-in-chief?

- Do you know how to cross-examine your opponent's witnesses?

---

d. CASE THEORY

Questions are organized in part in accordance with your case theory. A comprehensive case theory

- relies on known facts that lead to a logical conclusion
- does not contradict known facts
- explains unfavourable facts
- makes sense

The statements of claim and defence suggest the theories of both parties in this case.

Rita and Amir: The defendant negligently allowed his dog to run free, which caused injury to the plaintiffs and damage to their property.

Cramwell Brook: The injuries and damages were caused by the careless driving of the motorcycle operator.

Lawyers for both parties will attempt to construct questions that will present the court with the facts that support their case theory, while minimizing or offering alternative interpretations for the facts that contradict this theory.

e. EXAMINATION-IN-CHIEF

Facts in support of your case theory are established during examination-in-chief. The client's story is then challenged by the lawyer for the other party during cross-examination. It is beyond the scope of this chapter to discuss trial preparation in depth; this is a topic for law students who have already studied the rules of evidence.[23] However, the next section provides an example of the types of questions that might be asked during examination-in-chief to elicit the client's story and during cross-examination to challenge the factual claims made by the client.

Several witnesses may testify at trial. Ordering their testimony is critical because a story is constructed to provide a logical sequence of events. During examination-in-chief, consider the following:

- Have you structured your questions to answer the who, what, and why format discussed in Chapter 2 (e.g. Who is the witness? What information does he or she have to contribute?)?

- Do the questions follow a basic sentence structure (e.g. subject–verb, no compound sentences)? Are the questions short? Are they clear? Are they ordered so that the trier of fact can readily understand the story? Have you used transition statements to orient the witness and the court to a specific line of questioning? (Transition statements serve the same function as subheadings: e.g. "I would like you to turn your mind to the morning of July XX".)

f. CROSS-EXAMINATION

Your cross-examination challenges the evidence of the witnesses presented by your opponent. It may also support the evidence of your client.

Typically, cross-examination is narrowly focused on the points that you believe are the most damaging to your client's case. Usually, the questions in cross-examination lead either to a "yes" or "no" answer, or a response of no more than a few words; hence, they are called leading questions. Leading questions about the matter under dispute are not permitted during examination-in-chief.

Figure 14.8 presents questions posed to Amir during his examination-in-chief and cross-examination. The questions posed during examination-in-chief focus on Amir's identification of the dog that charged at his motorcycle. The questions posed during cross-examination focus on the suggestion that Amir was injured as a result of his inattentiveness while driving and the allegation that he was responsible for the accident.

---

23 See the following sources for in-depth trial preparation: Lee Stuesser, *An Advocacy Primer*, 3d ed (Toronto: Thomson Carswell, 2005), and Thomas A Mauet, Donald G Casswell & Gordon P Mac-Donald, *Fundamentals of Trial Techniques: Canadian Edition*, 2d ed (Toronto: Wolters Kluwer Law and Business, 2001). In addition, continuing legal education material for your jurisdiction may be available in your library or online through your local law society.

FIGURE 14.8 Sample Questions on Examination-in-Chief and Cross-Examination

Plaintiffs	
Theory of the case	The defendant was negligent and breached his duty of care by permitting Stormy to stray from the kennel, which caused damage to the plaintiffs.

Dog ownership	Examination-in-chief of Amir Shybani
	
	1. Do you know who owns the dog Stormy?
	   • The defendant
	2. How can you be certain that Stormy is owned by the defendant?
	   • I obtained a copy of Stormy's licence.
	3. Tender dog licence
	   a. Request permission to approach the witness:
	     Your Honour, may I approach the witness?
	   b. Authenticate the document:
	     Do you recognize this document?
	   c. Identify the document:
	     Can you tell the court what this is?
	     • It is the dog licence that I obtained from the Town of Kinnton Municipal Office.
	   d. Use the document to identify the dog.
	     Can you read the information written on the document?
	The licence identifies the dog Stormy as a Pomeranian owned by Cramwell Brook.

Defendant	
Theory of the case	The plaintiff's careless driving caused or contributed to their damages.

Plaintiff's careless driving	Cross-examination of Amir Shybani
	
	1. You testified that you and Rita Haddad were on your way to get married on the morning of July 13, 20XX?
	   • Yes.
	
	2. You were driving, and Rita was the passenger sitting behind you?
	   • Yes.
	
	3. You were looking forward to marrying Rita that day?
	   • Yes.
	
	4. You were excited, weren't you?
	   • Yes.
	
	5. You were thinking about Rita and how great your life was going to be as husband and wife?
	   • Yes.
	
	6. I bet the two of you were even discussing how great your life would be after marriage?
	   • Yes.
	
	7. In your excitement, you were looking at Rita as often as you could?
	   • No.
	
	8. So you were not focused on your driving but on your future wedding plans?
	   • No, I was focused on my driving.

g. POST-JUDGMENT: ENFORCEMENT OR APPEAL

At the conclusion of the trial, the judge renders a judgment. In the vast majority of cases, that is the end of the matter. However, always consider the possibility of an appeal if the case does not result in the outcome that you expected.

In a civil matter, securing judgment is only the first step in a successful outcome. Collection of the amount owing under the judgment is the final step.

In a clinic, students begin with a simple demand letter for this amount. If the demand is unsuccessful, the most common enforcement actions include:

- Garnishment—collecting an amount in increments on the basis of the judgment debtor's income or other liquid assets.
- Writ of seizure and sale of personal property or writ of seizure and sale of real property—collecting the judgment amount by selling the judgment debtor's assets.
- Examination in aid of execution—examining the judgment debtor about his or her liabilities and assets to determine the debtor's ability to pay the judgment amount. The court may order the debtor to pay a specified amount on the basis of the evidence disclosed in the examination.

Take as many enforcement proceedings as are applicable in the circumstances and likely to produce the desired result.

F. Closing the File

When all work is completed, prepare the file for closing. Draft a closing letter that summarizes the work done on the file. This letter is a complete record of all aspects of the file; it serves as a final report to the client. Follow the file-closing procedures of the clinic or office where you work and submit the file to the supervising lawyer for closure.

APPENDIXES

APPENDIX A
Sample Problem

I. Description

The fact pattern that follows is based on a more complex problem that was presented to one of the author's[1] Law I class in 2010. In the original problem, the issue of polygamy was examined in a number of contexts including family law, marriage, divorce, child welfare and best interests, and custody. In addition, as described in the following problem, the issue of polygamy was examined in the criminal law context.

The information in this appendix was prepared by two law students[2] who were in that original Law I class. They revisited the topic and described the research process they undertook, providing accompanying narrative for the decisions they made about their research process. The description that follows illustrates an approach to take when researching a topic of this nature; it is explanatory and not definitive.

II. Facts

Corfield, in the province of XXX, is home to the largest Canadian contingent of Idealights—that is, members of the faith organization Ideal Life Path (ILP). Idealights adhere to two related but distinct sets of principles of faith and values, referred to, respectively, as "Life Guides" and "Ways of Life".

Life Guides principles are subordinate to Ways of Life principles. Both are recommendations about how to live in accordance with the ILP faith. Among their beliefs, for example, are that Idealights must grow their own food and observe a strict 9:00 p.m. curfew. Breaches of these Life Guides precepts can result in fines, as well as in temporary suspensions from membership in ILP. The money collected from the fines is directed to an ILP fund dedicated to various causes. Breaching

---

1 Moira McCarney.

2 Chuck Andary and Andrew McLean, Law III, University of Windsor.

Ways of Life principles is a more serious matter; it can result in stronger sanctions, including permanent banishment from the ILP community.

Garnett Kane ("Kane") has been the leader of the ILP community for the last seven years. During his tenure, one of the Ways of Life principles—the one requiring Idealights to dedicate their lives to growing the membership of their community—has been variously interpreted. These differing interpretations have resulted in an escalating community conflict.

Two factions have emerged, with opposing viewpoints. One group, the traditionalists, has interpreted the community-growth principle as making polygamy mandatory for all Idealights. The other group, the progressives, view polygamy as a Life Guides principle that does not mandate permanent banishment for those who do not adopt the practice.

Kane knows that anyone practising polygamy in Canada faces prosecution under the *Criminal Code*. As a traditionalist member of the Idealight community, he has sought legal advice to determine whether the criminal sanction prohibiting polygamy could be successfully challenged as an unjustifiable infringement of his fundamental freedom of conscience and religion under the *Charter*.

III. Research Plan and Log

We started out by identifying legal concept keywords and fact keywords and then formulated the issue as described in Chapter 2, e.g. *Criminal Code*, polygamy, religion, faith, *Charter of Rights and Freedoms*, Ideal Life Path, Garnett Kane. In our research, sometimes we used online sources and sometimes we used print. We will describe what we found.

Although there are many ways to start legal research, e.g. consulting a legal encyclopedia, or searching for a secondary source on the topic of polygamy, both of which are explained in Chapter 7, we decided to look at the legislation first.

General Area/Topic of Law: Constitutional Law

Common Law? _X_   Civil Law? _____   Public? _X_   Private? _____

Jurisdiction: Federal? _X_   Provincial? ___   Municipal? ___   International/Foreign? ___

Legislation? _X_   Judicial Decisions? _X_   Unknown? ___

Issue 1: Does the prohibition against polygamy in section 293 of the *Criminal Code* unjustifiably violate Mr. Kane's fundamental freedom of conscience and religion under section 2(a) of the *Canadian Charter of Rights and Freedoms*?

Plan		Log	
Legal Information Required	**Online and Print Sources to Check**	**Checked (Date)**	**Findings (Append Results to Document)***
A. Essential elements of the crime of polygamy	*Criminal Code*		Section 293 of the *Criminal Code*.
B. Judicial interpretation of polygamy provisions	Case law—*Canadian Statute Citations*, *Canadian Abridgment*, CanLII, Quicklaw, Westlaw, CED, *Halsbury's*		Five cases consider the polygamy provisions.
C. Standing under the *Charter*	Case law		Three-part test to determine standing.
D. Relevant *Charter* section	*Constitution Act, 1982*		Section 2(a) of the *Charter*.
E. Purpose of polygamy provision	Backdate statute, consult *Hansard*		Provision originally enacted in 1890.
F. Case law on section 2(a) of *Charter*	*Canadian Abridgment*, *Canadian Statute Citations*, CanLII, Quicklaw, Westlaw, CED, *Halsbury's Laws of Canada*		A number of cases considering section 2(a) of the *Charter*. One case deals with polygamy violating section 2(a).
G. Secondary sources on polygamy and freedom of religion	ICLL, CLI		Several print and online articles to consider.
H. Limitations on section 2(a) rights	*Constitution Act, 1982*		Section 1 of the *Charter*.
I. Reasonable limits	Case law		Several cases interpret section 1 of the *Charter*.

* If additional questions are raised in the course of research, add them to column 1.

A. Essential Elements of the Offence of Polygamy

Recall from Chapter 4 that federal legislation can be found on the Department of Justice website. A search of "polygamy" identifies the *Criminal Code* as relevant legislation.

The *Criminal Code*, at section 293(1)(a)(i), makes it a crime to "consent to practice or enter into any form of polygamy". Under section 293(1)(a)(ii), it is also a crime to enter into "any kind of conjugal union with more than one person at the same time" regardless of whether it is recognized as a binding form of marriage. There is also a disjunctive rule under section 293(1)(b) that makes it a crime to do any activity that will "celebrate, assist or [be] a party to a rite, ceremony, contract or consent that purports to sanction" polygamy.

Polygamy is an indictable offence with a maximum penalty of five years imprisonment. Section 293(2) states that no proof of the method by which the alleged relationship was entered into is required for the purposes of the indictment or trial. Nor is it necessary to show that those charged had or intended to have sexual intercourse. The guilty act is to engage in a polygamous relationship.

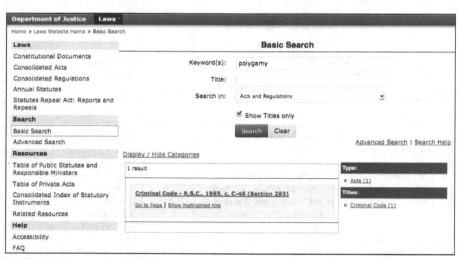

FIGURE A.1 Locate Legislation

B. Judicial Interpretation of Polygamy Provisions

Several sources can be consulted to locate case law. To ensure that all relevant considerations are brought to light, the following resources can be used:

- *The Canadian Abridgment*
- *Canadian Statute Citations*
- CanLII
- Quicklaw
- Westlaw
- *Canadian Encyclopedic Digest* (CED)
- *Halsbury's Laws of Canada*
- *Canadian Case Citations*

Recall that these sources are discussed in Chapter 7. The information they provide will overlap to some extent, and some sources may not provide any relevant information. But the competent researcher will exhaust all possible resources in an effort to become familiar with the issues. Only new information from each resource needs to be included; where resources overlap, the superfluous information can be omitted. Record the citation information for all cases so that they can be located at a later date.

1. Canadian Abridgment Digest Search

1. Using the *Canadian Abridgment*'s Key and Research Guide, available online and in print, locate polygamy under the section on criminal law. Note the classification code: VI. 117.

2. Locate the *Canadian Abridgment* volume on criminal law that contains VI. 117. This is volume 28B6, if using print sources.

3. Locate VI. 117. This section highlights several cases dealing with polygamy. Read the case summaries to find relevant cases.

Three convictions in Canada are relevant to this problem:

- *R v Bone* (1899), 4 Terr LR 173, 3 CCC 329—Earliest reported case of polygamy. Court found the accused guilty of polygamy for taking two wives in accordance with Aboriginal marriage customs.
- *R v Tolhurst*, [1937] OR 570, 68 CCC 319—Accused convicted. Notable that conjugal union means more than adultery; it means forming a union under the guise of marriage.

- *R v Harris* (1906), 11 CCC 254—Accused convicted. Marriage certificate sufficient proof of first marriage; provision applies because accused is living with another woman in open continuous adultery.

Note that these cases predate the *Charter* and the *Bill of Rights*.

Update the law, using the *Abridgment* digests. If using the print version, consult the July 2007-December 2011 volume and locate *Reference re Criminal Code, s 293*, 2010 BCSC 1308. Find this case, using any online reporter. This case deals with pre-trial matters in a polygamy constitutional reference.

When we completed our research using the *Canadian Abridgment* online, we found the same cases both in print and online except for the recent polygamy constitutional reference (which shows you how important it is to check all sources when updating the law):

- *Section 293 of the Criminal Code of Canada, Re*, 2011 BCSC 1588, 279 CCC (3d) 1—This case is directly on point, challenging the constitutionality of the polygamy prohibition. Provision determined to be constitutional. Note, however, that this was a trial level decision in British Columbia and was not appealed.

2. *Canadian Abridgment: Canadian Statute Citations: Search by Legislation Section*

Canadian Statute Citations (print) provides cases that have been decided pursuant to specific sections of legislation. At the time we did this research, we had already backdated our legislation and found out that the polygamy provisions were enacted in 1892. See section E below for a description of the backdating process. For this problem, two volumes are necessary: *Criminal Code 1892 to 1970* and *Criminal Code 1985 Section 254 to 519*.

1. In the first volume, locate the polygamy provision for the *Criminal Code*, RSC 1970, using the citation information you gather from backdating. Note that there are no cases.
2. Do the same for the *Criminal Code*, SC 1953-54. One case is listed, *Nicol v Prowse*. A search for this case in an online reporter shows that it is not relevant.
3. Do the same for the *Criminal Code*, RSC 1927. Two cases are listed, both of which you already found by using the *Abridgment*.
4. Do the same for the *Criminal Code*, RSC 1906. No cases are listed.
5. Do the same for the *Criminal Code*, SC 1892. Two cases are listed, both of which you already found by using the *Abridgment*.

6. In the *Criminal Code*, RSC 1985, locate the statute section. Two cases appear, but a quick search on an online reporter shows that they are not relevant.

7. Update the law using the updated digests in the *Canadian Statute Citations*. The October 2006–September 2011 volume provides several cases. *Reference Re Criminal Code, s 293* is something you have already found in the *Abridgment*. Finding these cases in an online reporter, you determine that *Blackmore v Blackmore* might be relevant to this matter but that the other cases are not.

3. CED: Overview

Locate the CED volume on criminal law. Find polygamy under "Marriage Related Offences". The entry on polygamy gives a brief overview of the elements to the crime and provides case citations. We had found all of these cases already, in the *Abridgment*. The online CED matches the print version.

4. Halsbury's Laws of Canada: Overview

Using the *Halsbury's Companion Guide and Consolidated Index*, find the reference for polygamy (HCF-165, HCR-335). The title index indicates that HCF refers to the *Conflict of Laws* volume of *Halsbury's*, while HCR refers to the *Criminal Law* volume. *Halsbury's Laws of Canada* is available in print and online.

Locate each volume and find each reference. The HCF reference discusses void marriages and is not relevant for the purposes of this problem. The HCR reference provides a brief overview of polygamy as it is dealt with in the *Criminal Code*. Both sections remained unchanged in *Halsbury's Cumulative Supplement* (print).

5. CanLII: Online Search

A keyword search of "polygamy" finds some of the cases that have already been found. We found no additional relevant cases.

6. Quicklaw and Westlaw: Online Search

A search for case law under "Legislation" and section 293 of the *Criminal Code* discovers only a few relevant cases, all of which we had already found with other sources. For historical research, a keyword search should be used.

7. Canadian Abridgment: Canadian Case Citations

Canadian Case Citations is a print research tool for noting up cases. This resource provides case details—name, citation, history, and judicial treatment—for both reported and unreported decisions from across the country. Remember to update using the supplement and monthly volumes. Noting up can also be done online; see Chapter 7.

R v Bone—Three cases cite *R v Bone*: (1) *R v Kahpeechoose*, (2) *Casimel v Insurance Corp of British Columbia*, and (3) *R v Church of Scientology of Toronto*. A search of these cases using an online reporter shows that they have no relevance to this problem. The January 2007–June 2011 supplement provides one case: *Manychief v Poffenroth*, but this is not relevant either.

R v Tolhurst—No cases cited.

R v Harris—No cases cited.

Reference Re Criminal Code s 293—The supplement volume for July 2011–March 2012 shows one case citation: *Carter v Canada (Attorney General)*, 2011 BCSC 1371. A search for this case using an online reporter shows that it is not relevant to this problem.

8. Case Analysis

At this stage, we summarized the relevant cases, preparing to incorporate the relevant law into the memorandum. For some cases, a statement of the *ratio decidendi* is all that will be required. For others, particularly those that outline a test to apply, a more detailed outline is required. (For a sample case-briefing layout, see Chapter 10.)

Criminal Code—section 293

Case Name and Citation: *R v Bone* (1899), 4 Terr LR 173, 3 CCC 329

Procedural History: Northwest Territories Superior Court

Facts: Mr. Bone married two women, in keeping with the Blood tribe's marriage customs.

Issue: Did Mr. Bone violate the polygamy provision of the *Criminal Code*?

Decision: The court found Mr. Bone guilty of practising polygamy.

Ratio: Regardless of how the marriages were performed (here, through Aboriginal ceremony), the accused entered into a polygamous union. Because this case was decided in the 19th century, its applicability is limited. The court of the day did not consider the customs and historical narrative underlying the Aboriginal practice of polygamy. Recall that Chapter 10 discussed critical perspectives on case law and legislation, including First Nations jurisprudence. This may provide an additional approach when researching this topic.

R v Tolhurst, [1937] OR 570, 68 CCC 319
"Conjugal union" means something more than adultery—it means forming a union under the guise of marriage.

R v Harris (1906), 11 CCC 254
Conviction entered; living with another woman in open, continuous adultery (guise of marriage).

Blackmore v British Columbia (Attorney General), 2009 BCSC 1299, [2009] BCWLD 7299
This case suggests a possible remedy if section 293 of the *Criminal Code* is found to be unconstitutional. Section 293 can be read down—i.e. narrowly interpreted— to apply to "only 'undesirable' polygamous relationships, such as those involving minors or allegations of physical or sexual abuse." The issue here is not whether the accused committed polygamy, but whether the law is constitutional.

Case Name and Citation: *Reference re: Section 293 of the Criminal Code of Canada*, 2011 BCSC 1588, [2012] BCWLD 1693

Procedural History: British Columbia Superior Court

Facts: Two men were charged with practising polygamy, and challenged the constitutionality of the provision.

Issues: Does the polygamy provision violate freedom of religion and, if so, is it saved under section 1 of the *Charter*?

Decision: While the provision violates section 2(a) of the *Charter*, it is saved by section 1.

Ratio: Public policy weighed heavily on the decision, with the prevention of harm to vulnerable groups (women and children) being the dominant deciding factor. This case is directly on point, but it comes from a trial level court in British Columbia and was not appealed; thus, although highly persuasive, it is not binding in any jurisdiction.

C. Standing Under the Charter

To find case law that judicially considers various sections of the *Charter*, we used both print and online annotated *Charter* resources, e.g. CanLII Charter Digest. To challenge a law and bring an issue before the Court, the applicant must have standing. In criminal cases, being charged automatically confers standing. In this case, assuming that Mr. Kane has not been charged, he will have to seek public-interest standing if he is to bring his issue before the Court.

The leading case with respect to public-interest standing is *Canadian Council of Churches v Canada*. It summarizes the law from a trilogy of standing cases.

Case Name and Citation: *Canadian Council of Churches v Canada (Minister of Employment and Immigration)*, [1992] 1 SCR 236

Procedural History: Supreme Court of Canada case, an appeal from the Federal Court of Appeal.

Facts: Canadian Council of Churches is an interest group representing several churches. It seeks standing to challenge portions of the *Immigration Act, 1976*.

Issues: Does the Council qualify for public-interest standing?

Decision: Council fails third part of test; standing denied.

Ratio: The test for public-interest standing is as follows:

1. Is there a serious issue raised as to the invalidity of the legislation in question?
2. Has it been established that the plaintiff is directly affected by the legislation, or, if not, does the plaintiff have a genuine interest in its validity?
3. Is there another reasonable and effective way to bring the issue before the Court?

D. Relevant Charter Section

Since an individual's religious freedom is at issue, the *Charter of Rights and Freedoms* becomes relevant.

Section 2(a) of the *Charter* states that "[e]veryone has the following fundamental freedoms: (a) freedom of conscience and religion".

Section 52(1) states that "[t]he Constitution of Canada is the supreme law of Canada, and any law that is inconsistent with the provisions of the Constitution is, to the extent of the inconsistency, of no force or effect".

E. Purpose of Polygamy Provision

At this point in our research, we recognized that backdating the polygamy provision was necessary in order to discover the legislative intent behind the creation of this section of the *Criminal Code*. Therefore, before we undertook any more case law research on the *Charter*, we backdated as described below.

1. Locate the *Criminal Code* in the 1985 RSC and find section 293. Note that the wording of the section is identical to the current wording. Record the citation that follows the section: RS, c C-34, s 257.

2. Locate the *Criminal Code* in the 1970 RSC using the citation from the 1985 RSC. Note that the wording is identical to the current wording. Record the citation that follows the section: 1953-54, c 51, s 243 (this is *not* an RSC citation).

3. Locate the *Criminal Code* in the 1953-54 SC using the citation information from the 1970 RSC. Note that the wording of this section is identical to the current wording. While no citation information follows the section, backdating must continue. The *Criminal Code* was repealed and reintroduced with several amendments in 1953-54.

4. The *Criminal Code* does not appear in the 1952 RSC. Recall from Chapter 4 the second backdating method, which uses the Table of Public Statutes. Occasionally, the method used here, while more efficient, does not provide all the information needed for backdating. Using the Table of Public Statutes in the 1952 SC, note the citation information for the *Criminal Code* in the 1927 RSC.

5. Locate the *Criminal Code* in the 1927 RSC, using the citation information from the 1952 SC. Section 310 deals with polygamy. Note that the wording is different from that in the current version. Note the citation information following the section: RS, c 146, s 310.

6. Locate the *Criminal Code* in the 1906 RSC, using the citation information from the 1927 RSC. Note that the wording of the section is identical to the wording in the 1927 RSC. Note the citation information following the section: 63-64 V, c 46, s 3. When doing historical research, citation information often lists the regnal year of the monarch rather than a specific SC year (63-64 V is the 1900 SC).

7. Locate *An Act to Further Amend the Criminal Code, 1892*, in the 1900 SC, using the citation information from the 1906 RSC. The section amends the *existing* polygamy provision. Note the wording of the polygamy amendment, which matches the wording in the 1906 RSC. Note the citation information in section 3 of the Act: 1892, c 29.

8. Locate the *Criminal Code* in the 1892 SC using the citation information from the 1900 SC. Note that there were only minor wording changes between the 1892 SC and the 1906 RSC. Note the citation information following the section: 53 V, c 37, s 11.

9. Locate *An Act to Further Amend the Criminal Law* in the 1890 SC using the citation information from the 1892 SC. Section 11 adds the polygamy provision to the *Criminal Code*. This is the original provision.

1. Hansard

The next step is to establish legislative intent by consulting *Hansard* from 1890. Use the *Hansard* index to find *An Act to further amend the Criminal Law*. The Minister of Justice of the time, Sir John Thompson, put forth the criminalization of polygamy. The resulting debate provides insight into why the provision against polygamy was enacted. The ban on polygamous relationships is purposely worded so that it does not only refer to marriage. This wording was a response to Mr. Edward Blake's contention that the Mormons would sometimes not seek marriage certificates.

There was concern among some House members that the Mormons immigrating to Canada from Utah would begin to engage in polygamous relationships. It is arguable that the initial goal of the legislators was to prevent further Mormon immigration to Canada, and they considered a law against polygamy as the best way to achieve this goal. Of course, there were House Members who disagreed with this goal but still agreed that polygamy was a social evil. As debate went on, supporters of the law softened their tone where immigration was concerned and joined the more moderate House members in arguing that the government was targeting polygamy, not the immigration of Mormons.

Consulting two annotated *Criminal Codes* yielded no information beyond what we had already ascertained from the wording of the legislation and from *Hansard*.

F. Case Law on Section 2(a) of the Charter

Applying the methods described previously for case law selection, we located several cases relating to section 2(a) of the *Charter* that were relevant to our case:

Case Name and Citation: *Syndicat Northcrest v Amselem*, 2004 SCC 47, [2004] 2 SCR 551

Procedural History: SCC case, on appeal from the Court of Appeal for Quebec

Facts: Tenants of a residential building placed *sukkah*s on their balconies, violating the building's bylaws against structures being built on balconies.

Issues: Does the bylaw violate the tenants' freedom of religion (this case deals with the Quebec *Charter of Human Rights and Freedoms*, but the *ratio* applies to the *Canadian Charter of Rights and Freedoms*).

Decision: Appeal allowed; erection of *sukkahs* is connected to the tenants' religious beliefs.

Ratio: From this case there emerges a basic principle, as well as a test for determining the scope of freedom of religion in individual cases. The Court ruled that, in order for a claimant to establish that his or her religious freedom has been infringed, he or she must demonstrate that (1) he or she sincerely believes in a practice or belief that has a nexus with religion, and (2) that the impugned conduct of a third party (or, as in this polygamy case, an impugned provision) interferes, in a manner that is non-trivial or not insubstantial, with the claimant's ability to act in accordance with that practice or belief. To qualify for this protection, a person must demonstrate that he or she sincerely believes in a practice or belief that has a nexus with religion.

The first step, therefore, in showing that a person's religious freedom has been infringed upon is to show that "he or she sincerely believes in a practice or belief that has a nexus with religion". This can be done in several ways—for example, by showing a consistency between the person's practice and his or her belief, and by establishing the claimant's credibility. Second, the claimant must show that the impugned provision (in this case, the law against polygamy) interferes, in a manner that is more than trivial or insubstantial, with the claimant's right to practice his or her religious beliefs. In this case, the court will impose limits on the practice if it infringes on the rights of others.

R v Big M Drug Mart, [1985] 1 SCR 295, 18 DLR (4th) 321
This case will be used for its discussion of legislative intent and shifting purposes. What a court must look at is the initial purpose for which legislation—in this case, the *Lord's Day Act*—was enacted. In *R v Big M Drug Mart*, the Court found that the legislation's purpose was to create a day of observance on the Sabbath for religious reasons. This made the legislation inconsistent with section 2(a) of the *Charter*. Even showing that the current effect of the law is secular in nature—in this case, a general day of rest—does not override the fact that there was an unconstitutional purpose behind the law. There can be no shifting purposes for legislation; the original intent is what will be scrutinized. This case also speaks to the scope of section 2(a) and demonstrates that, while it is not absolute, freedom of religion should be given a "generous" reading—thus giving it a broad scope.

R v S (M) (1996), 111 CCC (3d) 467, 84 BCAC 104
This is a case where the accused was charged with incest. He alleged that the ban on incest is in violation of section 2(a) of the *Charter* because it is rooted in a Judeo-Christian principle that he does not accept. Here, the court ruled that the fact that

the law is "rooted in a moral principle [that] developed within a religious trad-
ition" doesn't interfere with a freedom to believe or not to believe under the
Charter. This law protects others, and is thus not within the scope of section 2(a).

G. Secondary Sources on Polygamy and Freedom of Religion

Secondary research is an important way of gaining an understanding of a law's
effect on society. It is particularly important in *Charter* cases, where the purpose
and effect of the law will be under scrutiny. There are several resources for finding
treatises, scholarly articles, government documents, international treaties, and
other sources of legal interpretation.

1. Print Sources

We used legal periodical indexes to find scholarly articles. The following chart
outlines two widely used print periodical indexes:

Index	Currency	Availability	Usage
Canadian Abridgment— Index to Canadian Legal Literature (ICLL)	Cumulative volume (1985-2000), 2001-2011 supplement, monthly digest.	Also available online via Quicklaw and Westlaw.	Organized by topic and author, used for Canadian articles.
Current Law Index (CLI)	Cumulative volume, yearly supplement, monthly digests.	Also available online via LegalTrac.	Organized by topic and author, used for finding articles from Canada, US, Australia, UK, New Zealand, and Ireland. The most comprehensive of the print sources.

1. We used the keyword "polygamy" to search through these resources,
   starting with the cumulative volume, then updating through the
   supplements.

2. We recorded the titles of the articles found. Before choosing the articles
   to read, we reviewed and shortened the list. For example, in the ICLL
   2001-2011 supplement, there is an article from January 2010 entitled
   "Polygamy, Freedom of Religion, and Equality: What Happens When
   Rights Collide?", by Linda McKay-Panos and Brian Seaman. This seemed

relevant to the issues. However, another article on the list, Diane Klein's "Plural Marriage and Community Property Law", from the CLI June 2011 supplement, did not seem relevant.

3. We recorded the citation information for every potentially relevant article. Once the information was recorded, we looked for the articles either in print or online. Print articles, obtained from the library, are free, but the library may not have the journal you need. Finding articles online is much quicker, and they usually provide an abstract.

4. We read the remaining articles and noted relevant information that could be incorporated into the research memo.

2. Online Sources

Online sources are widely available and easily searchable; it is much more efficient to make use of them if possible. Searches usually produce an abstract, which makes the research process more efficient. The table below outlines four of the major searchable databases.

Source	Availability	Content
Scholar's Portal	Subscription; free for most Canadian university students.	Searches over 7,300 academic journals and resources from libraries across Canada that can be provided via interlibrary loan.
Quicklaw	Subscription; free for Canadian law students.	Searches for case commentary and journal articles with a focus on legal journals. Also includes Words & Phrases search.
Westlaw	Subscription; free for Canadian law students.	Searches for case commentary and legal journal articles through LawSource databases. Also includes Words & Phrases search.
HeinOnline	Subscription; free for most Canadian university students.	International database search; emphasis on historical content.

Searching print and online sources for articles on polygamy will generate many articles. For this reason, articles chosen for use in the memorandum will vary from person to person. A typical list might look like the following:

Bailey, Martha et al. *Expanding Recognition of Foreign Polygamous Marriages: Policy Implications for Canada*, Queen's Faculty of Law Legal Studies Research Paper Series, No 07-12 (Kingston, ON: Queen's University, 2006).

Bala, Nicholas. "Why Canada's Prohibition of Polygamy Is Constitutionally Valid and Sound Social Policy" (2010) 25:2 Can J Fam L 165.

Drummond, Susan. "Polygamy's Inscrutable Mischief" (2009) 47:2 Osgoode Hall LJ 317.

Foreign Affairs and International Trade Canada. "Canada's Commitment to Gender Equality and the Advancement of Women's Rights Internationally," online: (2012) Foreign Affairs and International Trade Canada <http://www.international.gc.ca/rights-droits/women-femmes/equality-egalite.aspx>.

Jütting, Johannes & Christian Morrisson. *Changing Social Institutions to Improve the Status of Women in Developing Countries*, OECD Development Centre: Policy Brief No 27 (OECD Publishing, Paris: 2005).

Al-Krenawi, A & JR Graham. "A Comparison of Family Functioning, Life and Marital Satisfaction, and Mental Health of Women in Polygamous and Monogamous Marriages" (2006) 52:1 Int J Soc Psychiatry 5.

H. Limitations on Section 2(a) Rights

Section 1 of the *Canadian Charter of Rights and Freedoms* "guarantees the rights and freedoms set out in it subject only to such reasonable limits prescribed by law as can be demonstrably justified in a free and democratic society".

I. Reasonable Limits

Using the same methods we had used previously led us to several relevant cases related to section 1 of the *Charter*:

Case Name and Citation: *R v Oakes*, [1986] 1 SCR 103, 26 DLR (4th) 200.

Procedural History: SCC case, on appeal from Ontario Court of Appeal.

Facts: Challenge to a law (the *Narcotic Control Act*) that created a reverse onus whereby possession of an illegal narcotic created a rebuttable presumption that there was intent to traffic. The issue was whether this presumption violates section 11(d) of the *Charter*.

Issues: Is a reverse onus a reasonable limit prescribed by law as defined by section 1 of the *Charter*?

Decision: No rational connection between possession and presumption of trafficking.

Ratio: This is the leading case regarding the application of section 1 of the *Charter*. *Oakes* outlines the test that should be used when determining whether an infringement on a right or freedom can be justified under section 1. An infringement must meet two criteria, with the burden of proof resting on the government:

1. The objective that the law seeks to achieve must be of pressing and substantial concern in a free and democratic society.

2. The means chosen must be reasonable and demonstrably justified.

   a. The measures must be rationally connected to the objective.

   b. The means chosen should impair as little as possible the right or freedom.

There must be proportionality between the effects of the measures and the objective.

RJR-MacDonald Inc v Canada (Attorney General), [1995] 3 SCR 199, 127 DLR (4th) 1

Decided after *Oakes*, this case imposes a stricter burden on the government to *demonstrate* why the right or freedom must be limited. The government cannot rely on abstract arguments; actual evidence must be presented to justify the limitation of the right or freedom in question. The Court takes a contextual approach with regard to the amount of deference that should be given to Parliament. The standard of proof required in a section 1 analysis is not a stringent one; it is similar to the standard of proof required in a civil case, where the Court will weigh the evidence on a balance of probabilities.

The rational connection test does not require scientific evidence of a relationship between the objective and the measures used to achieve that objective; rather, a causal link must be shown on the basis of reason or logic. In *RJR-MacDonald*, it was reasonable to draw a link between cigarette advertising and smoking.

RJR-MacDonald elaborates on the minimal-impairment criterion set out in the section 1 analysis. In *RJR-MacDonald*, the government had to show that the infringement impaired the right in question—the right to freedom of expression—as little as reasonably possible. In this instance, the Court recommended giving some leeway to the legislature; Justice McLachlin wrote, at para 160, that "if the law falls within a range of reasonable alternatives, the courts will not find it overbroad merely because they can conceive of an alternative which might better tailor objective to infringement".

Harper v Canada, [2004] 1 SCR 827, 239 DLR (4th) 193

This case can be used to further explain the first stage of the section 1 analysis. The Court suggests that, in characterizing the objective, the government should be as specific as possible. Definitive social science evidence is not needed to show harm.

Dagenais v Canadian Broadcasting Corp, [1994] 3 SCR 835, 120 DLR (4th) 12
This case is the authority for the final stage of the section 1 analysis. This part of the test is meant to determine whether the benefits of the limitation are proportional to the deleterious effects of limiting the *Charter* right. This part of the test is more effects-focused than the other parts of the section 1 analysis.

J. Summary

The results of the research that we obtained from following the processes described in this appendix were summarized and became the basis for a memorandum of law concerning Mr. Kane's legal issue.

APPENDIX B
Academic Success

I. Introduction

Much is expected of incoming law students. They are expected to read a great deal of legal material, learn a new vocabulary, memorize legal principles, and learn how to apply those principles in the appropriate form of legal argument, all with the goal of entering a profession that serves the public. A number of resources have described for students' benefit what to expect at law school, providing overviews of the law school academic culture.[1] In the following, we offer some practical precepts to help law students succeed.

In order to succeed at law school, students need to take a disciplined approach to legal studies. There are three concepts that are essential to success at law school: (1) effective habits and competence, (2) group work, and (3) hypothetical examinations.

II. Effective Habits and Competence

Students begin law school with certain goals and aspirations. Some have a traditional career path in mind. Some are considering an alternative career. Others are in search of personal growth and development. Even for those who are highly motivated, it is not uncommon for some students to experience difficulty in their first year of law school studies. Students' approach to their studies—their habits—can determine whether they struggle in law school or proceed smoothly through it. Furthermore, the habits a student adopts at law school can affect his or her future career. Adopting habits that promote learning is one way of enhancing competence, as is avoiding habits that inhibit learning and dissipate energy. Knowing how to evaluate your habits and modify them when appropriate is one way of developing competence.

---

1 Examples include Allan C Hutchinson, *The Law School Book: Succeeding at Law School*, 3d ed (Toronto: Irwin Law, 2009); and FC DeCoste, *On Coming to Law: An Introduction to Law in Liberal Societies*, 3d ed (Markham, ON: LexisNexis, 2011).

What do we mean by *habits*? Generally speaking, habits are behaviours that are adopted and practised until they become routine. Stephen Covey's work on the habits of highly effective people defines a habit as an "intersection of knowledge, skill, and desire".[2]

What are some useful habits for law students to have? No formula works for everyone, but some general guidelines may be helpful.

A. Planning

Managing time effectively is a challenge for lawyers and for law students. Both have competing demands on their time. The sooner lawyers and law students learn to manage time effectively, the sooner they will be able to enjoy the positive effects of a busy life and to manage the negative effects of situational stress. To this end, both lawyers and law students should consider

- using a calendar to diarize events, both personal and professional/academic
- deciding which activities cannot be missed (e.g. class attendance)
- knowing assignment due dates, and working to complete assignments ahead of deadlines
- anticipating that tasks will always take longer than planned and allowing sufficient time to review work before submitting it
- developing a reputation for strong time-management skills
- building free time into their calendars for "planned spontaneity", which will allow them to participate in events, personal and professional, that arise on short notice
- striving for balance between personal and professional activities, and making adjustments in this regard as needed
- reducing the tendencies of procrastination and perfectionism
- aiming for proactive time management instead of succumbing to reactive crisis management

---

2 Steven R Covey, *The Seven Habits of Highly Effective People: Restoring the Character Ethic* (New York: Simon & Schuster, 1989). See also Christian D Bareford, "Seven Habits of Highly Successful Law Students" (1999) 37 Duq L Rev 603. In Bareford's article, Covey's principles were considered from the perspective of law students beginning their legal studies. This article considers how law school accomplishments are supported by the adoption of effective habits.

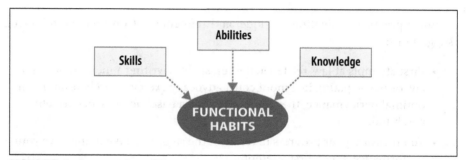

FIGURE B.1 Intersection of Competency and Habits

B. Prioritizing

This habit is linked to planning, but it differs in scope. Setting long-term priorities requires you first to think about what you need for both personal and professional satisfaction, and then to decide how you will achieve this vision. This process should also take into account the values you consider essential.[3] Once that is done, you can start setting specific goals and planning how to achieve them.

It may be necessary to set short-term priorities as well. Typically, you will need to do this when tasks and obligations exceed the time you have allotted for them. To help you in this process, consider

- distinguishing personal preferences from obligations to others, and ensuring that the latter are met before considering the former
- keeping the end goal in mind, and checking from time to time to make sure the right steps are being taken to achieve that goal
- recognizing that priorities differ from person to person and that you need to focus on your own requirements as you establish your personal priorities, and not be distracted by the choices of others (though advice from others may be helpful)

C. Practising/Persisting

A lawyer's work is frequently described as the "practice" of law. The practice of law includes performing numerous activities that lead to the resolution of a client's issue. Efficiencies and improved performance develop over time, and such development

---

3 Lawrence S Krieger, "The Inseparability of Professionalism and Personal Satisfaction (or Why the Wrong Values Will Mess Up Your Life)" (Paper delivered at the Annual Conference of the AALS Section on Legal Education, Vancouver, BC, 17 May 2003).

requires practice, evaluation, critique, and refinement. Consider the following suggestions:

- First attempts at law-related activities, such as writing a memorandum of law or participating in a moot court advocacy exercise, rarely result in an optimal performance; they merely provide a baseline on which to refine and build.
- You measure your progress in terms of the steps you take to improve your performance *after* a first attempt.
- It is useful to seek out and actively embrace critical and constructive feedback from your professors, peers, and mentors. Feedback allows you to develop—to improve your skills and increase your knowledge.
- Try to view your less successful efforts and experiences not as "errors" or "mistakes" but as positive opportunities to learn/develop.
- Persist with activities or tasks until the goal is achieved.
- If you practise law-related skills, such as making an oral argument at moot court or applying citation rules, your performance will improve.
- You can learn from observing others who are more experienced and skilled than you are.
- Recognize that these habits of practising and persisting are essential to life-long learning.

D. Self-Reflection

Self-reflection is essential for positive change. Consider the following suggestions:

- Reflecting involves thoughtful consideration of achievements and disappointments, observations, expectations, habits, values, experiences, hopes, goals, and plans. It grounds your thoughts. Keeping a record of your reflections allows you to review them later.
- Keeping a journal can help you develop a disciplined approach to self-reflection.
- Keeping a journal is a personal and solitary activity; in this way, it differs from tweeting, blogging, or other forms of social networking, although you may choose to share your private thoughts with trusted confidantes at some point.
- Once you develop a disciplined approach to self-reflection and it has become a settled habit, you may prefer not to continue journaling, though some adopt journaling as a lifelong habit.

Are these habits we have been describing effective for law students? What other habits should be developed? Consider the following thoughts from two current law students:

> Prior to starting law school I focused on self reflection and decided what was necessary to give me the best chance for success. Self reflection identified preparation, commitment and consistency as priorities for success. Based on these priorities I developed the habits that facilitated my success and limited any stress or anxiety.
>
> Quality preparation is absolutely necessary for success at law school and it takes many forms. Developing your own preparation style is necessary, but in my view the key is coming to class with a basic understanding of the material. This familiarity with the concepts allows you to understand the material in the lecture, ask questions to deepen your knowledge, and be able to apply the concepts later in the term. There is no short cut for this habit. You must be prepared everyday. During exams, this preparation paid off immensely; there was no stress from trying to learn concepts at the last minute, and I was able to spend my time reviewing and mastering the content.
>
> Commitment is another habit that produced success in my first year. Commitment is necessary to continually develop and improve the skills required of a competent lawyer. For me, being committed meant I had to critically analyze my abilities and determine where I needed to improve. I realized my writing skills needed to improve and I was committed to doing that. Whichever areas you identify, there are many resources available to improve on them. Being committed to improvement and growth means accepting feedback and critiques along with an honest assessment of your abilities.
>
> Consistency is a habit that ties all the other habits together. Law school does not allow you to cram, nor can you coast and then "turn it on". This consistency also reduces stress, and smoothes the distribution of your workload over the whole term. I chose to treat law school like a job. Therefore, I began everyday at 8 and worked until 6. This consistent effort allowed me to stay on top of all material, and when there was less work I got ahead. That way when things got busy I did not drown in the work. This simple habit was the single biggest contributor to my success.
>
> A.M., Law II student

• • •

Stephen Covey's *The Seven Habits of Highly Effective People* is not something that I would have given much attention to at the beginning of Law I. Looking back, however, I realize that my success in certain areas was due to good habits, and my struggles in other areas were due to poor habits. It shouldn't be surprising; I entered law school with similar credentials to my peers, but some students struggled much more than others. This wasn't due to pre-existing knowledge of the law or any other advantage; it came down to habits. There are several general keys to success that I could suggest; do your work early, don't commit any academic offences, study ... but you probably already know to do these things ... There are other habits that are not as obvious.

I entered law school knowing that it would be competitive. This didn't stop me, however, from treating my peers as my future colleagues rather than as my competition. I shared information, notes, and study tips. You're not going to be the best student in every class and you're probably not going to be able to make it to every class, so why not develop mutually beneficial relationships with your classmates? Thinking "win–win" is, in my opinion, the most important habit to embrace early in law school. There is a time and place for adversarial lawyering, but this is not it. Helping others shows that you are a person of integrity. No matter what type of student you are, there will be a time when you need assistance. Help your classmates and they will help you. It's win–win.

At my law school, first-year students take six full-year classes. Most of the time, it seems impossible to do everything that is expected of you— that is, attending all of your classes, doing all of your readings, making study notes and case briefs, and doing your assignments. I quickly had to learn how to prioritize my work so that I didn't miss any key information. First, above all else, I attended almost all of my classes. If I didn't go to a class, there was a good reason—and I obtained notes from a classmate. To me, prioritizing meant that I had to focus more on classes that I had trouble with. This may seem like a simple concept, but when you're behind in your readings, it is much easier to read something that you're comfortable with rather than something that you're struggling with. I knew that I had to be competent in all of these areas because my law career could go in any direction.

I found that there were two types of people in law school. There were those who, upon receiving a poor grade, would blame it on the professor, and those who would look back at how their own choices led to receiving that grade. I worked for a year prior to law school, and that helped me with doing assignments early and meeting deadlines. In my criminal law class, we were assigned to go to court, watch a hearing, and write up a court report. This was assigned on the first day of classes and it wasn't due until mid-November. The next week, I went to court, watched a few hearings, and wrote my report. A few days before the assignment was due, there were students who still hadn't even gone to court. Doing this assignment early was beneficial because, by this time, we had other assignments and readings to do. Taking a whole morning or afternoon to go to court was much more difficult in November than it was in September. Students who, on the day before the assignment was due, still hadn't gone to court were stuck. Most of these students were the ones that blamed the professor for making an assignment due so close to exams, apparently forgetting that it was assigned two months prior. The point is, you must take responsibility for your own actions. If you know you have something to do and you have the tools to do it, it's nobody else's fault if you delay. Doing an assignment the night before and receiving a mediocre grade is one thing (and is devastating for some), but getting a job at a firm and handing in a poorly written memo could be career altering. Get into the habit now of taking responsibility for your work and for your actions.

In my legal research class, we were assigned federal and provincial files which had us research various federal and provincial statutes and the case law surrounding those statutes. We wrote a memo on the provincial file. I found that my 12-page provincial memo took about as long as my 30-page final memo for the class. A large part of the reason for that was due to the work done prior to actually writing the memos. For the final memo, I took much more time to plan my research and my arguments. I knew where I wanted to go with the case, and actually wrote down the steps that I would take to get there. Everything in that memo was carefully planned beforehand—the issues, the relevant cases, the arguments. Taking a little more time to research and plan before actually writing the memo saved me an incredible amount of time afterward, and made for a much better and more structured argument.

During the federal research, we were placed into groups. I wasn't thrilled about the prospect because I work much better independently. Looking back, however, I realize that group work for this particular assignment was much more beneficial to my learning. Everyone in my group truly brought something different to the table. Undertaking research is not simply doing a web search and reporting what comes up; there are many aspects to legal research that are difficult to grasp early. Having group members master specific tasks and teach the rest of the group afterward allowed my group to finish the research very early. This particular group process—individual tasks, detailed reporting—worked extremely well for our group. We didn't start doing this until after our first plan failed—go into the library and try to do everything together. Different processes will work depending on the group dynamics and on the assignment; what is important is to find that group dynamic that works for your particular group. Our group received an excellent grade on this particular assignment, we were each very good at our particular task, and we all had a working familiarity with the tasks of other group members since we taught each other what we'd learned individually.

I did well in Law I, but I could have done better. Ironically, I believe that I would have done better if I did less work. I have spent countless hours studying and not retaining the information that I was studying because I lost balance in my life. Prior to entering law school, I played in a band, trained in mixed martial arts, and was active in political life in my community. From mid-September until the end of April, these things were put on hold. Looking back, I realize that continuing with these activities would have provided a much-needed break from legal studies. There are times during the year when you simply can't afford to step away from your studies, but this does not mean September until April. I realize now that I should have made time where thinking about law was prohibited, and I definitely should have kept up my pre-law school hobbies. Balance is where I did not succeed during my first year. If I could do it again, I would take certain nights off and pursue my interests.

The habits that you need to develop in law school are not necessarily habits that will help you understand the law better—maintaining the habits that got you here should do that. Social habits that help you to interact with others and habits that allow you to work more efficiently are the habits that you must develop early in Law I. Being organized, helping others, strengthening your weaknesses, and maintaining a proper balance are habits to get into that will assist you in being successful. Above all else, be a person of integrity. Do your work, go to class, be on time, and treat others with respect. It sounds simple, but if you brush this off, people will notice. Trust me.

C.A., Law II student

Commitment, quality preparation, and consistency are keys to succeeding at law school, as these two accounts from students demonstrate. Effective time management, which is related to good planning habits, promotes efficient use of time and is also essential to success. Consider the following strategies for enhancing time management at law school:

- Create a four-month large-scale semester calendar. As soon as you receive the course syllabus, record all course-assignment due dates and examination dates on the calendar. Where possible, note not just the day but the specific times that exams are being held and that assignments are due (e.g. 3:00 p.m.), and whether late penalties will be applied if assignments are submitted late. Keep the calendar easily accessible.

- Record the procedures you need to follow for rescheduling examinations and requesting extension of due dates for assignments. Do this for each course; the process may not be the same for all.

- Create a monthly calendar on the first day of the current month and include on it due dates, group meetings, as well as social events and appointments.

- Create a daily calendar on which you list all events and tasks for each day, including classes and readings. As you plan, fill in the gaps between classes with productive activities (e.g. schedule specific readings to be completed, or schedule a workout at the gym). Throughout the day, keep a textbook with you, so you can read during unexpected gaps in time or while waiting in long lines.

- Every evening, review the daily calendar, and carry forward to the next day any uncompleted task. Lawyers in practice also have a similar "bring-forward" system to ensure that they do not miss deadlines.

- In order to overcome procrastination, which is commonly a response to being overwhelmed by a large project, break down each assignment into small manageable tasks, and complete each task one at a time. Do this at a time of day when you work best and your energy level is at its highest—could be morning, afternoon, or evening. Prioritize your tasks for the day in such a way as to make this timing possible.

- Attend all classes. The legal knowledge and experience imparted in them is crucial to your development. A first-year law student must learn to "think like a lawyer".

- Prepare case briefs before class, bring them to class, and add the professor's in-class comments as notations directly onto the case brief. Do this in a different colour or font so that you can easily distinguish your own text from the professor's class comments.

- Be proactive. While reading for class, mark down any questions or concepts that you need clarified, and then, as soon as possible, meet with the professor to get your questions answered. Do not wait until the end of the semester; plan to do this weekly.

- Back up your class notes and all drafts of assignments in several locations—on several USB keys, for example—and regularly email these draft documents to yourself so that you can access them from a different computer if computer problems arise. Complete all assignments at least 24 hours in advance of the due date in order to avoid late submission penalties due to unexpected computer problems.

- Too many extracurricular events—e.g. overcommitment to volunteer activities and social events—may negatively affect your time management at law school and impede your academic success. Decline these extra events politely and focus on the academic work. When it comes to managing your time, self-discipline and the ability to discern what is in your best interest personally and academically are essential to success.

III. Group Work and Legal Practice: A Professional Obligation

In the previous section, the focus was on the individual's responsibilities. However, while law students and lawyers must sometimes work independently, legal work is essentially group-focused, with an emphasis on resolving disputes. Lawyers in their professional lives engage with others in many aspects of dispute resolution, including dispute avoidance. To facilitate dispute resolution, lawyers may benefit from understanding functional group dynamics and effective group processes; law students may benefit from acquiring this knowledge while in law school.

By its very nature, a dispute involves parties with unresolved differences of opinion and belief. If the parties cannot resolve their differences on their own, they have probably retreated to polarized positions.

Only a small number of disputes are resolved through a court or tribunal process. Most people find this formal adjudicative process to be distressing, expensive, and slow. Outcomes are often unsatisfactory, with no clear-cut winner; judges or other decision-makers rarely agree entirely with one side or the other. Instead of being settled through a formal court process, disputes may be settled through negotiation, mediation, or some other alternative dispute resolution process.

In any legal forum and at every stage of the process (e.g. pre-trial, trial, or appeal stages), the lawyer seeking to settle disputes must be able to work with other people—with, for example, the client, the other party (if unrepresented), the lawyer representing the other party, the lawyers on the same team, the judge or other decision-maker, the mediator, and the witnesses. In these circumstances, the lawyer has become a member of a group.

A. Developing Effective Group Processes

Group dynamics and group processes are a prominent area of social science study. It is an area that includes a discipline called organizational psychology, which studies issues related to both private and public sector organizations, large and small. All organizations require group effectiveness, and substantial scholarship in the field of organizational psychology concerns the study of effective group processes and what is involved in their success. Not just academics in this area but anyone who is involved in public administration, business, team sports, or social psychology will have learned that certain behaviours produce high-functioning groups and certain behaviours inhibit effective group processes. Whether or not an individual has had formal training in group psychology, he or she can—through study, practice, and self-reflection—develop the skills that facilitate group problem solving.

What are the features and habits of effective work groups? There is no definitive answer to this question. Work groups come together under various circumstances, for various purposes and for various lengths of time. The members themselves may bring varying levels of expertise, knowledge, and motivation to the group. Some groups may require a hierarchical structure, with roles clearly defined; others may require a more egalitarian structure, with members sharing the decision-making responsibility and seeking consensus. However, a feature common to all effective work groups is that they have established and developed their group structure before embarking on the tasks the group must achieve.

Individuals who assemble temporarily to perform a specific task—for example, lawyers attempting to resolve a dispute—collectively form an Ad Hoc Task Group. An Ad Hoc Task Group is brought together for a limited time and purpose; once the task is achieved, the group disbands. For this reason, these kinds of groups rarely have a chance to develop certain attributes, such as cohesiveness, that are found in well-functioning groups of long standing. This is a challenge for lawyers, whose group work is usually of the ad hoc variety.

Additional challenges may face the Ad Hoc Task Group. Some members may not wish to be part of the group and may not be fully committed to the group's tasks. Group members may not trust each other, and there may be little hope of establishing trust. This is especially true if the disputing parties have pre-existing experiences of conflict with each other. Group member roles may be undefined and fuzzy. Desired outcomes may differ. Some group members may not work well together. Some may adopt behaviour that interferes with a solution. In a legal context, if the difficulties cannot be worked out, the problem will be resolved by a judge or by another decision-maker, and the client will have to abide by the decision imposed.

Lawyers attempt to move disputing parties toward a resolution to their problem. Therefore, as a law student, one should consider some of the issues that arise in group dynamics, and some of the features of effective group processes. When the opportunity arises, practise the associated skills of effective group development to enhance effectiveness as a problem-solver within a group.

B. Stages

Effective Ad Hoc Task Groups have a life cycle. If the group is to achieve the set task for which it has been formed, group members should consider some common stages of group development, as discussed below.[4]

---

4   See Bruce Tuckman, "Developmental Sequences in Small Groups" (1965) 63 Pyschological Bulletin 384. Tuckman identified the stages as Forming, Storming, Norming, Performing, and Adjourning.

1. Formation: Planning

This stage focuses on creating the group structure. Group members come together to explore a common purpose. It is a discussion stage, not an action stage. It should permit members to resolve uncertainties about the tasks, the processes, and about each other. Discussion of goals, purposes, and expectations—of the process and of each other—is appropriate. Group members should have a preliminary discussion of what their respective roles are to be—defining the various roles and considering which group member will best fulfill each position. Discuss how the roles intersect. At this point, it may be appropriate for members to share information about their past group-work experiences, both positive and negative. Collectively, you can try to dissect the reasons for both the good and bad experiences and learn from them. This is an exploratory stage. Leave some time to reflect on this planning stage and to flag potential problems before proceeding to confirm group roles, processes, and tasks.

NB: The group formation stage is important. It will potentially set the template for such matters as trust, role clarity, and cohesiveness within the group, and these, in turn, will have a bearing on whether the task is successfully completed.

2. Confirmation: Regulating

This stage ensures that group members have had the opportunity to consider the preliminary discussion and are ready either to adopt the measures previously discussed or to work through remaining barriers or potential problems previously identified. This stage sets out rules and expectations, and otherwise regulates the group's operation. It can help resolve disputes before they occur. Disagreement is not unusual at this stage, and it can be beneficial as long as group members recognize that disagreement need not be disagreeable or unpleasant. Remain focused on the issues; avoid personal comments that can make a person feel that his or her contributions are unwelcome. Confirm roles and expectations. Fully examine the tasks to be completed and set out procedures for completing them. Build in an early review process, so planning errors can be corrected. Identify preliminary completion dates. Explore dispute-resolution options and decide on processes to help settle future disagreements. Devote the time necessary to reach consensus. Recognize that consensus does not mean majority rule; too much emphasis on majority decisions may result in silencing group members, and this can affect group cohesiveness. Compromise will be required.

NB: Proceeding to the task completion stage without careful consideration of group regulation can negatively affect such issues as trust, role clarity, cohesiveness, and, ultimately, successful task completion.

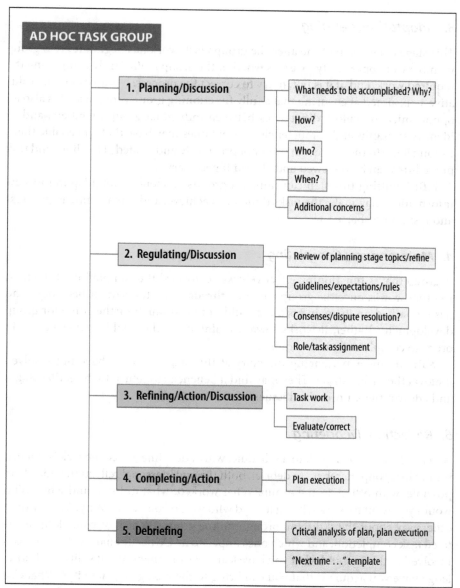

FIGURE B.2   Ad Hoc Task Group: Life Cycle

3. Adaptation: Refining

This stage occurs sometime after the group's task work has begun. It gives group members an opportunity to assess whether the group is efficiently completing the required work, and, if it is not, to try to correct the process. It is an essential evaluative step, aimed at ensuring that a fully functioning group is in place. It is also an opportunity to explore differences between individual group members, and to identify strengths and competencies certain ones may have that will enable them to contribute to the process in ways not previously anticipated. Timelines and task procedures can be reviewed and altered if necessary.

NB: Omitting this step can impair a group's efficiency. Not adapting to new information may make the tasks difficult to achieve, and it may impede progress and result in disharmony.

4. Maintenance: Completing

A group that is functioning effectively works toward the completion of the task. In other words, once the group has gone through the stages described above and has embarked on its main task, it should not need much further time for group development. Rather, it works toward maintaining the established structure in order to complete the task required.

NB: Groups experiencing difficulty at this stage typically have not resolved issues at the earlier stages. They may find it beneficial to return to the earlier stages and address these unresolved issues.

5. Reflection: Debriefing

Ad Hoc Task Groups work to a schedule, with a deadline. Once the task is done, it is time for group members to debrief, both through personal reflection and, where possible, with others in the group. What worked, what did not, and why? Who would you want to work with again and who would you avoid? Why? What would others say about the skills you brought to the group? Which of your skills facilitated task completion, and which ones impeded it? Critically analyze the processes involved in the task and what you have learned from them. What skills and knowledge have you acquired that you can bring to the next group activity? What else do you need to learn?

NB: As a lawyer, your reputation for effective dispute resolution will rest largely on your ability to function effectively in a group setting. Learning to work in groups is crucial for lawyers. Debriefing at the end of one group process can help you prepare for the next one.

C. Roles

At the first two stages of group-process development, group members should identify and confirm roles within the group and the tasks involved in each role. What responsibilities and obligations are shared by all? What individual roles are required? Who has the authority to make decisions; does that authority rest with one person or is it shared? Who organizes? Who schedules? Who compiles? Who does the task work? What skills are needed for specific tasks? Which member has prior experience with these tasks? Who focuses on group maintenance, identifying potential issues that will impede the group's work?

In Ad Hoc Task Groups, the members may share the various functions—proposing ideas to solve problems or reach goals, seeking information or opinions from others, clarifying, providing information or opinions, coordinating, summarizing, evaluating, motivating and encouraging, supporting, assisting, and recording.

Giving the role itself a title and attaching responsibilities to it rather than to the specific person assuming the role helps to delineate the task. Depending on the size of the group, one person may have multiple roles or a single role may require multiple members. The tasks associated with the roles may change during the process.

Groups whose members are goal-directed, motivated, and considerate can work through most organizational difficulties that arise. Sometimes, however, certain members of the group may engage in disruptive conduct that frustrates the group's work. This need not be a concern if infrequent. Disruptive conduct may include the following:

- Absenting—being either physically absent from meetings or physically present but failing to contribute to the group's work
- Dominating—seeking control to the extent of diminishing or negating others' contributions
- Attacking—engaging in personal criticism rather than focusing on the issues
- Distracting—making comments unrelated to either the group development or the task itself
- Avoiding—free-loading and persistently avoiding tasks despite seeming to share in the group goals

The group can address persistently disruptive behaviour in the following ways:

- Review the work completed at the first three stages to determine if making changes—correcting errors or omissions—may alter the group dynamic.

- Remain focused on the issues—identify the behaviour that is disruptive and seek to have it corrected, but do so without imputing motive, and refrain from responding in a way that contributes to further disruption.
- If the group member responsible for the disruption fails to correct the conduct, work around him or her—remain issue-focused.
- If attempts to solve the problem within the group are unsuccessful, and if there is someone with more authority in charge, consulting that authority may be appropriate.

IV. Preparing for Law School Hypothetical Examination Questions

The traditional law school exam question is called the "hypothetical" question (although other question formats, such as short answer, essay and multiple choice, are also used at law schools). The hypothetical question is a fact pattern not previously seen by students, set out in a description several paragraphs or pages in length, requiring students to identify and analyze the legal issues involved in the scenario. Students are expected to identify all legally relevant issues presented in the hypothetical and to apply the relevant law to the facts. This requires (1) substantive knowledge of the law, and (2) the ability to apply the law to new facts: in other words, a two-step process.

Preparing for hypothetical examinations in law school should begin very early in each semester, with the development of outlines or study notes. Reviewing class notes regularly and synthesizing their information into outlines is an essential part of preparing for these examinations. In this regard, consider the following strategies:

- When making study notes, students should prepare their own notes from the course readings and supplement them with the professor's in-class comments. They should not rely on commercial outlines or "canned" study notes created by other students. The law may have changed and/or the information may be inaccurate.
- Creating your own outline is a valuable aid to critical learning and enhances retention of material.
- Keep a copy of the textbook's table of contents and course syllabus accessible and check them before each class so that you know exactly where the professor is in the course. At the end of a chapter or part, review the material and, synthesizing your own reading notes with the professor's in-class comments, create an outline in one of the formats described below.

- Various outline formats exist: e.g. linear, flow chart, mind map, decision tree.[5] Which format you choose will depend on which learning approach you prefer and on the nature of the course material.

- Law school examinations can be either closed-book (no texts or notes allowed in) or open-book (in which case some additional material—e.g. text, outlines, notes—is allowed to be used during the exam). Each professor decides the exam format on a course-specific basis, and you need to ascertain in advance which format is being used.

- If your examination is an open-book one, prepare and bring to the exam an outline for which you have a detailed table of contents, so that you can quickly locate specific references. Keep in mind that time is of the essence in all examinations.

- The professor's examinations from previous years may be available. Try to locate them, and then write practice answers in real time.

- Write an outline to the answer prior to writing out the answer. The outline provides the framework for the answer, and it organizes the issues, the relevant law, the relevant facts, and the legal arguments.

- Your answer's application of the relevant law to the facts must be concise and clear. The following format, which was introduced in Chapter 10 for case briefing, can also be used to answer an issue. It is a suggested format *for each issue* in a hypothetical answer (although each professor may have his or her own prescribed format).

Issue 1: (IRAC format)

- **I**dentify the Issue (legal question raised by facts)
- **R**ule or law
- **A**nalysis (application of relevant law to specific facts; include both arguments and counter-arguments, referring to specific facts from the hypothetical)
- **C**onclusion (evaluate/answer issue)

Repeat this format for each relevant issue identified.

---

5 For further information and samples of law school outlines in various formats and for a description of learning approaches applied specifically to law school studies, see Martha M Peters & Don Peters, *Juris Types: Learning Law Through Self-Understanding* (Gainesville, FL: CAPT, 2007).

Glossary

act either a federal bill that has been passed by both the House and the Senate or a provincial/territorial bill passed by the legislature; also called an annual statute, unrevised statute, enacted version, or session law

advocacy the process by which a lawyer persuasively advances the client's position

affiant a person who makes an affidavit

affidavit an affiant's written statement of facts, made under oath before a person with authority to administer an oath or affirmation

amending statute a statute that is created to alter some aspect of an existing statute and that may (1) change some of its wording, (2) replace or repeal sections or entire parts of it, or (3) repeal it entirely

analogous case a case whose facts and legal issues closely resemble those of the client's case

authoritative sources of law government publications, other than those that disseminate statutes or judicial decisions, that are sources of legal authority (e.g. *Debates*)

backdating research method used to locate the historical origins either of a statute in its entirety or of a particular section of a statute

bill the form in which a prospective statute is first introduced to Parliament or a provincial/territorial legislature

binding authority a legal principle established by a higher court that a lower court, within the higher court's jurisdiction, is bound to apply

Canadian Abridgment a multi-function legal research instrument, available in print and online

Canadian Encyclopedic Digest a multi-function legal encyclopedia, available in print and online

CanLII a free online resource for legal research that provides unrestricted access to domestic primary law

case analysis the process of selecting and interpreting the principles from judicial decisions

case brief a summary of a judge's written decision that includes the case facts, the issues, and the legal reasoning

case comment analysis of a case, published in legal journals and in some commercial law reporters

CIF (coming into force) information statement statement that communicates the essential details about a statute's coming into force, sometimes referred to as the effective date

civil-law system system of law that provides the basis for the provincial legal regime in the province of Quebec

client-centred lawyering lawyer–client interactions that centre on active client decision making

closing letter a letter from the lawyer to the client confirming that the client–lawyer relationship has concluded, and that the lawyer's work is complete

coming into force (CIF) the final step in the process of a bill becoming law (i.e. becoming an act); acts may come into force or take effect immediately upon receiving royal assent, on proclamation, on specific dates, or in accordance with certain conditions

committee a committee of Parliament (House of Commons or Senate) or of a provincial/territorial legislature that has a particular mandate or area of expertise

committee bill a category of public bill that is introduced by the chair of the committee that produced the bill when considering the effect of prospective legislation during the bill passage process

common-law system a system of law in which principles arising from decided judicial cases are commonly applied to future cases

conflict of laws a body of law that concerns how to resolve issues arising from conflicts between laws of different jurisdictions

consolidated version of a statute the current version of a statute, including all amendments to it

counterargument viewing a client's case from the perspective of the other side of the dispute in order to identify weaknesses in the client's position (*see also* legal argument)

cultural competence being aware of the influence that cultural differences may have on legal decision making

debates discussion of a bill during its passage through Parliament or through the provincial legislatures

***Debates* of the House and Senate** transcripts of discussions held in Parliament and in the provincial/territorial legislatures during a bill's passage

digest a brief summary, ranging from one to several paragraphs, that explains a court's decision

dissent the opinion on the part of a judge or judges who disagree with the majority decision of the court

distinguishable cases prior cases whose precedents will not be followed because their facts and issues differ materially from those of the case at hand

enabling act the act from which the authority to make regulations is derived

fact analysis a process of analysis that involves (1) discovering the facts; and (2) sorting and organizing the facts and classifying them as either relevant or irrelevant to the dispute

factum the formal document filed with the court that sets out the facts, statutes, and case authorities that a party relies upon in support of its legal arguments

finding of fact a determination that an allegation made by one party to an action is true, even though that allegation is denied by another party; the finding must be based on a reasonable assessment of the evidence in the action

first-reading stage stage at which a new bill is introduced to Parliament or a provincial/territorial legislature and is thus made public

foreign law laws of a foreign country, which Canada's judiciary is not bound to apply to a domestic legal dispute

Gazette the official government newspapers in Canada that publish information about the federal, provincial, or territorial government's business, including recently enacted statutes and regulations, statutory orders, statutory instruments, and proclamations

government bill a public bill that is introduced by a member of the Executive Council (i.e. the Cabinet)

Halsbury's Laws of Canada   a multi-function legal encyclopedia-style reference; available in print and online

Hansard   official published report of the debates of Parliament and the provincial/territorial legislatures

headnote   a case summary or digest provided by the editorial staff of a case reports publisher; not primary law, and not to be cited as legal authority

instrument of ratification   a country's formal written confirmation of its intent to be bound by a treaty

IRAC   an acronym (Issue, Rule, Analysis, and Conclusion) that outlines one procedure for undertaking legal analysis

Journals of the House of Commons   formal record of House of Commons business for a given day, organized by legislative session number, that lists the following among other information: committee reports; the first, second, and third readings of a bill; and other significant dates of a bill's progress; journals also provide records of government business for provincial/territorial legislatures

Journals of the Senate   formal record of Senate business for a given day, organized by legislative session number, that lists the following among other information: committee reports; the first, second, and third readings of a bill; and other significant dates of a bill's progress

judicial decision   the written record of a court's judgment

judicial notice   a rule of evidence that allows a decision-maker to accept certain commonly known, indisputable, and uncontentious facts without requiring that they be proven with evidence

legal argument   the identification of the relevant legal principles, applied to the facts, that support a party's position (*see also* counterargument)

legal citation   identification, by an established reference form, of primary and secondary sources of law

legal competency   legal skills, abilities, and knowledge that can be applied to legal tasks

legal issue   a question that arises from the specific facts of a client's legal problem

LEGISinfo   an online tool from the Library of Parliament that tracks and provides information about bills in progress

legislation   the creation of law; the statutes, regulations, and bylaws passed by bodies of elected representatives or their delegates

Legislative Assembly an elected body of provincial/territorial legislators, also referred to as the legislature, with the authority to create provincial/territorial legislation

legislative comment critical analysis of specific legislation; frequently published as commentary in legal journals

legislative session a period during which sittings of Parliament and the provincial legislatures are held

letter of opinion a letter, usually to a client, that summarizes the lawyer's legal opinion about the issue for which the client is seeking advice

memorandum of law a document, usually internal to the law firm, that summarizes the relevant law as it applies to the facts of a client's problem

motion an application to a court or a judge for the purpose of obtaining an order directing that some kind of relief be granted to the party making the motion

neutral citation a standard citation, added by the court before the case is disseminated, that includes the year of decision (without brackets or parentheses), an acronym signifying the jurisdiction and court level, and a document number

noting up the process of determining the history of a case—e.g. verifying whether it is still relevant or has been reversed on appeal, or whether it has been criticized or overruled by subsequent cases

***obiter dictum* (pl. *obiter dicta*)** commentary in a judicial decision that does not constitute a legal principle but that may provide a useful context for the decision

objective legal writing legal writing that is done in a neutral style, intended to inform rather than persuade the reader

official case reporters published records of judicial decisions, prepared by the court and published by the Queen's Printer

official source of law a government or court publication that disseminates legislation or judicial decisions and that is the original source of the legal rules and interpretations of the law

operator a computer function command that allows researchers to connect words and phrases in order to refine an online search

period-in-time (point-in-time) research research that locates the version of legislation that appeared at a particular period or point in time

periodical index an index that provides citations to secondary sources of law, including articles and books

persuasive authority a legal principle from a case arising in another jurisdiction or a lower court in the same jurisdiction that is not binding but that a court finds convincing and incorporates into its decision

persuasive legal writing a style of legal writing meant to both inform and persuade the reader, not merely inform

plain language a style of writing that avoids jargon and uses various techniques to enhance clarity

precedential value the value of a case based on the extent to which subsequent judges have endorsed its legal reasoning

predictive writing outcome-predicting memorandum, based on an analysis of facts and law, regarding what will happen should a given matter be heard at court

preventive lawyering lawyering that focuses on ways to prevent legal risks from becoming legal problems

primary law the governing legal rules, derived from both legislation and judicial decisions

private bill a bill that grants powers, benefits, or exemptions from the general law to specific individuals, corporations, or local authorities

private member's public bill a type of public bill that is introduced by a member of Parliament or of a provincial legislature who is not a Cabinet minister and is not acting on behalf of the Executive Council

pro bono abbreviation of a Latin term, *pro bono publico*, meaning "for the public good," used where legal services are provided without remuneration, as a public service

procedural history summary of how a case was decided at every level of court at which it was heard

professional legal identity the professional image of a lawyer that is projected through his or her manner of practice, service to clients, and efforts in the public interest, as well as through his or her written work

public bill a bill that proposes laws in the public interest and is of general application

public international law the law between and among nations, primarily based on treaties and on international judicial decisions

question of law a question of what law applies, or how to apply or interpret the law in the circumstances of a case; in both jury and non-jury trials, questions of law are determined by judges

questions of fact a factual dispute; in jury trials, questions of fact are determined by the jury; in non-jury trials, questions of fact are determined by the trial judge

ratio decidendi the governing legal principle or rule on which a judge's decision in a case is based

regnal year formerly the means of identifying the date of legislation's enactment, the regnal year signified the number of years since the reigning monarch had ascended the throne

regulation the subordinate legislation whose existence and authority are derived from a governing statute but that performs important functions of its own and has the same force in law as a statute

research log record of the specific steps taken during research

research plan plan setting out the research to be done and the research processes to be used

reservation in the context of international law, a unilateral statement, made by a state when signing, ratifying, or acceding to a treaty, that purports to exclude or modify the legal effect of certain of the treaty's provisions with respect to its own obligations

revised statutes a consolidation and revision of annual statutes, undertaken when authorized by legislation

royal assent the final stage of the legislative process by which a bill becomes law after having passed all six readings in both the House and the Senate or, in the case of a provincial/territorial bill, three readings in the legislature

rules of statutory interpretation interpretive aids to statutory interpretation

second-reading stage stage of the legislative process where a draft of a bill is read for the second time; may be followed by debate

secondary sources of law sources of law that locate primary sources of law and that interpret its meaning or application

stare decisis the common-law principle that lower courts must follow precedent cases emanating from the higher courts in the same jurisdiction unless they are distinguishable

statement of claim a document prepared and filed by a plaintiff in a lawsuit that initiates the court action

statement of defence a legal document, filed by the defendant, that provides a response to the statement of claim.

Statutes of Canada the compilation, published annually, of all the federal acts of Canada passed by the Parliament of Canada; abbreviated as SC in legal citations

Statutory Instrument a regulation, order, or other instrument that is authorized by an act of Parliament; frequently referred to as an SI, and first published in the *Canada Gazette*, Part II

Statutory Orders and Regulations a statutory instrument as defined in the *Statutory Instruments Act*; frequently referred to as SOR, and published in the *Canada Gazette*, Part II

style of cause the name of the case or title of the proceeding, consisting of the names of the parties to the dispute

substantive statute a statute created to regulate some aspect of the law; in contradistinction to an amending statute, which is created to alter some aspect of a substantive statute

Table of Proclamations a listing of the acts that have been proclaimed in force during a specific time period, which provides the date and statutory instrument number reference to locate the CIF of an act

Table of Public Statutes a list of substantive statutes in force on the date that the Table was compiled; provides citations to amending statutes and their CIFs

third-reading stage the final review of a bill in the House or Senate before it is sent to the other chamber for review, or a provincial/territorial legislature's final review of a bill before enactment

transfer of learning transferring knowledge acquired in one setting to another setting

treaty accession the process by which a country that is not party to the original treaty expresses its intention to be bound

treaty succession process by which a newly formed country, whose predecessor state acceded to a treaty, assumes the obligations that its predecessor assumed

unofficial case reporters full texts of noteworthy judicial decisions, published in case law reporters by commercial publishers of legal information

unofficial source of law a source of law, such as a web-based or commercial publication, that is not official

unreported decisions judicial decisions that have not been published in commercial reporters but may be located by accessing the court file from the registry office where the case was originally heard

Index

Credits

Note: Reproductions of Government Canada works are copies of official works published by the Government of Canada and have not been produced in affiliation with or with the endorsement of the Government of Canada.

Chapter 1: Foundations

Figure 1.6 Adapted from *Canada's Court System, Figure: Outline of Canada's Court System, page 3.* <http://www.justice.gc.ca/eng/dept-min/pub/ccs-ajc/page3.html>. © Department of Justice Canada, 2005. Adapted with the permission of the Minister of Public Works and Government Services Canada, 2013.

Chapter 3: The Federal Law-Making Process

Figure 3.2 Parliament of Canada <http://www.parl.gc.ca/LEGISINFO/Home.aspx ?ParliamentSession=41-1>. Reproduced with permission.

Figure 3.3 Parliament of Canada <http://www.parl.gc.ca/LEGISINFO/Home.aspx ?ParliamentSession=41-1>. Reproduced with permission.

Task 3.2 Justice Laws <http://laws-lois.justice.gc.ca/eng/AnnualStatutes/index2005.html>.

Task 3.3 Canada Gazette <http://www.gazette.gc.ca/rp-pr/p3/2009/index-eng.html>; Canada Gazette <http://www.gazette.gc.ca/rp-pr/p3/2010/g3-03303.pdf>.

Task 3.4 Justice Laws <http://laws-lois.justice.gc.ca/PDF/2010_9.pdf>.

Task 3.5 Canada Gazette <http://publications.gc.ca/gazette/archives/p3/2002/g3-02405.pdf>.

Task 3.6 "Proclamations of Canada," *Statutes of Canada* 1995, vol II.

Task 3.7 Parliament of Canada <http://www.parl.gc.ca/HousePublications/Publication.aspx ?Pub=Hansard&Doc=lO&Parl=4l&Ses=l>.

Task 3.8 Canada Gazette <http://www.gazette.gc.ca/rp-pr/p2/2010/2010-12-23-x5/pdf/ g2-144x5.pdf>.

Chapter 4: Locating and Working with Federal Statutes and Regulations

Figure 4.3 *Revised Statutes of Canada* 1985, vol V, c H-6 at 1.

Figure 4.5 Canada Gazette <http://www.gazette.gc.ca/rp-pr/p2/2012/2012-06-30-c2/pdf/ g2-146c2-eng.pdf>.

Task 4.4 Justice Laws <http://laws-lois.justice.gc.ca/eng/TablePublicStatutes/A.html>.

Task 4.6 *Canada Gazette* Part II, vol 126, no 11-19, 1992, SOR/92-270 at 2048.

Task 4.7 Canada Gazette <http://www.gazette.gc.ca/index-eng.html>; Library and Archives Canada <http://www.collectionscanada.gc.ca/databases/canada-gazette/index-e.html>; Library and Archives Canada <http://www.collectionscanada.gc.ca/databases/canada-gazette/093/001060-119.01-e.php>. © Government of Canada. Reproduced with the permission of the Minister of Public Works and Government Services Canada (2013). Source: Library and Archives Canada's website, www.collectionscanada.gc.ca.

Task 4.8 Canada Gazette <http://www.gazette.gc.ca/rp-pr/p2/2011/2011-01-19/pdf/g2-14502.pdf>.

Task 4.10 Justice Laws <http://laws-lois.justice.gc.ca/eng/acts/>.

Task 4.12 Canada Gazette <http://www.gazette.gc.ca/rp-pr/p2/ci-ic-eng.html>; Canada Gazette <http://www.gazette.gc.ca/rp-pr/p2/2012/2012-06-30-c2/pdf/g2-146c2-eng.pdf>.

Task 4.15 Justice Laws <http://laws-lois.justice.gc.ca/Search/Advanced.aspx>.

Task 4.17 Justice Laws <http://laws-lois.justice.gc.ca/eng/regulations/SOR-2003-184/index.html>.

Task 4.18 Justice Laws Website <http://laws-lois.justice.gc.ca/eng/acts/B.html>.

Task 4.20 *Revised Statutes of Canada* 1985, vol VIII, c Y-1 at 1; *Statutes of Canada* 1980-81-82-83, c 110, s 80 at 3280; *Revised Statutes of Canada* 1970, vol V, c J-3 at 4631; *Revised Statutes of Canada* 1952 vol III, c 160 at 3507; *Statutes of Canada* 1929, c 46 at 218; *Revised Statutes of Canada* 1927, vol III at 2479.

Task 4.22 *Canada Gazette* Part II , vol 106, no 3 (January to June 1972) at 185.

Task 4.23 *Debates of the House of Commons*, 3rd Sess, 40th Parl, vol 145, no 27-40, 2010 at 2140.

Task 4.25 *Statutes of Canada*, 2005, vol I, c 17.

Chapter 6: Locating and Working with Judicial Decisions

Task 6.2 CanLII <http://canlii.org/en/databasesearch.html>. Reprinted by permission.

Task 6.3 LexisNexis Quicklaw <http://www.lexisnexis.com>. Reprinted with the permission of LexisNexis Canada Inc. All Rights Reserved.

Task 6.4 Westlaw Canada <http://canada.westlaw.com>. Reproduced by permission of Carswell, a division of Thomson Reuters Canada Limited.

Task 6.5 CanLII <http://canlii.org/en/databasesearch.html>. Reprinted by permission.

Task 6.6 Westlaw Canada <http://canada.westlaw.com>. Reproduced by permission of Carswell, a division of Thomson Reuters Canada Limited.

Task 6.7 LexisNexis Quicklaw <http://www.lexisnexis.com>. Reprinted with the permission of LexisNexis Canada Inc. All Rights Reserved.

Task 6.8 CanLII <http://www.canlii.org/en/index.php>. Reprinted by permission.

Task 6.9 CanLII <http://www.canlii.org/en/ca/scc/doc/2012/2012scc40/2012scc40.html>. Reprinted by permission.

Chapter 7: Researching Secondary Sources of Law

Task 7.4 Westlaw Canada <http://canada.westlaw.com>. Reproduced by permission of Carswell, a division of Thomson Reuters Canada Limited.

Task 7.5 Westlaw Canada <http://canada.westlaw.com>. Reproduced by permission of Carswell, a division of Thomson Reuters Canada Limited.

Task 7.6 Westlaw Canada <http://canada.westlaw.com>. Reproduced by permission of Carswell, a division of Thomson Reuters Canada Limited.

Task 7.8 LexisNexis Quicklaw <http://www.lexisnexis.com>. Reprinted with the permission of LexisNexis Canada Inc. All Rights Reserved.

Task 7.10 Westlaw Canada <http://canada.westlaw.com>. Reproduced by permission of Carswell, a division of Thomson Reuters Canada Limited.

Task 7.11 LexisNexis Quicklaw <http://www.lexisnexis.com>. Reprinted with the permission of LexisNexis Canada Inc. All Rights Reserved.

Task 7.12 LexisNexis Quicklaw <http://www.lexisnexis.com>. Reprinted with the permission of LexisNexis Canada Inc. All Rights Reserved.

Task 7.14 CanLII <http://canlii.org/en/index.html>. Reprinted by permission.

Task 7.15 CanLII <http://canlii.org/en/on/laws/index.html>. Reprinted by permission.

Task 7.17 Westlaw Canada <http://canada.westlaw.com>. Reproduced by permission of Carswell, a division of Thomson Reuters Canada Limited.

Task 7.19 Westlaw Canada <http://canada.westlaw.com>. Reproduced by permission of Carswell, a division of Thomson Reuters Canada Limited.

Task 7.20 LexisNexis Quicklaw <http://www.lexisnexis.com>. Reprinted with the permission of LexisNexis Canada Inc. All Rights Reserved.

Task 7.21 CanLII <http://canlii.org/en/ca/scc/doc/1995/1995canlii105/1995canlii105.html> [as of April 2013]. Reprinted by permission.

Task 7.24 Westlaw Canada <http://canada.westlaw.com>. Reproduced by permission of Carswell, a division of Thomson Reuters Canada Limited.

Task 7.25 Westlaw Canada <http://canada.westlaw.com>. Reproduced by permission of Carswell, a division of Thomson Reuters Canada Limited; LexisNexis Quicklaw <http://www.lexisnexis.com>. Reprinted with the permission of LexisNexis Canada Inc. All Rights Reserved.

Task 7.27 LexisNexis Quicklaw <http://www.lexisnexis.com>. Reprinted with the permission of LexisNexis Canada Inc. All Rights Reserved.

Task 7.28 Westlaw Canada <http://canada.westlaw.com>. Reproduced by permission of Carswell, a division of Thomson Reuters Canada Limited.

Task 7.29 HeinOnline <http://heinonline.org>. Image courtesy of HeinOnline.

Task 7.30 CanLII <http://canlii.org/en/commentary.html>. Reprinted by permission.

Chapter 8: Introduction to International and Foreign Legal Research in a Canadian Context

Task 8.1   Google <http://www.google.ca/advanced_search>.

Task 8.3   Canada Treaty Information <http://www.treaty-accord.gc.ca/search-recherche.aspx>; Canada Treaty Information <http://www.treaty-accord.gc.ca/details.aspx?id=105038>.

Task 8.4   United Nations <http://treaties.un.org/Pages/AdvanceSearch.aspx?tab=SEARCH>; United Nations <http://treaties.un.org/Pages/showDetails.aspx?objid=08000002800ac2f9>. © Copyright United Nations.

Task 8.5   United Nations <http://treaties.un.org/Pages/ParticipationStatus.aspx>; United Nations <http://treaties.un.org/Pages/ViewDetailsII.aspx?&src=TREATY&mtdsg_no= V~2&chapter=5&Temp=mtdsg2&lang=en>. © Copyright United Nations.

Chapter 10: Foundations of Statutory and Case Analysis

Figure 10.2   Justice Laws <http://justice.gc.ca/eng/dept-min/pub/legis/index.html> [as of April 2013].